HUMAN SECURITY AND HUMAN RIGHTS UNDER INTERNATIONAL LAW

Human security provides one of the most important protections; a person-centred axis of freedom from fear, from want and to live with dignity. It is surprising given its centrality to the human experience, that its connection with human rights has not yet been explored in a truly systematic way. This important new book addresses that gap in the literature by analysing whether human security might provide the tools for an expansive and integrated interpretation of international human rights. The examination takes a two-part approach. Firstly, it evaluates convergences between human security and all human rights—civil, political, economic, social and cultural—and constructs an investigative framework focused on the human security-human rights synergy. It then goes on to explore its practical application in the thematic cores of violence against women and undocumented migrants in the law and case-law of UN, European, Inter-American and African human rights bodies. It takes both a legal and interdisciplinary approach, recognising that human security and its relationship with human rights cuts across disciplinary boundaries. Innovative and rigorous, this is an important contribution to human rights scholarship.

Human Security and Human Rights under International Law

The Protections Offered to Persons Confronting Structural Vulnerability

Dorothy Estrada-Tanck

• H A R T •

OXFORD • LONDON • NEW YORK • NEW DELHI • SYDNEY

HART PUBLISHING
Bloomsbury Publishing Plc
Kemp House, Chawley Park, Cumnor Hill, Oxford, OX2 9PH, UK

HART PUBLISHING, the Hart/Stag logo, BLOOMSBURY and the Diana logo are trademarks of Bloomsbury Publishing Plc
First published in Great Britain 2016

First published in hardback, 2016
Paperback edition, 2018

A catalogue record for this book is available from the British Library.

Library of Congress Cataloging-in-Publication Data

Names: Estrada-Tanck, Dorothy, author.

Title: Human security and human rights under international law : the protections offered to persons confronting structural vulnerability / Dorothy Estrada-Tanck.

Description: Portland, Oregon : Hart Publishing, 2016. | Includes bibliographical references and index.

Identifiers: LCCN 2016024693 (print) | LCCN 2016025231 (ebook) | ISBN 9781849468824 (hardback) | ISBN 9781509902385 (Epub)

Subjects: LCSH: Humanitarian law. | Human security. | Human rights | International law.

Classification: LCC KZ6471 .E87 2016 (print) | LCC KZ6471 (ebook) | DDC 341.4/8—dc23

LC record available at https://lccn.loc.gov/2016024693

ISBN: HB: 978-1-84946-882-4
PB: 978-1-50992-880-4
ePDF: 978-1-50990-237-8
ePub: 978-1-50990-238-5

Typeset by Compuscript Ltd, Shannon

Preface

This book analyses whether human security may provide tools for an expansive and integrated interpretation of international human rights; State and non-State obligations in the context of structural vulnerability; and whether a gendered human rights-based approach can more accurately define the scope of human security and the types of violence and deprivation it considers. Human security has been qualified as 'the emerging paradigm for understanding global vulnerabilities'. Articulated by UN and regional bodies over the last 20 years, its person-centred axis of *freedom from fear*, *from want* and *to live in dignity* and its *protection* and *empowerment* strategies, suggest communicating bridges with human rights law. However, this connection has seldom been explored at a deeper level that transcends human rights as discourse or token. Thus, on the basis of an initial interdisciplinary reflection, this book critically evaluates the expressions of human security/human rights interaction in international law, particularly human rights law, with a cross-cutting emphasis on socio-economic vulnerabilities as authentic security concerns. Then it extrapolates the elements of such intersection to construct a general framework for thought and action, the 'human security–human rights synergy'. In a second part, the book explores the practical applications of this framework in the legal analysis of two thematic cores: 1) violence against women and girls, and 2) undocumented migrants and other non-citizens, converging in a particular examination of the conditions of undocumented female migrants; throughout the UN, and the Inter-American, European, and African systems of human rights, concentrating especially on the first two regional scenarios. In the last chapter, the book systematises this evidence to reveal and propose added values of human security to human rights law; and inversely, it indicates how human rights standards and indicators can deliver a needed more precise, normatively grounded and operational conception of human security. These identified *'interpretative synergies'* offer promise for shifting the boundaries of international human rights law: in constructing integrative approaches to fill legal gaps, better prevention and addressing protectively collective threats, and creating an 'enabling environment' to fulfil *all* human rights, especially for those not only confronting isolated moments of risk or individual human rights violations, but rather conditions of structural vulnerability affecting their everyday lives.

The first thematic core addressed in this book, violence against women and girls, is one of the most pervasive and widespread threats to a great sector of the population—more than half worldwide—even in well-off and/or democratic societies which are otherwise considered 'peaceful'. The second thematic core, risk conditions faced by undocumented migrants, also connects to most countries in the world, whether as sending, transit or host societies. It poses legal questions at the conceptual level in terms of the universality of human rights when considered in light of legal migratory status. Challenges also emerge in the practical sphere, whilst the lack of protection towards undocumented migrants has been aggravated with the economic crises in the US and Europe, together with new interrogations derived from the current exponential migratory flows from Syria, Iraq and Afghanistan, mostly to Turkey, Jordan and Lebanon and, to a much lesser extent, EU countries. Both themes, violence against women, and the human rights of undocumented migrants, meet again in a combined topic of review, namely, the heightened risks and vulnerabilities faced by undocumented migrant women and girls, and the particular compounded forms of discrimination and violence they experience, including sexual violence.

In light of recent events, the book may also contribute to palliate the need of more just, innovative, and coordinated proposals to address the fragile situation of undocumented migrants, several of them potential refugees, and their increased vulnerability to exploitation and violence. The appalling tragedy of thousands of people who have died at sea trying to reach the Mediterranean Coast, dramatically escalating in 2015,[1] or the mass graves of migrants discovered in northern Mexico[2] or Malaysia,[3] account for the global scale of the risks faced by people on the move who urgently require new solutions. I contend that legal human rights alone, accentuating mainly individual entitlements, are not enough to attend to their situation. It has become an issue of justice to tackle these threats with auxiliary and matching approaches: human security-inspired policy changes and normative reforms may provide widespread solutions to a widespread situation. Indeed, policy makers at the national, European, Inter-American, Middle Eastern and African levels need to deal with the recent wave of mass migration and rising death tolls in a satisfactory way from the human rights viewpoint. Practitioners and human rights defenders also need innovative strategies to tackle the magnitude of the current situation through more effective advocacy and litigation.

[1] International Organization for Migration (IOM), Missing Migrants Project, Migrant Fatalities Worldwide, available at https://missingmigrants.iom.int/latest-global-figures; and Brian, Tara and Frank Laczko (eds), *Fatal Journeys: Tracking Lives Lost during Migration* (IOM, 2014).

[2] Inter-American Commission of Human Rights (IACoHR), Annex to Press Release 82/11, 'Preliminary Observations of the IACHR's Rapporteurship on the Rights of Migrant Workers on its Visit to Mexico', 2 August 2011.

[3] BBC News, 'Asia Migrant Crisis: New Mass Graves on Malaysia-Thai Border', 23 August 2015, available at www.bbc.com/news/world-asia-34033474.

At the same time, I am aware of the fact that in 2016 the conditions in need of a global paradigm have changed dramatically, particularly in the Middle East and European context. Between the time of writing this work and updating it, the number of persons, especially from Syria, migrating in search of a safe haven and a better life has drastically increased, reaching the millions.[4] It would seem at first glance that there is little room for manoeuvre in terms of dialogue and implementation of a human security–human rights synergy. Still, this does not alter the guiding line of this text and its proposals. The human security–human rights framework exposes the links between structural vulnerability to human rights violations and conflict, including armed conflict. In that sense, it is alive and may prove useful. While by November 2014 over 155,000 people had reached EU shores—primarily those of Italy, but also Malta, Greece, Spain, and Cyprus—and Italy's Mare Nostrum operation had rescued tens of thousands of people from boats in distress,[5] Europe is today 'the world's most dangerous destination for "irregular" migrants', with the Mediterranean claiming the lives of over 3,700 migrants of the 5,400 migrant fatalities accounted for worldwide in 2015.[6] This is partly the result of substituting Mare Nostrum with EU border agency Frontex operations that did not prioritise the human security of migrants at sea, but rather aimed at impeding irregular migration.[7]

In light of the parallel events of the terrorist attacks by the 'Islamic State', ISIS, in Paris, Lebanon and Mali in November 2015, and in Turkey, Pakistan and Brussels in 2016, among many others, the armed response by several countries guided by hard-core national security doctrines, and the risk of further coarsening of migratory policy affecting all migrants, as well as asylum seekers and refugees, render the human security accentuation ever more necessary. New theoretical frameworks are called for; the human security–human rights symbiosis offers creative avenues for thought and action, and this will possibly be more so once the intensity of the 'crisis' has passed. When human insecurity is not attended to, violent conflict may follow. Many of the refugees of today, even when theoretically and legally deserving the status of refugee, will foreseeably be ignored, pushed-back, or rejected and become the undocumented migrants of tomorrow. But apart from this future risk, let us not forget

[4] See *2015 Situation Report on International Migration: Migration, Displacement and Development in a Changing Arab Region* (International Organization for Migration–UN Economic and Social Commission for Western Asia, 2015); and Berti, Benedetta, 'The Syrian Refugee Crisis: Regional and Human Security Implications' in *Strategic Assessment*, Vol 17, No 4, January 2015, 41–53.

[5] Human Rights Watch, *World Report 2015: European Union*, Events of 2014, available at www.hrw.org/world-report/2015/country-chapters/european-union.

[6] IOM, Missing Migrants Project (n 1). Bear in mind that, as the analysis points out, there are many more deaths unaccounted for.

[7] See Human Rights Watch Report (n 5).

that human insecurity is at this very moment a threat to the survival and well-being of the millions who suffer it; it is the greatest emergency of their lives.

The human security–human rights synergy is also highly useful at present for many parts of the world, e.g. those less affected by the immediate situation, such as the Inter-American region, Africa and parts of Asia, as well as EU countries less touched by the strongest effects of migratory pressure. At the same time, it provides arguments for prioritising the human security of women at risk of or suffering violence, regardless of their migratory status, and over existing migratory law or policy.

What I would suggest the reader to keep in mind is that too often international law has focused on 'peak moments of conflict' while leaving aside the analysis of and reaction to *quotidian structures of conflict and distribution* embedded in the economic and cultural global order.[8] Indeed, conceiving international law primarily as a 'crisis discipline', relevant overall to the highest crests of conflict and under certain reduced conceptualisations of 'conflict', is to impoverish its content and potentials. If exclusive or excessive focus is placed on the bellicose feature of the world through a reinforcement and consequent perpetuation of a state-based international law and politics, or on the human suffering caused by direct violence and armed conflict—as displayed in the reflections in this book—this prioritisation plays out to the detriment of other equally important concerns for international law: the respect and fulfilment of the whole spectrum of human rights, and the widespread gender-based violence, poverty, marginalisation, and discrimination brutally affecting an enormous portion of the global population. Concern within this book has thus been directed more to what Hilary Charlesworth has termed 'the international law of everyday life'.[9]

At the same time, this text has engaged in the study of the legal implications of conditions of structural vulnerability which, although constituting authentic 'crises' or 'emergencies' because of their severe and critical character, have become normalised to such an extent that they constitute the 'everyday' of the people who experience them, such as violence against women, insecure conditions of undocumented migrants, or poverty and grave socio-economic inequality. They are not exceptional situations but the rule. The human security–human rights symbiosis thus brings together the 'everyday' and the 'conflict situation' in a manner that is relevant for international human rights law and, more importantly, that

[8] Kennedy, David, 'Law and the Political Economy of the World' (2013) *Leiden Journal of International Law* 26, 33–34. Emphasis added.

[9] Charlesworth, Hilary, 'International Law: A Discipline of Crisis (2002) 65 *Modern Law Review* 3, 377, 389–92.

hopefully contributes to jointly constructing mechanisms for the better protection and empowerment of the persons living in these conditions.

This book sustains that the human rights situation of persons confronting structural vulnerability can be addressed more adequately if studied through the complementary lens of human security and not under human rights law alone. At the same time, human rights law provides the normative legal grounding usually lacking in human security. International human rights norms, mostly *individualistic and personal* in nature and firstly enacted more than 50 years ago, present limits which translate into a serious lack of protection and socio-economic marginalisation of undocumented migrants. As a result, the *collective or structural* conditions confronted by undocumented migrants can be better met through the broader and more recent notion of human security, which emphasises 'critical (severe) and pervasive (widespread) threats', and thus complement human rights law. Through the proposed human security–human rights framework, this book aims to expand the conceptual toolkit available to scholars and practitioners confronting new societal challenges.

The human security approach adds value to the traditional purely legal analysis of human rights: firstly, human security makes evident the risks faced by women and girls and by undocumented migrants, and also brings their voices to the fore through its two pillars of 'protection' (top-down) and 'empowerment' (bottom-up). This opens possibilities for transnational social networks, such as women, migrants' and human rights non-governmental organisations (NGOs) and institutions, to influence the shape of human rights law. Secondly, the human security ingredient facilitates exposing how migratory legal irregularity is in fact a source of risk that the conventional legal analysis ('law within the law') of human rights does not fully address.[10] Indeed, the current 'legal limbo' concerning undocumented migrants involves an aggravated risk to human rights violations and violence for undocumented migrants, especially female migrants.[11] The State-centred logic underpinning migration law and policy is not deeply nor fully challenged by human rights law. This allows for a 'State-constructed vulnerability' rendered fully detectable through a human security lens. Thirdly, with its emphasis on the need for *preventive action*, human security allows for *early warning* mechanisms to identify 'human rights at risk', be it due to State or non-State actors, and to avoid their violation or mitigate its effects. Placed in a continuum, human security would come first, providing a basis and rationale to human rights

[10] Refugee Council, *Remote Controls: How UK Border Controls are Endangering the Lives of Refugees* (UK, December 2008); Migrants' Rights Network, 'New Immigration Bill Will Push Irregular Migrants into a System of Modern Day Slavery', 21 May 2015, at www.migrantsrights.org.uk/.

[11] See, eg, Dauvergne, Catherine, *Making People Illegal: What Globalization Means for Migration and Law* (Cambridge, Cambridge University Press, 2008) .

governance (as a system), with human rights (as a legal tool) then delivering the detailed content and redress mechanisms needed in case of violations.

At the same time, a gendered human rights-based approach gives content to the human security concept and better defines its scope. One of the flaws of human security often signalled is the lack of accurate criteria for defining the threshold to be met in order to consider a given issue as a risk situation. The concept of violence against women and girls and its corresponding obligations of due diligence, normatively and jurisprudentially developed by international human rights law, provide a basis for better defining the boundaries of risk and types of violence and destitution to be considered as human security concerns. The jurisprudential reaffirmations of the universality of the rights of undocumented migrants, particularly from the Inter-American perspective—including the argument defending the *ius cogens* status of equality and non-discrimination as applied to them—are a necessary cornerstone for any human security argument that aims at countering the vulnerability faced by migrants. The interpretative outlines by human rights bodies giving content to economic, social and cultural rights in and of themselves or through the expansion of typical civil and political rights to also cover violations of a socio-economic character, ought to constitute an essential human security tool for framing poverty and inequality risks as a matter of vulnerability, as a global justice concern, but overall and foremost as an *issue of rights*. As a general stand, human security would benefit from considering the normative and jurisprudential human rights development of positive obligations of protection in order to implement its proposed 'top-down' strategy, precisely that of 'protection'.

A second contribution lies in human rights law's general standards and indicators as central elements to be included in the definition of human security and the measurement exercises to assess levels of (in)security. Thirdly, in addition to building on feminist theory, human security may profit from the ample experience of human rights advocates and legal practitioners in working with people to develop 'bottom-up' agency and human rights defence, thus implementing human security's strategy of 'empowerment'. Finally, the construction of human security on the basis of human rights law as a solid normative grounding and an objective reference point, limits the possibility of it being co-opted to legitimise abusive or oppressive aims through processes of securitisation of different subjects.

As such, the identified *interpretative synergies* advanced in the book may work as hermeneutic tools towards reinforced protection of the rights of women facing violence and undocumented migrants living in the context of structural vulnerability in their daily reality.

*****

Before moving to the content of the book, some words should be spared for the academic and personal motivation of this work. I am aware of the different theoretical positions regarding international law, in particular those fields connected to human rights. Let me then situate myself through the lens of personal and professional experience derived from the work I had the opportunity of carrying out at the Mexican Ministry of Foreign Affairs, the UN Office of the High Commissioner for Human Rights, the Case Matrix Network and mainly in the Mexico City Commission of Human Rights, a constitutionally autonomous institution (a certain model of expanded ombudsman) dealing with individual cases of human rights violations, as well as general programmes for the promotion, protection and fulfilment of all human rights in an immensely complex city of 20 million persons. I do not attempt to place myself as embodying any sort of paradigmatic experience in the human rights social and legal movement or its effects at the domestic level. Through my legal work in these institutions, though, I had the fortune of dealing with cases which allowed me to meet and learn from a variety of individual, social, economic and political actors. I would like to bring a few to the fore as the intellectual and personal origins for the interest in this work. They all illustrate the interrelated crossroads evidenced and argued in this book: the individual with the collective, the background stage with the distinct actors, and the immediately visible with the underlying. Although lived out as seemingly isolated single moments, they were experienced in the setting of daily work and are only a representative photograph of an ever-evolving reality.

Work related to indigenous peoples and to persons with disabilities gave me the chance to deepen my views on the need for intercultural and adaptable understandings of human rights and the richness of this joint inclusive construction of bridges, by contrast to monist, unilateral or excessively formalistic or positivistic conceptions of human rights. Through my work in the Mexico City Commission of Human Rights, I had the opportunity to meet the parents related to a case involving police negligence which resulted in the unwilling but foreseeable death of 12 people, among them nine young teenagers. Quite apart from the grave and impressive enough damage to the rights to life and personal integrity these families had suffered, surrounding it all was the additional realisation that there had been clear signs of discrimination based on socio-economic factors, that for myriad conditions this wouldn't have happened had their children not been poor, and if for some reason it had occurred to young people with a more 'favourable' background, the reaction by public authorities and the attempt to guarantee access to justice would have been radically different, as evidenced by analogous situations. This case brought with it particular insight of the pervasive effects poverty and inequality may hold as human rights violations in themselves and as a root cause of the structural vulnerability and human insecurity they entail.

I was also able to meet and talk with the mother of one of the girls who disappeared, and was sexually abused and killed in the *Cotton Field Case v Mexico* judgment by the Inter-American Court of Human Rights, analysed in this text, who experienced 'empowerment' amidst the terrible background of a fatal lack of 'protection'. A brave woman with a low literacy level, economically disadvantaged, who in the aftermath of her daughter's tragic death, faced authority denial, disregard and discrimination. At the beginning of the litigation process, she did not see herself as a political actor, much less as an agent of her case or a holder of rights, as she explained herself. She described her experience of the last 15 years involved in the case, how she had learned the meaning of 'strategic litigation', civil society, human rights, and the way in which her case was 'paradigmatic' in being able to open the path for other cases to be argued on the same basis. At the end of the conversation she wished to clearly summarise her experience: the enormous power she had found in her daughter's memory that had eventually turned her into another woman—a much better woman—and the struggle to find meaning in the middle of incommensurable pain: 'My daughter died so that I could be born'. It is these testimonies of human dignity that bring me to search for better paths in addressing our common humanity and accompany this struggle of people to construct justice.

Acknowledgements

The period in which I have converted my PhD thesis into a book has seen many changes and encounters and much enjoyment. From the person I was at the beginning of the PhD in Law at the European University Institute in Florence to the one I am now, I owe acknowledgment and gratitude to several people.

I thank my thesis supervisor, Professor Martin Scheinin, for challenging me to search for the legal aspects of my thinking and to deepen and refine my proposals. I am also grateful, Martin, for your broader support in developing my human rights work in general. To the external readers of the thesis, Professor Christine Chinkin from the LSE and Judge Antônio Augusto Cançado Trindade, I am extremely thankful to you for having agreed to review and comment upon this work, as well as for attending my oral defence: your presence was an honour and a real privilege, and your insightful observations a guide in modifying the thesis to convert it into a manuscript for publication. I especially wish to thank Professor Ruth Rubio Marin for believing in this project from the beginning, for your support, guidance and friendship throughout these years, with the hope of continuing to share issues of common interest and excitement.

I also wish to thank EUI Professors, Marise Cremona, Claire Kilpatrick, Francesco Francioni, Nehal Buhta and Dennis Patterson, for having listened to the views proposed in this project, as well as for their advice on academic life in general. Thanks are also owed to Judy Fudge, Fernand Braudel Professor at the EUI, who kindly agreed to discuss this research at the EUI and encouraged me to think and argue creatively.

My gratitude also goes to the 'Global Governance and Transnational Human Rights Obligations' Network (GLOTHRO), and to the participants at the Workshop on Human Rights of Persons with Disabilities in International and EU Law, organised by the EUI Human Rights Working Group and the Academy of European Law and held at the EUI in April 2012, for their opinions and ideas which have influenced this work. I especially thank Professor Margot Salomon from the LSE for agreeing to discuss my work and for her helpful observations. I owe my thanks to the members of the EUI Human Rights Working Group for their valuable feedback on this project, and to Annick Bulckaen, Françoise Thauvin, Machteld Nijsten and Ruth Gbikpi for their kind assistance at the EUI.

From my time as visiting researcher at Fordham School of Law in New York City in the spring of 2011, I am grateful to Vice Dean Sheila

Foster and to Assistant Dean Toni M Fine, as well as to Professors Jennifer Gordon, Paolo Galizzi, Chi Mgbako, Alena Herklotz and all at the Leitner International Human Rights Clinic at Fordham, for their warm reception, for making themselves available to discuss ideas about my work, and for their helpful and stimulating comments.

I thank Mehrnaz Mostafavi, Officer in Charge of the United Nations Human Security Unit within the UN Office for the Coordination of Humanitarian Affairs for agreeing to an interview in New York City in April 2011; this was very beneficial for better understanding the conceptual background and the practical application of human security at the UN. I am also thankful to the people at the Center for European and Policy Studies, particularly to Massimo Merlino, for discussing my work in June of 2011 and directing me to very useful documents on irregular migration and the EU. I owe my thanks to the different officials at the European Commission, for the conversations we had on the work of the EU in the fields covered by this project—particularly that of combating violence against women—and for their insightful observations. I thank Mient Jan Faber, Professor at the Free University (VU) Amsterdam, as well as his research assistant, Martijn Dekker, for granting me an interview in March of 2012 and providing me with academic viewpoints and vivid personal experiences relating to human security. I also am very grateful to Judge Allan Rosas and Judge Egils Levits from the Court of Justice of the European Union, and to Judge Vilenas Vadapalas from the General Court, for the discussions they kindly agreed to in the summer of 2012. I owe my gratitude particularly to the first two for their especially helpful insights on constructive proposals regarding public international law and human rights law.

I also thank Gijsbert Vonk, Professor of Social Security Law at the University of Groningen, Klaus Kapuy and the organisers of the Conference 'Access Denied' held in Amsterdam on 14 and 15 March 2012, for their valuable comments on my presentation on the rights of undocumented migrants. Similarly, I am grateful to the participants in the General Conference of the European Society of International Law held at Valencia in September 2012, particularly to Eva Brems, René Urueña and Marion Panizzon, for their very helpful comments on this work. I express my gratitude also to Professor Cesáreo Gutiérrez Espada from the University of Murcia for his encouragement and confidence in me.

To my colleagues in Mexico who introduced me to the human rights world as a profession and a commitment, whom I now am fortunate enough to count among my friends, I am thankful for having learned from you that with hard work, a sense of justice, sensibility and a bit of legal and political intuition, often even the unthinkable becomes possible. To Juan José Gómez Camacho, Salvador Tinajero, Sofía Lascurain, Patricia Olamendi, Luis González Placencia, José Guevara, Roberto de León,

Marcela Talamás, Regina Tamés, Tania Reneaum and Emilio Álvarez Icaza, many thanks for your presence, thoughtful guidance and companionship in these years.

A particular thank you goes to all the people at Hart Publishing. First of all, to Sinead Moloney for trusting me and the 'immutable elements' of the proposal of this book, and for providing such useful and timely advice: to Emily Braggins, for the daily exchange and support throughout the whole publication process and to Emma Platt, Mel Hamill, Tom Adams and John Hort for their assistance and patience in the editing, marketing and production of this work.

Grateful thanks to my family, uncles, aunts and cousins in Mexico and the US. In loving memory of my Aunt Teté, my Uncle Piquico, my Aunt Elinor and especially my Uncle and Godfather Mike. Thank you to my friends in Mexico and Murcia who gave me their support on this journey and were always there for me. I especially thank Marisa, Ale, Gaby, Magui, Elvia, Belena, Ana Laura, Analía, la Güera, as well as Rafa and Sol, Roger, Cynthia, Chucho Vázquez, Chabela, las Gabys, Carla, Adri, and Bony; as well as Rosa Marcela, Ari, Gaby, Amparo and Ana. I thank Dr Rodolfo Stavenhagen from El Colegio de México and Professor José Manuel Villalpando from Escuela Libre de Derecho for their academic and personal support. I particularly thank Jaime Del Arenal Fenochio for his intellectual guidance, personal advice and years of friendship since my time as a law student at Escuela Libre de Derecho; thanks also to my friends from the Mexican Foreign Service, Generación XIX, for their diplomatic and less formal advice in this period.

My friends at the EUI, particularly Emilie, Gonçalo, Fer, Juana, Germán, Mislavée, Matejjja, Tamara, Chiara (piccolina), Neja (Angelito), Susanna, Alex, Teimur (son), Lisa, Marina, Danai and Antonella, because I was fortunate enough to find real friendship during the PhD—your support and many wonderful times together played a great part in the completion of this work (and made the journey to reach this stage lots of fun!).

A Yolanda, una mujer inmigrante en España, que ha cambiado tiempo de su casa e hijos para ayudarme a cuidar a los míos y poder terminar este libro. Muchas gracias.

To the people from Spain who have now become part of my family, formally and because of the ties that unite us in the heart: to Dori and Jorge, Paqui, Antonio and Ana, I thank you for your generosity, joyfulness and patience in the ups and downs that were part of this work. For welcoming me so kindly from the beginning, for numerous trips to the airport at early hours, for sharing the affection for good food and music that define our nationalities and our times together, I thank you with all my heart.

To my Dad, for making me feel your love vividly even through these years of physical separation, for your wise and respectful advice, for being there in the happy and difficult moments these years have also carried with them, and for seeing me through them with faith and intelligence; for sharing the deep love for Mexico that partly inspired this project, for believing in its people, valuing what they have accomplished and hoping for more just times to come that dignify their real spirit and potential—mil gracias Papá.

Mom, of you I hope to have inherited more than a name. Thank you for all your support, for reading my work and always commenting perceptively, imaginatively and generously. During this work I have often recalled the story you told me of a rose fingered-dawn as Grandma wrote at the University of California at Berkeley in her college major in literature on Homer's Iliad. As you recounted, she was fond of this subject, but not as much as of chemistry, a degree that was denied to her in the California of the 1930s as considered an inappropriate subject for a woman. This book contains the story of many brave women that fervently fight for equality and justice. But this work is dedicated to you, my greatest testimony and example of meeting this task in softer, equally passionate, ways through your smile, your brilliant work as a historian, your heart and your tireless generosity and unbroken service to others.

Thank you to my best friends, Monica, Mary Fer and Isa for your encouragement and comments on my work and for walking hand in hand with me in so many ways in this period of our lives. Monica, I particularly thank you for your kindness, closeness and honest determination, Mary Fer for your caring attention to detail and your especially generous help with this book (remember the tables!) and Isa for your willingness to share everything and your ability to make me smile. Over the years you have woven a fabric around me, of a love so thick and so deep that it has kept my feet from getting wet in the paths of this world. ¡Gracias hermanitas!

My gratitude also goes to my brothers-in-law Memo and Alan: your support, advice and the fun times we always share make me see you as real brothers and for this I realise I am very lucky.

These years were also witness to the birth of my nieces and nephew. Jimena, I feel truly blessed to be your aunt and your godmother. Your smile, intelligence and courage have been an inspiration to me and this work. Thank you JuanFer for your fun and caring spirit, and for your precious friendship. Thank you Matilda, for your light-heartedness, sharing nature, and charming character. I cherish our moments together and I hope we continue to find loving ways of maintaining our ties, alive and growing, across the Atlantic.

Between the lines of this book, another narrative also developed—a love story of the kind I didn't know existed; the kind that makes you want to laugh and to cry; the kind that makes you want to be a better person; the kind you commit your whole life to. And we did! After our second year of the PhD, on a (slightly rainy) Saturday afternoon, my childhood church of La Sagrada Familia in overwhelming and beautiful Mexico City saw us

Table of Contents

Acronyms and Abbreviations

ACHPR – African Charter on Human and Peoples' Rights

ACoHR – American Convention on Human Rights (also known as Inter-American Convention on Human Rights)

AO 18/03 – Advisory Opinion OC-18/03 of the Inter-American Court of Human Rights, *Juridical Condition and Rights of Undocumented Migrants,* requested by the United Mexican States, 17 September 2003.

ASEAN – Association of Southeast Asian Nations

AU – African Union

Belém do Pará Convention/Convention of Belém do Pará – Inter-American Convention on the Prevention, Punishment, and Eradication of Violence against Women

CEDAW – Convention on the Elimination of All Forms of Discrimination Against Women

CHS – Commission on Human Security (body of independent experts and author of the 2003 report *Human Security Now*)

CJEU – Court of Justice of the European Union

CRMW – International Convention on the Protection of the Rights of All Migrant Workers and Members of their Families

ECHR – European Court of Human Rights

ECoHR – European Convention for the Protection of Human Rights and Fundamental Freedoms

ECOWAS – Economic Community of West African States

ESC Rights – Economic, Social and Cultural Rights

EU – European Union

HRW – Human Rights Watch

IACHR – Inter-American Court of Human Rights

IACoHR – Inter-American Commission on Human Rights

ICCPR – International Covenant on Civil and Political Rights

ICERD – International Convention on the Elimination of All Forms of Racial Discrimination

ICESCR – International Covenant on Economic, Social and Cultural Rights

ICJ – International Court of Justice

IHL – International Humanitarian Law

IHRL – International Human Rights Law

OAS – Organization of American States

OCHA – Office for the Coordination of Humanitarian Affairs (UN)

OECD – Organization for Economic Cooperation and Development

OHCHR – Office of the United Nations High Commissioner for Human Rights

OSCE – Organization for Security and Cooperation in Europe

PICUM – Platform for International Cooperation on Undocumented Migrants

R2P – Responsibility to Protect

UDHR – Universal Declaration of Human Rights

UN – United Nations

UN CAT – United Nations Committee Against Torture

UN Committee of CEDAW/CEDAW Committee – United Nations Committee on the Elimination of Discrimination Against Women

UN Committee on ERD – United Nations Committee on the Elimination of Racial Discrimination

UN Committee for ESC Rights – United Nations Committee for Economic, Social and Cultural Rights

UN Committee on RMW – United Nations Committee on the Protection of the Rights of All Migrant Workers and Members of their Families

UN CRPD – United Nations Convention on the Rights of Persons with Disabilities

UNDP – United Nations Development Program

UNGA – United Nations General Assembly

UNHCR – United Nations High Commissioner for Refugees

UN HRC – United Nations Human Rights Committee

UN OCHA – United Nations Office for the Coordination of Humanitarian Affairs

UN OHCHR – United Nations Office of the High Commissioner for Human Rights (also known as OHCHR)

UNSC – United Nations Security Council

UNSG – United Nations Secretary General

UNTFHS – United Nations Trust Fund for Human Security

VAW – Violence against women

Introduction

THIS BOOK USES as a starting point the following two basic questions: Whether human security may provide tools for an expansive and integrated interpretation of international human rights and their correlative State and non-State obligations, especially in the context of structural vulnerability; and whether a gendered human rights-based approach may contribute to a more accurate definition of the scope of human security and the types of violence and deprivation it takes into account.

Long-established concepts of national or military security, focusing on the territorial State, are unfit to analyse and address factors of risk, threat or sudden change in the daily lives of people—many of them transnational or not involving armed force[1]—such as poverty, environmental hazards, global epidemic diseases, natural disasters, and gender-based violence. All these elements of menace that affect people's rights and dignity, have usually not been considered as security-related risks which the State has an obligation to prevent or ameliorate, according to human rights standards as will be reviewed throughout this book. Such threats often become invisible in the public debate that generally centres its concerns on the national security of the State, or in some cases on public security related only to combating crime or violent conflict which employs armed force.

I argue that the fragmented attention to each of these problems does not offer a holistic approach to phenomena that are actually interrelated. Their individualised attention limits the development of more structural solutions to the violation of human rights that may derive from such situations. Thus, the notion of human security, centred on the individual instead of the State, but at the same time addressing widespread risks that transcend individual circumstances, emerges as a possible means to review and attend to all these conditions, whether or not they result from conflicts between States and independent of the fact that they occur within armed conflict.

Indeed, the notion of human security has been defended, arguing that the broad spectrum of perils that people confront in this global era cannot be understood nor fully tackled by traditional public policies and

[1] Fukuda-Parr, Sakiko, 'New Threats to Human Security in the Era of Globalization' in Chen, Lincoln, Sakiko Fukuda-Parr and Ellen Seidensticker (eds), *Human Insecurity in a Global World* (Harvard, Harvard University Press, 2003) 1–13.

concepts of national, military and state security.[2] More than 20 years after its inception in its contemporary form, advanced by the United Nations Security Council (UNSC) and the United Nations Secretary General (UNSG) in 1992, fully articulated by the United Nations Development Program (UNDP) in 1993 and 1994, and further developed by the Commission on Human Security (CHS) in its report of 2003, human security has been used in myriad ways. It has been addressed as a parallel concern for human development, as a foreign policy tool, as a guide in crisis management and peace-keeping operations, as an instrument for state-building projects, particularly in post-conflict societies, as an emerging right, as part of a wide understanding of the right to peace, as a motor for change in matters of global governance, as a light to render certain threats more visible—those of a socio-economic nature, violence against women and girls and risks faced by non-citizens among them—and not least as a catalyst for a broader understanding of security that covers individual and group security, but also collective security as contemplated by the UN Charter and public international law. The 2012 conceptualisation of human security by the UN General Assembly (UNGA) on the basis of *freedom from fear*, *freedom from want* and *freedom to live in dignity*, has operated in both a horizontal way as to the subject matter of security—the elements and conditions considered threats—and in a vertical way as to who should be the object of security—the actors worthy of protection: persons instead of States.

The 1994 formulation by the UNDP proposed, on the basis of the threats encountered by persons and communities, that human security encompassed seven types of security: economic security, food security, health security, environmental security, personal security, community security, and political security.[3] A decade later, the 2003 Report of the Commission on Human Security, *Human Security Now,* further defined human security and considered it to cover 'critical (severe) and pervasive (widespread) threats and situations'.[4] Human security escalated to a more important role in the international scene consolidated within the UN through the agreement reached by the UNGA in 2012 on a 'common understanding' of the notion which placed (legal) human rights at its core, a position confirmed by the UN Secretary General's third report on human security of 2013.[5] Human security thus comes forward as the first concept at

[2] See Alkire, Sabine, "Concepts of Human Security", in Chen, Fukuda-Parr and Seidensticker *ibid*, 15–39.

[3] UNDP, *Human Development Report* (UNDP, 1994) 23–25.

[4] Commission on Human Security, *Human Security Now* (New York, Commission on Human Security, 2003) 4.

[5] UNGA, 'Follow-up to Paragraph 143 on Human Security of the 2005 World Summit Outcome', A/Res/66/290, 10 September 2012, para 3 a) and c). UNSG, *Third Report of the UN Secretary General*, 'Follow-up to General Assembly Resolution 66/290 on Human Security', A/68/685, 23 December 2013.

the international level to encompass the traditional conceptions of three central propositions: security, development and human rights, to map their relations and also to fill the gaps between them.[6] This concept has also played a protagonist role in regional settings, through regional bodies at the European, Inter-American, and African level. What seems clear is that the concept of human security has been quite resistant and it is here to stay.

At this point it seems clear that at the UN level, the notion of human security will formally remain as a policy framework or at most, viewed from the perspective of positive law, as a meta-legal figure. Its impact has been and may further be to promote the inclusion of central elements of human security in legal instruments, even if not explicitly using the term, or building upon existing international legal obligations—mainly in the field of human rights law and refugee law, and to some extent in humanitarian law and criminal law—in order to promote coordination and partnerships to address widespread threats in a coherent manner and build resilience to confront them. Of course, nothing prevents the possibility of human security being applied as an orienting notion to complement and inform legal interpretation at the UN level, particularly in the actions of human rights bodies and mechanisms. On the other hand, proof indicates that at the regional level human security certainly plays a legal role in various settings.

The main focus of this book is not to defend the (absolute) legal character of human security or even the advantage of this option in all scenarios, but rather to build communicating bridges with its current relevance in light of public international law, particularly in international human rights law. Inversely, some ways in which human rights law, standards and indicators could contribute to better define the scope of human security are also identified. The links between human security and human rights are made visible through the element of *risk or vulnerability*, analysed as well in its legal dimension, with a particular and cross-cutting emphasis throughout the whole text on the vulnerabilities severely affecting economic, social and cultural rights (ESC Rights) and facilitated by conditions of extreme material deprivation and social marginalisation.

Indeed, often even

> among professionals working on world affairs, to speak of international law and human rights is often to evoke thoughts of countering terrorism, justifying humanitarian intervention or enforcing international criminal justice. What remains overlooked is that the machinery of international law when it comes to human rights applies, in multifarious and significant ways, to matters of world

[6] Summary given by Ms Mehrnaz Mostafavi, Officer in Charge of the United Nations Human Security Unit, New York; interview carried out on 8 April 2011. See also Klein Goldewijk, Berma, 'Why Human? The Interlinkages between Security, Rights and Development' (2008) 19 *Security and Human Rights* 1, 24–36.

poverty, inequality and development … they are (also) matters of 'international law and human rights'.[7]

The prioritised thematic cores of this book, violence against women and girls, and risks faced by undocumented migrants, particularly female migrants, and the cross-cutting concern with socio-economic vulnerabilities, constitute empirical realities of human suffering and structural challenges as global pressing concerns in the twenty-first century.

What should be pointed out at this initial stage is that the analysis stems not from a view to securitise human rights issues, but rather to humanise security.

I. LITERATURE REVIEW AND THE CURRENT DEBATE

Against this ample background, the UNGA considered human security as a 'right' in the *2005 World Summit Outcome*[8] and deriving from that, discussed a 'common understanding' of human security, later picked up in the *UN Secretary General's Second Report on Human Security*. The report was presented to the UNGA in April 2012, debated by this body in June 2012 and generally agreed upon by it in a resolution of September 2012. The 'common understanding' adopted by the UNGA defines human security as an *approach* to assist Member States in identifying and addressing *widespread* and *cross-cutting* challenges to the survival, livelihood and dignity of their people. It affirms that human security includes the *right* of people to live in freedom and dignity, free from poverty and despair, stressing that all individuals, in particular *vulnerable people*, are entitled to freedom from fear and freedom from want, with an equal opportunity to enjoy all their rights and fully develop their human potential. It specifically asserts that human security 'equally considers' civil, political, economic, social and cultural human rights.[9] (emphasis added) As such, the UNSG's 2012 Report and the UNGA's stand adopt a stronger legal human rights basis to ground the idea of human security than that contained in the 1994 UNDP and the 2003 CHS reports. The *UN Secretary General's Third Report on Human Security* of 2013, builds on the line of the UNGA 'common understanding' and stresses human security's potential for advancing the interconnected pillars of peace and security, development and human rights.

[7] Salomon, Margot E, 'The Future of Human Rights' (2012) 3 *Global Policy* 4, 455.

[8] Para 143 of the UNGA, *2005 World Summit Outcome*, A/RES/60/1, 24 October 2005. On human security as an 'emerging right', see Fernández Pereira, Juan Pablo, *La seguridad humana: un derecho emergente* (Barcelona, Ariel, 2006).

[9] UNGA (n 5) para 3 a) and c). See also UNSG (n 5) para 59.

On this basis, contributions that adopt a 'human security approach' as a general conceptual framework, and also as an orienting notion regarding the two thematic cores of this book, namely, violence against women and undocumented migrants, as well as its focus on socio-economic vulnerabilities, have also been made both from a scholarly perspective and as policy guidelines. The triangular relationship between human development, human rights and human security (under the short name of 'Human Derise' stemming from the three terms), has also been pointed out as a successful partnership used to improve life quality for disadvantaged sectors of society, for example, through poverty reduction strategies in certain national settings.[10]

The links between human security, national security and State security have been explored by different disciplines and through interdisciplinary approaches, including the impact of such relationship on human rights,[11] gender relations,[12] and migration.[13]

However, 'different from other academic disciplines, international law has been reluctant to respond to the rise of human security, and the potential of human security as a possible global normative framework has attracted less attention'; a fact worth noting if it is considered that 'human security ... does indeed pose a challenge to international law'.[14] In fact, 'despite its relevance to central questions of international law, human

[10] Hong Hai, Nguyen, 'Human Rights—Human Security—Human Development. Assessing the Inter-Relationships of Human Development, Human Security and Human Rights in Poverty Reduction in Vietnam', Document presented at the Human Security Conference, University of Thailand, 2007.

[11] See, eg Takahashi, Saul (ed), *Human Rights, Human Security, and State Security: The Intersection* (USA, Praeger Security International, 2014) Vol I.

[12] See Reardon, Betty A and Asha Hans (eds), *The Gender Imperative. Human Security vs State Security* (New Delhi/United Kingdom, Routledge, 2010); and Reardon, Betty A, 'Women or Weapons: The Militarist Sexist Symbiosis' in Kurtz, Mariam M and Lester R Kurtz (eds), *Women, War, and Violence: Topography, Resistance, and Hope* (USA, Praeger Security International, 2015) 99–109.

[13] See, eg, Pérez García, Nancy, 'Seguridad nacional *versus* seguridad humana: su impacto en la migración' in Sin Fronteras IAP (coord), *Cambiando perspectivas: de la gestión de flujos hacia la construcción de políticas de migración con enfoque de desarrollo* (México, Universidad Autónoma de Zacatecas, Sin Fronteras IAP, INCIDE Social, Miguel Ángel Porrúa, 2008) 113–73.

[14] Oberleitner, Gerd, 'Human Security: A Challenge to International Law?' (2005) 11 *Global Governance* 185–86; and by the same author 'Human Security: Idea, Policy, and Law', in Martin, Mary and Taylor Owen (eds), *Routledge Handbook of Human Security* (New York, Routledge, 2014) 319–30. See also Sunga, Lyal S, 'The Concept of Human Security: Does it Add Anything of Value to International Legal Theory or Practice?' in Frick, Marie-Luisa and Andreas Oberprantacher, (eds), *Power and Justice in International Relations. Interdisciplinary Approaches to Global Challenges* (England and USA, Ashgate, 2009) 131–48; and Owada, Hishasi, 'Human Security and International Law' in Fastenrath, Ulrich, Rudolf Geiger, Daniel-Erasmus Khan, Andreas Paulus, Sabine von Schorlemer and Christoph Vedder (eds), *From Bilateralism to Community Interest, Essays in Honour of Judge Bruno Simma* (New York, Oxford University Press, 2011) 505–20.

security has … received little attention from international lawyers',[15] although increasingly one may find reflections from legal scholarship on the human security conception and its relationship to international law,[16] though few in-depth studies on the subject, with the notable exception of the excellent book by Barbara von Tigerstrom.[17] Different aspects of human security as related to international law have been analysed as well in a variety of fields, such as the relevance of human security in the context of armed conflict, humanitarian law, peace-keeping operations, humanitarian aid, and UN Security Council activity;[18] the links of human security to non-State actors;[19] and on a more development-based approach, international intellectual property law and human security.[20]

Despite the attention drawn to some of these international legal bearings of human security, the specific relationship between human security and human rights in international law remains underexplored. The relevance of human security for the human rights framework and practice has been examined,[21] and specific analysis of the human security lens, or its main components, in relation to the two thematic cores of this book, has been advanced. For instance, the twin human security pillars of protection and empowerment have been applied to the human rights of women and girls.[22] The work edited by Alice Edwards and Carla Ferstman also

[15] Von Tigerstrom, Barbara, *Human Security and International Law. Prospects and Problems* (Studies in International Law) (Oxford and Portland, Oregon, Hart Publishing, 2007) Introduction page.

[16] Oberleitner (2005) and (2014) 319–30 (n 14). See also Sunga (n 14) 131–48; Owada (n 14) 505–20; and McClean, Emma, 'Human Security and International Law: Much Ado About Nothing?' in Banakar, Reza (ed), *Rights in Context: Law and Justice in Late Modern Society* (UK, Ashgate, 2010) 253–73.

[17] Von Tigerstrom (n 15).

[18] See, eg, Owada (n 14); and see also Oberleitner (n 14); and Breau, Susan and Indira Carr, 'Humanitarian Aid, Human Rights and Corruption' in Odello, Marco and Sofia Cavandoli (eds), *Emerging Areas of Human Rights in the 21*st *Century: The Role of the Universal Declaration of Human Rights* (USA and Canada, Routledge, 2011) 149–75, particularly 157–60.

[19] See Ryngaert, Cedric and Math Noortmann (eds), *Human Security and International Law: The Challenge of Non-State Actors* (Cambridge, Intersentia, 2014). See also Bruderlein, Claude, 'The Role of Non-State Actors in Building Human Security: The Case of Armed Groups in Intra-State Wars' (Geneva, Centre for Humanitarian Dialogue, 2000).

[20] Ramcharan, Robin, *International Intellectual Property Law and Human Security* (The Hague, Asser Press, Springer, 2013).

[21] See Ramcharan, Bertrand G, *Human Rights and Human Security* (The Hague, Martinus Nijhoff, 2002) and by the same author 'Human Rights and Human Security' (2004) *Disarmament Forum, Strengthening Disarmament and Security* 1, 39–48. See also Von Tigerstrom (n 15), particularly 65–68; Tadjbakhsh, Shahrbanou and Anuradha M Chenoy, *Human Security: Concepts and Implications* (London and New York, Routledge, 2007) Chapter 5; Benedek, Wolfgang, 'Human Security and Human Rights Interaction' in Goucha, Moufida and John Crowley (eds), *Rethinking Human Security* (UK, Wiley-Blackwell and UNESCO, 2008) 7–17; McClean (n 16) in her analysis on 270–71; and Howard-Hassmann, Rhoda E, 'Human Security: Undermining Human Rights?' (2012) 34 *Human Rights Quarterly* 1, 88–112.

[22] See Heyzer, Noeleen, 'Combating Trafficking in Women and Children. A Gender and Human Rights Framework' in Truong, Thanh-Dam, Saskia Wieringa and

creatively applies the human security umbrella to present a thorough analysis of national origin and legal status as risk factors for the human rights of non-citizens, comprising migrants, asylum seekers, refugees and stateless persons.[23]

However, the relationship between human security and human rights has usually been briefly quoted only as a general and abstract discursive framing. In the few in-depth academic studies of the linkages of human security to international law, and human rights law more particularly, human security has usually been viewed more as pinned to the 'basic rights' of life, personal integrity, or liberty or security of the person, as those that are understood to be more closely connected to 'survival, livelihood and dignity'; that is, even when person-centred it has adopted a more hard-core view of the values and rights incumbent to security, leaving out socio-economic rights.[24] Other recent publications share a more holistic understanding of the relationship between human security and human rights law, in a closer approach to that proposed in this book, such as vulnerability and its role in human rights law, particularly in ESC Rights.[25]

Other studies have focused on the relationship of human security to gender and women's experiences of vulnerability, including that of gender-based violence,[26] and through reflections from feminist theory,[27] although

Amrita Chhachhi (eds), *Engendering Human Security. Feminist Perspectives* (USA, Women Unlimited, India/Zed Books Ltd, 2006) 101–23.

[23] See Edwards, Alice and Carla Ferstman (eds), *Human Security and Non-Citizens: Law, Policy and International Affairs* (Cambridge, Cambridge University Press, 2010).

[24] See, eg, the analysis by Von Tigerstrom (n 15); Owada (n 14) 505–20; and Kempen, Piet Hein van, 'Four Concepts of Security—A Human Rights Perspective' (2013) 13 *Human Rights Law Review* 1, 1–23.

[25] See, eg, Chapman, Audrey R and Benjamin Carbonetti, 'Human Rights Protections for Vulnerable and Disadvantaged Groups: The Contributions of the UN Committee on Economic, Social and Cultural Rights' (2011) *Human Rights Quarterly* 33, 682–732. See also Peroni, Lourdes and Alexandra Timmer, 'Vulnerable Groups: The Promise of an Emergent Concept in European Human Rights Convention Law' (2013) 11 *International Journal of Constitutional Law* 1056–85; and González, Felipe, 'The Experience of the Inter-American Human Rights System' (2009–10) 40 *Victoria University* 1, 103–25.

[26] See generally Tripp, Aili, Myra Marx Ferree and Christina Ewig (eds), *Gender, Violence and Human Security: Critical Feminist Perspectives* (New York, New York University Press, 2013). See also Coomaraswamy, Radihka, 'Human Security and Gender Violence' (2005) 40 *Economic and Political Weekly* 44/45, 4729–36; the section on the security of women in Gasper, Des and Oscar A Gómez, 'Human Security Thinking in Practice: "personal security", "citizen security" and comprehensive mappings' (2015) 21 *Contemporary Politics* 1, 100–16; and Bunch, Charlotte, 'Foreword. Feminist Quandaries on Gender and Violence: Agency, Universality, and Human Security' in Bahun, Sanja and VG Julie Rajan (eds), *Violence and Gender in the Globalized World: The Intimate and the Extimate*, 2nd edn (England and USA, Ashgate, 2015) xiii–xviii.

[27] McKay, Susan, 'Women, Human Security, and Peace-Building: A Feminist Analysis', in Shinoda, Hideaki and Ho-Won Jeong (eds), *Conflict and Human Security: A Search for New Approaches of Peace-building, IPSHU English Research Report Series No.19*, (Hiroshima, Institute for Peace Science-Hiroshima University, 2004), 152–75; and Truong, Wieringa and Chhachhi (n 22). See also Reardon and Hans (n 12); and Reardon (n 12) 99–109.

less so on the specific link between human security and the human rights of women and girls,[28] and very rarely on human security and violence against women under human rights law.[29]

At the same time, while the process of securitisation of migration has been underlined in the last few years from a human rights perspective,[30] as well as the relevance of human security in the context of migration,[31] particularly in the field of migration and gender,[32] very few works have mapped and critically evaluated the links between the human security conception and human rights law as related to undocumented migrants.[33]

Regarding the focus of this book on the use of the human security lens to better identify socio-economic vulnerabilities, while several studies apply the human security perspective to different developmental issues that cover similar concerns, very few do so combining it with a human rights law perspective and particularly emphasising ESC Rights.[34]

Lastly, although there is scholarly analysis and institutional expressions of human security in different regional scenarios such as the EU, Inter-American or African Union bodies,[35] so far there is no work carried

[28] See Bunch, Charlotte, 'A Feminist Human Rights Lens on Human Security' (2004) 16 *Peace Review* 1, 29–34; and Ssenyonjo, Manisuli, 'Human Rights of Women in Africa: A Prerequisite for Human Security' in Abass, Ademola (ed), *Protecting Human Security in Africa* (Oxford, Oxford University Press, 2010).

[29] To my knowledge the only review of this relationship from the standpoint of human rights case-law and through a comparative regional perspective, is the chapter by this author, together with Rubio Marin, Ruth, 'Violence against Women, Human Security and Human Rights of Women and Girls: Reinforced Obligations in the Context of Structural Vulnerability' in Tripp, Ferree and Ewig (n 26) 238–59.

[30] Guild, Elspeth, *Security and Migration in the 21st Century* (Cambridge, Polity Press, 2009); Dembour, Marie-Bénédicte and Tobias Kelly (eds), *Are Human Rights for Migrants? Critical Reflections on the Status of Irregular Migrants in Europe and the United States* (New York, Routledge, 2011); and Mitsilegas, Valsamis, *The Criminalisation of Migration in Europe: Challenges for Human Rights and the Rule of Law* (Cham, Heidelberg, Springer, 2015).

[31] See Edwards and Ferstman (n 23), particularly the chapter by Lester, Eve, 'Socio-Economic Rights, Human Security and Survival Migrants: Whose Rights? Whose Security?' at 314–56; as well as Oberoi, Pia, 'Empowering Migrants: Human Security, Human Rights and Policy' in the same publication, at 227–72. See also Truong, Thanh-Dam and Des Gasper (eds), *Transnational Migration and Human Security: The Migration-Development-Security Nexus*, Hexagon Series on Human and Environmental Security and Peace (Berlin, New York, Springer, 2011) Vol 6.

[32] See, eg Truong, Thanh-Dam, Des Gasper, Jeff Handmaker, and Sylvia I Bergh (eds), *Migration, Gender and Social Justice: Perspectives on Human Security*, Hexagon Series on Human and Environmental Security and Peace (Berlin, New York, Springer, 2014) Vol 9.

[33] Notably the analysis by Lester (n 31) 314–56, touches both on the human security–human rights nexus in relation to undocumented migrants, and on socio-economic rights as well.

[34] Again, as a noteworthy exception, see Lester, *ibid.*

[35] See, eg, *A European Way of Security: The Madrid Report of the Human Security Study Group*, Human Security Study Group, presented to the EU High Representative for Common Foreign and Security Policy Javier Solana (Madrid, Spain, 2007); and Martin, Mary and Owen Taylor, 'The Second Generation of Human Security: Lessons from the UN and EU Experience' (2010) 1 *International Affairs* 86, 211–24; and Inter-American Commission on

out containing a comparative perspective between the Inter-American, European and African systems of human rights (and their links to the UN system). Neither is there a study that builds communicating bridges between human security and concrete human rights in the realm of normative instruments, as well as relevant case-law of the regional human rights systems, as addressed in this book.

II. THE ARGUMENT

This study aims at complementing the current debates surrounding human security by providing an integral evaluation of: **i)** the normative embodiment of the human security–human rights law interaction, and the potential and limitations of this relationship; **ii)** the impact of the notion of human security in the normative and jurisprudential developments on violence against women/migrant-related issues that (explicitly or implicitly) consider the human security–human rights interaction, at the UN level and regional levels of the Inter-American, European and African systems of human rights, mainly focusing on the first two regional systems; and **iii)** the contribution international human rights law can make to better delimit the scope of the concept of human security and the types of violence and deprivation it takes into account.

As such, the book proposes a framework for analysis and action, the 'human security–human rights synergy' to better address existing gaps and tackle issues of structural vulnerability in an interrelated and contextualised manner. I argue that human security is useful to bring light to threats that under the dominant security logic would otherwise remain invisible, such as violence against women, including domestic violence, as well as legal irregularity of migrants as a condition of risk; and generalised socio-economic inequality as a fertile ground that renders human rights violations possible. On the other hand, in engaging critically with the human security conception, I submit that it remains in need of a substantiated and precise normative grounding that can be provided by human rights law.

Of course, not merely the mentioned threats come to mind. Climate-change induced displacement, human trafficking, the dangers affecting children—the possibility of being recruited as a soldier, being affected by armed conflict, the sexual exploitation of children, especially girls, for commercial purposes—unimaginable global concerns in times of the Universal Declaration of Human Rights, have become sources of

Human Rights, Organization of American States, *Report on Citizen Security and Human Rights*, OEA/Ser.L/V/II, Doc 57, 31 December 2009; and Dersso, Solomon A (ed), *Promotion of Human Security in Africa. The Role of African Human Rights Institutions*, ISS Monograph Series, No 145, June 2008.

massive human suffering and harm to human rights. As such, I contend that modernising human rights and adapting them to current challenges may be done through human security acting as a complementary force to international human rights law.

On the other hand, there is no one unqualified and unequivocal meaning of security under international human rights law and, in fact, on occasions such uses may be contradictory.[36] Thus, human security is useful in giving a unified and orienting notion to bring together different understandings of 'human rights security' and provide them with direction. It works as a parameter of evaluation to assess outcome: does a given human rights norm or interpretation result in more effective protection and empowerment of those in conditions of structural vulnerability?

As a starting point to tackle this question, I argue that *all* human rights—civil, political, economic, social and cultural—should be considered within the human security conception, as confirmed by the UNGA's most recent position. My view is that to qualify as a human security concern, human rights should only be differentiated or prioritised according to identifiable and identified levels of risk and vulnerability on a context-specific basis.

Indeed, the element of *risk or vulnerability* allows for making the links between human security and human rights visible: through emphasising the interrelated risk factors and vulnerabilities affecting *all* human rights, the lack of enjoyment of political, cultural, social, civil and economic rights and the structural obstacles to their full realisation become security concerns for the State. The human security perspective holds potential as well for addressing other actors contributing to these risk-producing barriers, such as non-State actors—not only private individuals in cases of violence against women, for instance, but also other actors such as migrant-recruiting agencies or human smugglers. With this view, it also contributes to breaking down the vertical/horizontal divides in human rights law.

In this book a particular preoccupation with socio-economic vulnerability and situations of material deprivation and inequality, is displayed. However, poverty and inequality do not only affect economic, social and cultural human rights, and they are often also determined along gender, age, disability, and ethnic lines. Rather, poverty, social exclusion and socio-economic marginalisation have many faces, they cut through the whole set of human rights and they are deeply related to the rights of equality and non-discrimination and to the right of access to justice, as will be spelled out in this book. At this juncture, human security comes forward as a concept that may better capture the breadth and width of this relationship and transcend the traditional human rights divide of civil and political/ESC Rights.

[36] For the study of security as an unqualified good, see Kempen (n 24) 1–23; and Zedner, Lucia, 'Too Much Security?' (2003) 31 *International Journal of the Sociology of Law* 155–84.

The twin pillars of *protection* and *empowerment* embodied with the same force in the human security notion are both relevant not only from a conceptual, but also from a strategic perspective. In its axis of *protection*, the 'top-down' approach reinforces the role of the State as the primary duty-bearer in the protection of persons in conditions of vulnerability, but leaves open space to also engage other actors in a position of power, such as business corporations for instance, to also participate in guaranteeing human security. By emphasising 'bottom-up' construction through its element of *empowerment*, it echoes feminist discourse and opens up this second pillar as a wide-ranging condition necessary for realising human security for vulnerable, silenced or destitute persons and groups more generally. Indeed, the pillar of empowerment also drives us to build horizontal partnerships based on commonalities and create cooperative networks among persons and organisations working on similar issues, some of which have been essential for the legal advancement of women's rights, for instance.[37]

Although throughout this text it can be gathered that there are elements of human security present in the traditional primary sources of public international law—treaties, customary international law, general principles of law, as well as in the secondary sources, namely, jurisprudence and doctrine, or even in *ius cogens*—this book's main concern is not to address this legal analysis from the viewpoint of such sources. Rather, it attempts, firstly, to make explicit the intersections between the meta-legal concept of human security and the legal understanding of international human rights. Secondly, it explores the potential of this synergy for legal interpretation and practical implementation, focusing on persons in structural vulnerability. It does so by proposing a conceptual framework useful for action, the 'human security–human rights synergy', which identifies and gives shape to the intersections between human security and human rights and proposes certain guidelines that could further develop the reciprocal impact between them. In doing so, it moves across different issues relevant for public international law, such as State responsibility, the role of non-State actors, expansion of State positive obligations, and the procedural and substantive legal implications of the human security–human rights symbiosis.

Such framework is then applied to the two thematic cores of violence against women and the risks faced by undocumented migrants and other non-citizens, particularly to female migrants, emphasising socio-economic vulnerability throughout the analysis. This examination explores the actual and potential legal/policy implications for women at risk of or suffering violence and for undocumented migrants, as persons

[37] See Merry, Sally Engle, *Human Rights and Gender Violence: Translating International Law into Local Justice* (Chicago, University of Chicago Press, 2010). Note also her idea of 'vernacularization' of international law as the process of its appropriation by local actors and practices.

reflecting conditions of structural vulnerability. Through this thematic study the book reveals a set of *interpretative synergies* that can tackle the need for more just, protective, coordinated and effective fulfilment both of human rights and of human security.

Indeed, gender and legal status relating to entry into or residence in a given state, both continue to constitute risk factors increasing the possibility for women and girls, and for undocumented migrants, of experiencing human rights violations. The international legal human rights framework applicable to violence against women and to undocumented migrants and their implementation, present gaps which translate into a serious lack of protection. Thus, both topics present legal challenges in terms of bringing to life and making effective the human rights of the people covered by such norms. At the factual level, violence against women is still widespread and pervasive and apart from constituting a form of discrimination and a human rights violation in itself, it is also an obstacle for the enjoyment of other human rights. Concerning the theme of undocumented migrants, the human security quest for a new paradigm that adequately responds in a coordinated way to situations affecting people and transcending national borders, seems to fall directly in place with the transnational nature and the vulnerable condition deriving from undocumented migration. Undocumented migrants, whether moving across or within national frontiers, because of their status of legal irregularity, are at times placed in a situation of 'legal limbo' where their rights are purportedly undefined, they often live in a climate of fear and they confront constant threats or actual violations of their universally recognised rights. This is especially true of undocumented migrant women and girls, who suffer augmented risks of discrimination, violence, and other human rights violations, in many cases further aggravated by a lack of access to justice.

The two themes, violence against women and girls and the human rights of undocumented migrants connect to developed and developing countries, to liberal democracies and authoritarian regimes, to the context of peace or armed conflict, in different degrees and intensities, but with the common denominator of representing structural vulnerabilities worldwide. Moreover, the challenges of violence against women and the quandaries involved in upholding the rights of undocumented migrants render considerable sectors of the population defenceless, despite the fact that they are present in liberal democratic polities holding generally acceptable records regarding human rights. These vulnerabilities are confronted with gaps in human rights law and/or implementation that have been insufficient in addressing concerns on both topics. These cracks in the system allow for thousands of people to fall between norms, to remain unprotected and in some cases, to confront life-threatening situations. The human security proposal of *freedom from fear, freedom from want and freedom to live in dignity* seems to hold promise in adding value to identifying and addressing such collective vulnerabilities through offering an integrative approach to fill the relevant legal loopholes and fulfil the human rights of affected women and girls, undocumented migrants and other non-citizens in their everyday lives.

Also, the threats to human security in the form of socio-economic deprivation are a *cross-cutting issue*, placing both women and girls facing violence as well as undocumented migrants—often poor and socially marginalised—in heightened conditions of vulnerability. It is no coincidence that legal, philosophical, political and sociological scholarship, international and inter-governmental organisations' reports, universal and regional human rights mechanisms and multiple civil society activities have recently focused on prioritising both issues in their agenda. Thus, the present text affirms that international human rights law has something more to offer in the face of these challenges and, to do so more effectively, it must act in combination with human security in order to deliver the promises envisioned by the human rights spirit and the legal architecture constructed around it.

In contributing to identifying categories of vulnerability, the human security perspective provides for criteria to extend the boundaries of international human rights law and related areas of law such as refugee law: the human security notion may trigger and reinforce the State's (or other actors') human rights obligations to prevent, address and remedy violations. At the same time, the research signals limitations in the all-encompassing concept of human security, highlighting that to make it actually operational and valuable it is necessary for it to be tied to existing normative frameworks, languages and indicators, such as those developed in human rights law. It thus builds on key criticism towards the notion, but does not abandon the human security proposal, rather seeking to revisit it and complement it on the basis of the various insights it has contributed to strengthen or advance in four central identified points: **a)** its person-centred approach; **b)** its emphasis on intra-state violence and broader understandings of direct and indirect violence; **c)** its underlining of socio-economic vulnerabilities as authentic security concerns; and **d)** its emphasis on interrelatedness transcending individual conditions of human rights violations.

As reviewed above, the literature and academic scholarship, the positions of international and regional organisations, inter-governmental activity, and civil society initiatives approaching human security are vast and all-encompassing. It has been dealt with through the disciplines of development studies, political science, international relations, critical security studies and international law.

Thus, in terms of methodology, and to avoid the 'perils of "sectionalism"',[38] or fragmentary approaches to human security, this book

[38] See the critique to sectionalism in this field in Saul Takahashi's introduction in Takahashi (n 11) vii–xxiii.

is based on a first interdisciplinary approach incorporating international relations, sociology of law, political science, feminist theory, and migration studies, to the central area of legal analysis. It then particularly builds on international human rights law and scholarship, as well as on a comparative perspective between regional human rights instruments and case-law relevant to human security, especially on the themes of violence against women and the rights of undocumented migrants, also advancing the transnational dimensions of these links.

This book also aims at filling a gap usually present in the scholarship on human security: it is either only theoretical, for example, approaching it from the perspective of critical security studies, or when studying concrete engagements with human security, particularly those related to human rights, it focuses on UN activity or on one regional expression or another, but the literature is not 'talking to each other'. For instance, there is no publication to my knowledge that analyses the human security–human rights intersection in the existing regional institutional human rights' settings, namely the Inter-American, European and African systems of human rights.

This lack of academic exchange is possibly also due to linguistic reasons. To give an example, in none of the English language literature on human security did I find a reference to the 1995 Framework Convention on Democratic Security in Central America—one of the only international treaties specifically including State positive obligations attached to 'human security'.

The book wishes to trigger part of this much needed exchange by building one of the bridges for this dialogue, that of the English and Spanish-language scholarship, coupled by a deeper conversation between European and Inter-American, especially Latin American, human rights academy and jurisprudence. Given that we face some common challenges, their joint confrontation seems obvious. Apart from the contribution to legal pluralism, the functional value of this approach lies in providing further tools for the human security–human rights interaction to be constructed cooperatively through the experience of two of the main human rights systems and languages of the world, thus opening the door for advancing legal scholarship and practice.

III. CHAPTER SYNOPSES

This book is divided into two parts. Part I of the book is dedicated to presenting the conceptual outlines necessary for the construction of the human security–human rights synergy proposed in this book through the first three chapters.

Chapter 1 contains an overview of human security, its historical evolution, the main debate surrounding the concept, as well as the arrival in

2012 of a 'common understanding' of the notion by the UNGA. The text also includes key international, regional and national uses of the notion. A final part portrays the defence of a holistic understanding of human security, in light of the discussion on the advantages and setbacks of adopting a 'narrow' or a 'broad' definition. A broad idea of human security is advocated—comprising structural vulnerability caused by physical and indirect violence as well as by material deprivation—but making the case of placing *all* human rights at the core of the concept. As such, a section is reserved for a reflection on the human insecurities related to violations of ESC Rights and the vulnerability to poverty. At the same time, a threshold definition is defended considering the gravity, the widespread character and the high level of risk as the identifying element to qualify a given situation, including first and foremost human rights situations, as a human security concern. Some suggestions on the methodology to make such a concept operational in practice are included in the deliberation, highlighting the importance of incorporating human rights standards and indicators into human security assessments.

Chapter 2 analyses how human security relates to human rights and some concrete forms in which the elements of human security are reflected in international human rights law and their link to public international law more generally. A reflection on vulnerability and more particularly 'structural vulnerability' is presented, to open the way for the central approach of international human rights law to *risk* and *vulnerability*, essential elements of human security. These elements are analysed initially as a general umbrella under which the development of person-centred security concerns has taken place through noteworthy instruments and the case-law of international human rights and refugee law. The crucial features of this expression are systematised according to the subject matter they address. A reflection on human security, humanitarian intervention and the responsibility to protect is also presented with the view of clarifying their main consonances and dissonances for the purpose of this book's analysis. The relationship between human security and human rights is then examined through considering some of the main legal intersections between them. First, it looks at how human rights law has treated security in general through the embodiment of the rights to personal security, social security, security in tenure and food security, and sets the stage to ask whether human security is or should be a human right, finally exploring the human security–human rights interaction in light of the sources of public international law.

On the basis of the examination of the two previous chapters, Chapter 3 constructs the human security–human rights synergy proposed in this book. It does so through analysing Article 28 of the Universal Declaration of Human Rights and the contention that human security may be understood as a *facilitating environment* for human rights' realisation. It examines the idea of 'core content' in international human rights law and connects it to human security deriving the potential of the latter for acting as an integrating bridge among all human rights. The chapter then presents its proposal of the human security–human rights law intersection as a framework for thought and action and portrays a graphic illustration of this relationship. Finally, it lists the concrete points of the proposed framework and includes some suggestions on how to continue developing the symbiosis between human security and human rights in a resourceful and constructive manner for both.

In Part II, the book moves on to apply the proposed human security–human rights synergy, in relation to the two thematic cores of violence against women and girls, on the one hand; and on the other, the human rights of undocumented migrants and other non-citizens. Resulting from the intersection of these thematic cores, a third topic is analysed in considering the situation of undocumented female migrants, as well as some illustrative legal cases on the application of a human security approach to the conditions and human rights of undocumented migrants in general. This is carried out applying the propositioned framework through the review of these subjects in light of human rights law in the form of instruments and case-law of the UN system, as well as the regional Inter-American, European and African human rights systems, concentrating particularly on the two first regional scenarios.

In Chapter 4, the text will look more closely at the general conception of human security and the human security–human rights framework, in relation specifically to violence against women and girls and their human rights. It will first reflect critically on how a gendered human security would have to be shaped.[39] The chapter examines this relationship in the form of an in-depth thematic study covering the normative landscapes of the UN, the Inter-American, European and African human rights' systems. It also reviews paradigmatic cases resolved by the Inter-American and European Courts of Human Rights as exemplifying some of the potentials of the human security–human rights symbiosis. Considering the human security approach to critical risks and vulnerabilities, this chapter explores violence against women as one of the most pervasive and widespread threats worldwide. At the same time, the concept of violence against women and girls has been strongly developed by international

[39] It must be recalled that violence against women is conceived as a subcategory of gender-based violence. This last type of violence also covers, for example, the experiences of male violence against gay men, of violence based on gender by women or men against transgender persons, or of women against women in the absence of their performance of expected gender roles; in this sense see the analysis by Leach, Fiona and Sara Humphreys, 'Gender Violence in Schools: Taking the "Girls as Victims" Discourse Forward' in Terry, Geraldine and Joanna Hoare (eds), *Gender-Based Violence* (London, Oxfam GB, 2007) 106–20. However, women and girls 'constitute the majority of victims of gender-based violence and men the majority of perpetrators'; Hayes, Ceri, 'Tackling Violence against

human rights law, although seldom taken into account explicitly in human security concerns relating to violence. Thus, in the last part, the chapter examines the consequences of the interaction of applying a human security lens to the legal analysis of violence against women and their human rights, and of including the human rights definition of violence against women within the human security sphere, with the aim of fleshing out the added value of this dialogue and bringing to light the synergies between human security and human rights of women and girls.

Chapter 5 will analyse the existing international human rights law applicable to migrants, in particular undocumented migrants and other non-citizens, taking the UN standards as a central departing point and reviewing the regional standards on the subject. The chapter will then sketch out the interconnections between human security and human rights of undocumented migrant persons, at the empirical level as well as in legal analysis, by viewing legal irregularity as a source of risk. Similarly, it reflects on some of the specific risks confronted by asylum-seekers at a time when the economic crisis and mixed flows of migration, concretely in the EU context, have allowed for weakening protection of this group of non-citizens. More generally, the human security approach allows for identifying risks to several human rights of undocumented migrants, quite notably that of access to justice.

Chapter 6 addresses the concrete application of the gendered human security lens to spell out the particular risks and types of violence faced by undocumented migrant girls and women, as well as the vulnerabilities experienced more specifically by female undocumented migrant domestic workers and the legal regime that tackles them. In the last part of the chapter, the text will draw a picture of how some of the identified normative tools may be utilised to enhance human rights protection when applied through a human security-based approach. It will analyse illustrative quasi-judicial and judicial cases from the UN and regional human rights' systems in order to exemplify how a human security-sensitive perspective may orientate the interpretation of human rights when put to work in practice, as well as the consequences that may unfold when it is overlooked. The chapter concludes with some remarks on 'the right to have access to rights' as a necessary human security requirement for the respect and fulfilment of the universally recognised human rights of undocumented migrants.

Women: A Worldwide Approach' in Terry and Hoare, *ibid*, 2. Therefore, for the effects of our analysis, this text considers gender-based violence in its most frequent understanding as violence against women and girls (VAW). It concentrates on VAW as the most widespread and illustrative form of gender-based violence, and also as a human rights violation which has been dealt with extensively by international human rights law.

An initial clarification is in line regarding the meaning ascribed to 'individualist' human rights and 'collective' vulnerabilities considered under human security, as referred to in this book. True, human rights have worked for the protection of human beings and groups, and not only for individual persons. Think, for example, of the rights of minorities recognised in several human rights instruments, or of the 2007 UN Declaration on the Rights of Indigenous Peoples or instruments and case-law referring to them. Consider also how, particularly in the African tradition, human rights are to be understood also as community, and not only individual, entitlements. However, what human rights law does not, in itself, account for, are the interrelated social, economic, cultural, political and institutional conditions that facilitate human rights violations. In this sense, the personal and structural differentiation as proposed since the late 1960s by Johan Galtung in his conception of 'structural violence' may be more useful to illustrate this point.[40] Following this line of thought, I argue that the human security proposal better portrays this underlying interconnectedness and also emphasises the forms in which the human rights of some human beings are at a greater risk of being violated than the rights of other persons. As Paul Farmer puts it, while human rights are universal, 'the risk of having one's rights violated is not universal'.[41]

It is in the consideration of widespread and critical vulnerabilities of human security and the rights held by those affected by them as signalled by international human rights law that the two conceptions overlap and intersect. It is on this crossroad that this book is focused.

In a nutshell, the central core of this book, as studied in the six chapters, presents to the reader an analysis of the synergy between human security and human rights: portraying human security as (predominantly) a policy tool seen as a meta-legal concept offering a *collective and structural* outlook lacking in *individualist* or *personalist* human rights; and proposing human rights as a legally normative grounding for such an outlook, missing in the human security conception and operationalisation.[42] Various 'interpretative synergies' resulting from the human security–human rights interaction studied in the six chapters of this book are proposed in concluding Chapter 7.

[40] See Galtung, Johan, 'Violence, Peace, and Peace Research' (1969) 6 *Journal of Peace Research* 3, 167–91.

[41] Farmer, Paul, *Pathologies of Power: Health, Human Rights, and the New War on the Poor* (Berkeley, University of California Press, 2005) 231.

[42] See, eg, Paris, Roland, 'Human Security: Paradigm Shift or Hot Air?' (2001) 26 *International Security* 2, 87–102; Owen, Taylor, 'Human Security—Conflict, Critique and Consensus: Colloquium Remarks and a Proposal for a Threshold-Based Definition in *Security Dialogue* (Oslo, Norway, International Peace Research Institute, Sage Publications, 2004) Vol 35, No 3, 373–87.

Part I

Conceptual Outlines

1

Human Security: An Overview

I. HISTORICAL EVOLUTION OF HUMAN SECURITY

AS ALREADY SIGNALLED in the introduction, traditionally security had been considered a State matter, both as the subject in charge of providing it to the persons under its jurisdiction, as well as the object worthy of protection and regulation through laws and policies. The security of individual human beings, in contrast, was largely ignored.[1] While some authors trace the origins of human security to eighteenth century enlightened liberalism,[2] and one may also find explicit references to 'human security' in newspaper narratives of nineteenth century London,[3] it was not until the decades after World War II that the concept gained articulation on the international scene. The 1945 UN Charter, referring in its preamble to the Parties' commitment 'to promote social progress and better standards of life *in larger freedom*', served as inspiration for the subsequent understanding of security as linked to freedom from fear and from want, proposed by the United Nations Development Program (UNDP) in 1994. Since the late 1970s and early 1980s, though, changes in the traditional views of security were already being encouraged at the UN level.

The report of the Brandt Commission in 1980 had pushed for a non-military concept of security to be 'enlarged to include hunger, disease, poverty, environmental stress, repression, and terrorism, all of which endanger *human security* as much as any military provocation'. It emphasised that to meet that aim 'the international community has

[1] MacFarlane, Neil S and Yuen Foong Khong, *Human Security and the UN. A Critical History* (Bloomington, Indiana University Press, United Nations Intellectual History Project, 2006) 19.

[2] Owen, Taylor, 'Challenges and Opportunities for Defining and Measuring Human Security' in *Disarmament Forum* 3, (2004) 15–24.

[3] *The Times*, London, Wednesday, 18 October 1848, 4 (title not visible); 'Widow-Burning in India. Letter to the Editor from and East India Proprietor' *The Times*, London, 1831 (exact date and page not visible); *The Times*, London, Monday, 20 June 1842 (title not visible); *The Times* London, Wednesday, 18 October 1848, 4 (title not visible); *The Times*, London, Saturday, 20 January 1858 (title not visible); *The Times*, London, 'Criminal Court', 6 March 1862; and *The Times*, London,'Daylight Air Raid. 76 Killed and 154 Injured' Monday, 28 May 1917.

the responsibility to eliminate any social conditions that pose threats to the protection and dignity of people, before they erupt into armed conflict'.[4] Similarly, in 1982 the *Palme Commission Report on Disarmament and Security* and in 1987, the Brundtland Commission report, *Report of the World Commission on Environment and Development: Our Common Future,* noted that a

> comprehensive approach to international and national security must transcend the traditional emphasis on military power and armed competition. The real sources of insecurity also encompass unsustainable development, and its effects can become intertwined with traditional forms of conflict in a manner that can extend and deepen the latter.[5]

Such views were intended to impact on the traditional view of 'national security' stemming primarily from US political discourse in the mid-1940s after World War II. This concept considered the State as the referent and the acting unit of security, deriving from the balance of power consequent upon State behaviour and reaffirming its autarky. National security was thus defined in terms of 'national interest' and mostly guaranteed through military means, thus understanding 'military security' as a sub-type of national security.[6] The historical evolution of the conceptualisation of security in the UN advanced in parallel to shifts in theorising security by scholars from different disciplines within the growing field of security studies in the 1980s and 1990s.[7]

It was only after the Cold War that a political space was opened for a stronger institutional development of the notion of human security within the UN, alongside the trans-border phenomena deriving from a more interconnected world. Generally, the origin of the contemporary coining of the human security idea is traced back to the work done within UNDP in 1993 and 1994. True, the full articulation of human security at the international level finds its genesis in the UNDP. However, after the Cold War, the first mentions of human security within the UN institutional structure

[4] *Brandt Report*, examined in Quilligan, James Bernard, *The Brandt Equation: 21st Century Blueprint for the New Global Economy* (USA, Brandt 21 Forum, 2002) 13. See also the work done by Global Environmental Change and Human Security (GECHS), at www.gechs.org/.

[5] World Commission on Environment and Development, *Report of the World Commission on Environment and Development: Our Common Future*, UN Doc A/RES/42/187/Annex, 2 August 1987, p 4.

[6] See McSweeney, Bill, *Security, Identity and Interests: A Sociology of International Relations*, Cambridge Studies in International Relations (UK, Cambridge University Press, 1999) 19 and subsequently 28 and 34.

[7] See, eg, Buzan, Barry, *People, States and Fear: The National Security Problem in International Relations*, (USA, University of North Carolina Press, 1983) and the revised version by the same author, first published in 1991, *People, States and Fear: An Agenda for International Security Studies in the Post Cold War Era*, 2nd edn (UK, ECPR Press, 2007); Dorff, Robert H, 'A Commentary on Security Studies for the 1990s as a Model Curriculum Core' (1994) 3 *International Studies Notes* 19, 23–31; and McSweeney (n 6).

were actually suggested by the Security Council itself. Indeed, in 1992, 'at a time of momentous change', the UNSC expressed a strong commitment towards a human security agenda,[8] and then, in the first explicit mention of human security by one of the main UN bodies, it was addressed in the Secretary General's Report of that same year, *An Agenda for Peace. Preventive Diplomacy, Peacemaking and Peace-Keeping.*[9] In recognising the changing global context and the *new dimension of insecurity*, the Report stressed the necessity 'to address the deepest causes of conflict: economic despair, social injustice and political oppression' as each had 'a special and indispensable role to play in an integrated approach to *human security*'. The Report forwarded the view that the UN had to assess its own potential in maintaining international security 'not only in its traditional sense, but in the *new dimensions* presented by the era ahead'.[10] For this to be rendered possible, the Report details a set of early warning systems that should work as preventive tools, much in the spirit of the 'common understanding' of human security proposed by the UN Secretary General and endorsed by the UN General Assembly (UNGA) in 2012. The 1992 Report stressed the importance of such systems to be based on adequate fact-finding mechanisms and reports, including those of a socio-economic nature.[11]

The following year, human security was briefly referred to by the UNDP in its Human Development Report of 1993, *People's Participation*, and then fully constructed by Mahbub ul-Haq through the 1994 UNDP Human Development Report, called precisely *New Dimensions of Human Security.*[12] Thus, human security was initially envisioned as a parallel road and an indispensable companion for human development. Actually, the 1994 Human Development Report included a six-item agenda that reflected its concern with socio-economic equality and global justice as a means of ensuring what the document considered 'the peace dividend' of that time. Specifically underlining that 'the search for human security lies in development, not in arms', the Report included, amongst other items, the creation of a *global human security fund* to address the common threats to global human security, and the formation of a UN Economic Security

[8] Note by the President of the Security Council, UN Doc S/23500, 31 January 1992, pp 3–4.

[9] *An Agenda for Peace. Preventive Diplomacy, Peacemaking and Peace-Keeping*, Report of the Secretary-General pursuant to the statement adopted by the Summit Meeting of the Security Council on 31 January 1992, A/47/277—S/24111, 17 June 1992.

[10] *Ibid*, paras 13–16. Mention of human security in para 16.

[11] *Ibid*, paras 26 and following.

[12] UNDP, *Human Development Reports*, 1993 and 1994, available at http://hdr.undp.org/en/reports/. See UNDP 1993 Human Development Report, *People's Participation*, at pp iii; 2, 3 and 7 of Summary, and 12 of full report.

Council.[13] (emphasis in original) In a contemporary analysis, it would seem that over time the item to have reached a most successful outcome is that of a global fund for human security, through the existence of the UN Trust Fund for Human Security (UNTFHS), which in the last few years has dedicated an average of one million and a half USD for each regional project per year, adding up to a total of 22 million USD in the main ongoing national/regional projects (at different times between 2011–2015), plus many national projects with a specific budget for each one.[14] These are figures which seem to contrast starkly with the annual budget of approximately 186 million USD received annually by the UN Office of the High Commissioner for Human Rights (OHCHR) for the whole of its activities worldwide.[15]

The proposal to create an Economic Security Council is quite interesting, especially in light of the points raised by some human security detractors who fear that the concept will be utilised to justify some form of military intervention. In studying the actual official documents, it becomes clear that at least the intention of the first drafters, and a spirit that prevails today according to the 2012 UNGA 'common understanding' that will be reviewed, is clearly that of human security as a set of development features, notably socio-economic elements, as a pre-condition for peace and a strategic tool for its maintenance. In a deeper sense, it originally stemmed as a concern with global justice and the creation of a *new global ethic* based on the universalism of all human rights.[16]

Indeed, for the UNDP, following the original wording of the UN Charter, there are two conditions that can foster human security: *freedom from fear* and *freedom from want*.[17] Therefore, human security as defined by the UNDP includes two main aspects: 1) safety from such chronic threats as hunger, disease and repression; and 2) protection from sudden and hurtful disruptions in the patterns of daily life—whether in homes, in jobs or in communities. Such threats can exist at all levels of national income and development. Based on this definition, according to the Human Development Report of 1994, the threats to human security can be grouped into seven categories: economic security, food security,

[13] UNDP, *1994 Human Development Report, New Dimensions of Human Security*, Overview, pp 1, 5–6.

[14] This amount is calculated by adding the programmed budgets for the six main activities financed by the UNTFHS as described on its webpage; see www.un.org/humansecurity/.

[15] This amount is calculated on the basis of the volume of the regular UN budget allocated to the UN OHCHR for the biennium of 2010–2011, USD 151.6 million (less than 3% of the whole UN budget), that is, USD 75.8 million per year, plus the approximate amount of USD 111 million of voluntary contributions received by the OHCHR in 2011, to sum up, a total budget of the OHCHR of USD 186.8 million for 2011; see UN OHCHR Report 2011, pp 124–125, available at www2.ohchr.org/english/ohchrreport2011/web_version/ohchr_report2011_web/allegati/16_Funding.pdf.

[16] UNDP, *1994 Human Development Report* (n 13) pp 13–14 and 21.

[17] UNDP, *1994 Human Development Report* (n 13) p 24.

health security, environmental security, personal security, community security, and political security.[18] Of course, each one of these forms of human security is a world in itself. Specific types of human (in)security, the threats related to them and the affected human rights have been addressed on their own footing, such as the scholarly work and instruments on environmental security[19] and food security,[20] for example. However, the scope of this book will rather focus on understanding and demarcating human security, more in line with the 2003 and 2012 UN definitions.

After the release of the 1994 definition, different initiatives and institutional arrangements were put in place surrounding human security. The Human Security Network, a diplomacy-level lobbying initiative, was set up in 1998, mainly under the leadership of Canada. Its proposals supported goals more in line with the 'narrow' proponents of human security; that is, concentrating more on efforts related to address violent armed conflict.[21]

To consider further definitions of human security, let us review the 2003 Report which stemmed from an independent Commission on Human Security (CHS) established in 2001 by United Nations Secretary General (UNSG) Kofi Annan and integrated by a group of experts co-chaired by academic Amartya Sen, Nobel Laureate in Economics 1998, and Sadako Ogata, former UN High Commissioner for Refugees. After two years of deliberation, the Commission submitted its final report, *Human Security Now*, to the UNSG in May 2003. The Report, building from the *freedom from fear* and *freedom from want* ideals,[22] defines human security as protecting

> the *vital core of all human lives* in ways that enhance human freedoms and human fulfilment. Human security means protecting fundamental freedoms—freedoms that are the essence of life. It means protecting people from *critical*

[18] UNDP, *1994 Human Development Report* (n 13) pp 23–25.

[19] See for example Dalby, Simon, *Environmental Security* (University of Minnesota Press, 2002) in particular, 13–18; and 123–42. See by the same author, *Security and Environmental Change* (Cambridge, Polity Press, 2009); see also the analysis in Chapter 2 of the 2004 ECHR case *Oneryldiz v Turkey (GC)*, Application No 48939/99, Judgment of 30 November 2004.

[20] See for instance the 2003 Protocol to the African Charter on Human and People's Rights on the Rights of Women in Africa, the Maputo Protocol, dealt with in Chapter 4 of this book. See also Rome Declaration on World Food Security, Food and Agriculture Organisation, 1996, available at www.fao.org/wfs; and Declaration of Cochabamba on "Food Security with Sovereignty in the Americas", AG/DEC. 69 (XLII-O/12), Organisation of American States, 5 June 2012.

[21] See Behringer, Ronald M., *The Human Security Agenda: How Middle Power Leadership Defied U.S. Hegemony* (London, New York, Continuum, 2012) 22, 28. Note however that recently the Human Security Network has also backed sustainable development aims; see Press Release, 'High-level Meeting of the Human Security Network', New York, 29 September 2015, at www.un.org/humansecurity/human-security-unit/whats-new.

[22] Commission on Human Security, *Human Security Now* (New York, Commission on Human Security, 2003). It has been noted that the original UN objectives were formulated on the basis of the US President Franklin Roosevelt's position on 'the four fundamental

(severe) and pervasive (widespread) threats and situations. It means using processes that build on people's strengths and aspirations. It means creating political, social, environmental, economic, military and cultural systems that together give people the building blocks of *survival, livelihood and dignity*.[23] (emphasis added)

To do this, the 2003 CHS report proposed joint strategies of: 1) of *protection*, by crafting norms, institutions and processes that protect and advance human security, including the establishment of early-warning mechanisms, good governance and social protection instruments (top-down strategy); and 2) of *empowerment*, by building on people's perceptions of the risks they face and ensuring participatory processes that allow for individuals' roles in defining and implementing their essential rights, freedoms and responsibilities (bottom-up strategy).[24] As Sadako Ogata has put it, 'People protected can exercise choices. And people empowered can make better choices'.[25]

The CHS Report affirms that '*human rights* and the attributes stemming from human dignity constitute a normative framework and a conceptual reference point which must necessarily *be applied to the construction and putting into practice of the notion of human security*',[26] (emphasis added) although it doesn't provide deeper details on how exactly this could be achieved. The Report also stresses that State security and human security are complementary, given that the latter addresses insecurities that have not been considered as State security threats.[27] This of course may be considered as wishful thinking in cases where the State itself is directly the source of danger for people, or when State policy or practice, the bilateral or regional arrangements among States, or the global setting as a whole, construct vulnerability towards certain persons or groups, such as undocumented migrants or asylum seekers, and particularly

freedoms' [freedom of speech and expression, freedom of worship, freedom from want, and freedom from fear]; see Benedek, Wolfgang, 'Human Security and Human Rights Interaction' in Goucha, Moufida and John Crowley (eds), *Rethinking Human Security* (UK, Wiley-Blackwell and UNESCO, 2008) 7. Following this train of thought, the Universal Declaration of Human Rights (notably promoted by Eleanor Roosevelt) sets forth in its Preamble that 'Whereas disregard and contempt for human rights have resulted in barbarous acts which have outraged the conscience of mankind, and the advent of a world in which human beings shall enjoy freedom of speech and belief and *freedom from fear and want* has been proclaimed as the highest aspiration of the common people'.

[23] *Human Security Now* (n 22) p 4.

[24] *Human Security Now* (n 22) pp 10–11. See also Human Security Unit, *Human Security at the United Nations*, United Nations Trust Fund for Human Security (New York, OCHA, 2012) 5.

[25] Ogata, Sadako, 'Empowering People for Human Security', Presentation at the 56th Annual DPI/NGO Conference (no date) p 6, available at www.un.org/dpi/ngosection/annualconfs/56/ogata.pdf.

[26] *Human Security Now* (n 22) p 145.

[27] *Human Security No* (n 22) pp 1, 4 and 10. Quote taken from p 4.

undocumented female migrants, as will be analysed in Chapters 5 and 6 below.

Two years after the CHS Report, in 2005, former UNSG Kofi Annan issued the report *In Larger Freedom: Towards Development, Security and Human Rights for all*, as a guideline for global reforms regarding interrelated threats. The report included a third pillar, in addition to freedom from fear and from want, that of *freedom to live in dignity*, under which it deals with the rule of law, human rights and democracy.[28] (emphasis added) Notably, in the same year in the context of the *2005 World Summit Outcome*, in paragraph 143, entitled 'Human Security', the UNGA recognised

> the *right* of people to live in freedom and dignity, free from poverty and despair. We recognize that all individuals, *in particular vulnerable people*, are entitled to freedom from fear and freedom from want, with an equal opportunity to enjoy all their rights and fully develop their human potential.[29] (emphasis added)

Based on this paragraph, the Friends of Human Security (FHS), promoted by Japan and Mexico, was created in 2006 as an open-ended informal platform for Member States and UN organisations to discuss human security related themes and reach a 'common understanding' on the term. In contrast to the Human Security Network, the FHS promoted the 'broad' conception of human security, including concern for socio-economic and development issues.[30]

II. THE 2012 'COMMON UNDERSTANDING' OF HUMAN SECURITY AND BEYOND

Although before 2012, various UN and regional legal instruments had adopted what could be termed a 'human security approach',[31] it was not until then when the human security discussion reached a transformational moment. Indeed, in that year the UNGA arrived at a 'common understanding' of human security that allowed for consolidating the notion within the UN system and its follow-up through other actors.

This came into being on the basis of discussions promoted in the years following the 2005 World Summit. After informal thematic debates on the issue, in December 2010, the UNSG appointed Mr Yukio Takasu, former Ambassador of Japan to the UN, as Special Adviser on Human Security,

[28] Report of the United Nations Secretary General, *In Larger Freedom: Towards Development, Security and Human Rights for all*, A/59/2005, 21 March 2005, paras 78–81.

[29] UN General Assembly, *2005 World Summit Outcome*, A/RES/60/1, 24 October 2005, para 143.

[30] See www.mofa.go.jp/policy/human_secu/friends/index.html.

[31] Think for instance of the 1997 Ottawa Mine Ban Treaty or the 1998 Rome Statute of the International Criminal Court.

with the tasks of conducting close consultations with Member States, UN system organisations and other stakeholders to facilitate the achievement of a common understanding on the notion of human security and of coordinating his activities with the UN body created to harmonise human security efforts, the UN Human Security Unit located within the UN Office for the Coordination of Humanitarian Affairs (OCHA). The UNGA, under the coordination of its President and of Special Adviser Takasu, convened an informal thematic debate with a panel of experts to address these issues in an interactive dialogue with Member States, on 14 April 2011.

From this exchange, it could be gathered that a broad understanding of human security for the most part seemed to provoke general agreement between States. During the debate, States expressed consensus on this view and some like Pakistan, Costa Rica, Brazil and Thailand specifically highlighted the importance of maintaining economic, social and cultural rights (ESC Rights) inside the scope of the human security approach. Moreover, some of the experts of the panel, like Sonia Picado, Amitav Acharya and Andrew Mack, portrayed the idea that a very flexible definition would be necessary in order not to reduce the possibilities of practical action of human security. It was pointed out as well that the lack of a unanimous consensus up to that moment had not been an obstacle to implement dozens of projects under human security without a strict definition.[32] This broad understanding of human security was, in fact, the view confirmed by the 2012 UNSG Report and the UNGA.

The Report of the UNSG, of April 2012, confirmed the emergence of a level of consensus by which the concept of human security could be framed:

> …Member States understood the notion of human security to encompass a people-centred, *comprehensive*, context-specific and *prevention oriented* framework through which *national capacities* could be strengthened … As a result, a number of Member States considered that human security provided an *important lens* through which the United Nations can better address the *interface between security, development and human rights* in its activities.[33] (emphasis added)

In a similar way to the 1994 UNDP Report and the 2003 CHS Report, the 2012 UNSG Report depicts States' consensus on the broad view of human security as focusing on widespread and cross-cutting threats to people's *survival, livelihood and dignity*, in particular, the most vulnerable.

[32] Personal record taken at the informal UNGA debate.

[33] UNGA, *Second Report of the UN Secretary General on Human Security*, A/66/763, 5 April 2012, 'Follow-up to General Assembly Resolution 64/291 on Human Security. Report of the Secretary General', para 13.

Accordingly, human security draws attention to the root causes behind those threats (whether internal or external);[34] considers the impact of those threats on freedoms that are fundamental to human life—*freedom from fear, freedom from want and freedom to live in dignity-*; and highlights the actual needs, vulnerabilities and capacities of governments and people.[35] These freedoms are applicable to all people living under varied conditions of insecurity in developing and developed countries alike.[36]

As advanced above, the 'common understanding' formally adopted by the UNGA in September 2012 defines human security as an *approach* to assist Member States in identifying and addressing *widespread* and *cross-cutting* challenges to the survival, livelihood and dignity of their people. The UNGA also agreed that human security calls for prevention-oriented responses that strengthen the *protection* and *empowerment* of all people and all communities. It affirmed that human security includes the *right* of people to live in freedom and dignity, free from poverty and despair, stressing that all individuals, in particular *vulnerable people*, are entitled to freedom from fear and freedom from want, with an equal opportunity to enjoy all their rights and fully develop their human potential. It specifically asserts that human security 'equally considers' civil, political, economic, social and cultural human rights.[37] (emphasis added) Along these lines, the 2012 UNGA's position adopts a stronger legal human rights' foundation to base the idea of human security than that contained in the 1994 UNDP and the 2003 CHS reports.

The *UN Secretary General's Third Report on Human Security* of 2013, builds on the UNGA's notion of 'common understanding' and stresses human security's potential for advancing the interconnected pillars of peace and security, development and human rights. It adopts a practical view in presenting diverse experiences of national governments, non-governmental organisations (NGOs), regional organisations, and other actors in applying the human security approach. It summarises the principles of human security as 'protection and empowerment strategies that are people-centred, comprehensive, context-specific and prevention-oriented'.[38]

[34] On opposition to this view, see Statement by Mr Mohammad Hassani-Nejad, Representative of the Islamic Republic of Iran on the Report of the Secretary General on Human Security, New York, 4 June 2012; and 'Cuba advierte en ONU sobre amenazas a la Seguridad Humana', en *Digital Granma Internacional*, La Habana, 5 June 2012, at www.granma.cu/espanol/noticias/5junio-cuba-advierte.html.

[35] 2012 UNSG Report (n 33) para 24.

[36] 2012 UNSG Report (n 33) para 36 (f).

[37] UNGA, A/Res/66/290 'Follow-Up to Paragraph 143 on Human Security of the 2005 World Summit Outcome', 10 September 2012, para 3 a), b) and c).

[38] *Third Report of the UN Secretary General*, 'Follow-Up to General Assembly Resolution 66/290 on Human Security', A/68/685, 23 December 2013, para 59. See also paras 7 and 35.

On 8 May 2013, a high-level event on human security was convened in the UN to reflect on the added value and lessons learned from implementing the human security approach and consider the future integration of human security into the work of the UN and beyond. In early 2013, the UNTFHS had funded over 210 projects completed and underway in 85 countries, including regional projects, which were subject to an independent rapid assessment by the UNTFHS. According to this body, projects reviewed from around the world highlighted that, 'compared to the single support silo-driven responses, the human security approach has allowed for a new way of thinking to highlight the interconnectivity of the challenges faced by a broad range of communities'.[39] The Strategic Plan 2014–2017 of the UN Human Security Unit seeks to further human security as a fundamental concept that combines the agendas of peace and security, development and human rights in a more effective, efficient and prevention-oriented manner. Its main goals are to mainstream human security in the activities of the UN, and to extend global awareness of human security and the usage of the human security approach.[40]

Several actors within the UN and civil society movements also pushed for the adoption of a 'human security approach' as a comprehensive framework to guide the Post-2015 Sustainable Development Goals (SDGs). The SDGs, adopted by the UNGA in September 2015 and contained in the 2030 Agenda for Sustainable Development, reflect a human security vision on three fronts at least. Firstly, as the central goal is the eradication of all forms of poverty everywhere (Goal 1), the SDGs place 'freedom from fear and violence' at the same level as 'freedom from poverty'.[41] Secondly, they include the end of hunger and the achievement of 'food security' as Goal 2. Lastly, they adopt what one could call a 'prioritisation of the vulnerable' throughout the whole document: the guiding principles, the content, and the follow-up and review processes of the SDGs, all specify that they are projected for and 'have a particular focus on' the 'poorest and most vulnerable', they foster State building of resilience and risk reduction for 'those in vulnerable situations' and at the same time emphasise that 'people who are vulnerable must be empowered', thus reflecting both human security strategies of protection and empowerment.[42]

[39] Human Security Unit, *Strategic Plan 2014–2017* (United Nations, 2014) pp 9–10.

[40] *Ibid*, pp 12–13.

[41] UNGA, Resolution adopted by the General Assembly on 25 September 2015, *70/1. Transforming our World: The 2030 Agenda for Sustainable Development*, A/RES/70/1, Principle of 'Peace' (p 2); para. 7; and Goal 1.5.

[42] *Ibid*, see principle of 'Partnership' (p 2), paras 6, 8, 16, 23, 25, 33, 39, and 74; and Goals 1: 1.3, 1.4 and 1.5; 2: 2.1, 4.5, 6.2, 11.2 and 11.5.

III. INTERNATIONAL, REGIONAL AND NATIONAL USES OF HUMAN SECURITY

Human security proponents and advocates claim that the promotion of the concept has contributed to achieving different international initiatives and adoption of treaties or resolutions in the international law world, such as the 1997 Ottawa Treaty banning anti-personnel mines; the 1998 Rome Statute creating the International Criminal Court; and the 2009 UNSC resolutions on Children and Armed Conflict and on Women, Peace and Security,[43] this last one studied in Chapter 4 below. At the same time, in the realm of policy, different initiatives at the global level have focused on the human security proposal in its different dimensions, for instance, on the relationship between security and development.[44] Human security has also been used as a reference point to advance diverse global, regional or sub-regional aims such as the regulation of small arms and light weapons.[45] Human security has been applied in the political bodies and institutional arrangements at the EU, Inter-American and African Union levels, and to a lesser extent by the Association of Southeast Asian Nations (ASEAN) and the League of Arab States (LAS).[46] Similarly, civil society and academic initiatives implementing human security ideas and practice are varied and cover a plurality of subjects.[47] All these expressions of human security have been studied elsewhere.

Thus, the aim here is to review the uses of human security that connect directly with human rights, following the central concern of this book. And secondly, to explore some of the expressions of human security that I have not seen referred to in existing literature.

Human security's more specific relationship to the scope of legal human rights has been analysed at length by the Inter-American Commission on Human Rights, as one of the principal bodies of the Organization of American States (OAS);[48] in the African Union through the possibility

[43] See, eg, Behringer (n 21).

[44] World Bank, *World Development Report 2011: Conflict, Security and Development*, 11 April 2011, p 16. Also interesting is the analysis of data on the correlation between human rights abuses and future conflict risk (Box 2.8, p 82), although it mainly concentrates on violations to civil and political rights—arbitrary detentions, forced disappearances and extrajudicial killings; and the account of the gender-disaggregated impacts of violent conflict (Table 1.3, p 61).

[45] See, eg, Von Tigerstrom, Barbara, *Human Security and International Law. Prospects and Problems* (Studies in International Law) (Oxford, Hart Publishing, 2007) Chapter 6.

[46] See *Second Report of the UN Secretary General on Human Security*, A/Res/64/701, 8 March 2010, para 3.

[47] See, eg, Institute for Security Studies, Africa, at www.issafrica.org/iss-spotlight/tackling-new-threats-to-african-and-global-peace-and-security.

[48] See Estrada-Tanck, Dorothy, 'Human Security and Human Rights of Labour Migrants in the Americas' in Panizzon, Marion, Gottfried Zücher and Elisa Fornalé (eds), *Palgrave Handbook of International Labour Migration* (England, USA, Palgrave Macmillan, 2015) 253–96.

of intervention for the pursuit of human security goals, and through the actions by the African Commission for Human and Peoples' Rights;[49] and to a lesser extent the human security–human rights intersection has influenced the EU's position on security.[50] More importantly, some aspects of human security, such as food security or the right to peace for women, are in fact included in the human rights legal framework at the African level, as will be studied in Chapter 4 of this book.

Turning to the specific field of international human rights law, it may be highlighted that some of the seven different categories of human security identified by the UNDP in 1994 already reflected existing human rights law when formulated, such as the right to personal security, social security or security in tenure. Since then, other human security concerns have been further articulated in the language of human rights. Recent examples may be found, as mentioned above, in the right to food security or the right to peace for women, in the 2003 Protocol to the African Charter on Human and Peoples' Rights on the Rights of Women in Africa; or the humanitarian and poverty-related concerns explicitly framed as human security priorities in the binding Framework Treaty on Democratic Security in Central America of 1995; or the connection of human security to specific human rights, as elaborated in the 2009 *Report on Citizen Security and Human Rights* by the Inter-American Commission on Human Rights.

In fact, the 1995 Framework Treaty on Democratic Security in Central America (adopted a year after the UNDP Report on Human Security), is the first fully binding international legal instrument that explicitly endorses the (broad) human security notion on the basis of an 'absolute and indivisible democratic security'. Indeed, the Treaty considers that '*human security problems* in the region shall reflect a comprehensive and interrelated vision of all aspects of sustainable development' and deems poverty and extreme poverty as '*threats to the security of … peoples* and to the democratic stability of Central American societies'.[51] (emphasis added)

[49] See, eg, Tehindrazanarivelo, Djaboca L, 'The African Union's Relationship with the United Nations in the Maintenance of Peace and Security' in Yusuf, Abdulqawi A and Fatsah Ouguergouz (eds), *The African Union Legal and Institutional Framework: A Manual on the Pan-African Organization* (Leiden, Boston, Martinus Nijhoff Publishers, 2012) 375–413; Terwase Sampson, Isaac, 'The Responsibility to Protect and ECOWAS Mechanisms on Peace and Security: Assessing their Convergence and Divergence on Intervention' (2011) *Journal of Conflict and Security Law* 16 (3), 504–22.

[50] See, eg, *A European Way of Security: The Madrid Report of the Human Security Study Group*, Human Security Study Group, presented to the EU High Representative for Common Foreign and Security Policy Javier Solana, Madrid, Spain, 2007; Martin, Mary and Taylor Owen, 'The Second Generation of Human Security: Lessons from the UN and EU Experience' (2010) 1 *International Affairs* 86, 211–24; and Dersso, Solomon A (ed), *Promotion of Human Security in Africa. The Role of African Human Rights Institutions*, ISS Monograph Series, No 145, June 2008.

[51] Framework Treaty on Democratic Security in Central America, adopted on 15 December 1995 by the States of Central America: Costa Rica, El Salvador, Guatemala, Honduras,

At the level of the OAS, the Inter-American Commission on Human Rights (IACoHR), one of the six principal bodies of the organisation, issued in 2009 its report *Citizen Security and Human Rights*, in the context of the broader notion of 'democratic security'. This ample notion had been promoted by the OAS since the 2003 Declaration on Security in the Americas (also known as Declaration on Hemispheric Security), that adopted a 'multidimensional conception of security' building on human security ideas, notably in the context of the aftermath of 9/11.[52]

The 2009 Report by the IACoHR explains that the right to security from crime or interpersonal or social violence is not expressly protected under the international system of human rights law, but that the right to such protection can be inferred from the obligation of the State to guarantee the security of the individual as set forth in the Articles which refer to the *right to personal security*, as will be explained further on. As such, the Commission considers that 'the current basis of the obligations incumbent upon States is a *normative core* demanding the *protection of rights particularly vulnerable* to criminal or violent acts that citizen security policies are intended to prevent and control. This group of rights includes the right to life, the right to physical integrity, the right to freedom, the right to due process and the right to the use and enjoyment of one's property'.[53] (emphasis added)

Additionally, it clarifies that the expression 'citizen security' emerged, for the most part, as a concept in Latin America, as governments made the transition to democracy, as a way to distinguish the concept of security under a democracy from the notion of security under the earlier authoritarian regimes. In the latter case, the concept of security was associated

Nicaragua and Panama, and entered into force on 26 December 1997, Article 10 a) and d). The Treaty, which the six dominantly Spanish-speaking Central American countries are party to (Costa Rica, El Salvador, Guatemala, Honduras, Nicaragua and Panama—excluding Belize), also expressly contains positive obligations of the State in laying down that the Security Commission (composed of the Deputy Ministers for Foreign Affairs and Deputy Ministers in defense and public security of the Central American States) has the responsibility to 'Strengthen operational coordination mechanisms in the areas of defense, public security and humanitarian cooperation to deal with emergencies, threats and natural disasters' (Article 52 e)).

[52] OAS, Declaration on Security in the Americas, OEA/Ser.K/XXXVIII, 28 October 2003. For an account of the development of 'the multidimensional concept of security' that considers 'the human dimensions of security' and departs from the traditional State-focused conception, in the Americas in general and in the Latin American scenario, see the Interventions of the delegations of Argentina and Uruguay, under Issue 167 of the agenda: 'South-American Zone of Peace and Cooperation', 57 period of sessions of the UN General Assembly, 11 and 14 November 2002, respectively; and the Guidelines for the Policy of External Common Andean Security, Decision 587, adopted at the 13th Ordinary Meeting of the Andean Council of Ministers of Foreign Affairs (integrated by Bolivia, Colombia, Ecuador and Peru) on 10 July 2004.

[53] IACoHR, *Report on Citizen Security and Human Rights*, OEA/Ser.L/V/II, Doc 57 (Washington DC, Organization of American States, 31 December 2009), para 18.

with concepts like 'national security', 'internal security' or 'public security', all of which refer specifically to the security of the State. Under democratic regimes, the concept of security against the threat of crime or violence is associated with 'citizen security' and is used to refer to the paramount security of individuals and social groups.[54]

Also in the American hemisphere, at the national domain a State obligation to guarantee human security is included in the 2008 Constitution of Ecuador, setting forth that

> The State will guarantee *human security* through integrated policies and actions to ensure the peaceful coexistence of persons, promote a culture of peace and prevent forms of violence and discrimination and the commission of offenses and crimes. The planning and implementation of these policies will be entrusted to specialized bodies in the different levels of government.[55]

With these different expressions in mind, let us now turn to consider the appropriate definition of human security to adopt as a working understanding in this text.

IV. A HOLISTIC HUMAN SECURITY: *ALL* HUMAN RIGHTS AND A THRESHOLD DEFINITION

Human security has been criticised for being too broad to be academically useful and operational;[56] as a danger for watering down already established binding human rights obligations;[57] and, in its attempt to 'give a little to everyone', as having lost its grip as a critical and challenging tool for existing security conceptions.[58]

Proponents of a 'narrow conception' of human security advocate for focusing only on risks stemming from the threat or the use of armed force and on openly and physically violent conflict,[59] whereas defenders of the

[54] *Ibid*, para 21. However, it is worth noting that the Report explains in the same paragraph that 'the concept of "public security" is still widely used in the United States and Canada to also refer to the security of the individuals and groups who make up society. By contrast, as noted above, in Latin America the very same expression, "public security", refers to a different concept altogether, alluding to the security built by the State or, on occasions, the security of the State'.

[55] Art 393, Constitution of Ecuador, published in the Official Registry on 20 October 2008 (translation from Spanish by this author).

[56] See, eg, Paris, Roland, 'Human Security: Paradigm Shift or Hot Air?' (2001) *International Security*, 26(2) 87–102.

[57] Freitas, Raquel, 'Human Security and Refugee Protection after September 11: A Reassessment' (2002) 20 *Refugee: Canada's Periodical on refugees* 4, 36 and 37.

[58] Christie, Ryerson, 'Critical Voices and Human Security: To Endure, To Engage or To Critique?' (2010) *Security Dialogue* 41, 169–90.

[59] In particular, the idea of human security is still often limited to security as protection from violent conflict (both inter-State and increasingly also intra-State). See, eg, the *Human Security Report* initiated by Andrew Mack, and issued yearly since 2005, first by the University of British Columbia and later by the Simon Fraser University, Canada.

'broad conception' signal as one of human security's added values that of emphasising the indivisible character of physical and material security,[60] and its power in unmasking different types of conflict, such as domestic violence or those of a socio-economic nature.[61] However, in the conceptualisations of 'violent conflict' and 'violence'—the 'freedom from fear' pillar—mainstream ideas and measuring exercises of human security have adopted a restricted view confined to the utilisation of armed force by the State or by any other actor(s) in the context of contended issues.[62] And those who also place an emphasis on 'freedom from want' threats which do not necessarily involve armed force and often rightly highlight gender variables as important to orient analysis, do not consider that certain forms of extreme and structural deprivations may amount to violence.[63]

This text argues that a broad and integrated definition of human security has many advantages, as long as it is constructed on the basis of existing human rights law and encompassing all human rights.[64] This vision of human security, which does not primarily rest on the *a priori* hierarchical ordering of human rights, would relate to civil, political, economic, social and cultural rights depending on the evaluation of the circumstances of risk and vulnerability affecting each right in a given social context. I am thus not persuaded by the assertion of Von Tigerstrom, that only a limited set of rights, those 'basic rights' directly related

[60] See Glasius, Marlies, 'Human Security from Paradigm Shift to Operationalization: Job Description for a Human Security Worker' (2008) 39 *Security Dialogue* 1, 31–54. See also by the same author 'Human Security: A Shifting and Bridging Concept that can be Operationalized' in *Human Rights and Conflicts: Essays in Honour of Bas de Gaay Fortman* (Cambridge, Intersentia, 2012) 159–78. See also King, Gary and Christopher JL Murray, 'Rethinking Human Security' (2004) *Political Science Quarterly*, 586–610, who define human security as one's expectation of years of life without experiencing the state of generalised poverty.

[61] Basch, Linda, 'Human Security, Globalization, and Feminist Visions' (2004) 16 *Peace Review* 1, 5–12.

[62] See *Human Security Now* (n 22), in particular chapters 2 'People Caught up in Violent Conflict' and 4 'Recovering from Violent Conflict', Box 2.1 'Conflict Data are State-Centred, not People-Centred' at p 22, which also highlights that estimates of the number of people killed as a result of violent conflict usually reflect only battle-related deaths. But many more die from the consequences of conflict—from the destruction of infrastructure, the collapse of essential health services and lack of food. However, those data are not available or included. The World Bank–Human Security Research Group, *Miniatlas on Human Security 2008* (Canada, Simon Fraser University-School for International Studies, 2008) Notes on Terminology, 66, specifically equates 'violent conflict' to 'armed conflict', which is defined as 'political violence between two parties involving armed force, and causing at least 25 reported battle-deaths a year'.

[63] Human Security Index; see Hastings, David A, 'The Human Security Index: An Update and a New Release', HumanSecurityIndex.org, 2012, available at www.humansecurityindex.org/wordpress/wp-content/uploads/2012/02/hsiv2-documentation-report1_1.pdf.

[64] On these same lines, arguing that human security as a holistic concept can contribute to counter the fragmentation of international law, see Noortmann, Math, 'Human Securities, International Laws and Non-State Actors: Bringing Complexity Back In' in Ryngaert, Cedric and Math Noortmann (eds), *Human Security and International Law: The Challenge of Non-State Actors* (Cambridge, Intersentia, 2014) 13–27.

to 'survival, livelihood and dignity', should be considered within human security.[65]

The need for specifying rights would appear to fall back into the classical hierarchical division between civil and political rights/ESC Rights, generally surpassed by now, as will be detailed in the next section. Additionally, to adopt the position of differentiating 'basic rights' would seem somewhat dangerous given there already exists a legal regime in place, through international human rights law and international humanitarian law, that defines the derogable/non-derogable rights in situations of peace and armed conflict, as will be studied in Chapter 3 of this book. I thus propose that human security is formed by the junction between the 'core content' of each human right as defined by international human rights law, in the form explained in detail in such chapter.

At the same time, I suggest that the incorporation of human rights norms, standards and indicators may partly contribute in the task of better defining the scope of human security and providing tools for the assessment of concrete situations. The evaluation as to which threats are to be considered in relation to which rights will depend on the critical and widespread nature of the risk affecting a certain right or set of rights and the level of vulnerability experienced by certain persons or groups, and this will determine the prioritisation and course of action that the realisation of human security and human rights require in each context-specific case.

Although the construction of a full measuring methodology to do so exceeds the purpose of this book and has been developed elsewhere[66] (not least through global governance indicators),[67] I advance some guidelines that could prove useful. The methodology to identify such risks factors and conditions of vulnerability would be built upon quantitative and qualitative proposals closer to a holistic appraisal, such as development, respect for human rights and effects of violent or armed conflict.[68]

[65] Von Tigerstrom (n 45) 43.

[66] eg, The *Human Security Report* proposed by Andrew Mack (n 59).

[67] See Human Security Index (n 63). For global governance indicators more generally, see Davis, Kevin E, Benedict Kingsbury and Sally Engle Merry, 'Indicators as a Technology of Global Governance', IILJ Working Paper 2010/2 Rev, Finalised 08/02/2011, International Law and Justice Working Papers, Institute for International Law and Justice, New York University School of Law.

[68] For example, from UN human rights mechanisms, the annual reports of Charter-based and treaty-based monitoring bodies; from international organisations, the Annual Human Development Index of UNDP, the World Development Report of the World Bank; from the academic and civil society sector, the Human Security Index, the Human Security Report Project, the Peoples Under Threat Report, the annual reports of Human Rights Watch or Amnesty International. Depending on the kind of threat and situation under review, the same type of analysis could be replicated at the regional, national or local level, looking at the equivalent institutions, and including national human rights institutions and judicial

It would go a step further in specifically incorporating UN human rights norms and indicators, as well as sources of diagnosis such as reports by regional human rights bodies, national and local human rights institutions, and civil society documentation defining protection standards and delimiting State obligations in human rights law. Such an exercise could be carried out by integrating, for example, the 2012 *UN OHCHR Guide to Human Rights Indicators*, and escalating an additional stage to develop threshold criteria of 'risks to rights' and levels of vulnerability of particular persons or groups that could direct us, for instance, to estimating low, medium or high levels of human (in)security on a context-specific basis, and thus, orient appropriate *preventive, protective and reparative* action in that regard.[69] Jurisprudential and interpretative criteria by human rights mechanisms and courts such as those analysed in the following chapters of this book would have to form part of the assessment and could be further developed along the same lines as the 'human security–human rights synergy' proposed in this text.

Still, as mentioned above, the inclusion of the whole panoply of human rights in the sphere of human security preoccupation has raised reasonable concerns as to whether the notion we end up with is too broad to be workable. Under such views, a narrow definition mainly concerned with the risks produced by violent conflict and related to civil and political rights would be necessary to make human security operational. It is therefore worth exploring some attempts to surpass a constricted conception of human security, while at the same time searching for a functional definition that enables its practical use.

A threshold-based conceptualisation, such as that proposed by Taylor Owen, would determine threat inclusion by *severity*, rather than by *cause* (socio-economic vs political) and would thus bridge the divide between the broad and narrow proponents, addressing the critiques of the concept and providing a clear policy agenda operating on various scales.[70] As Owen puts it, 'Human security threats should be included not because they fall into a particular category, such as violence, but because of their actual severity'. In this conception, what human security means 'is not defined by an arbitrary list, but by what threats are actually affecting people'.[71] Indeed, as Shahrbanou Tadjbakhsh has argued, 'Thresholds of

decisions by human rights courts in the applicable cases. See also *Human Security Handbook* (UNTFHS, OCHA, 2009).

[69] UN OHCHR, *Human Rights Indicators: A Guide to Measurement and Implementation*, HR/PUB/12/5, UN, New York and Geneva, 2012.

[70] See Owen, Taylor, 'Human Security—Conflict, Critique and Consensus: Colloquium Remarks and a Proposal for a Threshold-Based Definition' in *Security Dialogue* (Oslo, Norway, International Peace Research Institute, Sage Publications, 2004) Vol 35, No 3, 373–87.

[71] Owen (n 2) 20.

human security are not to be defined in terms of isolated violent acts or by sporadic human rights violations, but as *structural* in nature'.[72] (emphasis added)

Security, not least human security, is an inter-subjective phenomenon. As such, the identification of a human security concern should consider two factors: subjective security—what people perceive as the main threats affecting them; and objective security—risk assessment based on external criteria. This moves in line as well with the 'empowerment' and 'protection' strategies integrated in the human security notion. But the exercise of identification is also political

> as it points up a wide range of issues for the national and international actors who are responsible for providing human security as a public good. A threshold-based definition recognizes that certain threats cannot be dealt with by traditional institutions but are severe enough to require immediate action, both in the short term to handle the crisis and in the long term to prevent reoccurrence.[73]

Thus interpreted, what the notion of human security mostly allows for is to identify situations of serious threat, which we could generically call *risk situations*. The factors that may come together in generating a risk situation might be several and can include the gravity of the violation of certain human rights; the widespread or systematic nature of a certain type of violation and/or the fact that the violation targets or have a disparate impact on what we could call a vulnerable population, meaning a population living in *structural* conditions of inequality or disadvantage, with a whole set of rights insufficiently guaranteed, and hence more susceptible to be severely affected by particular risk factors. Through the identification of the risk factors affecting concrete rights and, consequently, of the 'rights at risk', the State's human rights obligations would be triggered, translating the human security assessment into specific legal duties. This diagnosis would also involve threats stemming from 'private' actors, such as individuals perpetrating violence against women, or business corporations, employers or recruitment agencies creating vulnerable conditions for undocumented migrants.

A broad idea of human security seems to hold more promise in making visible the threats to persons or groups that would otherwise remain unseen on two fronts: **a)** all the other categories of widespread threats that do not necessarily involve the cases of harm considered most grave by

[72] Tadjbakhsh, Shahrbanou, 'Human Security: Concepts and Implications with an Application to Post-Intervention Challenges in Afghanistan' (2005) *Les Études du CERI*, N° 117–18, 9. See by the same author 'In Defense of the Broad View of Human Security' in Martin, Mary and Taylor Owen (eds), *Routledge Handbook of Human Security* (New York, Routledge, 2014) 43–57.

[73] Tadjbakhsh, Shahrbanou, 'Human Security: Concepts and Implications with an Application to Post-Intervention Challenges in Afghanistan' (2005) (n 72).

international law: genocide, crimes against humanity, and war crimes (as already covered by international criminal and humanitarian law), but that represent nonetheless severe risks to persons or populations, for example, systemic forms of violence that are frequently shadowed to the public eye, as certain forms of violence against women, mainly domestic violence; or (extreme) poverty, not sufficiently covered by existing categories and mechanisms (eg discrimination law); and **b)** the threats affecting certain parts of the population, such as women and girls, or certain sectors of society, such as undocumented migrants—both analysed in this text—that because of their non-membership or contingent relationship to ethnic, linguistic or religious minorities, become trapped in the middle of other existing categories, and the particular risks confronted by them are underrepresented or rendered invisible. In these cases, gender and legal immigration status related to entry or residence in a given State—possibly added to class, race, national origin, ethnicity or skin colour—become the two driving factors for discrimination and other human rights violations, a risk which human security may highlight in a more coordinated, efficient, and less rigid manner.

Indeed, conditions of human insecurity may be signalled without carrying the weight of having to prove the existence of specific human rights violations—as they may have not yet occurred and are only likely to be materialised—and because the identification of a human insecurity situation does not involve the technical legal requirement that the diagnosis of human rights violations entail.

Human security thus understood would have to incorporate gender in its constitutive content, its strategies and its implementation. The concrete forms of doing so and the legal implications of this incorporation for human rights are spelled out in Chapter 4 of this book.

At this point, some words should be spared for the element of socio-economic vulnerability as part of a broad human security conception, a transversal concern dealt with throughout the whole book.

A. ESC Rights, Human Insecurity and Vulnerability to Poverty

Roughly one out of every eight persons in the world lives at or below $1.90 USD a day.[74] In terms of inequality, scandalous figures indicate that 50 per cent of the world's wealth is concentrated in one per cent of the world's population, and 50 per cent of the world's poorest hold one per cent of

[74] See www.worldbank.org/en/topic/poverty/overview: In 2012, 12.7% of the world's population lived at or below $1.90 a day … This means that, in 2012, 896 million people lived on less than $1.90 a day.

global wealth.[75] For an enormous amount of the people in the world, the risk of death from hunger, preventable diseases or meagre maternal health care is as high as or higher than that of armed conflict. In the examples, right to life, right to food and women's right to health are inextricably woven together in cumulative forms of disadvantage. As such, from the human security–human rights perspective, it is not only that ESC Rights relate to civil and political rights insofar as poverty and inequality carry the risk of deteriorating into violent conflict. It is that poverty *is a risk in itself* for her or him who experiences it. Viewed from the perspective of her or him who suffers it, whether you die from a bullet or from starvation is irrelevant, what matters is that you die. The common feature between the two is that we are facing preventable causes of death.

Conscious that poverty involves the whole spectrum of human rights and not only ESC Rights,[76] I consider nevertheless that ESC Rights deserve a particular mention in relation to human security for various reasons: **i)** the historical difficulties faced in relation to the conceptualisation or to the justiciability of these human rights, which has in itself represented a barrier to their confirmation as proper legal rights; **ii)** the fact that within the debate on human security, some of the ongoing and influential practical measuring exercises focus on the 'narrow definition' of human security, only concentrating on the aspect of violent conflict (*freedom from fear*), whereby an integrated consideration that also incorporates socio-economic aspects (*freedom from want*), or even the overarching pillar of *freedom to live in dignity*, merit further attention; and **iii)** the close relationship that has been highlighted between poverty, especially extreme poverty, and human rights,[77] which calls for a deeper analysis of issues of poverty and socio-economic inequality, but viewed from international law and translated into the legal terminology and criteria of rights.

The close links between the risks to civil and political rights and ESC Rights brought to light through the cases analysed in this book opens the path for the proposed human security–human rights lens. Such a perspective can constitute a useful tool to identify and analyse levels of widespread vulnerability, including that of a socio-economic nature, and reaffirm the consequent heightened obligation of protection, firstly by the

[75] *Credit Suisse Wealth Report 2015*, Credit Suisse Research Institute, available at www.credit-suisse.com/es/en/about-us/research/research-institute/news-and-videos/articles/news-and-expertise/2015/10/en/global-wealth-in-2015-underlying-trends-remain-positive.html.

[76] UN Human Rights Council, *Guiding Principles on Extreme Poverty and Human Rights* (contained in the Final Draft submitted by the Special Rapporteur on extreme poverty and human rights, Magdalena Sepúlveda Carmona, UN General Assembly Resolution A/HC/21/39, 18 July 2012), endorsed by UN Human Rights Council in Resolution 21/11 of 27 September 2012, para 3.

[77] See the *Report of the UN Independent Expert on the Question of Human Rights and Extreme Poverty*, Magdalena Sepúlveda, UN General Assembly, A/64/279, 11 August 2009.

State, but also in terms of inter-State duties within a broader view of the transnational and international dimensions of human rights enjoyment.

But what precisely would a concrete human security analysis applied to legal interpretation look like in the case of extreme poverty and socio-economic vulnerability? Several of the cases by human rights mechanisms and courts, reviewed in the following chapters, deal indirectly or openly with socio-economic vulnerability and provide criteria for assessing related risks and addressing them from a human rights viewpoint. To advance some of them, consider an illuminating paragraph from the 2010 case of *Xakmok Kásek Community v Paraguay* by the Inter-American Court of Human Rights (IACHR), which referred to the extreme situation of death of several members of an impoverished indigenous community, including children, in which the Court highlighted that

> the fact that the State is currently providing emergency aid does not exempt it from international responsibility for having failed to take measures in the past to *prevent the risk* of a violation to the right to life *from materializing*. The Court therefore must examine which of the deaths are attributable to the State for failing in its duty to prevent them. This examination will ... stem from a perspective that allows for the situation of *extreme and particular vulnerability*, the *cause of death*, and the corresponding *causal link* between them *to be connected*, without placing on the State the *undue burden* of overcoming an *indeterminate or unknown risk*.[78] (emphasis added)

The IACHR had already developed in detail the study of extreme vulnerability in its case-law. Indeed, cases like *Barrios Altos v Peru*, *Plan de Sánchez Massacre v Guatemala*, *Moiwana Community v Suriname*, the cases of the massacres of *Mapiripán v Colombia* and *Ituango v Colombia*, and *La Cantuta v Peru*, together constitute a whole cycle of jurisprudence on massacres, illustrative not only of life-threatening vulnerability, but even of an acute state of defencelessness.[79]

[78] IACHR, *Xákmok Kásek Indigenous Community v Paraguay*, Judgment of 24 August 2010 (Merits, Reparations and Costs), para 227. See also IACHR, *Case of the Sawhoyamaxa Indigenous Community v Paraguay*, Judgment of 29 March 2006 (Merits, Reparations and Costs), Separate Opinion of Judge AA Cançado Trindade, supporting his argument on the work of Stavropoulou, M, 'Searching for Human Security and Dignity: Human Rights, Refugees, and the Internally Displaced' in Stamatopoulou, Danieli E and CJ Dias (eds), *The Universal Declaration of Human Rights: Fifty Years and Beyond* (Amityville/New York, Baywood Publishing Co, 1999) 181–82, para 14, fn 20.

[79] IACHR, *Barrios Altos v Peru*, Judgment of March 14, 2001 (Merits); IACHR, *Plan de Sánchez Massacre v. Guatemala*, Judgment of April 29, 2004 (Merits), and regarding the same case the Judgment of November 19, 2004 (Reparations); IACHR, *Moiwana Community v. Suriname*, Judgment of June 15, 2005 (Preliminary Objections, Merits, Reparations and Costs); IACHR, *"Mapiripán Massacre" v. Colombia*, Judgment of September 15, 2005 (Merits, Reparations, and Costs); IACHR, *Ituango Massacres v. Colombia*, Judgment of July 1, 2006, (Preliminary Objections, Merits, Reparations and Costs); and IACHR, *La Cantuta v Peru*, Judgment of 29 November 2006 (Merits, Reparations and Costs). For a full analysis of this jurisprudence,

The human security–human rights framework proposed in this book would also be in line with the interpretation by the UN Committee on ESC Rights which details the circumstances in which a *reversal of the burden of proof* is allowed or even called for. States are under a legal obligation, according to the International Covenant on Economic, Social and Cultural Rights (ICESCR), to use the maximum of their available resources to assure rights, privileging the most vulnerable groups and those with the most urgent needs. In this respect, diligence in the adoption of these measures cannot be presumed and States must demonstrate the steps they are taking to prioritise the protection of at least the minimum core of such rights even in time of crisis or resource constraints.[80] Note the similarity between the language of 'minimum core' of rights used by the Committee and that of the 'vital core' of all human lives as proposed by the human security definition.

From the more general standpoint of the human security–human rights interaction, one may also underline that the *lack of full justiciability* of ESC Rights is in itself a *risk for their full enjoyment*, given that the absence of access to justice (not only at the factual but also at the institutionalised level) undermines the whole concept of 'legal right'.[81] In this sense, in terms of the justiciability of such rights, the UN Committee of ESC Rights had reaffirmed since 1998 that

> the adoption of a rigid classification of economic, social and cultural rights which puts them, by definition, beyond the reach of the courts would thus be arbitrary and incompatible with the principle that the two sets of human rights are indivisible and interdependent. It would also drastically curtail the capacity of the courts to protect the rights of the *most vulnerable and disadvantaged groups in society*.[82] (emphasis added)

see Cançado Trindade, Antonio A, *State Responsibility in Cases of Massacres: Contemporary Advances in International Justice*, Inaugural address as Honorary Professor to the Chair in 'International and Regional Human Rights Courts', delivered on 10 November 2011 at Utrecht University.

[80] See Article 2.1 of the ICESCR and UN Committee on ESC Rights, General Comment No 3, *The Nature of States Parties Obligations (Art 2, par 1 of the Covenant)* (contained in Document E/1991/23), 14 December 1990, paras 10–13. See also UN Committee on ESC Rights, General Comment No 9, *The Domestic Application of the Covenant* (contained in Document E/C.12/1998/24, General Comments), 3 December 1998, on the burden of proof in relation to the duty to give effect to the Covenant in the domestic legal order, para 3.

[81] On the *integrated approach* underlining interdependence and interaction of all human rights, see Krause, Catarina and Martin Scheinin, 'The Right Not to be Discriminated Against: The Case of Social Security' in Orlin, Theodore, S, Allan Rosas and Martin Scheinin (eds), *The Jurisprudence of Human Rights Law: A Comparative and Interpretive Approach* (Turku/Åbo, Finland, Institute for Human Rights, Åbo Akademi University, 2000) 255.

[82] UN Committee on ESC Rights, General Comment No 9 (n 80) para 10.

Much of this risk, however, has been surpassed by the adoption in 2008 and entry into force in 2013 of the Optional Protocol to the ICESCR, which includes an individual complaints mechanism regarding violations of ESC Rights, bringing them to the same level of international justiciability as civil and political rights, and fulfilling the post-Cold War political affirmation of the Vienna Declaration of 1993 that 'all human rights are universal, indivisible and interdependent'.[83] The Optional Protocol also includes the mechanism of inquiry procedure which the UN Committee on ESC Rights may initiate upon receipt of reliable information on *grave or systematic violations* by a State party (Article 11). Such procedure may offer advantages over individual communications for addressing situations of structural human rights violations. The adoption of the Protocol and the inclusion of both enforcement mechanisms give closure to a historical discussion on the hierarchy between rights and open the door to a new stage in international human rights law where all rights enjoy equal legal status and protection. Human security can thus act as a buttress to this process or linger behind in the somewhat passé discussion of division and relevance of rights.

Let us turn to the scope of the State's general obligations in relation to ESC Rights. In this respect, the body in charge of interpreting the Covenant, the UN Committee on ESC Rights,[84] has indicated that the State has, as minimum duties towards these rights that are immediately enforceable: **i)** the obligation to take steps to apply all the provisions of the Covenant observing the principles of progressivity and non-regressivity;[85] and **ii)** the obligation of non-discrimination. The positive and negative obligations with regard to ESC Rights have been extensively analysed,[86] and within the legal examination carried out by human rights bodies, the

[83] Article 5 of the Vienna Declaration and Program of Action, UN General Assembly, World Conference on Human Rights, A/CONF.157/23, 12 July 1993.

[84] The Committee was established under United Nations Economic and Social Council (ECOSOC) Resolution 1985/17 of 28 May 1985 to carry out the monitoring functions assigned to the ECOSOC in Part IV of the ICESCR, in particular, Articles 16.1 and 16.2.a); 17.1; and 18–22.

[85] On these two obligations and principles, see UN Committee on ESC Rights, General Comment No 3 (n 80) paras 2 and 9; Courtis, Christian, 'La prohibición de regresividad en materia de derechos sociales: apuntes introductorios' in Courtis, Christian (compilador), *Ni un paso atrás: La prohibición de regresividad en materia de derechos sociales* (Buenos Aires, Editores Del Puerto, 2006) 3–52; and Abramovich, Victor and Christian Courtis, *Los derechos sociales como derechos exigibles* (Prologue by Luigi Ferrajoli) (Spain, Editorial Trotta, 2002).

[86] See, for eg, Liebenberg, Sandra, 'South Africa: Adjudicating Social Rights under a Transformative Constitution' in Langford, Malcolm (ed), *Social Rights Jurisprudence. Emerging Trends in International and Comparative Law* (Cambridge, Cambridge University Press, 2008) in particular 82–95.

extent of these obligations has also been developed further.[87] However, because of its accent on interrelatedness, it is particularly useful to look at human security and human rights borrowing from the concept of the *continuum* of obligations, proposed especially in the context of ESC Rights. This continuum covers a series of legal obligations, ranging from negative (State abstention) to positive (State action), in relation to all human rights, and thus reaffirms the interdependent nature of all these rights,[88] and their equal relevance for human security assessments, as illustrated at the start of this section.

Reflections on socio-economic risks and vulnerabilities from the human security perspective can thus feed into and complement ongoing discussions on the legal obligation to alleviate world poverty as a pressing human rights and global justice concern.[89] Human security may prove helpful and even necessary as a bridging conception to shape and unify current debates on (the right to) development, global justice and the role of the international trading, investment and financial systems, and the involvement of non-State actors, such as transnational and other business corporations, in the field of human rights. Prioritising critical and widespread vulnerability as its axis, regardless of whether it is State-produced or not, I argue that human security may indeed act as a centripetal force to bring together several contemporary debates and social movements that

[87] See IACoHR, *Access to Justice as a Guarantee of Economic, Social, and Cultural Rights: A Review of the Standards Adopted by the Inter-American System of Human Rights,* Organization of American States, OEA/Ser.L/V/II.129, Doc 4, 7 September 2007. On ESC Rights in the Inter-American system, see also Rossi, Julieta and Víctor Abramovich, 'La tutela de los derechos económicos, sociales y culturales en el artículo 26 de la Convención Americana sobre Derechos Humanos' in Martin, Claudia, Diego Rodríguez-Pinzón and José A Guevara B (eds), *Derecho Internacional de los Derechos Humanos* (Ciudad de México, Universidad Iberoamericana Mexico City, American University Washington College of Law and Distribuciones Fontamara, 2004) 457–78.

[88] See Sepúlveda, Magdalena, *The Nature of the Obligations under the International Covenant on Economic, Social and Cultural Rights* (Anvers, Oxford, New York, Intersentia, 2003) Chapter V; and Koch, Ida Elisabeth, 'Dichotomies, Trichotomies, or Waves of Duties?' (2005) *Human Rights Law Review* 5/1, 81. On the interconnectedness of human rights, see also *Legal Consequences of the Construction of a Wall in the Occupied Palestinian Territory*, Advisory Opinion, 9 July 2004, International Court of Justice, Reports 2004, paras 106 and 112; and OHCHR, 'Of all Places … a Toilet', World Toilet Day, 19 November 2012, available at www.ohchr.org/EN/NewsEvents/Pages/DisplayNews.aspx?NewsID=12806&LangID=E.

[89] See, for eg, Pogge, Thomas, 'Severe Poverty as a Human Rights Violation' in Pogge, Thomas (ed), *Freedom from Poverty as a Human Right: Who Owes What to the Very Poor* (Oxford, Oxford University Press-United Nations Educational, Scientific and Cultural Organisation, 2007); and Salomon, Margot E, 'International Human Rights Obligations in Context: Structural Obstacles and the Demands of Global Justice' in Andreassen, Bard A and Stephen P Marks (eds), *Development as a Human Right: Legal, Political and Economic Dimensions*, 2nd edn (Antwerp, Intersentia, 2010) and by the same author, *Global Responsibility for Human Rights: World Poverty and the Development of International Law* (Oxford, Oxford University Press, 2007).

share the common concern of appalling material deprivation and marginalisation experienced by millions of persons worldwide. The human security–human rights framework proposed in this book may foster such a conversation under a common umbrella that covers these different preoccupations and confronts them preventively in a timely manner.

From this viewpoint, human security would form part of a long line of legal and political instruments that have been used in modern law and discourse to forward social justice and equality. Indeed, it may be seen as part of a shared ethical and legal project based on the common value of human dignity, what could be termed 'humanity's law'. This quest for the most fundamental values of humanity has been worked upon, among other disciplines, through international law—especially in its more recent development throughout the twentieth and early twenty-first centuries—in using the theoretical and methodological approach of placing people, and not the State, at the centre of these norms.[90]

Thus, what appears to hold promise in the human security approach, if it is to be relevant and add value to existing conceptions and methodologies, is its capability to highlight the *interrelatedness* between conditions that would otherwise be analysed in an isolated, and therefore incomplete, manner.

[90] On the use of this type of 'moral cosmopolitanism', see Von Tigerstrom (n 45) 54–57.

2

Human Security, International Law and Human Rights

I. INTERNATIONAL LAW, RISK AND STRUCTURAL VULNERABILITY

ONE MAY BROADLY think of the normative and legal dimensions of security in trying to address the question of how the law responds to risk.[1] Generally speaking, if one looks at the human security agenda and its central elements of risk and vulnerability, such dimensions have been enclosed in one way or another by international norms and principles. International law as a general stand has put forward considerations of *risk* and *vulnerability* with a person-centred approach—even when not always defining such conceptions in detail but rather leaving them open to legal interpretation by competent bodies. Indeed, risk and vulnerability have been applied by international law to situations, persons and groups that it deems worthy of a certain reinforced obligation directed to prevent harm, protect the affected subject if the risk is materialised or granting redress when an injury from an unsafe situation has already occurred. Consider the norms containing duties of rescue at sea,[2] or those targeting the protection of groups of persons, such as children in armed conflict,[3] or women subjected to discrimination and violence as will be studied in Chapter 4.

Lyal S Sunga has pointed out that a notion of human security that is wholly informed by international human rights law, international humanitarian law, international criminal law and international

[1] For a series of essays on the subject of law and security, see Scheinin, Martin, et al, *Law and Security –Facing the Dilemmas*, EUI Working Paper Law 2009/11 (Florence, European University Institute, 2009).

[2] See UN International Maritime Organisation's Safety of Life at Sea Convention of 1974 (SOLAS) and the 1979 International Convention on Maritime Search and Rescue, and the obligations of rescue at sea and international cooperation contained therein, and complemented by the 1982 UN Convention of the Law of the Sea, particularly relevant for the current situation of thousands of migrants and potential refugees from the Middle East and Africa attempting to reach European countries by sea.

[3] Optional Protocol to the UN Convention on the Rights of the Child on the Involvement of Children in Armed Conflict, adopted by UN General Assembly Resolution A/RES/54/263 of 25 May 2000 and entered into force 12 February 2002.

refugee law, and which considers the relevant international legal norms prohibiting the use of force in international relations, will probably prove more valuable to international legal theory and practice in the longer term, than a notion of human security which does not meet these conditions because these areas of law embody the objectified political will of States.[4] Some elements of these four branches of international law, usually deemed as the block of protective norms of human beings—an 'international law of humankind'—intersect and overlap with human security in their person-centred approach and in the widespread vulnerabilities they address.

Actually, Judge Cançado Trindade has similarly considered that the three main veins of protection of the human person within international law, namely international human rights, humanitarian, and refugee law, converge in their concern for security of the person, and thus the junction of these three branches of law could be considered in fact human security.[5] Certainly, human security holds the potential of bringing together person-centred values, goals and legal norms under a common overarching framework. Building from this idea, the aim here is to explore how this conception could provoke new ways of understanding international legal expressions and render them operational in ways that are relevant for international law.

In this context, elements and expressions of human security may be found, whether explicitly or indirectly, in the traditional primary sources of public international law—treaties, customary international law, general principles of law –, as well as in the secondary sources of jurisprudence and doctrine, or even in *ius cogens*,[6] as gathered from the analysis throughout the book. As explained from the outset in the Introduction, however, this book's main concern is not to address the legal implications of human security from the viewpoint of such sources. Rather, it attempts firstly, to make explicit the intersections between the meta-legal concept of human security and the legal understanding of international human rights. Secondly, it proposes concrete ways in which this interaction could be further developed and mutually beneficial for both human security and human rights. In that sense, human security is explored in its potential as a hermeneutic and heuristic tool for the legal understanding of human rights.

In considering the international legal focus on human security-relevant risks, a reference must also be made to the relationship of human security

[4] See Sunga, Lyal S, 'The Concept of Human Security: Does it Add Anything of Value to International Legal Theory or Practice?' in Frick, Marie-Luisa and Andreas Oberprantacher (eds), *Power and Justice in International Relations. Interdisciplinary Approaches to Global Challenges* (England/USA, Ashgate Publishers, 2009) 131–48.

[5] Cançado Trindade, Antonio Augusto, *A humanizaçao do direito internacional* (Brazil, Editora del Rey, 2006) 322–24.

[6] Art 38 of the Statute of the International Court of Justice. For *ius cogens*, see Art 53 of the 1969 Vienna Convention on the Law of Treaties.

to international humanitarian law (IHL). As the normative framework dealing with armed conflict, indeed some of the situations IHL envisions overlap with the human security concern. Because of the gravity of some of the circumstances described in the text, and the relationship they hold with the threshold of 'risk situation' as a criteria to activate human security and human rights duties, an outlook could indeed be conceived from the standpoint of IHL. This book does, when applicable, partially analyse IHL or the humanitarian aspects of certain norms (for example, Resolutions 1325 and 1820 of the UN Security Council (UNSC) on women in armed conflict and peace-building and peace-keeping contexts, as reviewed in Chapter 4 below). However, given that IHL is deemed as a regime of exception where narrower standards are applicable, the more ample perspective from the general standards of international human rights law (IHRL) is fitting with the holistic notion of human security upheld in this text, as one that contains at its core the protection of all human rights: civil, political, economic, social and cultural. Indeed, since the main focus of the book is to explore the structural and widespread conditions of vulnerability present at different levels in all societies, the perspective of IHRL has been preferred, precisely as the broader normative framework that opens the door for innovative questions in terms of the potentials and limitations of the notion of human security.

As such, this chapter presents some reflections as to the levels of encounter between human security and human rights and their effect in the specific area of IHRL and secondly on international refugee law, understood as the application of human rights law to the concrete situation of refugees.[7] This section unpacks the approach of these fields of international law to *risk* and *vulnerability*, central elements of human security, as a general umbrella under which the development of security concerns related to the protection of persons has taken place. Indeed, 'human security is defined by international human rights norms, which give it content'.[8]

For an understanding of *risk*, let us first turn to its general conception within the social sciences, which defines it as 'the *possibility* of experiencing a negative outcome or a significant damage as a consequence of one (or more) factors (called "risk factors")'.[9] (emphasis added) Likewise, risk

[7] For a development of this understanding, see Chetail, Vincent, 'Are Refugee Rights Human Rights? An Unorthodox Questioning of the Relations between Refugee Law and Human Rights Law' in Rubio Marín, Ruth (ed), *Human Rights and Immigration* (Oxford, Oxford University Press, 2014) 19–72.

[8] UNSC Provisional Verbatim Record of the 4784th Meeting, S/PV.4784, July 7, 2003 (Address by UN Acting High Commissioner for Human Rights, Bertrand Ramcharan, to the UN Security Council, calling for action against impunity relating to gross human rights violations in the Democratic Republic of the Congo).

[9] Ranzi, Costanzo, 'Social Vulnerability in Europe' in Ranzi, Costanzo (ed), *Social Vulnerability in Europe. The New Configuration of Social Risks* (London, Palgrave Macmillan,

analysis in the social sciences introduces the concept of *vulnerability* to explain how the effect of the same risk factor can be different for equally exposed individuals. In this sense, vulnerability gives an account of the distribution of a negative outcome on a population in relation not to the cause (the risk factor) that determined it, but to the greater or lesser exposure of the population to suffering the consequences of this cause.[10] Thus, vulnerability as a general term can be characterised as the *degree of exposure to damage* that may result from a risk being actualised.

In a way, this would contrast with the 'vulnerability approach' proposed by Martha Fineman from the standpoint of feminist legal theory. While a full examination of legal theory exceeds the scope of this book, let us reflect briefly on vulnerability analysis as directly related to the human security approach. Fineman considers vulnerability as a universal and constant feature of the human condition more generally and, as such, wishes to release the understanding of vulnerability from its negative connotations as a sign of exceptional weakness, dependency, or pathology. Viewing vulnerability as a universal characteristic, this approach sustains, positions us in relation to each other as human beings and also suggests a relationship of responsibility of the State and its institutions towards the individual.[11] Such a perspective, at first glance, is in line with the universal and egalitarian concern of human security as a concept covering risks and threats affecting *all* persons. Still, the human security approach stresses the call to focus 'particularly on vulnerable people',[12] considering persons or groups in vulnerable conditions as a distinct category to be singled out and prioritised among *all* people or any or every person indeterminately.

I consider that Martha Fineman's position has done a great deal to clarify the limits of formal equality and to point to the need for measures to achieve substantive equality. I also share with her the concern for bringing light to systemic obstacles to equality. Indeed, incorporating 'structural and institutional arrangements' to the analysis, transcending individual conditions or identities, as she urges us to do, leads us to assess 'the state's response to situations of vulnerability before indicting the individual'.[13] In fact, other factors such as institutional precariousness or lack of an

2010) 14. Also from a sociological perspective, see the classic work of Beck, Ulrich, *Risk Society. Towards a New Modernity* (London, Sage, 1992).

[10] *Ibid*, 16–17.

[11] Fineman, Martha Albertson, 'The Vulnerable Subject: Anchoring Equality in the Human Condition' (2008) 20 *Yale Journal of Law and Feminism* 1, 8–9.

[12] UN General Assemby (UNGA), A/RES/66/290, 'Follow-Up to Paragraph 143 on Human Security of the 2005 World Summit Outcome', 10 September 2012, para 3, a): '… All individuals, *in particular vulnerable people*, are entitled to freedom from fear and freedom from want, with an equal opportunity to enjoy all their rights and fully develop their human potential'.

[13] Fineman (n 11) 18.

effective State power may also sit at the core of the severe and critical threats considered by human security and often materialising into harm to human rights.[14]

Taking into account these reflections, this book, however, is concerned with studying vulnerability as an element of human security primarily from the position of *human rights law*. Although vulnerability may admittedly be seen as a common human attribute, possibly more so than the classical liberal conception of individual autonomy, I argue that different factors such as gender, legal immigration status and/or socio-economic deprivation, as reviewed in this text, may entail structural conditions of risk that place some individuals or groups in a position which has a *higher degree of exposure to human rights' violations*—in a more vulnerable position—than others.

In consideration of 'structural' vulnerability as differentiated from a merely personal or individual status, I build on Johan Galtung's conception of 'structural violence' proposed since the late 1960s. Galtung sets apart personal or direct violence as that where there is an actor that commits the violence from the case where there is no such actor and thus we are in the presence of structural or indirect violence. He acknowledges that in both cases individuals may suffer injury, but whereas in the first case this can be traced back to concrete persons as actors, in the second case this is no longer meaningful. There may not be any person who directly harms another person in the structure. Indeed, as Galtung warns,

> the violence is built into the structure and shows up as unequal power and consequently as unequal life chances … Resources are unevenly distributed, as when income distributions are heavily skewed, literacy/education unevenly distributed, medical services existent in some districts and for some groups only, and so on.

As he emphasises, 'Above all the power to decide over the distribution of resources is unevenly distributed'.[15]

According to this line of thought, I argue that some persons or sectors of the population such as those analysed in this book, are 'structurally' situated at an intensified level of risk to suffering violations to their human rights. This is thus not an essentialist or identitarian conception of vulnerability, but a relational one, directly dependent on the stronger level of possibility of a person or group to being negatively affected in

[14] See Turner, Bryan S, *Vulnerability and Human Rights* (Pennsylvania, Pennsylvania State University Press, University Park, 2006) 4–15.

[15] See Galtung, Johan, 'Violence, Peace, and Peace Research' (1969) 6 *Journal of Peace Research* 3, 170–71. See the analysis Paul Farmer presents using Galtung's conception of structural violence as a starting point to reveal the contemporary harm suffered by the poor in their right to health, in *Pathologies of Power: Health, Human Rights, and the New War on the Poor* (Berkeley, University of California Press, 2005).

their rights. As such, 'structural vulnerability' is understood in this study as *the heightened and endemic degree of exposure to experiencing human rights violations*.

Under this notion, in this section the treatment of risk and vulnerability as human security elements is reviewed in its expressions in international human rights and in international refugee law. The selected instruments and case-law in these two sections are not exhaustive and rather intend to illustrate the concrete forms in which a 'human security approach' is embedded in these normative legal expressions, and the potentials of this relationship. Lastly, a reflection on human security and its (possible) relationship to humanitarian intervention and the responsibility to protect (R2P) is also presented with the aim of clarifying the main similarities and differences between them.

A. International Human Rights Law

Using the concepts of risk and vulnerability as touchstones for the analysis, what could be termed a 'human security approach' may be found in different human rights instruments. For a more systematic analysis, these are grouped roughly on the basis of the subject matter they tackle, in the following sections.

i. Socio-Economic Risks and Poverty

The *Guiding Principles on Extreme Poverty and Human Rights*, adopted in 2012 by the UN Human Rights Council, highlight that:

> Persons living in *poverty* are often *exposed* to both *institutional and individual risks of violence* and threats to their physical integrity from State agents and private actors, causing them to live in constant *fear and insecurity*. Continued *exposure and vulnerability to violence* affect a person's physical and *mental health* and impair his or her economic development and *capacity to escape poverty*. Those living in poverty, with little or no economic independence, have *fewer possibilities* of finding security and protection. Law enforcement agents often profile and deliberately target persons living in poverty … Moreover, poverty is a cause of *preventable* death, ill-health, high mortality rates and low life expectancy, not only through *greater exposure to violence but also material deprivation* and its consequences, such as lack of food, safe water and sanitation.[16] (emphasis added)

[16] UN Human Rights Council, *Guiding Principles on Extreme Poverty and Human Rights* (contained in the basis of the Final Draft submitted by the Special Rapporteur on extreme poverty and human rights, Magdalena Sepúlveda Carmona, UN General Assembly Resolution A/HC/21/39, 18 July 2012), endorsed by UN Human Rights Council in Resolution 21/11 of 27 September 2012, para 63.

Expressed in human security language and spirit, certain economic, social and cultural rights (ESC Rights) also open the door to reinforced protection of persons in contexts of structural socio-economic vulnerability. The right of 'everyone' to *freedom from hunger*, for example, is specifically contemplated as the content of the right to food in Article 11.2 of the International Covenant on Economic, Social and Cultural Rights (ICESCR).[17] In further developing this right, the UN Special Rapporteur on the Right to Food has proposed criteria to guarantee 'food security' and a dignified life *free from hunger and free from fear*.[18] Risk is particularly considered in the Revised European Social Charter which includes, in Article 30, a right to protection against poverty and social exclusion, that translates into a State obligation to take measures to promote the effective access 'of persons *who live or risk living* in a situation of social exclusion or poverty, as well as their families, to, in particular, employment, housing, training, education, culture and social and medical assistance'.[19] In the academic field, health security as a subtype of human security has also been examined from the perspective of human rights law by Rebecca Cook, for instance.[20]

The European Court of Human Rights (ECHR) dealt with another issue close to the human security concern, as related to its environmental dimension and the vulnerability experienced in the context of urban poverty.[21] In the 2004 case of *Oneryldiz v Turkey*, the Court emphasised the positive obligation of the State to take measures to *prevent risks*, particularly life-threatening ones, when it was knowledgeable of the existence of such threats. The case involved the explosion of a municipal rubbish tip which resulted in the loss of life of 39 people living in a contiguous irregular settlement, facts that led the ECHR to conclude that 'there was *practical information available* to the effect that the inhabitants of certain slum areas … were faced with a *threat* to their physical integrity on account of the technical shortcomings of the municipal rubbish tip'. It further emphasised that 'the Turkish authorities at several levels *knew or ought to have*

[17] International Covenant on Economic, Social and Cultural Rights (ICESCR), adopted and opened for signature, ratification and accession by UN General Assembly Resolution 2200A (XXI) of 16 December 1966 and entered into force on 23 March 1976.

[18] See, eg, the press release on his country visit to Cameroon, Olivier De Schutter, UN Special Rapporteur on the Right to Food, 'Cameroon: Stricter Taxes for Companies Drawing on Natural Resources to Better Tackle Hunger—UN Special Rapporteur', 23 July 2012, available at www.ohchr.org/EN/NewsEvents/Pages/DisplayNews.aspx?NewsID=12385&LangID=E

[19] Revised European Social Charter (RESC), CETS No 163, opened for signature by the Member States of the Council of Europe on 3 May 1996 and entered into force on 1 July 1999.

[20] Cook, Rebecca J, 'Human Rights Dimensions of Health Security' (2003) 97 *American Society of International Law Proceedings* 101–06.

[21] On human security and urban poverty, see Liotta, Peter H and Aybüke Bilgin, 'Why Human Security? The Case for Resilience in an Urban Century' in Martin, Mary and Taylor Owen (eds), *Routledge Handbook of Human Security* (USA and Canada, Routledge, 2014) 109–22.

known that there was a *real and immediate risk* to a number of persons living near the … municipal rubbish tip'.[22]

Along these lines, in the cases of the massacres of *Mapiripán* and *Ituango*, of 2005 and 2006, both against Colombia, the Inter-American Court of Human Rights (IACHR) developed the 'doctrine of the known risk' or 'of the preventable and avoidable/created risk', building from previous European human rights case-law and incorporating elements of the Inter-American reality.[23] This concept of the 'known risk' is picked up in the analysis of this book to illustrate the relationship between potential violations involving human rights at risk, and those which actually become materialised due to a lack of attention of the State to the risks it 'knew' or 'ought to have known' about, an obligation that is reinforced regarding persons or groups in conditions of extreme vulnerability.

This dimension of the 'known risk' is also picked up in later cases involving the analysis of poverty and socio-economic conditions, such as *MSS v Belgium and Greece* of 2011, by the ECHR, as will be reviewed in detail in Chapter 6 of this book.

ii. Precautionary, Provisional or Interim Measures

Apart from these specific provisions, in the arena of more general stands by human rights law, one may also find a first general approximation to risk in the procedural power granted to some international judicial bodies to issue an order of *precautionary, provisional or interim measures* that suspend the procedure on the grounds of the need to avoid an imminent risk of irreparable harm. This procedural competence evidences the consideration of risk as a condition worthy of legal consideration that may generate positive obligations for the State. In the case of both the IACHR and the ECHR, this faculty has been used frequently.[24]

To provide an illustrative example relating to the thematic core of migration approached in Chapter 5 of this book, let us refer to the case

[22] See ECHR, *Oneryldiz v Turkey (GC)*, Appl No 48939/99, Judgment of 30 November 2004, paras 98 and 101.

[23] See IACHR, *Case of the Massacre of Mapiripán v Colombia*, 15 September 2005, Series C, No 134, and *Case of the Massacre of Ituango v Colombia*, 1 July 2006, Series C, No 148, analysing paramilitary intervention in the face of lack of evidence of direct agency of State officials, and concluding nonetheless on responsibility of the State on the basis of complicity regarding a 'known risk'. Along the same lines, see also IACHR, *Case of the Massacre of Pueblo Bello v Colombia*, 31 January 2006, Series C, No 140.

[24] See González, Felipe, 'The Experience of the Inter-American Human Rights System', (2009–10) 40 *Victoria University Wellington Law Review* 1, particularly section D. Urgent Measures at the Commission and Court 123–24; and statistics on request and granting of interim measures by the ECHR under Article 43 of the European Convention on Human Rights and Fundamental Freedoms (ECoHR) in www.echr.coe.int; see also Joint Dissenting Opinion of Judges Tulkens, Bonello and Spielmann in *N v UK*, at fn 1 (*N v United Kingdom*, Appl No 26565/05, 27 May 2008).

before the IACHR concerning the massive expulsions and deportations that Haitians and Dominicans of Haitian origin were being subjected to by the Dominican authorities, in cases wherein such activity endangered the life and the physical integrity of those deported, as well as their family members left behind, particularly those minors who were abandoned as a result. The Court then issued *precautionary measures* and ordered the Dominican Republic to adopt whatever actions necessary to protect the life and personal integrity of a series of concrete persons and to abstain from deporting or expelling from its territory one of the children involved in the case. It also ordered the State to permit the immediate return to its territory of one of the affected men so as to make the reunion between himself and his son possible.[25] This case dealing with the rights to nationality, legal personality and non-discrimination precedes what would later, in 2005, become a contentious case before the Court in the realm of both non-citizen and gender considerations, the *Case of the Yean and Bosico Girls v Dominican Republic*, as will be examined in Chapter 6 of this book.

iii. Particularly Vulnerable Groups

On substantive grounds, the IACHR has also dealt with different groups as particularly vulnerable to human rights violations. In the *Case of the 'Street Children' (Villagrán Morales et al) v Guatemala*, of 1999, the Court considered children as especially vulnerable, and characterised children living on the street as *at-risk children*, a situation which compelled the State to take positive measures for enhanced protection under Article 19 of the American Convention on Human Rights (American Convention), referred to the rights of the child, and interpreted in light of the UN Convention on the Rights of the Child.[26]

In facing the facts of five murdered street children, four of them tortured, presumably by police agents in 1990 in Guatemala City, the Court concluded that the State violated the rights of the child, as well as its general obligation to respect rights (Article 1.1.) in relation to the rights

[25] See IACHR, *Provisional Measures, Haitians and Haitian Origin Dominicans in the Dominican Republic*, Orders of 14 September 2000; 12 November 2000; and 26 May 2001. Think also of precautionary measures at the national level within procedures of legal or Constitutional protection of fundamental rights, for example, through the suspension of an arrest warrant affecting the right to liberty and security, or of an eviction order as related to the right to housing, involving negative duties of the State. Orders of precautionary measures may also require the active intervention by the State to protect an individual's life or personal integrity and translate into positive obligations that the State must carry out.

[26] IACHR, *Case of the 'Street Children' (Villagrán-Morales et al) v Guatemala*, Judgment of 19 November 1999 (Merits), paras 185–91. Reference is made to the UN Convention on the Rights of the Child, adopted and opened for signature, ratification and accession by General Assembly Resolution 44/25 of 20 November 1989, and entered into force on 2 September 1990, in accordance with Article 49.

to life (Article 4), to humane treatment (Article 5), and to the personal liberty (Article 7) of the children; as well as the rights to a fair trial (Article 8.1) and judicial protection (Article 25) of the children's families, based on the provisions of the American Convention. It also considered these grave occurrences as a violation of the right to personal integrity under Articles 1, 6 and 8 of the Inter-American Convention to Prevent and Punish Torture.

The Court framed the violations suffered by the five individual children and the members of their families against the broader social background prevailing at the time of the events, recognising

> as a *notorious and public fact* that … there was a *systematic practice* of aggression against 'street children' in Guatemala carried out by members of State security forces; this included threats, persecution, torture, forced disappearance and homicide.[27] (emphasis added)

Thus, the Inter-American Court expanded the scope of positive obligations of protection to cases in which the State *knew* or *ought to have known* of such situations of systemic vulnerability. This criteria, at work since the beginning of 1999, would be taken up by the Court in later cases of violence against women from 2001 onwards, and especially from 2009 to the present date, addressing similar State obligations of prevention through the due diligence notion and transcending the traditional public/private divide to also cover State responsibility in cases of actions carried out by private parties in which the State was not directly the perpetrator of the violations, as will be specified in Chapter 4 of this book.

a) Reinforced Positive Obligations of Protection

The expansive interpretation of the IACHR in the *Case of the Street Children v Guatemala*, using the formula of when the State *knew or ought to have known*, is also in line with general principles of interpretation of public international law. The Inter-American Court indicated that 'when interpreting a treaty, not only the agreements and instruments formally related to it should be taken into consideration (Article 31.2 of the Vienna Convention), but also the system within which it is (inscribed) (Article 31.3)'. It related the criteria generally informing normative legal systems specifically to international human rights law,

> which has advanced substantially by the evolutive interpretation of international protection instruments … consequent with the general rules of the interpretation of treaties embodied in the 1969 Vienna Convention … human rights treaties are living instruments, the interpretation of which must evolve over time in view of existing circumstances.

[27] *Case of the Street Children* (n 26) para 189. See also paras 59 c) and 79.

Under this reasoning, the Court concluded that both the American Convention and the UN Convention on the Rights of the Child form part of a very comprehensive international *corpus juris* for the protection of the child that should help the Court establish the content and scope of the general provision established in Article 19 of the American Convention.[28]

In their Joint Concurring Opinion, Judges Cançado Trindade and Abreu-Burelli emphasised the interpretation of the Court and detailed the reasoning for the broad interpretation of the scope of the right to life of the street children as understood by the Court's judgment:

> The duty of the State to take positive measures is *stressed* precisely in relation to the protection of life of *vulnerable and defenseless persons, in situation of risk*, such as the children in the streets. The arbitrary deprivation of life is not limited, thus, to the illicit act of homicide; it *extends* itself likewise to the *deprivation of the right to live with dignity*. This outlook conceptualizes the right to life as belonging, at the same time, to the domain of civil and political rights, as well as economic, social and cultural rights, thus illustrating the interrelation and indivisibility of all human rights.[29] (emphasis in first two phrases in original, emphasis in fourth and fifth phrase added)

The *Case of the Street Children v Guatemala* of the IACHR resonates with the preoccupations expressed by the UN Committee on the Rights of the Child (in charge of reviewing State compliance with the Convention on the Rights of the Child and its Optional Protocols).[30] The UN Committee has pointed out its concern (concretely in its State review of Togo) on the lack of measures taken to avoid 'children at risk', as the Committee calls them, including children living in extreme poverty or on the street, from becoming victims of sexual exploitation, pornography and trafficking, according to their obligations of *prevention* set forth in Article 9, paragraphs 1 and 2, of the Optional Protocol to the Convention on the Rights of the Child on the Sale of Children, Child Prostitution and Child Pornography. The Committee goes further to also stress the links between gender-based discrimination and violence as a fertile ground for children, particularly girls, being placed at risk of sexual exploitation. Indeed, in analysing State

[28] *Case of the Street Children* (n 26) paras 192–94. The sentence refers to the Vienna Convention on the Law of Treaties, adopted in Vienna on 23 May 1969, entered into force on 27 January 1980, United Nations, Treaty Series, vol 1155, 2005, p 331.

[29] *Case of the 'Street Children' v Guatemala*, Joint Concurring Opinions of Judges AA Cançado Trindade and A Abreu-Burelli, para 4.

[30] Articles 43–45 of the UN Convention on the Rights of the Child; Article 8, paragraph 1, of the Optional Protocol to the Convention on the Rights of the Child on Involvement of Children in Armed Conflict; and Article 12, paragraph 1, of the Optional Protocol to the Convention on the Rights of the Child on the Sale of Children, Child Prostitution and Child Pornography, adopted and opened for signature, ratification and accession by General Assembly Resolution A/RES/54/263 of 25 May 2000, entered into force on 18 January 2002.

obligations in this respect, the UN Committee specifically recommended that under the provisions of the Convention, the State should

> Take effective measures to *identify* groups of children, including *girls, children living in extreme poverty and children in street situations, at risk* of being victims of the offences prohibited under the Optional Protocol, and provide them with the necessary support and assistance.
>
> Eradicate gender-based discrimination and violence, and in particular repeal laws still in force that discriminate against women…[31] (emphasis added)

Turning back to the Inter-American level, the Court has also straightforwardly addressed the State's obligation to take active measures to tackle risk in the field of socio-economic vulnerability. In the cases of *Moiwana v Suriname, Saramaka People v Suriname, Yakye Axa v Paraguay, Sawhoyamaxa v Paraguay*, and *Xákmok Kásek v Paraguay*, involving indigenous and traditional communities,[32] the Court stressed the risk and vulnerability arising out of extreme poverty, coupled with the membership of persons to indigenous communities or minority ethnic groups. Consequently, it interpreted the State's obligations regarding the rights to life, personal integrity and judicial protection, to encompass positive obligations to mitigate risk conditions in order to *prevent* violations to human rights and to adopt *protective measures* to confront such threats, thus affirming the State's reinforced obligation of protection. It also gave due regard to the communal conception of property of these indigenous groups as a condition that allowed them to confront risk and ensure the possibility of economic survival, building from its pivotal case of *Awas Tingni Community v Nicaragua*, of 2001.[33]

In the 2006 case of the *Sawhoyamaxa Indigenous Community v Paraguay*, involving non-citizens, namely internally displaced persons, Judge Cançado Trindade even gave life to a concrete mode of applying the human security–human rights symbiosis through judicial interpretation.

[31] UN Committee on the Rights of the Child, CRC/C/OPSC/TGO/CO/1, 8 March, 2012, Fifty-ninth session, held on 16 January—3 February 2012, 'Consideration of reports submitted by States parties under article 12, paragraph 1, of the Optional Protocol to the Convention on the Rights of the Child on the sale of children, child prostitution and child pornography. Concluding observations: Togo', para 21, c) and d).

[32] IACHR: *Moiwana Community v Suriname*, Preliminary Objections, Merits, Reparations, and Costs, Judgment of 15 June 2005, Series C No 124, para 133; *Saramaka People v Suriname*, Preliminary Objections, Merits, Reparations, and Costs, Judgment of 28 November 2007, Series C No 172, para 164; *Yakye Axa Indigenous Community v Paraguay*, Merits, Reparations, and Costs, Judgment of 17 June 2005, Series C No 125, paras 38 a, b, c, and d, and 39; *Sawhoyamaxa Indigenous Community v Paraguay*, Judgment of 29 March 2006 (Merits, Reparations and Costs); and *Xákmok Kásek Indigenous Community v Paraguay*, 24 August 2010 (Merits, Reparations and Costs).

[33] IACHR, *Case of the Mayagna (Sumo) Awas Tingni Community v Nicaragua*, Judgment of 31 August 2001 (Merits, Reparations and Costs).

In this case, based on an academic study on human security and human dignity, Judge Cançado reminds us that

> The problem of internally displaced people … is actually a human rights problem. Displaced people are in a *vulnerable situation* precisely because of the fact they are under the jurisdiction of the State … (their own State) that did not adopt enough measures to *avoid* or *prevent* the situation of virtual desertion they came to suffer.[34] (emphasis added)

Similarly to the analysis done by the IACHR, the ECHR has addressed the concern for vulnerability and to date has identified three 'vulnerable groups': persons with mental disabilities, the Roma people, and asylum-seekers.[35] Related to the thematic cores of this book, some of these cases involve elements of gender-based discrimination and more notably, of human rights violations in relation to race, ethnic and national origin. The case of asylum-seekers will be examined more closely in Chapter 5 of this book, so let us now turn to view some of the assessments on vulnerability in cases concerning the Roma people and persons with mental disabilities.

As an illustrative case, *Connors v the United Kingdom* may be recalled, where the Court concluded a violation of Article 8 (private and family life) deriving from the eviction of a gypsy man and his family from a caravan site viewed as lacking due protection of the gypsy way of life, considering the 'vulnerable position of gypsies as a minority'. Similarly, in *Chapman v the United Kingdom*, the Court concluded that there is a positive obligation of States under Article 8 of the European Convention for the Protection of Human Rights and Fundamental Freedoms (ECoHR) to facilitate the gypsy way of life. In a more recent case, *Aksu v Turkey*, of 2012, the ECHR evaluated whether Turkey complied with its positive obligation under Article 8 to protect the applicant's private life from alleged interference by a third party, namely the author of a book and two dictionaries which were—according to the applicant's claim—demeaning and offensive to the gypsy/Roma community and its lifestyle, and reflected anti-Roma racist sentiment. In this case, though, even when the Court recognised that the '*vulnerable position* of Roma/Gypsies means that special consideration should be given to their needs and their different lifestyle, both in the relevant *regulatory framework* and in reaching *decisions in particular cases*', it concluded there had not been a violation, as the State had adequately

[34] *Sawhoyamaxa* (n 32), Separate Opinion of Judge AA Cançado Trindade, supporting his argument on the work of Stavropoulou, M, 'Searching for Human Security and Dignity: Human Rights, Refugees, and the Internally Displaced' in Danieli, Y, E Stamatopoulou and CJ Dias (eds), *The Universal Declaration of Human Rights: Fifty Years and Beyond* (Amityville, New York, Baywood Publishing Co, 1999) 181–82; at para 14, fn 20.

[35] See the excellent article by Peroni, Lourdes and Alexandra Timmer, 'Vulnerable Groups: The Promise of an Emergent Concept in European Human Rights Convention Law' (2013) 11 *International Journal of Constitutional Law* 1056–85.

balanced the applicant's right to private life against the author's freedom of expression, which prevailed.[36] (emphasis added)

In the case of *Muñoz Díaz v Spain*, of 2010, the Court had held precisely that 'the *vulnerable position* of Roma means that some special consideration should be given to their needs and their different lifestyle both in the relevant *regulatory framework* and in reaching *decisions in particular cases*'. In this instance it concluded that the State had violated Article 14 of the ECoHR (non-discrimination) in relation to Article 1 of Protocol 1 to the Convention (peaceful enjoyment of possessions) by denying a Roma woman her entitlement to a pension on the basis of not recognising the Roma marriage to her defunct husband (while such marriage had been accepted as valid through various acts by the Spanish authorities).[37] (emphasis added)

b) Indirect Discrimination and Reversal of Burden of Proof

Vulnerability and discrimination should not be confused, the latter being an *actual* unjustified distinction, whereas vulnerability is situated in the realm of the *possible* or the *susceptible*. Under international human rights law, discrimination may be understood as

> any distinction, exclusion, restriction or preference or other differential treatment that is directly or indirectly based on the prohibited grounds of discrimination and which has the intention or effect of nullifying or impairing the recognition, enjoyment or exercise, on an equal footing, of human rights and fundamental freedoms.

Such prohibited grounds for discrimination include sex, gender, race, colour, descent, culture, language, religion, political opinion, national or ethnic origin, immigrant status, disability, or any other status which has the mentioned intention or effect.[38]

[36] Cases by the ECHR: *Connors v the United Kingdom*, Appl No 66746/01, 27 May 2004, para 84; *Chapman v the United Kingdom* (GC), Appl No 27138/95, ECHR, 18 January 2001, paras 92 and 96; *Aksu v Turkey* (GC), Appl Nos 4149/04 and 41029/04, 15 March 2012, paras 75, 61, and 81–89.

[37] *Muñoz Díaz v Spain*, Appl No 49151/07, 8 December 2009 (Final 8 March 2010), paras 61 and 69–71.

[38] UN Committee on Economic, Social and Cultural Rights (UN Committee on ESC Rights), General Comment No 20, *Non-Discrimination in Economic, Social and Cultural Rights (art. 2, para. 2)*, E/C.12/GC/20, 10 June 2009, para 7, in combination with the definitions of discrimination under Article 1 of the 1965 International Covenant on the Elimination of Racial Discrimination (ICERD); Article 1 of the 1979 Convention on the Elimination of Discrimination Against Women (CEDAW); and Article 2 of the UN Convention on the Rights of Persons with Disabilities. The UN Human Rights Committee comes to a similar interpretation in General Comment No 18, paras 6 and 7. On the right to non-discrimination on the basis of immigrant status, see also UN Committee on the Elimination of Racial Discrimination, *General Recommendation No 30: Discrimination Against Non Citizens*: 01/10/2004 (General Comments), available at Compilation of General Comments and General Recommendations adopted by Human Rights Treaty Bodies. Addendum, HRI/GEN/1/Rev.7/Add.1, 4 May

There are cases that remind us, however, that a higher level of exposure to risk factors, namely, vulnerability, may in itself amount to discrimination, particularly indirect discrimination. In the prominent case of *DH and Others v the Czech Republic*, the ECHR acknowledged the concept of *indirect discrimination* in examining whether the disproportionately high placement of Roma students in schools for the learning disabled ('special schools') in the Czech Republic was a violation of their right, under Article 2 of Protocol 1 (right to education), read in conjunction with Article 14 (non-discrimination) of the ECoHR, to be free from racial discrimination in the realm of education. The Court concluded on that basis that the State was actually responsible for such violations and that it had a positive obligation to protect the Roma as a vulnerable people. The Court emphasised that discrimination means treating differently, without an objective and reasonable justification, persons in relevantly similar situations. The

> 'lack of objective and reasonable justification' means that the impugned difference in treatment does not pursue a 'legitimate aim' or that there is not a 'reasonable relationship of proportionality' between the means employed and the aim sought to be realised.[39]

At times, though, this attention by the Court to vulnerable groups has not been uniform or wholly coherent, especially and disturbingly regarding cases of violence against Roma people.[40]

In the case by the ECHR of *Horváth and Kiss v Hungary*, of January 2013, the Court found a violation of the right to education in relation to the right to non-discrimination, following the line of *DH and Others*, in this case affecting two Roma men who as children had been placed in 'special schools' on account of a 'mild mental disability'. In this case, the Court noted that Roma children had been overrepresented among the pupils at the remedial primary and vocational school attended by the applicants and that Roma children had generally been overrepresented in the past in remedial schools in Hungary due to the systematic misdiagnosis of mental disability. The underlying figures were uncontested by the Hungarian Government. This situation had to be seen *in the context of a long history of misplacement of Roma children* in special schools in Hungary and other European countries. While it could be argued that

2005. The concept and interpretations of discrimination against women as related to violence against women will also be reviewed in Chapter 4 of this book.

[39] See ECHR, *DH and Others v the Czech Republic (GC)*, Appl No 57325/00, 13 November 2007, paras 181, 175 and 196.

[40] See Möschel, Mathias, 'Is the European Court of Human Rights' Case Law on Anti-Roma Violence "Beyond Reasonable Doubt"?' (2012) 12 *Human Rights Law Review* 3, 479–507, for an account of the reluctance of the Court to deal with these cases as racial discrimination cases under Article 14 of the ECHR, as well as a useful table that illustrates the Court's response to such cases at 483.

the situation resulting from the applicants being treated differently—the school assessment testing—might have a similar effect on other socially disadvantaged groups, there was nevertheless, at first glance, a case of *indirect discrimination*. The Government therefore had *to prove* that that difference in treatment had *no disproportionately prejudicial effects*. It also concluded that Roma children were often 'misdiagnosed because of *socio-economic disadvantage or cultural differences*'. In line with the human security blueprint, the judgment even contains a whole part dedicated to analysing the 'societal context' of the case.[41] While this case is a 'good case' in terms of equality and non-discrimination on the basis of ethnicity and takes due regard of the context of vulnerability experienced by Roma people, doubts can be cast leading it to be considered as a 'questionable case' in terms of the human rights of persons with disabilities.[42]

With regard to the specific vulnerability of persons with *mental disabilities*, the Court has also based its assessment of this condition on their 'past history of discrimination and prejudice' and clarified that this results in heightened obligations for the State when placing limitations on their rights. In the case of *Alajos Kiss v Hungary*, it indicated that

> [I]f a restriction on fundamental rights applies to a *particularly vulnerable group* in society, who have suffered *considerable discrimination* in the past, such as the *mentally disabled*, then the State's margin of appreciation is substantially narrower and it must have very *weighty reasons* for the restrictions in question.... [T]he treatment as a single class of those with intellectual or mental disabilities is a questionable classification, and the curtailment of their rights must be subject to *strict scrutiny*.[43] (emphasis added)

Thus, apart from reinforcing obligations of protection in the context of structural social vulnerability, this approach also holds the effect of reducing the margin of appreciation available to the State. Converging with a human security lens, the prioritisation should be targeted at the rights of those that are most vulnerable and not at the State's space of discretional interpretation, even when such legal option is usually available.

[41] ECHR, *Horváth and Kiss v Hungary*, Appl No 11146/11, 29 January 2013, paras 104,105 and 115; and section 1.B.

[42] Although the case did not involve a specific disability-related analysis, it is quite unfortunate that the schools for children with mental disabilities were classified by the judgment as 'inferior' (para 115). The Court did so in referring to the Report on Hungary of the European Commission against Racism and Intolerance (ECRI) quoted in para 75 of the judgment, although the ECRI did not describe such schools with that adjective. Note also that the UN Convention on the Rights of Persons with Disabilities, to which the EU has been a party since 2010, was not even mentioned in the judgment's paragraphs related to the subject (72–76), thus constituting a missed human security opportunity for reaffirming and harmonising general equality and non-discrimination rights. Such an analysis could have also set the stage for further definition of the threshold of protection of the rights of persons with disabilities in the European context.

[43] ECHR, *Alajos Kiss v Hungary*, Appl No 38832/06, 20 May 2010, paras 42 and 44.

The identification of certain vulnerabilities, however, calls for an exception to this legal margin and triggers a *reversal of the burden of proof* on the State, as it rests on this actor to justify the differential treatment of the vulnerable group or its members. The reversal of the burden of proof regarding persons in extreme vulnerability and urgent need has also been reaffirmed by the UN Committee on ESC Rights as recounted in Chapter 1 above, and is addressed in other cases of structural vulnerability and/or discrimination as analysed in the following chapters.

iv. Collective Stereotyping and Harm: Collective Responses

From a wider outlook concerning vulnerability of other groups, it should be noted that the phenomenon of collective stereotyping, demonisation or criminalisation of certain groups, through targeting or highlighting certain—real or supposed—characteristics of the group's members,[44] would seem to require responses that take into account the collective dimension of the group's vulnerable situation. Sadly, some of the expressions of collective stereotyping have come in the form of official measures exactly contrary to human rights law, for example, the collective expulsion of Roma people by the French Government in 2011, which seems to echo some of the policies reviewed by the IACHR in the case of expelled Haitians or Dominicans of Haitian origin from the Dominican Republic, mentioned above.

It is true that human rights law and international law more generally have responded to this with the protection of group rights, in some cases to be exercised by *the collective itself* and not the individual, or the individual insofar as a member of a group. Think, for instance, of the right to communal land to be exercised by indigenous peoples—a proper 'collective right'—under Article 26 of the 2007 UN Declaration of the Rights of Indigenous Peoples. Group protection has also taken form through international criminal law in the protective regime of the 1948 Genocide Convention and 50 years later in the 1998 Rome Statute of the International Criminal Court, concerning national, ethnic, religious and linguistic groups. International law and several legal regimes at the regional and domestic level take group membership into account as one of the elements either for non-discrimination law or for direct protection measures understood more broadly as a mechanism for substantive equality.[45]

At the UN level, consider the protection of the rights of minorities under Article 27 of the International Covenant on Civil and Political Rights (ICCPR) and Article 30 of the Convention on the Rights of the Child, and

[44] See Peroni and Timmer (n 35).

[45] See Lerner, Natan, *Group Rights and Discrimination in International Law*, 2nd edn (The Hague, Brill-Martinus Nijhoff Publishers, 2005).

particularly, the UN Declaration on the Rights of Persons Belonging to National or Ethnic, Religious and Linguistic Minorities; although in all these cases the right is to be exercised *individually* by the group member. Also, as indicated above, the ECHR has worked on group vulnerability mainly in certain groups such as Roma people and asylum-seekers. The IACHR has deepened the analysis of socio-economic vulnerability as a cross-cutting feature transcending ethnic, religious or linguistic membership. The Inter-American region was also the first to consider violence against women as an endemic problem requiring a specific legal regime of protection, embodied in the 1994 Inter-American Convention on the subject, dealt with in Chapter 4 below.

It would seem, however, that certain political or social expressions of stereotyping, present in authoritarian regimes, but also in democratic ones, especially in times of economic crisis, escape the existing legal regimes or do not fully enjoy the characteristics for classical group rights' legislation, and thus are left invisible, shadowed or unprotected. This is especially the case for undocumented migrants, as will be seen in Chapter 5 of this book.

In the face of expressions of collective stereotyping, closely touching the border-lines of racial or ethnic discrimination, a collective response is needed. This should account for more than the sum of individual sufferings or human rights violations, and rather involve an insight that duly weighs and connects these collective dimensions. I argue that one of the possibilities for such an insight is offered by the human security conception, understood in terms of the more precise definition of the 2003 report by the Commission on Human Security (CHS), *Human Security Now*, and complemented by the 2012 UN General Assembly Resolution, as submitted in this text. A way to implement this definition here is that of using *public policies* with a human security/human rights-based approach, these measures from the executive being the archetypical tool to address 'macro' problems of a more collective and widespread nature.[46] As explored above, some judicial decisions such as *Muñoz Díaz v Spain*, by the ECHR, for example, timidly start to refer to *regulatory frameworks* as possible necessary instruments to protect groups in conditions of vulnerability and facilitate their lifestyle and consequent exercise of rights. The relationship between public policies and the fulfilment of human rights

[46] Commission on Human Security (CHS), *Human Security Now* (New York, CHS, 2003). Work in the area of human rights as policy-prescriptive and orienting to confront structural challenges in the realm of action of the executive—transcending the classical study of judicial or legislative human rights' protection—has recently started to be explored, especially in the Inter-American Human Rights' System; see Vázquez, Daniel and Domitille Delaplace, 'Public Policies from a Human Rights Perspective: A Developing Field' (2011) 8 *Sur—International Journal on Human Rights* 14; and Abramovich, Víctor, 'De las Violaciones Masivas a los Patrones Estructurales: Nuevos Enfoques y Clásicas Tensiones en el Sistema Interamericano de Derechos Humanos' (2009) 6 *Sur, Revista Internacional de Derechos Humanos* 117–40 (also available in English).

has also begun to unfold through its inclusion in certain wide-ranging normative instruments referring to women's rights at the regional level, as described in Chapter 4 below.

B. International Refugee Law

While the analysis of this book is not directly centred on international refugee law, rather applying human rights law as the general legal regime, the particular vulnerability of refugees warrants attention. Indeed, possibly the archetypical reaction when considering human security risks and relating them to human rights, is thinking of refugees—they hold in the very definition of their normative categorisation the reference to fear and risk of persecution. The two basic instruments of international refugee law, the 1951 Convention on the Status of Refugees and its 1967 Protocol, define a refugee as a person who is outside his or her country of nationality or habitual residence; has a well-founded fear of being persecuted because of his or her race, religion, nationality, membership of a particular social group or political opinion; and is unable or unwilling to avail him or herself of the protection of that country, or to return there, for fear of persecution.[47] Their situation is often so dangerous and intolerable that they cross national borders to seek safety in nearby countries, and thus become internationally recognised as 'refugees' with access to assistance from States, the UN High Commissioner for Refugees (UNHCR), and other organisations. People who fulfil the refugee definition deserve State protection (generically called 'asylum'—hence the term 'asylum-seekers') and are entitled to the rights and bound by the duties contained in the 1951 Convention.[48]

Let us also recall that Article 33 of the Convention sets forth an obligation of protection of refugees through prohibiting States from expelling or returning them when they face a risk to their life or freedom ('*refouler*'). In a complementary manner, Article 3 of the 1950 ECoHR, Article 3 of the

[47] See Article 1A(2) of the Convention relating to the Status of Refugees, adopted on 28 July 1951 by the UN Conference of Plenipotentiaries on the Status of Refugees and Stateless Persons convened under General Assembly Resolution 429 (V), and entered into force on 22 April 1954. See also Protocol on the Status of Refugees, approved in New York on 31 January 1967 and entered into force on 4 October 1967, in conformity with Article VIII. The Protocol opens up the definition of refugee of the 1951 Convention to universal application, by suppressing the reliance on occurrences having happened before 1 January 1951 and by eliminating any geographic limitation in the applicability of the 1951 Convention (given the 1951 definition is confined only to Europe).

[48] On the recognition of the status of refugee as a declaratory (and not constitutive) act, as well as on the institution of asylum as predating the international legal regime for refugees, see Gil-Bazo, María Teresa, 'Refugee Status, Subsidiary Protection, and the Right to be Granted Asylum under EC Law', Research Paper No 136, Refugee Studies Centre, Oxford University, UK-UNHCHR Policy Development and Evaluation Service, November 2006.

Convention Against Torture and Article 7 of the ICCPR, all include an obligation of protection of any person confronting a risk of torture or inhuman or degrading treatment, an obligation that is not subject to exception and constitutes *ius cogens*. The expansion of the status of 'refugee' under this definition grounds the entitlement of the person to 'subsidiary protection' from the State. Thus, both under refugee law and human rights law, risk of persecution affecting life or freedom and risk of torture or ill-treatment have become well-established conditions for triggering an obligation of protection from the State under the principle of *non-refoulment*.[49] A recent interpretation from the UN CEDAW Committee, of 2014, suggests a further enhancement of the applicability of the *non-refoulment* obligation to cover cases of 'serious forms of discrimination against women, including gender-based violence', as detailed below.

i. Principle of Non-Refoulment: Transcending Individual Circumstances

To give but a few orienting examples of the application of such obligation, to be explored in more detail in Chapter 5 of this book, we may find a reaffirmation of this principle in the realm of judicial interpretation of the ECHR. In *N v Finland*, a case of 2005 involving an applicant who had carried out services under President Mobutu of the Democratic Republic of Congo (DRC), and faced a possible expulsion from Finland (his country of residence), the Court deemed that the *risk of ill-treatment* to which the applicant would be exposed if he returned to the DRC at the moment under consideration might not necessarily emanate from the authorities of that time, 'but from relatives of dissidents who may seek revenge on the applicant for his past activities in the service of President Mobutu'. Thus, in a human security-sensitive approach that transcended potential time limitations to grant protection to the applicant, the ECHR concluded that

> sufficient evidence has been adduced to establish substantial grounds for believing that the applicant would be exposed to a *real risk* of treatment contrary to Article 3, if expelled to the DRC at this moment in time. Accordingly, the enforcement of the order issued to that effect would violate that provision for as long as the risk persists.[50]

The Court did consider a violation of Art 3 in the case of *N v Finland*, although in the comparable case of *HLR v France*, decided previously in

[49] See the analysis by Duffy, Aiofe, 'Expulsion to Face Torture? *Non-refoulment* in International Law' (2008) 20 *International Journal of Refugee Law* 3, 373–90. See also American Convention on Human Rights, Art 22, para 8; and African Charter on Human and Peoples' Rights, Art 5.

[50] ECHR, *Case of N v Finland*, Appl No 38885/02, Judgment, 26 July 2005 (Final 30 November 2005), paras 163 and 167.

1997, it had concluded that there was not enough evidence of a substantive risk to a person to be deported back to Colombia. In this last case, the Court did not rule out the possibility that Article 3 may also apply where the danger emanates from persons or groups of persons who are not public officials and held that even in such a scenario it must be shown that the *risk is real* and that the authorities of the receiving State are not able to obviate the risk by providing appropriate protection (in that applicant's case against reprisals by drug traffickers). The *general situation of violence existing in the country* of destination (Colombia) would not in itself entail a violation of Article 3 in the event of the applicant's deportation. In addition, the Court found no relevant or sufficient evidence to support the claim that his personal situation would be worse than that of other Colombians, were he to be deported.[51] The shift towards a more protective standard at play in *N v Finland* suggests positive evolutions that may point towards an integral appreciation of the collective dimensions of risks and the consequent human rights obligations that emanate from a more human security friendly vision of individual cases that also considers contextual elements in its legal evaluation.

Similarly, important from a human security perspective and transnational duties in the context of migration, is the conclusion reached in 2014 by the CEDAW Committee in its General Recommendation No 32, *The Gender-Related Dimensions of Refugee Status, Asylum, Nationality and Statelessness of Women*. The Committee clarifies that

> States parties [are bound] to protect women from being exposed to a real, personal and *foreseeable risk* of serious forms of discrimination against women, including gender-based violence, irrespective of whether such consequences would take place *outside the territorial boundaries* of the sending State party: if a State party takes a decision relating to a person *within its jurisdiction*, and the necessary and foreseeable consequence is that the person's basic rights under the Convention will be seriously at risk in *another jurisdiction*, the *State party itself* may be in violation of the Convention. The *foreseeability of the consequence* would mean that there was a *present violation* by the State party, even though the *consequence* would not occur *until later*.[52] (emphasis added)

As such, in terms of the applicability of the *non-refoulment* principle, the CEDAW Committee ascertained that

> States parties have an obligation to ensure that no woman will be expelled or returned to another State where her life, physical integrity, liberty and security of person would be threatened, or where she would risk suffering *serious forms*

[51] ECHR, *Case of HLR v France (GC)*, Appl No 24573/94, Judgment, 29 April 1997, paras 40–42.

[52] CEDAW Committee, General Recommendation No 32, *The Gender-Related Dimensions of Refugee Status, Asylum, Nationality and Statelessness of Women*, CEDAW/C/GC/32, 14 November 2014, para 22.

> *of discrimination, including serious forms of gender-based persecution or gender-based violence.*[53] (emphasis added)

This enhancement of the scope of the principle of non-refoulment to also cover the risk of violence against women is highly relevant as a development in international human rights law and a benefit for a gendered human security construction.

ii. Generalised Human Insecurity: Expanding the Concept of 'Refugee'

Circumstances causing a *generalised state of human insecurity* have also been dealt with by African and Inter-American instruments on refugees, transcending and complementing an individualist view of protection. Let us look at the Inter-American case, as an expression with a strong human rights-based approach and 'one of the most encompassing approaches to the refugee question'.[54] The concrete context of some Central American countries like Guatemala, Nicaragua and El Salvador in the 1980s, torn by civil war and armed violence, provoked a shift in the legal answers provided by the regional system to the reality of massive flows of people seeking asylum. Indeed, structural situations, rather than only individual ones, were also included in the 1984 Cartagena Declaration on Refugees. Notably, although the broadening of the conception of refugee is analogous to that made by the former Organization of African Unity's 1969 Convention on Refugee Problems in Africa—to cover those compelled to leave their country of origin on account of external aggression, occupation, foreign domination, or events seriously disturbing public order—the Cartagena Declaration emerged not out of the regional system, but out of an *ad hoc* group of experts and representatives from Latin American governments that met in a colloquium in Cartagena, Colombia and adopted the Declaration, which was later endorsed by the Organization of American States (OAS) and the Inter-American human rights system.[55]

The text of the Cartagena Declaration explains what should be understood by refugee, as well as the sources and objectives of this expanded concept:

> ...in view of the experience gained from the massive flows of refugees in the Central American area, it is necessary to consider *enlarging the concept of a refugee*, bearing in mind, as far as appropriate and in the light of the situation prevailing in the region, the precedent of the OAU Convention ... and the doctrine employed in the reports of the Inter-American Commission on Human Rights. Hence the *definition or concept of a refugee to be recommended for use in the region* is

[53] *Ibid*, para 23.

[54] Goodwin-Gill, Guy S and Jane McAdam, *The Refugee in International Law*, 3rd edn (Oxford, Oxford University Press, 2007) 38.

[55] *Ibid*, 37–38.

> one which, in addition to containing the elements of the 1951 Convention and the 1967 Protocol, includes among refugees persons who have fled their country because their *lives, safety or freedom have been threatened by generalized violence, foreign aggression, internal conflicts, massive violation of human rights* or other circumstances which have seriously disturbed public order.[56] (emphasis added)

This broadening of the definition of refugee, although contained in a 'soft-law' instrument, represents State endorsement of the applicable standards of protection and assistance, and through the Inter-American human rights system such standards have actually become entrenched in the basic principles of asylum and the recognition of 'the fundamental right of the individual to seek asylum from persecution and be heard in making that presentation'.[57] Echoing the human security concern of freedom from fear, be it *generalized violence, internal conflicts, or massive violation of human rights*, the expanded Cartagena definition, complemented by the reassessments of the 1994 San José Declaration and the 2004 Mexico Declaration,[58] was a decisive tool in assuring in practice the effective protection of hundreds of persons deemed refugees, and thus, unfolding a set of consequent legal obligations deriving from that status. The focus on people placed in vulnerable conditions due to structural conditions affecting their basic well-being, allowed for a much broader and far-reaching scope of protection of persons, regardless of an individualised risk of persecution to each one of them—a politically generous and legally creative response which could work as a reference for the EU's position of 2015 in the face of Syrian and other refugees.

C. Human Security, Humanitarian Intervention and the Responsibility to Protect

Before turning to the direct relationship between human security and human rights, some words should be reserved for the link between human security and humanitarian intervention, more concretely through the concept of the responsibility to protect (R2P).

The World Summit of 2005 had actually proposed for the UN General Assembly (UNGA) to discuss two concepts: that of Human Security and that of R2P, the latter envisioned in 2001 by the International Commission

[56] *Cartagena Declaration on Refugees*, Colloquium on the International Protection of Refugees in Central America, Mexico and Panama, adopted by the Colloquium on the International Protection of Refugees in Central America, Mexico and Panama, held at Cartagena, Colombia from 19– 22 November 1984.

[57] Inter-American Commission of Human Rights (IACoHR), 'Report on the Situation of Human Rights of Asylum Seekers within the Canadian Refugee Determination System', OEA/Ser.L/V/II.106, Doc 40 rev, 28 Feb 2000, para 118. See also Goodwin-Gill (n 54) 38.

[58] For an account of this development, see Cançado Trindade (n 5) 281–86.

on Intervention and State Sovereignty (ICISS) as a reinterpretation of sovereignty and a criteria-setter for humanitarian intervention, in the form of military intervention. As is well known, this position proposes a different content for the concept of sovereignty of the State as a 'responsibility to protect' individuals. The ICISS, established by the Government of Canada in September 2000 and supported by then UN Secretary General, Kofi Annan, forwarded the idea that the protection of individuals through humanitarian intervention by collective action of the international community, via the channels foreseen in the UN Charter, is required as a last resort in the cases of certain large-scale humanitarian crises: 1) genocide, 2) ethnic cleansing, 3) war crimes, and 4) crimes against humanity; in order to prevent further violations or to face the ones already taking place.[59] The UN R2P proposal, further developed over the years through reports by the UNSG and reviewed by the UNGA, specifies that such responsibility may and should be carried out in cases where the State primarily exercising jurisdiction is unwilling or unable to protect its people.[60]

In many scenarios, it is the polemic concept of R2P which has captured much attention because of its political implications, especially in light of the events of the last few years in Libya and Syria,[61] though it must not be forgotten that this is only one of the proposals for grounding a principled and legally valid foundation of humanitarian intervention, aiming at coherence with Chapter VII of the UN Charter and public international law.[62] At the same time, while it is true that the ICISS Report begins framing the R2P notion in its relationship to the distinct concepts of human rights and human security, it only does so at the beginning of the Report and as part of the construction of the broader argument that the protection of individuals has recently become a political priority for the international community.[63] It subsequently moves on to develop the R2P concept,

[59] See *The Responsibility to Protect*, Report of the International Commission on Intervention and State Sovereignty (ICISS), New York, December 2001.

[60] UNGA, 'Implementing the Responsibility to Protect: Report of the Secretary-General', A/63/677, 12 January 2009. See subsequent UNSG reports: 'Early Warning, Assessment and the Responsibility to Protect' of 2010; 'The Role of Regional and Sub-Regional Arrangements in Implementing the Responsibility to Protect' of 2011; 'The Responsibility to Protect: Timely and Decisive Response' of 2012; 'Responsibility to Protect: State Responsibility and Prevention' of 2013; and 'Fulfilling our Collective Responsibility: International Assistance and the Responsibility to Protect' of 2014.

[61] Consider, for example, the use of the R2P doctrine in UN Security Council's Resolution No 1973, of 17 March 2011, as a basis for authorising military intervention in Libya, and endorsed by the League of Arab States. See also *R2P: The Next Decade* (The Stanley Foundation, 2012).

[62] For an alternative view that challenges R2P (and other legal and moral proposals) as the appropriate notions to guide humanitarian intervention, and rather proposes grounding decisions in this field on equitable principles as general principles of law, see Burke, Ciarán, *An Equitable Framework for Humanitarian Intervention*, (Studies in International Law) (Oxford, Hart Publishing, 2013).

[63] See *The Responsibility to Protect* (n 59) 14–15.

an elaboration in which human security is mentioned only once, in reference to the responsibility to *prevent* and thus to attend the 'root causes' of conflict.[64]

Due to the somewhat parallel historical development of human security and R2P in the international arena, and their shared people-centred approach towards protection from severe threats and critical destructive harm to human beings, the relationship between certain cases of human insecurity and humanitarian intervention might come to mind.[65] Indeed, for some, human security and R2P are 'two sides of the same coin'.[66] It is true as well that a case of mass repression may lead to thinking of an R2P scenario. A case of mass starvation, though, would not entail R2P consequences under its current conceptualisation, although both mass repression and mass starvation are genuine human security concerns. For some, the human security approach may provide a normative basis for humanitarian intervention, independently of its legal character as defensive or authorised by the Security Council under Chapter VII of the UN Charter, that is, human security working as a modern form of Just War doctrine.[67]

A deeper analysis of humanitarian intervention, *ius bellum*—as the right to war—and *ius bello*—as the law during war—is not a part of the central focus of this book.[68] What should be pointed out, though, is that the examination carried out throughout this text reveals that actually most of the literature and UN official documents over the years dealing with human security have not approached the hypothetical human security–humanitarian intervention link in a significant manner, perhaps because of two reasons.

Firstly, the debate on the link between mass human rights violations and military intervention for humanitarian purposes has been dominated in the political agenda and in academic examination mostly by the concept of R2P. And secondly, it is understandable that human security has not been primarily considered in this debate, in light of its pacifist

[64] *Ibid*, 23.

[65] See Reveron, Derek S and Kathleen A Mahoney-Norris, *Human Security in a Borderless World* (USA, Westview Press, 2011) 20: 'The R2P construct … rests on human security as being the central concern'; and Glusac, Luka, 'Humanitarian Interventions in the Concept of Human Security' (2010) *Western Balkans Security Observer* 16, 80–92; and Axworthy, Lloyd, 'Human Security in the R2P Era' in Martin, Mary and Taylor Owen (eds), *Routledge Handbook of Human Security* (New York, Routledge, 2014) 149–158.

[66] See, eg, the account of this position given by Kerr, Pauline, 'Human Security' in Collins, Alan (ed), *Contemporary Security Studies*, 3rd edn (Oxford, Oxford University Press, 2013) 104–16.

[67] Farer, Thomas, 'Human Security: Defining the Elephant and Imagining its Tasks' (2011) 1 *Asian Journal of International Law* 1, 49.

[68] For this analysis, see, eg, Cassese, Antonio, *International Law*, 2nd edn (Oxford, Oxford University Press, 2005), particularly Chapter 20, 'Legal Restraints on Violence in Armed Conflict'; and Remiro Brotóns, Antonio, *Derecho Internacional* (Valencia, Spain, Tirant lo Blanch, 2007), Chapter XXX, 'El Derecho Internacional Humanitario/Los crímenes internacionales'.

vocation since its initial conceptualisation: in none of its foundational documents or practical applications at the UN level, has human security been used as a trigger or justification for military intervention. Quite the contrary: because of its emphasis on all types of vulnerabilities that affect people's human rights and impede them from living both free from fear and free from want, human security seeks to create the conditions necessary to eliminate or ameliorate such risk situations and build resilience to confront them, not only as valuable goals in their own right, but also to *prevent* them from escalating to a situation of physical violence or use of armed force, whether locally, nationally or internationally. Of course critical human insecurity may well be the background curtain against which certain scenarios of widespread human suffering develop. Grave and systematic violations of human rights may lead to considerations of the need for humanitarian intervention that, according to R2P, would be carried out only in the very limited cases of genocide, ethnic cleansing, war crimes and crimes against humanity. But when this occurs, *human security has failed.*

As Hilary Charlesworth put it in 2002, under alternative visions

> security would mean the absence of violence and economic and social justice. If the idea of security is understood more broadly, the futility of the standard form of international collective action becomes clear. Military intervention is an inappropriate mechanism if the causes of insecurity are poverty, discrimination and violence protected by structures within the state.[69]

As I have argued, the human security–human rights lens makes visible the human suffering caused by direct and indirect violence, all forms of conflict—armed and otherwise—regarding equally important concerns for international law than those stemming from 'crisis moments'. The identification and correct diagnosis of these other forms of conflict provided by the human security–human rights intersection would in turn allow for well targeted, non-armed preventive action by international, regional and national actors, as also promoted by the R2P position. The differences between the two concepts, however, should continue to be underlined.

In fact, the 2012 UNSG report, based on informal debates with experts and input from States, and endorsed by the UNGA, carefully and explicitly excluded any possibility of humanitarian or military intervention to foster human security goals. The 2012 UNGA Resolution itself specifies the notion of human security as distinct from the responsibility to protect and its implementation, given that human security does not entail

[69] Charlesworth, Hilary, 'International Law: A Discipline of Crisis' (2002) 65 *Modern Law Review* 3, 391–92. See also Chandler, David, 'Resilience and Human Security: The Post-Interventionist Paradigm' (2012) *Security Dialogue* 43 (3), 213–14, for a criticism towards the narrative of thinking strictly in terms of the binary R2P/military intervention, and human security/development activities.

the threat or the use of force or coercive measures.[70] As such, the risk of human security being used as a justification for armed action or as the basis for humanitarian intervention under any doctrine, including that of R2P, seems far-fetched. While scholarly discussion on the issue may have been in line in previous years, the fact of the matter is that the 2012 UNGA Resolution reflecting State consensus leaves little room for placing in doubt the conceptual—and political—differences between human security and R2P. The official documents in the same vein, as well as the empirical experience to date, are also evidence of this assumption. In this context, it is also worth mentioning the debates of recent years on the right to peace within the UN Human Rights Council that incorporate features of a 'broad' human security understanding and recognise 'a right to human security' within the 'right to peace of persons and peoples'.[71]

At the same time, a critical account is called for regarding UN human security documents. I have argued before for the inclusion of human rights law standards and indicators in the definition of the scope and content of human security. Interestingly enough, the need to turn to human rights indicators, to profit from the extensive work already developed in this field, and to build upon the coordination carried out by the United Nations Office of the High Commissioner for Human Rights (OHCHR), was actually highlighted more distinctly in the 2009 R2P Report of the UNSG than in the 2010 and 2012 analogous UNSG Reports on Human Security. The human security advocates would possibly benefit from looking at the work by their neighbouring companions from the R2P world.

II. HUMAN SECURITY AND HUMAN RIGHTS

To begin exploring the intersections between human security and human rights, one could question if the two can actually sit comfortably together, when the first is a notion articulated originally in the field of development, political science, and international relations, and thus more useful in the public policy realm, whereas human rights enjoy a strong international

[70] UNGA A/Res/66/290, para 3, d) and e).

[71] See *UN Draft Declaration on the Right to Peace*, contained in Human Rights Council, *Report of the Human Rights Council Advisory Committee on the Right of Peoples to Peace*, A/HRC/20/31, 16 April 2012 and UNGA Resolution A/HRC/RES/20/15, 17 July 2012. Along these lines, it has been argued that human security with a human rights-based approach would entail constructing it on the basis of the human rights to peace and development to enable its effective implementation; see Paupp, Terrence E, *Redefining Human Rights in the Struggle for Peace and Development* (UK, Cambridge University Press, 2014) 475 and subsequent pages, particularly 491 and 513. See also Schabas, William A, 'Freedom from Fear and the Human Right to Peace' in Keane, David and Yvonne McDermott (eds), *The Challenge of Human Rights. Past, Present and Future* (USA/UK, Edward Elgar, 2012) 36–51.

normative architecture constructed mainly over the last 60 years and providing for legally binding obligations.[72]

This would be, however, a partial representation of the relationship. As analysed, numerous legal and 'soft-law' expressions refer to human security and are normative in content and spirit. Legally binding human security obligations are also contained in regional and sub-regional instruments. All such instruments jointly constitute a public basis for State action and social agency and as such impact on human rights enjoyment or limitation. The involvement of legal scholarship in this reflection is called for given that human security, it is suggested in this text, even when viewed only as an orienting notion, has influenced human rights' legal norms and interpretation and holds the potential to keep on doing so.

Human rights as one of the main drivers of the development of modern international law,[73] shares with human security its person-centred teleology, as opposed to prioritising State-focused goals. Both constructs, human security and human rights, serve common purposes and are therefore 'mutually reinforcing'.[74] Indeed, as the 2003 CHS Report had already noted, 'Human security helps *identify the rights* at stake in a particular situation. And *human rights* help answer the question: How should human security be promoted.'[75] (emphasis added)

Despite the potential of the human security–human rights link as a reciprocal symbiosis, as has been explained, while most human security ideas relate to human rights at the general or discursive level, they do not connect at a deeper level and they do not adopt a human rights-based approach when measuring levels of human security. In a similar way to the human rights-based approaches that have been suggested in relation to development, as well as in relation to ESC Rights,[76] a human rights-based approach to human security—and moreover a gendered and

[72] See Dahl-Eriksen, 'Human Security: A New Concept which Adds New Dimensions to Human Rights Discussions?' (2007) 16 *Human Security Journal*; and Howard-Hassmann, Rhoda E, 'Human Security: Undermining Human Rights?' (2012) 34 *Human Rights Quarterly* 1, 88–112.

[73] See Cassese (n 68) 45.

[74] Von Tigerstrom, Barbara, *Human Security and International Law: Prospects and Problems*, (Studies in International Law) (Oxford and Portland, Hart Publishing, 2007) 39.

See also Benedek, Wolfgang, 'Human Rights and Human Security: Challenges and Prospects' in Ferrándiz, Francisco and Antonius CGM Robben (eds), *Multidisciplinary Perspectives on Peace and Conflict Research: A View from Europe* (Bilbao, University of Deusto, 2007) 29–50.

[75] *Human Security Now* (n 46) p 10.

[76] See *The Millennium Development Goals and Economic, Social and Cultural Rights; a Joint Statement by the UN Committee on Economic, Social and Cultural Rights and the UN Commission on Human Rights' Special Rapporteurs for Economic, Social and Cultural Rights*, November 2002, in www2.ohchr.org/english/bodies/cescr/docs/statements/MDGandESCRs-2002.doc; Alston, Philip, 'A Human Rights Perspective on the Millennium Development Goals', paper prepared as a contribution to the work of the Millennium Project Task Force on Poverty and Economic Development, 2004; and Alston, Philip and Mary Robinson, *Human Rights and Development: Towards a Mutual Reinforcement* (Oxford, Oxford University Press, 2006).

human rights-based approach as I have defended—would bear fruitful results, but has seldom been explored.

In line with the recent emphasis on focusing on human rights implementation,[77] the connection between human security and human rights under this perspective would also contribute to the possibility of constructing public policies with a human rights-based approach. Such public policies, being of a widespread nature, would include the aspect of *prevention* and *attention* to serious threats and risks that cause situations of structural vulnerability. The human security approach introduces a practical framework for identifying the specific rights that are at stake in a particular situation of insecurity and for considering the institutional and governance arrangements that are needed to exercise and sustain them.[78] It is true that legal and policy measures based on human rights standards are in line with the triple State duties of 'respecting, protecting and fulfilling', already articulated in human rights law (and studied in Chapter 3 of this book). Still, the State sovereignty logic contained in human rights norms themselves limits the manoeuvring space to seriously challenge certain forms of State-constructed vulnerability—eg, that stemming from restrictive migration law and policy—from the standpoint of human rights law alone. In light of this, human security as a sui generis policy-normative concept holds the potential to defy—hand in hand with human rights standards—unjust measures, and to promote equally widespread measures to address them such as legal reforms and public policies. Continuing with the example, human security/rights-sensitive measures would include policies of prevention of and attention to violence against undocumented migrant women and girls, regardless of their immigration status.

In line with the current 'common understanding' of human security reflected in the UNSG's Report and the UNGA's position of 2012, I have argued for an integrated approach that considers *all* human rights potentially at the centre of human security, with no *a priori* definition of which one is to be taken into account and which one is to be excluded. The differentiating element, the one that unites the two notions and therefore makes it significant both for rights and for security, is the component of *serious threats, risk situations and vulnerabilities*, as pointed out in the 'broad' threshold of understanding above.

[77] See the OHCHR's work on indicators of human rights implementation at www.ohchr.org/EN/Issues/Indicators/Pages/HRIndicatorsIndex.aspx. See also Abramovich, Víctor, *Los estándares interamericanos de derechos humanos como marco para la formulación y el control de las políticas sociales* (Buenos Aires, Anuario de Derechos Humanos, 2006); and UN, 'The Second Interagency Workshop on Implementing a Human Rights-based Approach in the Context of UN Reform', Workshop Report, Stamford, 5-7 May, 2003.

[78] See UN Trust Fund for Human Security (UNTFHS), *Human Security in Theory and Practice. Application of the Human Security Concept and the United Nations Trust Fund for Human Security* (Human Security Unit, Office for the Coordination of Humanitarian Affairs, United Nations, 2009) 9.

Let us now turn to explore the concrete ways in which international human rights law has dealt with some of the different dimensions of security in conceptualising them as rights.

A. Is Human Security a Human Right? A Survey of Security in Human Rights Law

Several international human rights instruments refer to security, both at the UN and the regional levels. Let us take a panoramic view of the legal provisions in those spheres that cover security in its different understandings linked to human rights.

Kempen identifies at least four different concepts of security within human rights law: (i) international security; (ii) negative individual security against the State; (iii) security as justification to limit human rights [national security]; and (iv) a positive State obligation to offer security to individuals against State officials and private parties. He signals rightly, in my view, how several of these concepts are at odds with each other and some of them only offer diffuse or even vague perspectives on security. He points out, however, that these 'human rights security concepts' can make a valuable contribution to political and legal discourses on security since they have a common basis: all these concepts imply that the referent for security ultimately is the individual. 'Combined, these concepts could have the potential to offer what may be called a human rights approach to security, and by doing so help to give substance and direction to the human security discourse.'[79] One would have wanted to see added to this interesting analysis the notion of 'social security' as recognised by human rights law. Apart from the conceptual weak spots of prioritising civil rights, as discussed above, as of today this distinction lacks a strong foundation in international human rights law: with the adoption of the Optional Protocol to ICESCR, the right to social security is normatively protected on an equal footing to the right to personal security of ICCPR, and would thus also feed into the human security discourse as suggested by the author.

The core international human rights instruments—the Universal Declaration of Human Rights (UDHR),[80] as well as the two main Covenants within the UN human rights system, the ICCPR and the ICESCR—[81] all

[79] Kempen, Piet Hein van, 'Four Concepts of Security—A Human Rights Perspective' (2013) 13 *Human Rights Law Review* 1, 1–23, quote from 23.

[80] Universal Declaration of Human Rights, proclaimed by the United Nations General Assembly in Paris on 10 December 1948, General Assembly Resolution 217 A (III).

[81] ICCPR and ICESCR, adopted and opened for signature, ratification and accession by UN General Assembly Resolution 2200A (XXI) of 16 December 1966 and entered into force on 23 March 1976.

recognise the right to security in one way or another. Certainly, one of the most important legal intersections between human security and human rights is considering security (with no preceding adjective) as a human right. Let us now turn to unpack in further detail the types of security recognised by human rights law.

The ICCPR acknowledges the 'right to liberty and *security* of person' and indicates that no person 'shall be subjected to arbitrary arrest or detention' nor 'shall be deprived of his liberty except on such grounds and in accordance with such procedures as are established by law' (Article 9.1).[82] This provision has also been interpreted to protect the right to security of the person outside the context of a formal deprivation of liberty.[83] The right to personal liberty and security is also recognised by regional human rights instruments, in Article 5.1 of the 1950 ECoHR; Article I of the American Declaration on the Rights and Duties of Man (ADRDM); Article 7.1 of the 1969 American Convention on Human Rights (ACoHR or Pact of San José); and Article 6 of the 1981 African Charter on Human and Peoples' Rights (ACHPR or Banjul Charter).[84]

On the other hand, the ICESCR recognises in a broad way 'the right of everyone to *social security*, including social insurance' (Article 9) and prescribes the widest possible protection and assistance by the State to the family, which is the natural and fundamental group unit of society, particularly for its establishment and while it is responsible for the care and education of dependent children (Article 10.1). It also stipulates the obligation of granting special protection to mothers during a reasonable period before and after childbirth and mentions that during such period working mothers should be accorded paid leave or leave with adequate *social security* benefits (Article 10.2). Also, Article 11.1 on the right to an adequate standard of living relates to social assistance and other needs-based mechanisms of social benefits in cash or in kind to anyone without adequate resources.

There is thus a narrow and a broad understanding of the right to social security, the first one relating more to income and situation-based 'earned'

[82] Emphasis added in this and all of the subsequently quoted instruments in this section.

[83] See UN Human Rights Committee, *Dias v Angola*, Communication 711/1996, UN Doc CCPR/68/D/711/1996, 2000, para 8.3; and the case of *Delgado Páez v Colombia*, Communication No 195/1985, 12 July 1990, reviewed in more detail below; as well as the general analysis of the right to liberty and security of the person in Conte, Alex and Richard Burchill, *Defining Civil and Political Rights: The Jurisprudence of the United Nations Human Rights Committee*, 2nd edn (Aldershot, England, Ashgate, 2004) 112–18.

[84] European Convention for the Protection of Human Rights and Fundamental Freedoms (ECoHR), CETS No 005, opened for signature by the Member States of the Council of Europe on 4 November 1950 and entered into force on 3 September 1953; American Declaration on the Rights and Duties of Man (ADRDM), Organization of American States (OAS) Res XXX 1948; American Convention on Human Rights (ACoHR), OAS Treaty Series No 36, adopted on 22 November 1969 and entered into force on 18 July 1978; African Charter on Human and Peoples' Rights (ACHPR), adopted on 27 June 1981, Organization of African Unity Doc CAB/LEG/67/3 rev. 5, 21 I.L.M. 58 (1982), and entered into force on 21 October 1986.

social security benefits of workers and their families, usually in the form of cash benefits (also referred to as 'social insurance'), and the second also including individuals or groups receiving need-based assistance from public funds, raised through tax revenues ('social welfare' or 'social assistance'). In terms of international treaties, the right to social security has been interpreted in the latter manner to cover both types of social security as a *right*, more explicitly by the European Social Charter[85] and through the interpretation of the UN Committee on ESC Rights, the ICESCR's monitoring body, in the forms specified below.

The right to social security or of non-discrimination in relation to social security, is also confirmed in other UN treaties, such as in various conventions of the International Labour Organization (ILO), the main one being the Social Security (Minimum Standards) Convention of 1952 (No 102), although there are many more.[86] This is possibly why the text of the ICESCR was drafted with a rather general content in dealing with social security, in light of the existence of well-developed ILO standards in the field and the possibility for the ILO to continue exercising its faculties on standard-setting and implementation.[87] With the 2008 General Comment on *The Right to Social Security* of the UN Committee on ESC Rights, however, further criteria for the interpretation of this human right were provided from within the human rights world, given that the Committee specified the 'Core Obligations' of States in relation to this right.[88]

Also, with the adoption of the 2008 Optional Protocol to the IESCR and its entry into force in 2013, the existence of an individual complaints mechanism regarding violations of ESC Rights allows for the right to social security and the related right to an adequate standard of living to be fully justiciable also (or possibly primarily) within the realm of UN human rights protection mechanisms. This would open the door for subsequent interpretations of the core content of these rights in human rights understanding, not a minor task in the context of the recent economic crisis.

Other UN human rights and human-centred instruments confirm the right to social security in relation to specific groups such as refugees, children, women, stateless persons, and migrants.[89] This same right to

[85] See Scheinin, Martin, 'The Right to Social Security' in Eide, Asbjorn, Catarina Krause and Allan Rosas (eds), *Economic, Social and Cultural Rights. A Textbook*, 2nd revised edn (The Netherlands, Martinus Nijhoff Publishers, 2001) 212–14. See for example European Committee on Social Rights, Conclusions XIX-2, Luxembourg, 22 December 2009.

[86] See also ILO Conventions 35, 36, 38, 39, 40, 48, 67, 70, 71, 103, 118, 128, 131, 156, 157, 167, 165, 168 and 183, available at www.ilo.org/ilolex/english/convdisp1.htm.

[87] In this respect, see Scheinin (n 85) 214–15. The author also explains how the UN Committee on ESC Rights has used the ILO's Reporting Guidelines as a reference point in its own work for defining State obligations.

[88] See UN Committee on ESCR, General Comment No 19, *The Right to Social Security (Article 9)*, E/C.12/GC/19, 4 February 2008, paras 59–61.

[89] Article 5,e) iv of ICERD; Articles 11 and 13 of the 1979 CEDAW; Article 27 of the 1989 Convention on the Rights of the Child; Articles 27, 45 and 54 of the 1990 International

social security is recognised in regional human rights instruments, in Articles 12, 13, 16, 17 and 27 of the Revised European Social Charter (ESC); Article XVI of the ADRDM; Article 9 of the Additional Protocol in the Area of Economic, Social and Cultural Rights to the ACoHR (Protocol of San Salvador); and Article 18.4 of the ACHPR.[90]

Notably, the European Committee of Social Rights monitors compliance of Council of Europe Member States that have ratified the European Social Charter (43 States), and may decide not only individual complaints, but also complaints against those States that have chosen to accept the Committee's *collective complaints* procedures. Such mechanism seems to echo the human security approach of providing collective responses to collective problems.

Different contents can be found for the right to security, depending on the nature of the Covenant and the values each one wishes to protect with regards to human dignity, in one case, more related to physical liberty and integrity, and in the other, more linked to social support networks and socio-economic well-being. However, these are both expressions of an individual right to safeguards and certainties enjoyed in different spheres of human life, in relation to which the State holds positive obligations of protection.

These aspects of the right to security were originally conceived by the 1948 UDHR,[91] which affirmed that 'Everyone has the right to life, liberty and *security* of person' (Article 3), and that

> Everyone, as a member of society, has the right to *social security* and is entitled to realisation, through national effort and international co-operation and in accordance with the organization and resources of each State, of the economic, social and cultural rights indispensable for his dignity and the free development of his personality (Article 22).

It also set forth that

> Everyone has the right to a standard of living adequate for the health and well-being of himself and of his family, including food, clothing, housing and medical care and necessary social services, and the *right to security* in the event of unemployment, sickness, disability, widowhood, old age or other lack of livelihood in circumstances beyond his control.

Convention on the Rights of All Migrant Workers and Members of their Families (CRMW); Article 24 of the 1951 Convention relating to the Status of Refugees; and Article 24 of the 1954 Convention relating to the Status of Stateless Persons.

[90] European Social Charter, CETS No 035, opened for signature by the Member States of the Council of Europe in Turin on 18 October 1961 and entered into force on 26 February 1965; and Revised European Social Charter (RESC), CETS No 163, opened for signature by the Member States of the Council of Europe on 3 May 1996 and entered into force on 1 July 1999; Additional Protocol in the Area of Economic, Social and Cultural Rights to the ACoHR (Protocol of San Salvador), signed 17 November 1988 and entered into force 16 November 1999.

[91] Adopted by the UN General Assembly on 10 December 1948, Resolution 217 A (III).

The UDHR also set out that 'Motherhood and childhood are entitled to special care and assistance' (Article 25, 1 and 2).

Security is also mentioned in both Covenants of 1966 as a justifiable restriction to the exercise of certain rights, under the auspices of 'national security'. The two instruments generally prescribe that these rights shall not be subject to any restrictions except those which are provided by law, are necessary to protect *national security* in a democratic society, public order (*ordre public*), public health or morals or the rights and freedoms of others, and are consistent with the other rights recognised in the Covenant (Articles 12.3; 13; 14; 19.3, a) and b); 21; and 22.2 of the ICCPR; and Article 8.1, a) and c) of the ICESCR).

It is important to note, though, that the possibilities of using the security of the State as a legitimate restriction of rights, was not mentioned at all in the UDHR, which sheds light on the fact that in the Cold War period in which the two Covenants were adopted, the political fear of threats posed by the exercise of rights such as liberty of movement, freedom of expression, right to information in the context of criminal proceedings or freedom of association (in the case of the ICCPR), or the right to form trade unions (in the case of the ICESCR), was probably higher than in the immediate aftermath of WWII, or than (arguably) it is today, at least in the democratic world.

Consequently, in legal terms, apart from these limited exceptions, State actions aimed at attaining security could consequently not override the human rights contained in international law or other constitutional or legal instruments at the national or local level. In an analogy to what occurs in the field of development, it seems useful to recall the Vienna Declaration and Programme of Action to the effect that 'while development facilitates the enjoyment of all human rights, the lack of development may not be invoked to justify the abridgement of internationally recognized human rights' (Part I, para 10). Similarly, in a holistic view of threats affecting persons and communities as that proposed by the human security conception, other concerns of a reductionist view of security, such as 'national' or 'military security' could not be argued as a basis for limiting or watering down international human rights, as it has been attempted in some contexts, for example, regarding indigenous peoples' rights.[92]

[92] In the field of indigenous peoples' human rights, it has been pointed out that 'Pitting security against the collective human rights of indigenous peoples would contradict existing international human rights law and be "dangerous". It could seriously jeopardize the notion of "human security" [of such peoples]', that encompasses many elements, inter alia, physical, spiritual, health, religious, cultural, economic, environmental, social and political aspects; see Henriksen, JB, 'Implementation of the Right of Self-Determination of Indigenous Peoples Within the Framework of Human Security' in MC van Walt van Praag and O Seroo (eds), *The Implementation of the Right to Self-Determination as a Contribution to Conflict Prevention*, (Barcelona, Centre UNESCO de Catalunya, 1999) 226, quoted in UN Commission on Human Rights, Report of the second expert seminar 'Democracy and the Rule of Law', Geneva, 28 February–2 March 2005, Note by the secretariat, E/CN.4/2005/58, 18 March 2005, p 15, para 45.

Following the human-centred view already described, if we understand security as the protection from severe threats, risks and vulnerabilities that can negatively affect the daily lives, rights and dignity of people, then we can consider not only the threats stemming from physical violence which harm the human rights to life, liberty or personal integrity, but we may also view security in relation to the risks to ESC Rights (whether they originate from violent conflict or not), as considered in the right to social security, for example.

In the realm of these last types of threats to the fulfilment of ESC Rights, it is worth noting Article 30 of the Revised ESC in this precise sense. The European Social Charter, originally adopted in 1961, included in its revised version of 1996, the 'right to protection against poverty and social exclusion', mentioned above. Thus, the Revised ESC, apart from including the autonomous rights to social security, education and housing, it also set forth this provision that recognises the interconnected nature of the rights affected by poverty and social exclusion. It goes one step further in acknowledging the right to protection against poverty and social exclusion not only in relation to persons already confronting this situation, but Article 30 additionally includes the positive obligation of States to 'take measures ... to promote the effective access of persons who ... *risk living* in a situation of social exclusion or poverty, as well as their families, to, in particular, employment, housing, training, education, culture and social and medical assistance'.

Following a similar line, more recently *food security for women*, as one of the types of human security, and the *right to peace for women*, inextricably linked to the human security notion, have both been specifically considered as human rights under Articles 15 and 10 respectively, of the 2003 Protocol to the ACHPR on the Rights of Women in Africa, the Maputo Protocol. Comparably, within the regional context of the OAS, the States in the Americas adopted in 2012 the Declaration of Cochabamba on 'Food Security with Sovereignty in the Americas'[93] and the Resolution 'Excessive Commodity Price Volatility and its Consequences for Food Security and Sustainable Development in the Americas',[94] which both endorse a broad idea of security as encompassing the human right to food.

See UN Commission on Human Rights, Sixty-second session, E/CN.4/2005/WG.15/CRP.2, 24 November 2005, Working group established in accordance with Resolution 1995/32, Eleventh session, Geneva, 5–16 December 2005, 'General Provisions' of the Draft UN Declaration on the Rights of Indigenous Peoples, pp 19–20.

[93] Declaration of Cochabamba on 'Food Security with Sovereignty in the Americas', AG/DEC. 69 (XLII-O/12), OAS General Assembly, adopted at the fourth plenary session, held on 5 June 2012.

[94] OAS General Assembly, 'Excessive Commodity Price Volatility and its Consequences for Food Security and Sustainable Development in the Americas', AG/RES. 2757 (XLII-O/12), agreed at the fourth plenary session, held on 5 June 2012.

In line with the human security conception, the UN Committee on ESC Rights has also affirmed the existence of a *right of tenants to security of tenure* as part of its interpretation of the right to adequate housing deriving from Article 11 of the ICESCR.[95] Although not specifically contained in the Covenant, this right to security of tenure does arise from the legal interpretation of the competent supervisory body of these rights and thus constitutes an authoritative source to reason on the current understanding of one of the dimensions of security under human rights law.

Thus, under general international human rights law, as it stands today, there is legal basis to affirm that security is a human right, but limited to the *right of personal security* and the *right to social security*, as well as the *right to security of tenure* (derived through the interpretation of the UN Committee on ESC Rights). We should also include the *right to food security* as a general right in certain instruments of the OAS and, more specifically, a *right to food security for women* in the binding regional legal framework of the African human rights' system.

B. Human Security and Human Rights in Public International Law

I have sustained above that this book's central focus is not to give full evidence of the normative embodiment of human security in the traditional sources of public international law, but rather to deepen the analysis of the legal implications of the human security–human rights symbiosis. One of the central concerns of contemporary public international law, however, is the area of international human rights law. As such, I will briefly refer to the sources of public international law and the way human security relates to them in the concrete sphere of human rights.

According to Article 38.1 of the Statute of the International Court of Justice (ICJ), traditionally regarded as the foundation for the sources of public international law,[96] the Court can decide the cases brought before it 'in accordance with international law', applying:

a) international conventions, whether general or particular, establishing rules expressly recognised by the contesting States;
b) international custom, as evidence of a general practice accepted as law;

[95] See General Comment No 4, *The Right to Adequate Housing (Art 11 (1) of the Covenant)*, 13 December 1991 (Contained in document E/1992/23); and General Comment No 7, *The Right to Adequate Housing (Art 11 (1) of the Covenant): forced evictions*, sixteenth session 1997, Contained in document E/1998/22, annex IV, 20 May 1997.

[96] See, eg, Kaczorowska, Alina, *Public International Law*, 5th edn (Oxon and New York, Routledge, 2015) 26–28; and Schachter, Oscar, *International Law in Theory and Practice* (The Netherlands, Martinus Nijhoff Publishers, 1991) 35–38.

c) the general principles of law recognised by civilized nations;
d) judicial decisions and the teachings of the most highly qualified publicists of the various nations, as subsidiary means for the determination of rules of law.[97]

Usually, the first three are regarded as primary sources of international law given the specific mention in point d of judicial decisions and the teachings of the most highly qualified publicists (doctrine) as 'subsidiary' means for the Court's legal determinations.

Worth noting, however, is that this orthodox classification has been criticised from a feminist perspective. Hilary Charlesworth and Christine Chinkin argue that this formal categorisation of sources and its defence by States, lawyers and academics have left new law-making and law-impacting bodies and procedures 'outside' the realm of law, normally to the detriment of women. Indeed, they present the example of violence against women to reveal the difficulty of opening traditional and mainstream views concerning the (valid) sources of international law.[98] For the purposes of this section, though, the classical categorisation will be followed in order to use these sources as a starting point and then build from them the analysis of the human security potential to point to 'non-traditional' sources of evidence and argumentation in international human rights law, as explained in Part II of this book.

Thus, in light of ICJ sources of public international law, one may recall that the content of the UDHR and both International Covenants of 1966 studied above—on Civil and Political Rights, and on Economic, Social and Cultural Rights, jointly known as the 'International Bill of Rights'—are now generally considered binding international law, either directly through the obligations adopted by States parties in international treaties, or in the form of customary international law[99] or of general principles of law.[100] This is of course relevant in the sense of determining the rights and obligations of non-parties of international human rights treaties at the State level, on the one hand, as well as the entitlements of individual persons or groups contemplated in international customary norms, on the

[97] Statute of the International Court of Justice (ICJ), annexed to the Charter of the UN, of which it forms an integral part.

[98] Charlesworth, Hilary and Christine Chinkin, *The Boundaries of International Law. A Feminist Analysis* (UK, Juris Publishing, Manchester University Press, 2000) 70–79.

[99] Schachter (n 96) 335–42.

[100] See Meron, Theodore, 'On a Hierarchy of International Human Rights' (1986) 80 *The American Journal of International Law* 1, 1–23; see also the conclusion by the ICJ in the sense that ESC Rights are an essential part of human rights law to be complied with by States, even in the context of armed conflict; analysis of the ICJ's Advisory Opinion of 2004, *Legal Consequences of the Construction of a Wall in the Occupied Palestinian Territory*, below.

other. Another important consequence of this affirmation is that 'the recognition of human rights in customary law allows not only the treaty non-parties, but also the parties to have recourse to international law remedies not provided for in the treaties'.[101]

In this respect, all human rights contained in these legal instruments, as a minimum standard, form an essential part of international law, and some of them, such as the absolute prohibition of torture developed in additional instruments and analysed in detail in Chapter 6 of this text, even constitute peremptory norms of general international law, that is, *ius cogens* norms. Such norms are defined in Article 53 of the 1969 Vienna Convention on the Law of Treaties as those which are 'accepted and recognized by the international community of States as a whole as a norm from which no derogation is permitted and which can be modified only by a subsequent norm of general international law having the same character'. Thus, they enjoy an absolute character and are non-derogable and opposable *erga omnes*, that is, their compliance can be claimed from the whole of the international community and not only from a specific State.[102] As the ICJ has recognised, the reason behind this legitimate concern of all States is the nature of the issue at stake: 'In view of the *importance of the rights* involved, *all States* can be held to have a *legal interest* in their protection; they are obligations *erga omnes*'.[103] (emphasis added)

Following this line of thought, it has also been argued that *ius cogens* norms—following a similar logic to the basis of customary international law, but with a legally binding character of a higher degree—are immune to persistent objection by any given State or minority group of States. In this sense,

> it seems clear that there are elements of the present international legal system that are not based on the consent of the states involved … Jus cogens norms are seen … as a sort of superinternational law, trumping other forms of law and only able to be changed by the evolution of a new rule of jus cogens. Moreover, these norms are viewed as capable of [being] binding by all and against all (not just by and against those who have consented to the creation of the norms).[104]

[101] Schachter (n 96) 335.

[102] Vienna Convention on the Law of Treaties, 23 May 1969, entered into force on 27 January 1980, United Nations, Treaty Series, vol 1155, 2005, p 331. See the analysis of *ius cogens* done by Alfred Verdross since the 1930s and revisited a few years before the adoption in 1969 of the Vienna Convention, in 'Jus Dispositivum and Jus Cogens in International Law' (1966) 60 *American Journal of International Law* 55–82; see also a current examination in Duffy (n 49).

[103] ICJ, *Case Concerning The Barcelona Traction, Light and Power Company, Limited, Belgium v Spain*, Judgment 5 February 1970, para 33.

[104] Moises Penalver, Eduardo, 'The Persistent Problem of Obligation in International Law' (2000) *Stanford Journal of International Law* 36, 282.

Ius cogens norms have also been examined in light of human rights by concluding that

> In the context of the sweeping language of human rights, *certain human rights principles* are recognized as jus cogens peremptory norms of international law. Jus cogens norms are fundamental tenets of international law considered accepted by and binding on all states, from which no derogation is permitted.[105] (emphasis added)

It could be then argued that other human rights, and certainly at least the 'core content' of all human rights, including ESC Rights, have reached the level of *ius cogens*.[106] Whether there is enough evidence in this direction or if (some) human rights remain at the stage of customary international law or general principles of law as primary sources of international law, constitutes a debate which is not at the centre of this book. What remains clear in considering the international legal norms referring to the rights and protection of human beings is that they now constitute one of the pivotal standpoints of the whole of public international law more generally. While traditionally international law had been deemed as mainly regulating the relationships between States, as Antonio Cassese has pointed out, historical development shows that 'international law increasingly covers issues of human rights and binds States not only among each other, but moreover States in respect to the persons subject to their jurisdiction'.[107] Judge Cançado Trindade has extensively developed the 'international law of humankind' both from an academic perspective, and based on international and regional jurisprudence and legal practice.[108] This position is confirmed through work by Ruti G Teitel, who recognising a post-Cold War shift from the State to the 'human security perspective', has termed the crossover points of international norms in human rights, humanitarian and criminal law, as *humanity's law* more generally, and consequently has identified jurisprudential and normative expressions of a human security framework at work.[109]

[105] Humes-Schulz, Stacy, 'Limiting Sovereign Immunity in the Age of Human Rights' (2008) *Harvard Human Rights Journal* 21, 110.

[106] In this sense, see the convincing arguments on the right to health as *ius cogens* presented in Gunn, Patricia C, 'Health Care Refugees' (2009) 6 *Loyola University Chicago International Law Review* 339. See also Galtung, Irene, *Lawyers or Liars? Is World Hunger Suable in Court?*, PhD Thesis in Law (Florence, European University Institute, 2011), who argues that the core content of the right to food, namely, freedom from hunger, is a *ius cogens* norm.

[107] Cassese, Antonio, *International Law*, 2nd edn (Oxford, Oxford University Press, 2005) 45.

[108] See the classical Cançado Trindade, Antônio Augusto, *International Law for Humankind: Towards a New Jus Gentium* (The Netherlands, Martinus Nijhoff Publishers, 2010).

[109] Teitel, Ruti G, *Humanity's Law* (Oxford, Oxford University Press, 2011) 35–69; 105–38 and the analysis of the 'human security turn' to global justice at 139–64.

At the same time, it must also be acknowledged that the international legal framework of human rights itself presents gaps and shortcomings that are especially identifiable in the case of undocumented migrants and other non-citizens, and in some of the cases involving women and girls, as reviewed in this text. It is in these instances that human security can play its most powerful role, I argue, as an orienting and complementing concept to broaden the boundaries of international law, to use Hilary Charlesworth's and Christine Chinkin's language, and provide tools for more connected and expansive legal interpretations of human rights and reinforced protective measures for persons and groups living in conditions of structural vulnerability.

3

The Human Security–Human Rights Synergy

I. ARTICLE 28 OF THE UDHR AND HUMAN SECURITY: AN ENABLING ENVIRONMENT

AGAINST THE REVIEWED background of Chapter 2, analysing the links between human security and human rights under public international law, I propose to consider with more detainment Article 28 of the *Universal Declaration of Human Rights* (UDHR) which, since 1948, set forth that

> Everyone is entitled to a social and international order in which the rights and freedoms set forth in this Declaration can be fully realized.[1]

Similar phrasing is also used in the 1986 *UN Declaration on the Right to Development*[2] and in the more recent 2011 *Maastricht Principles on Extraterritorial Obligations of States in the area of Economic, Social and Cultural Rights*. Although not a legally binding instrument, the Maastricht Principles constitute an authoritative source for debate given they were drafted and adopted by experts in international law and human rights from the academic field and international and regional practice. Moreover, they were thought of and discussed on the basis of the binding treaty of the *International Covenant on Economic, Social and Cultural Rights* (ICESCR) considered in light of modern problems and challenges. The Maastricht Principles specifically contain in Article 29 a State 'obligation to create an international enabling environment'.[3]

[1] Universal Declaration of Human Rights, proclaimed by the United Nations General Assembly in Paris on 10 December 1948, General Assembly Resolution 217 A (III).

[2] UN Declaration on the Right to Development, A/RES/41/128, 97th plenary meeting, 4 December 1986, Article 1, 1) and 2).

[3] *Maastricht Principles on Extraterritorial Obligations of States in the area of Economic, Social and Cultural Rights*, adopted on 28 September 2011. See also the analysis in Langford, Malcolm and Jeff A King, 'Committee on Economic, Social and Cultural Rights: Past, Present and Future' in Langford, Malcolm (ed), *Social Rights Jurisprudence. Emerging Trends in International and Comparative Law* (Cambridge, Cambridge University Press, 2008) 477–516.

Thus, the idea of an enabling collective and global environment that facilitates the full realisation of human rights for 'everyone' seems to go in line with the human security notion—human security coming to the fore as a stage in which such realisation of rights is at *critical risk*. Under human security, because of such risk situation, the 'entitlement' to this enabling social and international order is not actually being enjoyed by everyone or is in danger of being harmed. As a result, State action, this text argues, should be taken under human security's 'protection' strategy, for these threats to be prevented, ameliorated, due reparations granted, and further avoided, especially for those who are most vulnerable. Such a position would strengthen the fulfilment of Article 28 of the UDHR.

This Article of the UDHR has been termed an 'intriguing provision' in that it 'seems to straddle the line between the substantive rights of the Declaration and the last few articles, which do not speak of rights themselves, but rather of duties and limitations'.[4] Although not literally framed in terms of a 'right' but an 'entitlement', there is proof in the drafting history of this Article to indicate that the original phrase used had been 'everyone has the right' but was later replaced by 'everyone is entitled' on a stylistic argument on the account that the terminology of rights was used twice in the Article, but not pursuant to any substantial discussion on this issue.[5] On this basis, for the effects of this book, I consider Article 28 as embodying a right to the content thereby expressed.

Article 28 would seem to also stem from the acknowledgement that human rights cannot be understood in a vacuum but that they are actually experienced in a determined social, economic and political context. Not only is the individual linked to the community in which she or he is born into or lives, but also at a broader level, in a world composed of States as the form of political organisation *par excellence*, as early as 1948 the view was that one State is not isolated from the other. Indeed, the perspective was that in fact an international order, a relationship between States (and/or other international actors), is to be found, and such order is an underlying factor for the realisation or not of an individual person's human rights.

In this sense, Article 28 'raises many questions … such as individual versus group and collective rights, and the duties of developed versus developing countries'.[6] In what seems to be an answer to some of these

[4] Curtis, Josh and Darcy, Shane, 'The Right to a Social and International Order for the Realisation of Human Rights: Article 28 of the Universal Declaration and International Cooperation' in Keane, David and Yvonne McDermott (eds), *The Challenge of Human Rights. Past, Present and Future* (USA/UK, Edward Elgar, 2012) 9.

[5] *Ibid*, 12.

[6] Rosas, Allan, Review of the book, *Exploring Social Rights: Between Theory and Practice*, by Daphne Barak-Erez and Aeyal M Gross (eds) (Oxford, Hart Publishing, 2007), (2009) 42 *Israel Law Review* 1, 209. I thank Judge Allan Rosas of the Court of Justice of the European Union for referring me to this review.

questions, recent work has addressed the duty-bearers of the right encompassed in Article 28 from the perspective of 'international cooperation', as an organisational principle in international law and as an important aspect of human rights law, particularly in the fields of development and economic, social and cultural rights (ESC Rights).[7] Certainly, this issue can be approached from the standpoint of considering the fairness and suitability (or not) of the current international trading, economic and financial system as an ideal or even adequate forum for full realisation of human rights according to Article 28, as well as through reviewing the role of transnational business corporations or other business enterprises, as recent UN debate has done, among others, through the 2011 *Guiding Principles on Business and Human Rights: Implementing the United Nations 'Protect, Respect and Remedy' Framework*, also called the Ruggie Principles following their proponent's name.[8]

Turning to the questions approached directly in this book, in looking at Article 28 of the UDHR, the right to an *enabling environment* leads us to human security territory and it can bring us to reflect on the *contextual and collective dimensions* of the realisation of human rights in people's everyday lives. Such dimensions were conceived since the foundations of international human rights law, as this Article of the UDHR evidences, followed by both Covenants—the International Covenant on Civil and Political Rights (ICCPR) and ICESCR.[9] Indeed, as reviewed in the previous chapter, both ICCPR and ICESCR take into account social and structural factors, and in a similar vein other human rights legal instruments do so as well, for example, on violence against women (VAW) or migrant workers, as will be reviewed in Chapters 4, 5 and 6 of this book. Specifically in the field of women's human rights, as will be seen in detail in Chapter 4, certain instruments provide for the duty of States to take action to comply with such rights within *an environment that guarantees safety and human security*.

[7] Curtis and Darcy (n 4) 10 and subsequent pages.

[8] *Ibid*, 13–20. See Ruggie, John, *Guiding Principles on Business and Human Rights: Implementing the United Nations "Protect, Respect and Remedy" Framework*, presented in the Report of the Special Representative of the Secretary-General on the issue of human rights and transnational corporations and other business enterprises, John Ruggie, UN Human Rights Council Resolution A/HRC/17/31, 21 March 2011, and endorsed by the UN Human Rights Council in June of 2011, in UN General Assembly Resolution 17/4 'Human Rights and Transnational Corporations and other Business Enterprises", 6 July 2011, OP 1. See also Estrada Tanck, E Dorothy, *Régimen jurídico internacional de las empresas transnacionales en la esfera de los derechos humanos*, Breviarios Jurídicos, núm. 36 (México, Editorial Porrúa, 2005); and Salomon, Margot E and Ian Seiderman, 'Human Rights Norms for a Globalized World: The Maastricht Principles on Extraterritorial Obligations of States in the area of Economic, Social and Cultural Rights' (2012) 3 *Global Policy* 4, 460.

[9] ICCPR and ICESCR, adopted and opened for signature, ratification and accession by UN General Assembly Resolution 2200A (XXI) of 16 December 1966 and entered into force on 23 March 1976.

Thus, it is submitted that human security as a *relational* concept may contribute to shedding light on such collective or societal aspects that at times are so unfavourable to human rights, and their nature so critical or widespread that they amount to risks or threats to the enjoyment of an individual or group's human rights. Such risks can be characterised as potential violations to human rights or in some cases, as violations in themselves. This linking ability of human security in turn strengthens the principle of interdependence and indivisibility of human rights, as one of the axioms informing the legal interpretation of human rights from the perspective of public international law, as described above.

Human security in a *positive sense* then constitutes the existence of a series of societal conditions that allow for the respect, protection and fulfilment of human rights, a type of collective guarantee for their realisation; whereas in the *negative sense*, human security—or rather human insecurity—points out the absence of such conditions in terms of the risks, threats and vulnerabilities that affect human rights and provides elements for their proper identification.

'Human security' as such has also been considered as 'an emerging right', which would consist of the individual's claim to the protection against the seven types of threats correlated to the categories of insecurities identified by the 1994 United Nations Development Program (UNDP) Report.[10] From the stand of a *moral* right owed to people as a means to live free from fear, free from want and free to live in dignity, it is submitted that there is a valid ethical entitlement to human security as a necessary condition for the enjoyment of human rights. As has been described above, this 'right' is recognised as such by Member States of the UN General Assembly in paragraph 143 of the 2005 World Summit.[11]

In a parallel way, human security could be characterised as a 'programmatic' right in the sense that although it does not yet provide for unequivocal and general obligations, it sets aspirations and new demands as societies change.[12] According to that perspective, human security could be the flesh and bones of Article 28 of the UDHR, a modern conceptualisation in a globalised world of the original meaning of a right to a certain international and social order, a *facilitating environment*, for the fulfilment of all human rights by every person.

[10] Fernández Pereira, Juan Pablo, *La seguridad humana: un derecho emergente* (Barcelona, Ariel, 2006) 107 and 118. This author also includes violence against women as one of the necessary indicators to be developed in assessing a society's level of human (in)security, as suggested in Chapter 4 of this book.

[11] *2005 World Summit Outcome*, UN General Assembly, A/RES/60/1, 24 October 2005.

[12] On the programmatic right of political participation, see Rosas, Allan, 'Democracy and Human Rights', in Rosas, Allan and Jan Hegelsen (eds, with the collaboration of Donna Gomien), *Human Rights in a Changing East-West Perspective* (London and New York, Pinter Publishers, 1990) 50.

II. HUMAN SECURITY AND 'CORE CONTENT' OF HUMAN RIGHTS

Following this view, human security could also contribute to the reflection on determining the non-derogable elements of human rights, the 'core content' which may not be affected under any circumstance, and whose mere placing *at risk* produces a 'disabling' environment contrary to Article 28 of the UDHR and related standards and provisions. The concept of 'core content' or 'minimum core' in the human rights legal framework has been developed in relation to ESC Rights.[13] To provide an example, on the basis of Article 11 of the ICESCR and General Comment No 3 of the UN Committee on ECSR reviewed in Chapter 1, it is generally considered that *freedom from hunger* is the baseline and the 'minimum core content' of the right to food. Other aspects of the right would involve having access to adequate and nutritious food, for instance.[14] The rationale of the 'core content' developed in relation to ESC Rights has also been used in relation to other rights. Indeed, the concept of core obligations in human rights law has also been expressed more recently in the interpretation of the Convention on the Elimination of Discrimination against Women (CEDAW),[15] a cross-cutting instrument covering both civil, and political, as well as ESC Rights. This core content developed in human rights law is also close to the definition of human security adopted by the UN Commission on Human Security (CHS) in 2003, as the protection of the 'vital core' of all human lives, and later endorsed by the UN Secretary-General's Second Report on Human Security of 2012. This intersecting feature between human rights and human security opens the door for a deeper exploration of its legal implications, while at the same time confronting the reasoned criticisms towards the human security conception for being too broad to be operational, as also described in Chapter 1.

[13] See UN Committee on ESC Rights, General Comment No 3, *The Nature of States Parties Obligations (Art 2, para 1)*, 14 December 1990 (contained in Document E/1991/23) especially para 10; see the 'Core Obligations' defined by the UN Committee on ESC Rights regarding the right to health in its General Comment No 14, *The Right to the Highest Attainable Standard of Health (Article 12 of the International Covenant on Economic, Social and Cultural Rights)*, E/C.12/2000/4, 11 August 2000, paras 43–45. The Committee specifically stresses that these 'core obligations' are considered 'non-derogable'; see para 47.

[14] UN Committee on ESC Rights, General Comment No 3 (n 13). See, eg, Künnemann, Rolf, 'The Right to Adequate Food: Violations Related to its Minimum Core Content' in Chapman, Audrey and Sage Russell (eds), *Core Obligations: Building a Framework for Economic, Social and Cultural Rights* (Oxford/New York, Antwerp, Intersentia, 2002) 171; and Randolph, Susan and Shareen Hertel, 'The Right to Food: A Global Perspective' in Minkler, Lanse (ed), *The State of Economic and Social Human Rights: A Global Overview* (UK, Cambridge University Press, 2013) 23–24.

[15] CEDAW Committee, General Recommendation No 28, *The Core Obligations of States Parties under Article 2 of the Convention on the Elimination of All Forms of Discrimination against Women*, CEDAW/C/GC/28, 16 December 2010.

Consequently, let us turn to the differentiation between derogable and non-derogable rights or elements of rights, ie, when only certain features of the right are considered non-derogable, and other aspects of the right may be subject to restrictions. In this respect, Martin Scheinin has distinguished between the rules and principles related to human rights considering 'the rule as the *inviolable core* of the right, whereas the other dimensions of the same right [the principle] would fall *outside the core* and be, for instance, subject to permissible limitations through a process of weighing and balancing'.[16] (emphasis added)

The derogable/non-derogable classification of rights has traditionally been defined, firstly, through the provisions of international human rights law (IHRL) itself. Indeed, Article 4 of the ICCPR, for instance, refers to states of emergency and the non-derogable rights under the Covenant in such situation: life, freedom from torture, freedom from slavery, prohibition of imprisonment for non-fulfilment of contractual obligations, due process rights in criminal law, equality before the law and freedom of thought, conscience and religion.[17] Article 4 of ICESCR also stipulates that

> States Parties to the present Covenant recognize that … the State may subject [ESC Rights] only to such limitations as are determined by law only in so far as this may be compatible with the nature of these rights and solely for the purpose of promoting the general welfare in a democratic society.

Secondly, the distinction between derogable and non-derogable rights is also understood through the boundaries of IHRL as a general standard, and of international humanitarian law (IHL) or the rules of armed conflict and protection of civilians, as a standard of exception. Thus, IHL comprises principles and non-derogable rights as defined in common Article 3 of the 1949 Geneva Conventions on *minimum* applicable standards in armed conflict and related provisions and interpretations.[18]

[16] Scheinin, Martin, 'Terrorism and the Pull of "Balancing" in the Name of Security', in Scheinin, Martin, et al, *Law and Security-Facing the Dilemmas*, EUI Working Paper Law 2009/11 (Florence European University Institute, 2009) 55. The author uses as a reference point the well-known model of rules and principles developed by Robert Alexy.

[17] See Article 4 of the ICCPR and the non-derogable rights under the Covenant: Articles 6, 7, 8 (paragraphs I and 2), 11, 15, 16 and 18.

[18] Convention (I) for the Amelioration of the Condition of the Wounded and Sick in Armed Forces in the Field; Convention (II) for the Amelioration of the Condition of Wounded, Sick and Shipwrecked Members of Armed Forces at Sea; Convention (III) relative to the Treatment of Prisoners of War; and Convention (IV) relative to the Protection of Civilian Persons in Time of War, all adopted in Geneva on 12 August 1949, and entered into force on 21 October 1950; see also Protocol Additional to the Geneva Conventions of 12 August 1949, and relating to the Protection of Victims of International Armed Conflicts (Protocol I); and Protocol Additional to the Geneva Conventions of 12 August 1949, and relating to the Protection of Victims of Non-International Armed Conflicts (Protocol II), both adopted on 8 June 1977 and entered into force on 7 December 1978; as well as Protocol additional to the Geneva Conventions of 12 August 1949 relating to the Adoption of an Additional Distinctive Emblem (Protocol III), adopted on 8 December 2005 and entered into force on 14 January

Rather than examining the differences between relevant standards in armed conflict and non-armed conflict contexts and their implications already dealt with extensively in legal scholarship,[19] in line with the concrete goals of this book, an exploration of the link between human security and the *core content* of rights is called for in light of human security's potential to highlight interrelated elements of structural risk or vulnerability and incorporate them into the analysis of such essential content.

In this respect, human security could serve a purpose in advancing a protective interpretation of human rights in general and the non-derogable elements of said rights in particular (see also the figure at the end of this section). This would not substitute the set of rights to be upheld in each given context, including those of armed conflict, generalised conflict situation or state of emergency. It would, however, allow for consideration of risk situations, particularly structural ones, affecting the core content of rights which the State *knew* or *ought to have known* about and, consequently, provide more extensive criteria to trigger its obligations of prevention, taking measures and/or granting reparations.

To give an example of a protective standard-setting exercise, the UN Human Rights Committee, monitoring body of ICCPR, in its General Comment No 29, *States of Emergency (Article 4)*, offered a progressive interpretation by considering that the requirement of court review over the lawfulness of detention constitutes a *non-derogable element* in Article 9 of the ICCPR, even when this Article is not referred to in Article 4, para 2, of the ICCPR, as a non-derogable right during a state of emergency.[20]

Human security could then prove useful in analysing the non-compliance of the State with *positive obligations* of taking measures directed to *risk prevention and attention* and it may provide guidance with regard to the causes of violations of rights, through *actions* or through *omissions*, especially concerning these positive obligations. For instance, in the famous *Case of the Mayagna (Sumo) Awas Tingni Community v Nicaragua*, of 2001, regarding State action which was damaging to the collective property of an indigenous community, the Inter-American Court of Human Rights (IACHR) indicated that according to 'the rules of law pertaining to the international responsibility of the State and applicable under International

2007; see also International Committee of the Red Cross, at www.icrc.org/en/war-and-law/treaties-customary-law/geneva-conventions.

[19] See, for example, Schachter, Oscar, *International Law in Theory and Practice* (The Netherlands, Martinus Nijhoff Publishers, 1991) Chapters VII and VIII; and Remiro Brotóns, Antonio, *Derecho Internacional* (Valencia, Spain, Tirant lo Blanch, 2007) Chapter XXIX, 'La protección internacional de los derechos humanos' and Chapter XXX, 'El Derecho Internacional Humanitario/Los crímenes internacionales', on the differences and relationship between IHRL and IHL.

[20] See UN Human Rights Committee, General Comment No 29, *States of Emergency (Article 4)*, CCPR/C/21/Rev.1/Add.11, 2001, para 16.

Human Rights Law, *actions or omissions* by any public authority, whatever its hierarchic position, are chargeable to the State'.[21] (emphasis added)

Similarly, in the case of *Oneryldiz v Turkey*, of 2004, mentioned in Chapter 2 and involving the explosion of a municipal rubbish tip which resulted in the loss of life of 39 people living in a contiguous irregular settlement, the European Court of Human Rights in an expansive interpretation of the right to life (Article 2 of the European Convention on Human Rights and Fundamental Freedoms (ECoHR)), considered

> The positive obligation to take all appropriate steps to safeguard life ... entails above all a primary duty on the State to put in place a legislative and administrative framework designed to provide *effective deterrence against threats* to the right to life.[22] (emphasis added)

In relation to the obligation to guarantee an 'effective judicial system' (Article 13 ECoHR) to deal with these violations, the Court sustained that Article 2 involved this duty particularly in the context of *dangerous activities*,

> when lives have been lost as a result of events occurring under the responsibility of the public authorities, which are often the only entities to have *sufficient relevant knowledge* to *identify and establish the complex phenomena* that might have caused such incidents.

In relation to the right to protection of peaceful enjoyment of possessions (Article 1 of Protocol 1 to ECoHR), the Court pointed out that

> the *causal link* established between the *gross negligence* attributable to the State and the *loss of human lives* also applies to the engulfment of the applicant's house ... the resulting infringement amounts not to 'interference' but to the breach of a positive obligation, since the State officials and authorities did not do everything within their power to protect the applicant's proprietary interests.[23]

Apart from the human rights explicitly under consideration by the Court, this case holds evident broader correlations to environmental rights, an important connection which the human security idea could contribute to emphasise openly, as part of a more reciprocal connection between civil and political rights and ESC Rights.

In light of these cases, the possibility of the human security–human rights exchange is considered especially necessary in relation to ESC Rights, and to promote a more direct and fruitful connection between these rights and civil and political rights, more so in the context of developing countries, or countries in a transition to democracy. These societies

[21] IACHR, *Case of the Mayagna (Sumo) Awas Tingni Community v Nicaragua*, Judgment of 31 August 2001 (Merits, Reparations and Costs) para 154, referring to the obligations of States under Article 1.1 of the American Convention on Human Rights.

[22] See ECHR, *Oneryldiz v Turkey (GC)* Appl No 48939/99, Judgment of 30 November 2004, para 89. In all further references to the case, emphasis added by this author.

[23] *Ibid*, paras 93 and 135.

everyday still face, to different levels and degrees, civil and political rights violations, such as cases of torture, arbitrary detention, forced disappearance, restrictions to freedom of expression, and breaches of the right to due process of law or access to justice. Hence, the first and most urgent concern is usually the attention to these types of cases involving these civil and political rights, whereas the violations of ESC Rights have traditionally been treated through the right to non-discrimination or the right of equality,[24] occasionally through the focus on direct violations of ESC Rights and rarely through the perspective of violations of a positive duty to prevent.[25]

Indeed, in the arena of civil and political rights, the 'right to security of person', or 'right to personal security' (Article 9, 1 of the ICCPR), has been broadly interpreted in relation to the *duty to prevent* a violation from taking place. For instance, this right was considered by the UN Human Rights Committee (HRC), the monitoring body of the ICCPR, as applicable independently of the context of deprivation of liberty. In the 1990 case of *Delgado Páez v Colombia*, in which the State of Colombia had not taken proper measures to ensure the person's right to security in spite of the death threats he had received, the Committee affirmed that

> State parties have undertaken to guarantee the rights enshrined in the Covenant. It cannot be the case that, as a matter of law, States can ignore *known threats* to the life of persons under their jurisdiction, just because … he or she is not arrested or otherwise detained. State parties are under an obligation to *take reasonable and appropriate measures to protect* them.[26] (emphasis added)

Thus interpreted, the right to personal security would encompass a positive duty to prevent the violation, as part of the binding non-derogable content of this right.

This position was actually confirmed by the recent General Comment No 35 of the HRC, *Article 9 (Liberty and Security of the Person)*, of 2014, which clarified that the right of personal security entailed a State obligation 'to protect individuals from *foreseeable threats* to life or bodily integrity

[24] See Krause, Catarina and Martin Scheinin, 'The Right Not to be Discriminated Against: The Case of Social Security' in Orlin, Theodore, S, Allan Rosas and Martin Scheinin (eds), *The Jurisprudence of Human Rights Law: A Comparative and Interpretive Approach* (Turku/Åbo, Finland, Institute for Human Rights, 2000).

[25] Interesting work however has been developed recently in this area; see for example Salomon and Seiderman (n 8). For an account from a political theory perspective, see Pogge, Thomas, 'Severe Poverty as a Human Rights Violation' in *Freedom from Poverty as a Human Right: Who Owes What to the Very Poor* (Oxford, Oxford University Press, 2007). See also the book covering a broad range of questions in this area: Langford, Malcolm, Wouter Vandenhole, Martin Scheinin and Willem van Genugten (eds), *Global Justice, State Duties. The Extraterritorial Scope of Economic, Social and Cultural Rights in International Law* (UK, Cambridge University Press, 2013).

[26] UN Human Rights Committee, Communication No 195/1985, *Delgado Páez v Colombia*, 12 July 1990, para 5.5.

proceeding from any governmental *or private actors'*.[27] (emphasis added) This exemplifies how a protective interpretation, consistent through time, can end up shaping the law and expanding the boundaries of a given human right.

The lack of more direct judicial connections between all human rights—civil, political and ESC Rights—as well as the minimisation of the implications of the relationships between their core content, has often proved detrimental for the protection of human rights, especially of the most vulnerable, as reviewed throughout this book. In this context, let us recall that violations of human rights may be caused through *actions* or through *omissions* of the State in breach of any of its general international obligations to *respect, protect and fulfil* human rights. This 'trichotomy' of human rights obligations was first proposed by Asbjorn Eide in his reports on the right to food under ICESCR and then introduced in 1999 in General Comment No 12, *Right to Adequate Food*, of the UN Committee on ESC Rights.[28] However, some authors have reflected that this classification may be inadequate in facing the complexity of today's human rights violations and the involvement of many non-State actors in activities affecting them, for example, development projects, privatisation of services like water or electricity or severe cuts in welfare allowances, which could potentially violate the three duties of respecting, protecting and fulfilling human rights.[29]

In this scenario, the concept of *continuum* of obligations (ranging from negative to positive),[30] regarding all human rights, becomes a useful tool. Given that the triple typology to respecting, protecting and fulfilling 'might be considered unworkable or an *oversimplification of the interconnected nature* of certain problems',[31] (emphasis added) it is submitted that the human security notion may be deemed as a complement to provide criteria for filling-in protection gaps and adapting this triple categorisation to interdependent realities in the current globalised world.

In turn, this may contribute to provide a more realistic picture of the *widespread* situation of human (in)security in a given society, and the conditions of *vulnerability* to human rights' violations that certain persons or groups find themselves in—a context which may become invisible if dealing primarily with *actual* violations of *individual* human rights that have *already* taken place.

[27] UN Human Rights Committee, General Comment No 35, *Article 9 (Liberty and Security of the Person)*, CCPR/C/GC/35, 16 December 2014, para 9.

[28] See Eide, Asbjorn, UN Special Rapporteur on the Right to Food, *The Right to Food (Final Report)*, E/CN.4/Sub.2/1987/23, 1987, paras 66–69; and UN Committee on ESC Rights, General Comment No 12, *Right to Adequate Food*, E/C.12/1999/5, 1999, para 15.

[29] See Langford and King (n 3) 484–86.

[30] See Sepúlveda, Magdalena, *The Nature of the Obligations under the International Covenant on Economic, Social and Cultural Rights* (Oxford, New York, Anvers, 2003) Chapter V.

[31] See Langford and King (n 3) 485.

Given that the proposed conception of human security would look at the severity of the threat or condition of structural vulnerability in order to decide when there is a risk situation, the declaration of a risk situation would act as a 'detonator' activating the human rights' obligations of the State, especially to take preventive measures, to address the violations of human rights that have already taken place as soon as possible and to grant reparations that redress individuals and communities for the harm they have suffered while seeking to address the systemic shortcomings. In this sense, the idea of human security risk would function as a kind of 'red alarm' or state of exception, but in an inverse way, meaning that the State would have reinforced obligations to prevent, protect and remedy in light of an endemic situation of violation of human rights amounting to serious threats of basic human well-being.

This understanding of human security would have implications for poverty-stricken, marginalised or at risk sectors of the population, such as women and girls in danger of or experiencing violence, or undocumented migrants, both addressed in this text. As we will see, identifying severe threats to their basic well-being, whether they be linked to the variety of human rights that are often not adequately guaranteed, the seriousness or systematic nature of some of the violations they suffer, but also the compounded effect of the violations in situations in which they encounter multiple and structural forms of discrimination, promises to deliver a much more complex picture than the one provided by an analysis that looks at different individual human rights violations as separate events affecting isolated individuals. It also renders obvious the need to give due visibility to threats stemming from private actors, by reinforcing State *due diligence obligations* in view of the fact that, in situations of risk, the State *knew or should have known* about existing conditions of vulnerability.

Now, if we are to accept the protection of *all human rights*—civil, political, economic, social and cultural—as the central element of *security concerns*, and combine it with the principle of interdependence of all human rights in an integrated manner, then it follows that at a minimum a 'core content' of all human rights would have to be taken into account in any understanding of security (in armed conflict or not),[32] in connection with the identification of serious threats and risks that cause *structural vulnerabilities* in a context-specific approach (see graphic representation below).

According to this view, the notion of human security would form part of a long line of legal and political instruments that have been used in modern law and discourse to forward social justice and equality.

[32] For a defence of a 'broad and interconnected interpretation of the core of rights', including ESC Rights, in the context of the UNSC activity, see De Wet, Erika, 'Human Rights Limitations to Economic Enforcement Measures Under Article 41 of the United Nations Charter and the Iraqi Sanctions Regime' (2001) 14 *Leiden Journal of International Law* 277–300.

Consequently, apart from the conceptual validity of the connection, there seems to be a clear *strategic advantage* in exploring further the links in international law between human security and human rights and viewing them as part of a shared ethical and legal project based on the common value of human dignity.

III. THE FRAMEWORK IN A NUTSHELL

Law cannot and should not remain indifferent in the face of risk. As has been argued in this part of the book, the main distinctive element between human security and human rights is the element of *risk* or *vulnerability*. In this sense, following from the universality, interdependence and indivisibility of human rights, it has been proposed to consider through an integrated approach that *all* human rights sit at the centre of human security. The differentiating element, and at the same time the one that unites the two notions and therefore makes it significant both for rights and for security, is precisely the component of serious threats or risk situations that allow for conditions of structural vulnerability.

I have suggested in this text that human security reaches spaces which the concepts of personal security, social security and citizen security do not. In terms of human rights, human security includes all human rights and covers therefore the rights to personal security, social security, security of tenure and food security (for women) as contemplated in international human rights law. But it also extends to risks, threats and sudden changes not fully considered by these concepts or by these specific rights. To give but a few examples, one may think of forced displacement due to climate change, or risks to the right to health or the right to a healthy environment.

It is then not enough to look at each right separately or to examine them in a joint manner simply as the sum of many rights, to fully grasp their level of enjoyment or understand the nature of the violations that affect them. As such, it has been submitted that human security has the potential to function as an *integrating bridge* between correlated ideas and norms, in this case, those that allow attention to interrelated risks to human rights that place persons in a situation of vulnerability.

As was reviewed in the previous chapter, there is not enough substantiation at the moment to consider that there is a full positive *legal* human right to human security in all its breadth and scope. Nonetheless, human security relates to public international law, at least, in a bi-directional manner:

(i) in its articulation as an *enabling environment* allowing for the full realisation of all human rights, as a form of contemporary embodiment of Article 28 of the UDHR and related standards (see **Figure 1** below); and

(ii) as an orienting notion for more protective, expansive and integrated interpretations of the core content of human rights and their non-derogable elements.

The concrete ways in which both potentials may unfold in practice, as well as the wider possibilities of the human security–human rights intersection in legal analysis, will be further discussed in this book, particularly in the thematic topics reviewed in Chapters 4, 5 and 6 of the text.

In any case, it may not even be desirable for the whole concept of human security, flexible as it is, to become a human right with an autonomous legal foundation—at least in the current dominantly individualistic human rights architecture—if we wish for human security to retain its power as a unifying, transforming idea, useful to understand in an integrated manner collective and interconnected realities such as the rights affecting structural vulnerabilities approached in this text. At the same time, it is argued in this book that human rights law may complement the human security proposal, and grant it needed specificity in scope and normative grounding, in order to translate it into State and other actors' concrete obligations.

Regarding the first articulation of human security as an *enabling environment*, referred to above, it is submitted that human security may work in a dual way, or if one wishes, in a triple manner if we are to consider its ability as a *connecting* conception.

First, it is useful for providing criteria to identify risk situations and conditions of structural vulnerability, through what could be termed the *negative sense* of human security, that is, for assessing circumstances as lacking an adequate environment for general well-being and human rights realisation, and therefore activating duties primarily of *prevention*, but also of *protection* and/or *reparation*, when violations are already taking place.

It is also argued that human security has the potential to function as an *integrating bridge* between correlated ideas and norms, in this case, those that focus attention on interrelated risks to human rights that place persons in contexts of vulnerability.

Lastly, I propose that the result of looking at the connection between the *core content* of human rights and viewing them integrally may be considered in fact *human security*. In light of this, human security refers not only to the protection from severe threats and risks, but in a *positive sense*, also becomes a *guarantee* at the collective level, a general condition which is necessary to allow the full enjoyment of all human rights by all persons.[33] In this understanding, human security may act as the modern

[33] In the case of indigenous peoples, '[T]he desirable *human security situation* [for indigenous peoples] exists when the people concerned and its individual members have adequate *legal and political guarantees* for their fundamental rights and freedoms, including the right of

materialisation of the right to an *enabling social and international environment* foreseen in Article 28 of the UDHR, and thus complement the predominantly individualist basis of human rights. This view of the human security–human rights symbiosis may be represented graphically with some exemplifying human rights, as shown in **Figure 1** below:

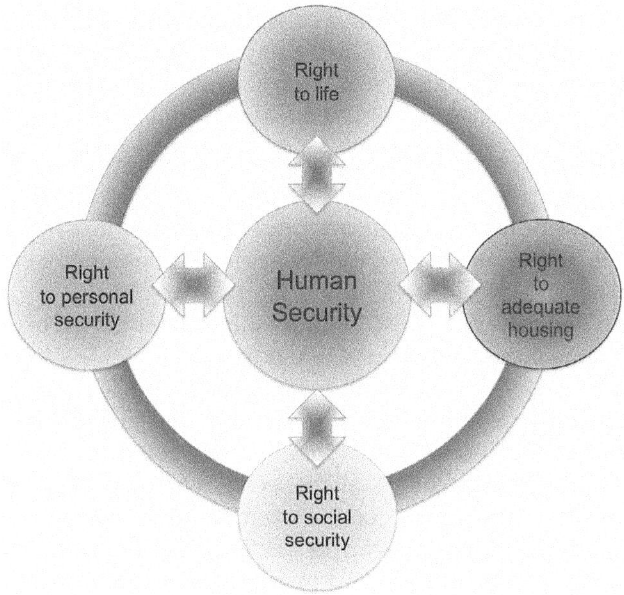

Figure 1: Exemplifying Rights in Human Security–Human Rights Synergy as an Enabling Environment[34]

The figure may be considered an 'aerial' view of the human security–human rights interaction: human security understood as the *core content* of every human right—congruent with the 2003 CHS definition of human security as the 'vital core' of human lives—and at the same time human

self-determination'; see Henriksen, JB, p 226, quoted in UN Commission on Human Rights, Sixty-second session, Working group established in accordance with Commission on Human Rights Resolution 1995/32, Eleventh session, Geneva, 5–16 December 2005, 'General Provisions' of the Draft U.N. Declaration on the Rights of Indigenous Peoples, E/CN.4/2005/WG.15/CRP.2, 24 November 2005, pp 19–20.

[34] The rights represented are only included by way of illustration. As analysed throughout the book, the human security–human rights synergy includes *all* human rights and as such, the understanding proposed in this book is that human security relates to each and every human right in this way.

security as the *bridge* between these minimum contents, in order to create altogether a facilitating environment for the fulfilment of all human rights in the spirit of Article 28 of the UDHR, as explained in the preceding paragraph.

I present to the reader a summarised list of the concrete arguments in favour of the proposed 'human security–human rights synergy', the main points of its content, and some suggestions on how to continue developing this interaction in a resourceful and constructive manner for both human security and human rights. The list also presents aspects of this framework for thought and action that are particularly relevant to the situation of women at risk of or facing violence and of undocumented migrants:

— The human security perspective allows an integrated analysis of the widespread risks and collective threats that facilitate human rights violations of individual persons, and highlights the interrelatedness between conditions that would otherwise be examined in an isolated manner.
— Human security may thus work as a hermeneutic tool providing a more unified and holistic understanding of the State's human rights obligations in the context of vulnerability, and identifying or constructing those of non-State actors, and through this proposal broaden existing boundaries of international human rights law.
— As such, human security should be seen as a pre-condition and at times a necessary complement for the exercise and enjoyment of human rights. It may be understood as an 'enabling environment' for the realisation of human rights—a modern materialisation of Article 28 of the UDHR.
— Human security can be seen as the result of looking at the connection between the *core content* of *all* human rights and viewing them *integrally*.
— In a *negative sense*, it means assessing circumstances as lacking an 'enabling environment' for general well-being and human rights realisation, and therefore activating duties primarily of *prevention*, but also of *mitigation* and *attention*, when violations are already taking place.
— In a *positive sense*, it also becomes a *guarantee* at the collective level, a general condition which is necessary to allow the full enjoyment of all human rights by all persons.
— Human security expedites the triggering of 'red alarms' and highlights the need for early warning mechanisms and responses when human rights 'at risk' have been identified, in order to avoid further escalation of crisis and actual/continued human rights violations.
— The synergy obliges a *prioritisation of the most vulnerable*: in situations of different vulnerabilities, such as that of the State and that of individual persons, the human security–human rights synergy directs us to prioritise persons, and among them, the most vulnerable.

— In focusing on risk situations and structural vulnerability to human rights violations, it reinforces the State's *positive obligations of protection* of persons and groups in identified and identifiable vulnerable conditions.
— As such, it covers the first human security 'top-down' strategy of 'protection'.
— It provides a language and a conceptual framework for civil society to advocate for blocking policies and laws that place human rights *at risk*, even when not openly breaching human rights.[35] Thus, it induces not only coordination among common values and interests, but also the tools to clarify 'red lines' that are not to be crossed.
— As such, human security may benefit from the ample experience of human rights advocates and legal practitioners in working with people to realise 'bottom-up' agency, capacity-building and human rights defence, thus implementing human security's second strategy of 'empowerment'.
— The concept of human security becomes more precise with the incorporation of the standards and indicators of international human rights law, and thus is able to define more clearly its scope and content, making it an operational approach in practice.
— The construction of human security on the basis of human rights law as a solid normative grounding and an objective reference point, limits the possibility of it being co-opted to legitimise abusive or oppressive aims through processes of securitisation of different subjects.
— Through its understanding of security as freedom from all forms of violence, independent of the State-related threat or the context of armed conflict, it contributes to making VAW and girls visible, and accounting for gendered experiences of exposure and exploitation.
— In viewing security not only as absence of physical harm, but also as freedom from material deprivation and precariousness, human security builds stronger links between civil and political rights, and ESC Rights, thus reinforcing universality of all human rights and revealing paths for studying poverty-related causes of insecurity.
— In focusing on risk, it contributes to revealing human rights violations by *omission*, including in the field of ESC Rights, thus focusing

[35] In the context of migrants trying to reach Europe by sea, think of the work done by civil society in late 2014 warning about the risks of moving from the Italian coordinated search-and-rescue operation of Mare Nostrum, to operation Triton led by the EU border agency Frontex, minimising rescue goals directed primarily to curbing irregular migration; contrasted with the disastrous results in the exponential increase of deaths at sea in 2015; see European Council of Refugees and Exiles, http://ecre.org/component/content/article/70-weekly-bulletin-articles/1040-eus-response-to-situation-in-mediterranean-fails-refugees-and-migrants-say-ngos.html; and www.bloomberg.com/graphics/2015-migrant-rescue-in-the-mediterranean/.

on State responsibility of *prevention*, rather than only concentrating on reactive approaches.

— Human security places poverty as a risk in itself and a deterring environment for human rights realisation.
— It also makes visible the diverse forms of VAW and the risks confronted by women and girls vulnerable to violence or already experiencing it.
— The 'human security–human rights synergy' aims to bring together existing initiatives, boosting their shared objectives under a common coherent framework, and providing further tools to better confront human rights challenges.
— It thus creates a space for constructive dialogue between a plurality of actors that already develop human security initiatives, and human rights research, defence or policy work—in this case, in the areas of VAW and/or undocumented migrants, and combatting poverty and inequality—but which usually do not talk to each other or explore collaborative potentials.
— The human security–human rights synergy acts as a framework to address situations of total *defencelessness* where the vulnerability reaches such a degree that a person's agency to fulfil her or his basic needs and rights is completely eliminated.[36]
— The synergy facilitates bringing together different existing studies of a quantitative nature, giving elements for the qualitative analysis of threats that emerge from the mapping of diverse reports and sources. As such, it favours fact-finding and evidence-based work as part of preventive strategies founded on a diverse range of sources, including non-traditional sources of international law, such as civil society reports or those from national human rights institutions.
— Human security acts as a counterbalance to national security, shifting the focus to the vulnerabilities suffered by persons instead of the State.
— Human security may work as a bridge between security advocates and discourses and the human rights agenda. The synergy allows for presenting a clear conceptual profile and a strong normative content provided by human rights law, which shields human security from merging into national security discourse—instead of the classical (false) dilemma of 'security v liberty', or 'security v rights', the debate may be framed as '(national/military/State) security v human security (containing human rights)'.

[36] In this sense, see the concept of 'structural human rights violations', proposed by Ho, Kathleen, 'Structural Violence as a Human Rights Violation' (2007) 4 *Essex Human Rights Review* 2, 1–27.

— The synergy better promotes the fulfilment of obligations of international cooperation envisioned originally in the UN Charter and human rights instruments such as the ICESCR.[37] According to this view, different practical initiatives could be promoted.[38]
— In *procedural legal terms*, the human security emphasis on risk and its holistic focus encompassing socio-economic vulnerabilities may prompt an expansion of the practice of international judicial bodies to issue orders of *precautionary, provisional or interim measures* that suspend the procedure on the grounds of the need to avoid an imminent risk of irreparable harm, including possible irremediable damage to ESC Rights and not only to right to life, personal integrity or liberty, as currently implemented under human rights instruments.
— The synergy facilitates a reversal of the burden of proof on the State: It is the State that must justify the differential treatment of the vulnerable group or its members—and not the person or group that has to prove a situation of vulnerability or an actual human rights violation.
— It pushes for legal interpretations recognising the collective and interconnected dimensions of human rights, including the issue of *reparations*. This entails viewing legal remedies in human rights law as a means to transform the social and institutional context in which violations took place.
— The human security–human rights synergy thus facilitates viewing human rights obligations as a *continuum* ranging from State abstention to State action, covering the respect, protection and fulfilment of human rights, but also emphasising a spectrum moving from strong obligations of *prevention*, to large-scale measures of *protection*, and finally to broader means of collective *reparation*.
— It contributes to the 'transnationalisation' of human rights protection surpassing the traditional understanding of State human rights obligations set in neatly defined territorial jurisdictions.
— As a strategic advantage and a methodological standpoint, the human security–human rights synergy opens doors for further dialogue between the Inter-American, European and African political bodies, human rights systems, and civil society organisations. Since human security has been explored and relied upon in the different regional scenarios, the use of the joint framework allows for further innovative exchanges than those which occur on each front separately.

[37] And consider the more recent wording of this obligation in Art 32 of the 2006 UN Convention on the Rights of Persons with Disabilities.

[38] Think about, for instance, the possibility of creating trust funds for human insecurity victims, a recurrent mechanism in the case of human rights violations, or more recently, of victims of corruption. See the proposals in Olaniyan, Kolawole, *Corruption and Human Rights Law in Africa*, (Studies in International Law) (Oxford and Portland, Hart Publishing, 2014) 337 and subsequent pages.

— Human security may also act as a filter to bring light to human rights violations by action and by omission that may fall not only under the field of international human rights/refugee law, but also in other legal arenas such as international criminal law through the identification of grave human rights violations and systematic patterns of abuse that could eventually constitute crimes against humanity.[39]
— The human security–human rights synergy advances a 'rule of rights' instead of only a 'rule of law' (*Estado de derechos v Estado de Derecho*).
— The human security–human rights synergy acts together as a person-centred approach advancing 'humanity's law' and 'the principle of humanity' already alluded to in doctrine and case-law.[40] It thus helps to unlock the creative potential of human security and human rights law to search for new answers to new challenges that stress human dignity as their common element and axiological foundation.

As will be seen in detail in the following chapters dedicated to the thematic cores of the book, VAW and risks to undocumented migrants and other non-citizens, the human security–human rights synergy applied to such topics advances some basic perspectives. The full scope of this second list of points will be presented in concluding Chapter 7 in the form of *interpretative synergies* deriving from the normative and jurisprudential analysis regarding these thematic cores:

— Measures that reinforce human rights and establish a viable institutional system in order to increase the individual's life options—in this case, the woman or migrant's vital realm of choice—to be able to surpass her condition of structural vulnerability and fully experience *freedom from fear, from want and to live in dignity.*
— The reinforcement of the continuum of human rights obligations to give cohesion to responses towards human rights at risk or actually violated in the case of VAW, operates, for example, regarding the State's 'due diligence obligation', developed in international human rights law interpretations and jurisprudence.

[39] Think, for example, of the case of the mass graves of migrants found in Northern Mexico in recent years. See, eg, Robinson, Darryl, 'The Mexican War on Drugs and the Boundaries of Crimes Against Humanity', in *CMN-ICJ Toolkits Blog*, 19 May 2015, at https://blog.casematrixnetwork.org/toolkits/eventsnews/op-ed/op-ed-robinson-on-crimes-against-humanity/.

[40] See, eg, Teitel, Ruti G, *Humanity's Law* (Oxford, Oxford University Press, 2011); and IACHR, *Case of the Sawhoyamaxa Indigenous Community v Paraguay*, Judgment of March 29, 2006 (Merits, Reparations and Costs), Separate Opinion of Judge AA Cançado Trindade, supporting his argument on the work of Stavropoulou, M, 'Searching for Human Security and Dignity: Human Rights, Refugees, and the Internally Displaced' in Danieli, Y, E Stamatopoulou and CJ Dias (eds) *The Universal Declaration of Human Rights: Fifty Years and Beyond* (Amityville, New York, Baywood Publishing Co, 1999) 181–82; at para 14, fn 20.

— Specific human rights instruments and legal interpretations, for instance on the right to 'food security for women' in the African context, transcending 'human rights' only as general discourse or token, provides human security with a normative scaffold that can spell out the relationship between human security and human rights better.[41]
— In the specific context of migration, human security represents a renovating counterweight force to the national security discourse often used to justify restrictive measures.[42]
— The collaborative implications of viewing issues like undocumented migration as transnational phenomena with normative consequences would entail the obligation of joint State action, and international cooperation, to prevent situations of risk and accentuating the shared responsibility in human rights fulfilment of migrant persons.
— Through its two pillars of 'protection' and 'empowerment', human security makes evident the rights of undocumented migrants and also brings their voice to the fore, thus pushing forward their inclusion in the policy and norm-making processes that impact on them, and opening avenues for exploring their participation in transnational civil society organisations.
— The human security lens reveals the State-constructed vulnerability derived from rigid and restrictive migration norms and policies. Human security can do so in a more straightforward way than human rights law alone, given the rationale of human rights partly based on State sovereignty.
— The human security ingredient facilitates exposing how migratory legal irregularity is in itself a source of risk, in a way that the sole analysis of the 'law within the law' would not be capable of doing. This State-created 'legal limbo' involves an aggravated risk of violence and other violations for undocumented female migrants.[43]
— Human security's focus on 'widespread risks' allows for highlighting the multiple threats, entwined forms of vulnerability and intersectional discrimination suffered by undocumented female migrants.
— As such, and with its emphasis on *preventive action*, regardless of the State or non-State source of the threat, the human security–human

[41] On the embeddedness of human rights in the human security framework, see Tomuschat, Christian, *Human Rights: Between Idealism and Realism*, 3rd edn (Oxford, Oxford University Press, 2014) 63–65.

[42] See, eg, Pérez García, Nancy, 'Seguridad nacional *versus* seguridad humana: su impacto en la migración' in Sin Fronteras IAP (coord), *Cambiando perspectivas: de la gestión de flujos hacia la construcción de políticas de migración con enfoque de desarrollo* (México, Universidad Autónoma de Zacatecas, Sin Fronteras IAP, INCIDE Social, Miguel Ángel Porrúa, 2008) 113–73.

[43] See, eg, Dauvergne, Catherine, *Making People Illegal: What Globalization Means for Migration and Law* (Cambridge, Cambridge University Press, 2008).

rights framework fosters measures of legal reform and/or public policy, vital for instance, in the case of undocumented migrant women and girls, particularly those who are at risk of, or suffering, violence.

— The human security potential to highlight possible human rights obligations by non-State/private actors, or strengthen existing ones, points in these cases to perpetrators of violence against women, and to human smugglers or traffickers, migrant recruitment agencies, or abusive companies/employers, in the case of undocumented migrants.

— The human security–human rights synergy as a framework of analysis, constitutes a mechanism of social innovation that could expand the conceptual toolkit available to scholars and practitioners confronting new challenges, many of them unexpected at the time of negotiation and drafting of existing human rights legal instruments, eg, hundreds of migrants dying at sea or the discovery of mass graves of migrants presumably murdered by organised crime or human trafficking/smuggling groups.

— The need for the *prioritisation of the most vulnerable* is exemplified in the case of the current great influx of migrants and refugees to Middle Eastern and European countries: the public policy and material challenges faced by States are a second priority, whilst the life, security and rights of undocumented migrants and of refugees—their human security—must be guaranteed in the first place.

— The synergy attempts to provide argumentation for creative strategies for real-life defence and advocacy by organisations and human rights bodies, and also contributes to articulating guiding criteria for VAW/migration law and policies.

Part II

Practical Applications of the Human Security–Human Rights Synergy in Legal Analysis

4

Violence against Women, Human Security and Women's Human Rights

Gender-based violence is perhaps the most wide-spread and socially tolerated of human rights violations. It both reflects and reinforces inequities between men and women and compromises the health, dignity, security and autonomy of its victims

UN Population Fund[1]

I. INTRODUCTION

IT HAS BECOME clear in recent years that women are often the worst victims of violence in times of conflict: they form the majority of civilian deaths, the majority of refugees, and are often the victims of cruel and degrading practices, such as rape and other forms of sexual violence.[2] However, women's basic well-being is also severely threatened in daily life by unequal access to resources, services and opportunities, not to mention the many forms of violence women experience under 'ordinary circumstances'. By making the security and basic well-being of persons its main concern, the concept of human security is able to capture this broader range of threats and risks and to raise the need to address violence, whether interpersonal, inter-group, internal or international, as

[1] UN Population Fund, 2005, quoted in Nedelsky, Jennifer, *Law's Relations: A Relational Theory of Self, Autonomy, and Law* (New York, Oxford University Press, 2011) 198. I am aware of Jennifer Nedelsky's very interesting proposal of 'relational autonomy' as a path to transcend the liberal individualist view of autonomy and better understand the human condition. Her perspective also sheds light on the dynamics of social interaction and the relationship between individuals, groups, the State and other forms of power, including in the issue of violence against women. The present work has, however, chosen the frame of human security with its consequent accent on vulnerability as the relevant avenue to explore violence against women, with the hope of also contributing to the reflection of forms to adequately weigh social context as the facilitating background of individual human rights violations and experiences of harm, violence and deprivation.

[2] See the report *Global Burden of Armed Violence 2011*, specifically Chapter 4, 'When the Victim is a Woman', Geneva, Geneva Declaration Secretariat, 113–44.

well as systemic and extreme forms of deprivation and precariousness. It is therefore not surprising that the appearance of the concept was celebrated as offering a new lens through which to understand the difficulties women and girls encounter to live a life free from fear and deprivation.[3]

Although there is a general understanding that a human security analysis and the human rights framework somehow intersect, the bodies of literature that deal with each have so far failed, for the most part, to adequately spell out more specifically the ways in which the two concepts can mutually reinforce each other. They have also fallen short in examining how such reinforcement may contribute in the fight against the multiple forms of violence women and girls experience. Thus, this chapter wishes to further stress the need to provide the notion of human security with a stronger human rights and gender component. At the same time it seeks to flesh out ways in which the notion of human security can contribute to a more comprehensive understanding of human rights of women and girls and the set of State obligations that their protection requires. The chapter then presents some proposals on how to advance fruitful synergies between both notions, spelling out some of the benefits that this may specifically entail for women and girls in general and for their right to live a life free from violence in particular.

To give substance to the relationship between human security, violence against women (VAW) and human rights, section II reviews the emerging and competing conceptions of human security presented succinctly in Chapter 1, and assesses their strong points and limitations in view of their potential to duly reflect VAW as a basic threat to women's and girls' security. In particular, this chapter argues for the added value of a human rights-based approach to human security and its gender implications (II A) and defends a definition of human security which, by focusing on the severity of threats and risks, invites a gendered and human-rights dimension to come to the fore (II B).

Thus, it must be recalled that VAW is conceived as a subcategory of gender-based violence. This last type of violence also covers, for example, the experiences of male violence against gay men, of violence based on gender by women or men against transgender persons, or of women against women in the absence of their performance of expected gender roles.[4] However, women and girls 'constitute the majority of victims of

[3] See Basch, Linda, 'Human Security, Globalization, and Feminist Visions' (2004) 16 *Peace Review* 1; and O'Manique, Colleen, 'The "Securitization" of HIV/AIDS in Sub-Saharan Africa: A Critical Feminist Lens' in MacLean, Sandra J, David R Black and Timothy M Shaw (eds), *A Decade of Human Security. Global Governance and New Multilateralisms* (England/USA, Ashgate, 2006) 161–76.

[4] See Leach, Fiona and Sara Humphreys, 'Gender Violence in Schools: Taking the "Girls as Victims" Discourse Forward' in Terry, Geraldine and Joanna Hoare (eds), *Gender-Based Violence* (London, Oxfam GB, 2007) 106–20.

gender-based violence and men the majority of perpetrators'.[5] Therefore, for the effects of our analysis, this text considers gender-based violence in its most frequent understanding as violence against women and girls and concentrates on VAW as the most widespread and illustrative form of gender-based violence, and also as a human rights violation which has been dealt with extensively by international human rights law.

Once the gendered human security–human rights synergies have been unpacked, the rest of the chapter attempts to exemplify the potential of the mutual reinforcement of the concepts of human security and human rights of women. In particular, section III discusses the concepts of violence under human security and that of violence against women under human rights law and suggests that international human rights instruments on the rights of women and girls, may serve to give content and precision to a gender sensitive idea of human security. Finally, section IV explores the relationship of the ways in which the concept of human security can contribute to the understanding of women's human rights and resulting State obligations in contexts of structural vulnerability, through the analysis of paradigmatic cases from the European and Inter-American human rights systems. The chapter finishes by suggesting that there are certain *synergies* to be found between human security and human rights which may prove useful in achieving the goal of women's and girls' lives to be free of violence, as developed further in the concluding Chapter 7 of this text.

II. HUMAN SECURITY AND ITS GENDER IMPLICATIONS

As discussed in Chapter 1, security of the State was commonly interpreted as protecting its territorial integrity and its sovereign powers, but the security of individual human beings, and in particular women and girls, was largely ignored.[6] We have also gone through the history of how the modern idea of human security emerged as a post-Cold War answer to threats that had been overlooked by State-centred conceptions of national, military and territorial security,[7] as well as to new risks posed by the process of globalisation and other transnational phenomena, intra-State violence, sudden economic downturns, environmental dangers and global infectious diseases such as HIV/AIDS, all of which create mutual and interlinked vulnerabilities for persons around the world.

[5] Hayes, Ceri, 'Tackling Violence against women: A Worldwide Approach' in Terry and Hoare (n 4) 2.

[6] See, eg, Florea Hudson, Natalie, *Gender, Human Security and the United Nations: Security language as a Political Framework for Women* (New York, Routledge, 2010).

[7] MacFarlane, Neil S and Yuen Foong Khong, *Human Security and the UN. A Critical History* (Bloomington, Indiana University Press, United Nations Intellectual History Project, 2006) 20.

In the face of these new realities, the contemporary idea of human security was first born in connection with development. As has already been described, it was initially referred to by the UN Security Council (UNSC) and the UN Secretary General (UNSG) in 1992, presented as an autonomous concept in 1993 by the United Nations Development Program (UNDP), and then fully articulated through the 1994 UNDP Human Development Report.[8] The concept coined in the Report was ambitious and sought to express in a comprehensive manner the possibility of multiple threats to individuals' and groups' basic well-being. Following-up on the account of the Report presented in Chapter 1, three forms of comprehensiveness of the concept as formulated by the UNDP are worth underscoring.

First, and in the context of the 1993 Vienna Declaration and Programme of Action which affirmed the universality, indivisibility and interdependence of human rights, the Report contributed to bridge the civil-political/socio-economic and cultural divide or hierarchy of rights and interests. It achieved this through following the original wording of the 1945 United Nations (UN) Charter which expressed in its Preamble the Parties' commitment 'to promote social progress and better standards of life in larger freedom', as well as the views of the founders of the UN that considered security as covering both *freedom from fear* and *freedom from want*. Given that after 1945, especially in the Cold War context, the international community had tilted in favour of freedom from fear in addressing security matters, the UNDP recovered the initial UN values and considered that both types of freedoms are essential components of human security.[9] Thus, as defined by the UNDP in 1994, threats to human life also had to include those related to hunger, disease and repression and not only those related directly to international war or use of armed force.

Second, by focusing on the individual, instead of the State, the UNDP Report's proposed idea of human security unsettled conventions about what were considered 'ordinary' and 'extraordinary' threatening events, making sure that protection from sudden and hurtful disruptions in the patterns of daily life—whether in homes, in jobs or in communities—would be given due consideration.[10] Indeed, the Report

[8] UNDP, *Human Development Reports*, 1993 and 1994 available at http://hdr.undp.org/en/reports/.

[9] UNDP, *1994 Human Development Report, New Dimensions of Human Security*, p 24, at http://hdr.undp.org/en/media/hdr_1994_en_chap2.pdf. See also Article 5 of the Vienna Declaration and Program of Action, UN General Assembly, World Conference on Human Rights, A/CONF.157/23, 12 July 1993.

[10] As was explained in Chapter 1, based on this definition, the Human Development Report of 1994 grouped the threats to human security into seven categories: 1. Economic security, 2. Food security, 3. Health security, 4. Environmental security, 5. Personal security, 6. Community security, 7. Political security. UNDP, *Human Development Report*, 1994, pp 23–25.

explicitly highlighted the fact that 'for most people, a feeling of insecurity arises more from worries about daily life than from the dread of a cataclysmic world event'.[11]

Finally, although in a less self-conscious manner, the Report identified threats of human security stemming not only from the *disruption* of people's ordinary lives, but also from the *affirmation* of normalised violence and discrimination in persons' lives.

This multifaceted understanding of the notion of threats to human security accounts for the relative success of the notion among feminist scholars. Whereas classical security visions had focused on external military threats to the State, by looking at the individual, the human security concept opened the door for addressing the security concerns of both women and men equally, shedding light on the many forms of severe deprivation and violence that women encounter.

Sharing the main concern of this chapter, some feminist authors have argued that gender approaches deliver more credence and substance to a wider security concept, but also enable a theoretical conceptualisation more reflective of security concerns that emanate from the 'bottom up'.[12]

Indeed, feminist thinking has traditionally focused on the security of the individual rather than the State—broadly defining security as freeing individuals and groups, particularly women and girls, from the social, physical, economic, cultural and political constraints that prevent them from living an autonomous life project. Accordingly, the notion of human security was welcomed as having a clear potential to act as a driving force for critical thought regarding mainstream security concerns and the way they had systematically overlooked women and girls, allowing critical security studies to be brought in line with feminist security studies.[13] Human security has also been appreciated by civil society and some governments as a motivator for social and political change and as a unifying language for legal reform favouring women and girls vis-à-vis national or State security.[14]

[11] UNDP, *1994 Human Development Report* (n 9) p 1.

[12] See Hoogensen, Gunhild and Kirsti Stuvøy, 'Gender, Resistance and Human Security' (2006) 37 *Security Dialogue* 2, 207–28. See also Stuvøy, Kirsti, 'Human Security and Women's Security Reality in Northwest Russia' in Hoogensen Gjørv, Gunhild, Dawn Bazely, Marina Goloviznina, and Andrew Tanentzap (eds), *Environmental and Human Security in the Arctic* (London and New York, Routledge, 2014) 231–49.

[13] In this sense, see Florea Hudson (n 6) 34. On the need to further develop the links between human security and VAW, see also Bunch, Charlotte, 'Foreword. Feminist Quandaries on Gender and Violence: Agency, Universality, and Human Security' in Bahun, Sanja and VG Julie Rajan (eds), *Violence and Gender in the Globalized World: The Intimate and the Extimate*, 2nd edn (England and USA, Ashgate, 2015) xiii–xviii.

[14] See, eg, the history behind the intent of inclusion of human security, particularly of women and girls, in the Draft Constitution of Fiji of 2012, and its final exclusion from the approved Constitution of 2013 to be substituted by the concept of national security, in *Equality, Development and Peace: Women's Human Security First*, A FemLINKPACIFIC Policy

Although failing to give a comprehensive account of violence against women and its impact in terms of human security, the 1994 UNDP Report explicitly raised the question of the many forms in which women experienced high chances of becoming victims of violence just because of their gender.[15] The Report stated that,

> (i)n no society are women secure or treated equally to men. Personal insecurity shadows them from cradle to grave ... At school, they are the last to be educated. At work, they are the last to be hired and the first to be fired. And from childhood through adulthood, they are abused because of their gender.[16]

And while the Report recognised that women were making progress in the domain of education and employment, it also underlined that there are still many shocking practices contributing to women's insecurity, including the widespread practice of genital mutilation, the custom of expecting women to be the last to eat in the household, as well as that of systematically disregarding health security issues relating to childbirth. In regards to this last aspect, as the Report underlined, 'a miracle of life often turns into a nightmare of death just because a society cannot spare the loose change to provide a birth attendant at the time of the greatest vulnerability and anxiety in a woman's life'.[17] Certainly, conflict, epidemics, natural disasters, or the complete breakdown of a country's health system are crises faced by millions of patients around the world every day, 'But a maternal death: that's the avoidable crisis'.[18] When crisis is escalated to become the everyday, that is, when women's death rates by these causes are so high that 'maternal mortality *is* the emergency',[19] a clear connection can be traced between protecting women's human rights as a generalised social need, and not only as a state of exception, in order to guarantee their human security.

As was emphasised in Chapter 1, another important milestone in the coining of the idea of human security was the 2003 Report of the UN Commission on Human Security (CHS): *Human Security Now*. In the Report, State security and human security appeared as complementary, the latter trying to focus on insecurities that have traditionally not been considered

for Peace Report, Fiji Islands, 2009–2014, 2014. See also Korany, Bahgat, Hania Sholkamy and Maya Morsy (eds), *Women in the Concept and Issues of Human Security. Arab and International Perspectives*, Proceedings of the Second Conference of the Arab Women Organisation Abu Dhabi, United Arab Emirates, 11–13 November 2008, Vol II, AWO, Egypt, 2010; and *Patriarchal Violence—an Attack on Human Security*, Government Offices of Sweden, Stockholm, 2005.

[15] UNDP, *1994 Human Development Report* (n 9) p 22.

[16] UNDP, *1994 Human Development Report* (n 9) p 31.

[17] UNDP, *1994 Human Development Report* (n 9) p 28.

[18] Medecins Sans Frontieres, *Urgent Delivery—Maternal Deaths: The Avoidable Crisis*, Special Report, 7 March 2012, p 4. Underlined in original.

[19] *Ibid*, p 25.

as State security threats.[20] Not unlike the UNDP Report, the concept tried to capture the original UN spirit of viewing security comprehensively as including protection of both *freedom from fear* and *freedom from want*.[21] Indeed, the CHS referred to threats coming from violence, but as it was explained, also from poverty, ill health, illiteracy and other maladies, and highlighted the fact that conflict and deprivation are interconnected.[22] It also underlined abrupt change as a risk to security, rather than just absolute levels of deprivation, for example, in the case of sudden economic downturns.[23]

This conception of human security allowed the 2003 Report to give due recognition to the multiple threats to women's basic well-being during violent conflict and its aftermath, including those with a disparate impact on some sectors of the population such as refugees and internally displaced persons. The Report made in passing reference to the many forms of gender-based violence including rape, sexual violence, enforced prostitution and trafficking and also raised questions relating to the economic security and social protection of women, underlining the importance of land security and addressing the problem of gender disparity in education and literacy rates.[24]

In spite of this, the *Human Security Now* Report has been subject to criticism for failing to address violence against women specifically, as well as for not paying specific attention to women as subjects or constituency. This presumably resulted in issues that predominantly affect women, such as the complex set of questions surrounding women's bodily integrity, especially with regard to reproductive health and violence, being side-lined. For instance, whereas the Report does mention the harm to women's physical integrity due to maternal mortality and malfunctioning of systems of reproductive health,[25] it fails to relate this directly to general situations of violence against women or to analyse in depth the question of women's reproductive autonomy. This failure to address violence against women specifically, Charlotte Bunch has argued, allowed

[20] Commission on Human Security (CHS), *Human Security Now* (New York, CHS, 2003) pp 1, 4 and 10.

[21] We may recall that considering the concept the Report asserts that 'Human security means to protect the *vital core* of all human lives in ways that enhance human freedoms and human fulfillment. Human security means protecting fundamental freedoms—freedoms that are the essence of life. It means protecting people from *critical (severe) and pervasive (widespread) threats and situations*. It means using processes that build on people's strengths and aspirations. It means creating political, social, environmental, economic, military and cultural systems that together give people the building blocks of survival, livelihood and dignity' *ibid*, p 4.

[22] *Ibid*, *Outline of the Report*, p 1.

[23] *Ibid*, Box 1.3 'Development, Rights and Human Security', p 8.

[24] *Ibid*, pp 23, 25, 61, 65, 77–79, 81, 107, 114 and 122.

[25] *Ibid*, Box 6.2 'Ensuring Human Security for Women: Reproductive Health', p 100.

the connection between violence against women and other kinds of domination and insecurity in the world to be masked. The way in which a culture of violence at the domestic level furthers tolerance towards the violence of war, militarism, and other forms of domination that the *Human Security Now* Report discusses, is not given due visibility.[26]

This is why the idea of human security simply as a supplement to State security has also been problematised from a feminist perspective. It has been argued that the notion of State security, as traditionally coined (ie with an emphasis on military security), is not only too narrow but actually contrary to that of human security, especially if one considers the close links between gender and war and the way in which the current security system is rooted in patriarchal hierarchy. From this perspective it has been said that 'the present highly militarized global system of state security is not only incompatible with human security, but represents the foremost barrier to planetary security'.[27] As Betty A Reardon puts it, the State system represents 'an arms addicted patriarchy versus a human security partnership'.[28]

Similarly, Tamar Pitch pressingly critiques the 'security society', as she calls it, taking some elements from Ulrich Beck's 'society of risk', and highlighting the possibilities that the current global securitised system opens up for a numerous amount of people to be considered threats to security and thus to live outside of the law. Refugees and undocumented migrants enter the list, the disparate impact on women and girls being signalled as well as an effect of the security society.[29]

While the study of VAW has helped to acknowledge the intersection between racism and sexism, human security may also bring forward the horizontal similarities of VAW worldwide. Because it contributes to breaking down the national and cultural differences and rather accentuates the shared features of the phenomenon of VAW as a form of discrimination against women—as has been legally recognised in General Recommendation No 19 of the UN Committee on the Elimination of Discrimination Against Women (CEDAW Committee)—it thus sets VAW against the background of broader forms of communal violence, structural violence and symbolic violence, common (in different degrees) to all societies.

[26] See Bunch, Charlotte, 'A Feminist Human Rights Lens on Human Security' (2004) 16 *Peace Review* 1, 29–34.

[27] See Reardon, Betty A and Asha Hans (eds), *The Gender Imperative. Human Security vs State Security* (New Delhi/United Kingdom, Routledge, 2010) 3.

[28] See Reardon, Betty A, "Women or Weapons: the Militarist Sexist Symbiosis' in Kurtz, Mariam M and Lester R Kurtz (eds), *Women, War, and Violence: Topography, Resistance, and Hope* (USA, Praeger Security International, 2015) 100.

[29] Pitch, Tamar, *Pervasive Prevention. A Feminist Reading of the Rise of the Security Society* (UK, Ashgate, 2010) 112–14. In a similar sense on the security society, see Den Boer, Monica, 'Preventive Empires: Security Dynamics at Multiple Levels of Governance' (2011) 3 *Amsterdam Law Forum* 3, 102–13.

Actually, the research-led *Human Security Report*, of 2012, duly highlights the shortcomings of traditional conceptions of violence, and even of violence against women as too often reduced only to sexual violence in dominant scholarship and measurement attempts. According to the Report, the dominant narrative assumes that conflict-related sexual violence is on the rise, and that rape is increasingly being deployed as a 'weapon of war'. Such narrative would suggest that the experience of the small number of countries afflicted by extreme levels of sexual violence is the norm for all war-affected countries. The Report then argues that the mainstream narrative ignores domestic sexual violence in wartime, which is far more pervasive than that perpetrated by combatants—and which victimises a far greater number of women.[30]

However, caution should be exercised when considering this Report. As Fionnuala Ní Aoláin has signalled, the Human Security Report Project contains parts which may be considered highly provocative. She deems that the Report rightly identifies an incentive structure in conflict-afflicted societies that encourages media, non-governmental organisations (NGOs) and international institutions to disproportionately (according to the Report) concentrate on conflict-related sexual violence distorting our general understanding of sexual violence in zones of conflict. In her view, applying a critical lens to general orthodoxy in policy or scholarly endeavours, as the Report does, is to be encouraged. At the same time, she rightly warns that little attention has been paid in most societies to appropriately and systematically documenting the scale and forms of violence experienced by women. National crime studies and statistical gathering methods evidence bias and limitation in their capture of female sexual harms. Few myths are said to exist about these pervasive and common fault-lines and they rarely capture the attention of the myth-breakers. So, there is reason to be tepid when the myth-breakers turn to conflict-related sexual violence and loftily pronounce the need to remedy all procedural deficiencies. She signals that it should be obvious that the short history of interest and measurement of sexual violence directed in conflict is a mere shadow to the long histories of silence over centuries, a reflection which is swiftly brushed away by the authors of the Report.[31]

Thus, to try to remedy some of the dominant shortcomings of VAW analysis in bringing specific women's experiences to the fore, a gendered human security may well represent a renovating force, both as an analytical framework and as a political project of emancipation, as has been duly

[30] See *Human Security Report 2012*, Human Security Report Project, 2012, available at http://hsrgroup.org/press-room/latest-news/latest-news-view/12-10-10/New_Report_Greatest_Source_of_Wartime_Sexual_Violence_Ignored.aspx.

[31] Ní Aoláin, Fionnuala, 'Some Caution in Reading Human Security Report', 15 October 2012, Blog posted in *IntLaw Grrls. Voices on International Law, Policy and Practice*, available at www.intlawgrrls.com/2012/10/some-caution-in-reading-new-human.html#more.

argued by Heidi Hudson. In defending a position based on identity politics, she advocates for more fluid context-based interpretations of gender in human security, for example, through alternative feminist approaches, such as those rooted in the African context.[32] As the present chapter illustrates, this would seem to echo with some of the human security concerns that have found their way into specifically African legal instruments, such as the inclusion of a 'right to food security' in the 2003 Protocol to the African Charter on Human and Peoples' Rights (ACHPR) on the Rights of Women in Africa.

This book wishes to concentrate on this expression of human security in human rights legal provisions and judicial/quasi-judicial interpretations, and the connections between them. Consequently, throughout this chapter and the following two, the text reveals a series of *interpretative synergies* that are then presented in a summarised list in concluding Chapter 7. Such synergies reflect the interaction operating between the two concepts, human security and human rights, specifically regarding women and girls at risk of or suffering violence, and undocumented migrants and other non-citizens. As a result, the study identifies limitations of this relationship and also advocates for its potential in expanding the human rights' agenda and improving its applicability to alleviate real-life situations of extreme risk and vulnerability faced by human beings.

A. Added Value of a Gendered Human Rights-Based Approach to Human Security

The notions of human security enshrined in the 1994 UNDP Report and the 2003 CHS Report, and later picked up in the 2012 UNSG Report and UNGA Resolution,[33] are still worth defending, especially in view of competing and narrower notions enshrined elsewhere endorsing the dichotomous approach to the 'freedom from fear' or the 'freedom from want' dimension of human security. This said, it is my understanding that the concept could be improved and surmount some of the expressed feminist criticism if it were able to duly take advantage of the way in which human

[32] Hudson, Heidi, '"Doing" Security As Though Humans Matter: A Feminist Perspective on Gender and the Politics of Human Security' (2005) 36 *Security Dialogue* 2, 155–74.

[33] See UNGA, *Second Report of the UN Secretary General on Human Security*, A/66/763, 5 April 2012, 'Follow-up to General Assembly Resolution 64/291 on Human Security. Report of the Secretary General' para 13; and UNGA, A/Res/66/290 'Follow-Up to Paragraph 143 on Human Security of the 2005 World Summit Outcome', 10 September 2012, para 3 a), b) and c). See also in the same lines as the 2012 UNGA Resolution, the *Third Report of the UN Secretary General*, UNGA, 'Follow-Up to General Assembly Resolution 66/290 on Human Security. Report of the Secretary General', A/68/685, 23 December 2013, especially paras 7, 35, and 59.

rights standards and indicators can contribute in the definition and assessment of the levels of protection of human security in general, and of the human security of women in particular.

In principle, there seems to be nothing particularly surprising about this. As has been emphasised, being person-centred constructs, it is clear that both human security and human rights serve common purposes and can therefore be mutually reinforcing notions.[34] However, although the 2003 CHS Report made a general reference to the relationship between human security and human rights and viewing these as a 'normative framework and a conceptual reference point' for human security,[35] it did not endorse a human rights-based approach. In developing its findings, the Report limited itself to describing the factual situations it identified as threats, failing to incorporate a normative assessment related to the condition of enjoyment of human rights and the risks faced with regards to their protection, as well as the level of compliance of States with their human rights obligations. This is not unique. Rather, we find that in most theoretical articulations of the notion of human security, as well as in most existing exercises of human security assessment, human rights are considered, but only at the discursive level, or in their character of a general normative reference point. Few works have actually attempted to draw, in any serious way, the connection between human security threats and the failure to ensure human rights.

One may find some expression in the existing human rights normative framework of the growing awareness of the interconnection between human rights protection and human security goals, with the coining of certain new rights or the linking of traditional rights to the notion of human security. For instance, the Protocol to the African Charter on Human and Peoples' Rights on the Rights of Women in Africa, of 2003, the 'Maputo Protocol',[36] seems to echo human security concerns and duly underscore the relevance of general conditions for the enjoyment of rights when it sets forth, inspired partly by UNSC Resolution 1325, *a right to peace for women*, consisting of 'the right to a *peaceful existence* and the right to participate in the promotion and maintenance of peace' (Article 10).

[34] Von Tigerstrom, Barbara, *Human Security and International Law: Prospects and Problems* (Studies in International Law) (Oxford and Portland, Oregon, Hart Publishing, 2007) 39.

[35] '... human rights and the attributes stemming from human dignity constitute a normative framework and a conceptual reference point which must necessarily be applied to the construction and putting into practice of the notion of human security. In the same manner, without prejudice to considering the norms and principles of international humanitarian law as essential components for the construction of human security, we emphasize that the latter cannot be restricted to situations of current or past armed conflict, but rather is a generally applicable instrument". CHS, *Human Security Now* (n 20) p 145.

[36] Adopted by the 2nd Ordinary Session of the Assembly of the Organization of the African Union in Maputo, 11 July 2003, entered into force on 25 November 2005, available at www.achpr.org/instruments/women-protocol/.

Similarly, the Maputo Protocol refers to the *right to food security* of women (Article 15).

This can be understood in viewing some of the grave challenges and gross human rights violations faced by women in the African context, so much so that the promotion and protection of the human rights of women has been qualified as 'a prerequisite for human security in Africa',[37] considering that

> Violence against women and girls has assumed unprecedented levels across Africa ... Harmful traditional practices against women and girls such as female genital mutilation, virginity tests, early and forced marriages and widow inheritance continue to bedevil continental efforts towards gender equality and women's empowerment. The situation of women in conflict situations in Africa is deplorable. Gross human rights violations are perpetrated against civilians in general but against women and girls in particular.[38]

The situation of gender inequality and violence against women is not exclusive to the African continent, it is—to different levels and degrees—ongoing and pervasive in all societies, developed and developing, from the North to the South, in peace or in violent conflict.[39] Indeed, none are completely exempt from gender inequality and violence against women, which are in themselves human rights' violations and in turn facilitate further violations. These circumstances create different types of vulnerabilities for women and girls worldwide, and when they become systematic, they allow for a generalised state of human insecurity at the societal level.

Thus, it is submitted in this chapter that incorporating human rights parameters can fulfil several purposes, all of which are relevant in order to duly engender the notion of human security. Firstly, it can help in providing the notion of human security with a more precise content. Secondly, and at least to the extent that the human rights system has made progress in reflecting women's needs, it can ensure that the notion of human security is defined without leaving behind those threats to basic well-being that affect women and girls disparately. Finally, the human rights perspective helps to underscore the empowerment of citizens who in this way come to be seen not only as in need of assistance, but also and more importantly as rights holders.

[37] See Ssenyonjo, Manisuli, 'Human Rights of Women in Africa: A Prerequisite for Human Security' in Abass, Ademola (ed), *Protecting Human Security in Africa* (Oxford, Oxford University Press, 2010), taken from OXFORD SCHOLARSHIP ONLINE (www.oxfordscholarship.com). See also 'An African Spring? Human Rights and Security in Times of Change' in *Human Security Perspectives 1 (2014)* (European Training and Research Centre for Human Rights and Democracy (ETC), 2014).

[38] Statement by the African Union Chairperson, Professor Alpha Oumar Konare, in Celebration of the International Women's Day of 8 March 2007, quoted by Ssenyonjo (n 37) 179–80.

[39] In this respect, see the World Bank Report, *World Development Report 2012: Gender Equality and Development*, available at http://econ.worldbank.org.

In view of this, the incorporation of human rights standards to the content of human security can be particularly important for those groups who, like women, have traditionally been marginalised. From this angle, the human security aspiration becomes not only that of catering to distinctive basic needs for a broadly conceived notion of human well-being, but also and primarily that of affirming citizenship by 'ensuring fundamental human entitlements—social, economic, and political—in ways that expand human choices and promote human well-being and empowerment'.[40] For this to happen, a gendered understanding of human security requires that this notion be measured in the light of the particular violations of human rights of women and girls and the actual conditions of systemic vulnerability which they face. In this task, it is argued, the application of international legal human rights standards can serve to shed light on women´s experiences and needs; be a useful tool to interpret and clarify the concrete meaning of human security for the lives of women and girls and empower women and girls as citizens and rights holders.

B. Profile of a Gendered Human Security

It was argued in Chapter 1 that a broad definition of human security has many advantages and that the incorporation of human rights standards may partly contribute in the task of narrowing down the meaning and providing tools for the assessment of concrete situations. Both things, it is claimed, hold promise for women and girls.

In looking at Taylor Owen's proposal of a threshold-based conceptualisation, it was noted how he submitted the idea that human security may work 'as a threshold beyond which a wide range of issues become something similar, something requiring the unified policy response granted to security threats'.[41]

Thus interpreted, it has already been argued that what the notion of human security mostly allows for is to identify situations of serious threat, which we could generically call *risk situations*. The factors that may come together in generating a risk situation may be several and can include the gravity of the violation of certain human rights; the widespread or systematic nature of a certain type of violation and/or the fact that the violations

[40] Heyzer, Noeleen, 'Combating Trafficking in Women and Children. A Gender and Human Rights Framework' in Truong, Thanh-Dam, Saskia Wieringa and Amrita Chhachhi (eds), *Engendering Human Security. Feminist Perspectives* (USA, Women Unlimited, India/Zed Books Ltd, 2006) 112.

[41] Owen, Taylor, 'Human Security—Conflict, Critique and Consensus: Colloquium Remarks and a Proposal for a Threshold-Based Definition' in *Security Dialogue* (Oslo, Norway, International Peace Research Institute, Sage Publications, 2004) Vol 35, No 3, 384.

target or have a disparate impact on what we could call a vulnerable population, meaning a population living in structural conditions of inequality or disadvantage, with a whole set of rights insufficiently guaranteed, and hence more susceptible to be severely affected by particular risk factors.

In the first chapter of this study, I argued in favour of a vision of human security which does not primarily rest on the hierarchical ordering of human rights.[42] According to this position, emphasis should be placed on the State's obligation to carry out primarily actions of *prevention*, as well as actions of *mitigation* and *attention*, against risks and vulnerabilities affecting people's overall level of security. The possibilities of human security to act as a 'detonator' in triggering the human rights obligations of the State, are particularly relevant for the analysis of this chapter, especially in relation to the State's duties to take preventive measures, to address the violations of human rights that have already taken place as soon as possible and to grant reparations that redress women and girls, as well as communities, for the harm they have suffered while seeking to address the systemic shortcomings.

The identification of severe threats to persons' basic well-being and the compounded effect of the violations in situations in which they encounter multiple and structural forms of discrimination, offers in this chapter a picture which, it is suggested, captures in a richer way the harm to human rights and well-being suffered by the women and girls in the analysed cases, than the one which would be provided looking only at the different individual human rights violations as separate events affecting various individuals. This type of examination also brings to light the actions of private actors, by reinforcing State *due diligence* obligations in cases in which the State *knew or should have known* about the risk situations faced by women and girls and partly caused by the intervention of private actors.

Based on this, the text now moves to exemplify the way in which the human rights of women and girls and a gendered notion of human security can intersect and mutually reinforce each other, by looking at two issues: first, the adequate conceptualisation of the notion of violence against women and its due recognition as a security concern; and second, the content and interpretation of the State's obligations regarding the human rights of women and girls in the context of systemic or structural vulnerability. As we shall see after such analysis, in both issues a series of *interpretative synergies*, useful for both human security and for human rights concepts, come to the fore.

[42] Affirming the universality, interdependence and indivisibility of human rights, this integrated approach envisions that potentially all human rights can be at the centre of human security. As it has been pointed out, the differentiating element, and the one that links the notion of human rights and human security together, is the component of risk or structural vulnerability contained in the idea of serious threat.

III. VAW UNDER HUMAN RIGHTS LAW: DEMARCATING THE SCOPE OF HUMAN SECURITY

It has been pointed out that the idea of human security looks at a broad range of insecurities that individuals and communities face in the context of violence, embracing a broad notion of violence which encompasses interpersonal, intergroup or international violence. Looking at gender relations through the lens of human security—rather than or in addition to a rights-based frame—may raise new questions or offer different strategic choices, some of which have recently been examined in scholarly analysis.[43] One of these questions is the need to increase the awareness about the interrelationship between interpersonal violence and inter- or intra-state conflict, as the 2003 CHS Report rightly did.[44]

Also, an increasing focus on the security of persons has almost inevitably contributed to shedding light on the manifold ways in which inter and intra-state armed conflict affects the lives of women and girls. There are indeed promising signs that reflect a growing awareness about the need to incorporate women's needs and views in conflict and post-conflict situations. Paradigmatic is of course Resolution 1325, issued by the UN Security Council in 2000, which focuses on the impact on women and girls in situations of armed conflict, as well as the need for gender mainstreaming in peace-keeping operations that duly address the needs and human rights of women and girls, and the importance of the participation of women in conflict resolution and peace-building.[45] Worth mentioning is also Resolution 1820 of the Security Council adopted in 2008, underscoring the urgent need to protect civilians, particularly women and girls, against *widespread or systematic* sexual violence in the context of armed conflict or post-conflict situations.[46] (emphasis added) As a follow-up to Resolution 1820, the UN Security Council in 2009 passed Resolution

[43] See generally Tripp, Aili, Myra Marx Ferree and Christina Ewig (eds), *Gender, Violence and Human Security: Critical Feminist Perspectives* (New York, New York University Press, 2013).

[44] CHS, *Human Security Now* (n 20) p 23. The Report explicitly states that '[i]n and immediately following conflict, crime rates soar. So do incidents of gender-based and sexual violence … The increases arise from the trauma of conflict and its impact on *interpersonal relations* and community networks, and from the broader issues of the breakdown of law and order … But the influence works both ways. High levels of *interpersonal violence* also appear to affect the likelihood for violent conflict. High rates of communal violence may reflect growing inequalities among communities as well as the manipulation of identity politics … Increases in gender-based and sexual violence may mark a rise in poverty and the collapse of social safety nets. And although by itself interpersonal violence will not lead to conflict, combined with other factors it leads to a widespread sense of insecurity easily manipulated along identity lines'. (emphasis added)

[45] UNSC, Resolution 1325, S/Res/1325 (2000), 31 October 2000, especially OP 1, 10, 16, and 17.

[46] UNSC, Resolution 1820, S/Res/1820 (2008), 19 June 2008, especially PP 8 and OP 1.

1888 on Women, peace and security, relevant for our topic because of its requirement for more detailed and *systematic reporting* to *detect trends* on sexual violence against women in conflict.[47] (emphasis added) In a broad understanding, such monitoring would encompass economic, social and cultural rights, as well as civil and political rights, given that assessments related to the first type of rights may provide insight on structural factors of discrimination that have been proven to constitute powerful generators of sexual violence against women,[48] A similar view seems to be strengthened by subsequent UNSC Resolution 1889, also of 2009, which recognises the role of 'socio-economic factors' such as lack of access to education and health services, as obstacles to women's participation in conflict-prevention, decision-making and peace-building processes.[49]

Subsequent UNSC resolutions have been adopted building on the previous ones, Resolution 2122 being particularly noteworthy for its mirroring of human security concerns under the 'broad' view and the emphasis on 'empowerment' strategies. The Resolution expresses concern 'at the *full range of threats and human rights violations* and abuses experienced by women in armed conflict and post-conflict situations' and also recognises that women 'who are particularly vulnerable or disadvantaged may be specifically targeted or at *increased risk of violence*'. The Resolution also recognises the importance of the economic empowerment of women for peace-building and requests the UNSG's representatives to 'consult with women's organizations and women leaders, including *socially and/or economically excluded* groups of women'.[50]

International civil society has also taken into account the idea of human security, specifically in promoting the right and duty for reparations to violations of women's and girls' rights in the context of armed conflict. The *Nairobi Declaration of the Right to Remedy and Reparation of Women's and Girls' Rights*, of 2007, bearing in mind 'the terrible destruction brought by armed conflict, including forced participation in armed conflict, to

[47] UNSC, Resolution 1888, S/RES/1888 (2009), 30 September 2009, focused on women as victims (see especially OP 24). See also UNSC, Resolution 1889, S/RES/1889 (2009), 5 October 2009, centred more on women as peacemakers; and UNSC, Resolution 1960, S/RES/1960 (2010), 16 December 2010, addressing specifically sexual violence against women and children (while subsequent Resolution 2106 deals with men and boys as victims of sexual violence. UNSC, Resolution 2106, S/RES/2106 (2013), 24 June 2013). For a full comparative analysis of all these resolutions, see Engle, Karen, 'The Grip of Sexual Violence: Reading UN Security Council Resolutions on Human Security', in Heathcote, Gina and Dianne Otto (eds), *Rethinking Peacekeeping, Gender Equality and Collective Security*, Series Thinking Gender in Transnational Times (UK, Palgrave Macmillan, 2014).

[48] See in this respect Organisation for Security and Cooperation in Europe (OSCE), Office for Democratic Institutions and Human Rights (ODIHR), *Gender and Early Warning Systems: An Introduction* (OSCE/ODIHR, 2009) 10.

[49] See UNSC, Resolution 1889, S/RES/1889 (2009), 5 October 2009, at PP 8, 9 and 10; and OP 1, 10 and 15.

[50] UNSC, Resolution 2122, S/RES/2122 (2013), 18 October 2013, PP 8 and OP 7,a).

people's physical integrity, psychological and spiritual well-being, economic security, social status, social fabric, and the gender differentiated impact on the lives and livelihoods of women and girls', explicitly includes in its declarative point No 6 that 'national governments bear primary responsibility to provide remedy and reparation within an *environment that guarantees safety and human security*, and that the international community shares responsibility in that process'.[51] (emphasis added)

Similarly, in the UN setting, human security has been taken up in addressing security policy affecting women in the context of armed conflict, as a useful tool that seems to reach further than just stressing the need for a human rights-based approach to security policy, and rather calls for another formulation of 'security' altogether. The UN Civil Society Advisory Group on Women, Peace, and Security (CSAG), was established in 2010 to advise the UNSG on ensuring a coherent and coordinated approach by UN agencies and entities to protecting women's rights during armed conflict and ensuring their full participation in all conflict prevention, peace-building, and post-conflict reconstruction processes. With the aim of implementing the substantial responsibilities of the international community under UNSC Resolutions 1325 and 1820 for preventing and responding to sexual violence against women displaced by armed conflict, it specifically recommended that

> International and national policymakers *should fully consider issues of human security*, and in particular the potential impact of their security decisions on women, when formulating security policy. Most significantly, they should refrain from ill-advised and ineffective actions against insurgent groups if they are likely to result in massive retaliation against civilian populations, including killings, rapes, and large displacement of women and women-led households.[52]

Indeed, the gendered dynamics of war and peace are increasingly understood as a problem of security and a contributing factor for relapse into

[51] The Declaration was issued at the International Meeting on Women's and Girls' Right to a Remedy and Reparation, held in Nairobi from 19 to 21 March 2007, by women's rights advocates and activists, as well as survivors of sexual violence in situations of conflict, from Africa, Asia, Europe, Central, North and South America, at www.womensrightscoalition.org/site/reparation/signature_en.php. The Nairobi Declaration was actually taken into account by the African Commission on Human and Peoples' Rights in its Resolution on the Right to a Remedy and Reparation for Women and Girls Victims of Sexual Violence; see ACHOR/Res 111 (XXXXII) 07.

[52] International Crisis Group, 'Working Paper on Preventing and Responding to Sexual Violence against Women Displaced by Conflict' by Donald Steinberg, 12 July 2010, Recommendation No 14, available at www.crisisgroup.org/en/regions/op-eds/working-paper-on-preventing-and-responding-to-sexual-violence-against-women-displaced-by-conflict.aspx. A gendered human security approach that duly considers human rights law and standards, I suggest, would have to integrate concrete human rights and humanitarian criteria addressing gender-based violence, if it is dealing with human security in the context of armed conflict, for example, the *Guidelines for Gender-based Violence Interventions in*

conflict. Nonetheless, more than fifteen years after the adoption of UN Security Council Resolution 1325 on Women, Peace and Security, women remain severely underrepresented in peace-building. While today there are general calls being made for the inclusion of women, women are still routinely excluded. A need remains to critically examine gender power relations that uphold the *status quo*, and investigate the process by which certain issues are put on the peace agenda while others are not. Fortunately, some efforts are being carried out in this domain, notably under the logo 'Equal Power-Lasting Peace'.[53]

Without doubt, armed conflict has a huge impact on women and girls, and provides the scenario of widespread gender-based violence, particularly rape and other forms of sexual abuse.[54] However, as it has been emphasised in this research, there are various forms of pervasive violence against women that also occur in contexts of 'peace' (viewed under the State-centred logic), and that may be the result of a continuum of gender-based violence involving structural discrimination and the violation of a wide set of interrelated human rights. In this respect, one may think of domestic violence for example, or human trafficking of women and the way they experience (in)security in such settings,[55] the violence arousing from extreme poverty in itself and in the different forms of violence it facilitates, especially if one takes into account the millions of avoidable deaths every year that derive from sources not directly related to armed force.[56]

Nevertheless, as reviewed in Chapter 1, in their consideration of 'violent conflict' and 'violence', several human security ideas adopt a narrow view confined to the utilisation of armed force by the State or by any other actor(s) in the context of contended issues. In other words, those who focus on 'freedom from fear', limit themselves to violence expressed in inter or intra-State violence, and those who also place an emphasis on 'freedom from want' threats which do not necessarily involve armed force and often rightly highlight gender variables as important to

Humanitarian Settings: Focusing on Prevention of and Response to Sexual Violence in Emergencies, developed and adopted by the Universal Declaration of Human Rights and Office for the Coordination of Humanitarian Affairs, which refer to 'food security and nutrition' (including fuel for cooking), among other human security-relevant components.

[53] *Equal Power-Lasting Peace. Obstacles for Women's Participation in Peace Processes*, The Kvinna till Kvinna Foundation, Sweden, 2012.

[54] UNSC, Resolution 1325 (n 45), OP 10.

[55] Coomaraswamy, Radihka, 'Human Security and Gender Violence' (2005) 40 *Economic and Political Weekly* 44/45, 4729–36.

[56] Along these lines, see eg Roberts, David, *Global Governance and Biopolitics: Regulating Human Security* (London, Zed Books, 2010) 13 and 16. See also Persaud, Christine and Hye Jin Zumkehr (eds), *Gender and Security: Guidelines for Mainstreaming Gender in Security Risk Management*, Briefing Paper (European Interagency Security Forum, 2012).

orientate analysis, do not consider that certain forms of extreme and structural deprivations may amount to violence.

In doing so, it is argued, the dominant concepts of human security do not sufficiently take into account the evolution of the concept of violence against women under human rights law, an evolution which has gradually broadened it to include many forms of harm, including of physical, psychological or sexual, but also of an economic nature, in both the public and the private realms,[57] both during times of peace and armed conflict,[58] and as a form of discrimination.[59]

Indeed, conceptualising VAW as a form of discrimination was a major step towards viewing it as a human rights violation and more broadly as a breach to equality. This outlook advanced in General Recommendation No 19 of CEDAW Committee, of 1992, was based on the Committee's consideration of VAW as 'acts that inflict physical, mental or sexual harm or suffering, *threats of such acts*, coercion and other deprivations of liberty' and its conclusion that such violence constitutes a form of discrimination against women within Article 1 of the relevant Convention, which actually deals with the 'Elimination of Discrimination Against Women', and not directly with VAW.[60] Although the Convention itself does not present VAW as a form of discrimination, as Christine Chinkin has noted, through providing this interpretation, CEDAW Committee creatively placed VAW within the realm of human rights, opening the door for its consideration as a State obligation. In an important realisation in *human security* terms, she highlights how this 'rights-based approach recognizes that women are entitled to be free from violence and the *fear of violence*, and that State parties have a legal obligation to ensure this right'.[61] In this

[57] See Art 1 of the UN 1993 *Declaration on the Elimination of Violence against Women* (UN General Assembly, A/RES/48/104); Arts 1 and 3 of the 1994 Inter-American Convention of Belém do Pará; Art 1 of the 2003 Protocol to the African Charter on Human and Peoples' Rights on the Rights of Women in Africa; and Arts 1, 3 and 4 of the Council of Europe Convention on Preventing and Combating Violence against Women and Domestic Violence. See also UN CEDAW Committee and Committee on the Rights of the Child, *Joint General Recommendation No 31 of CEDAW/General Comment No 18 of the Committee on the Rights of the Child on harmful practices*, CEDAW/C/GC/31/CRC/C/GC/18, 14 November 2014.

[58] See Art 1 of the 2003 Protocol to the African Charter on Human and People's Rights on the Rights of Women in Africa.

[59] See, eg, General Recommendation No 19 of UN CEDAW Committee, 1992 (11th session, 1992), available at www.un.org/womenwatch/daw/cedaw/recommendations/recomm.htm#recom19; and Art 6 of the 1994 Inter-American Convention of Belém do Pará.

[60] CEDAW Committee, General Recommendation No 19 (n 59) paras 6 and 7.

[61] Chinkin, Christine, 'Violence Against Women' in Freeman, Marsha, E, Christine Chinkin and Beate Rudolf (eds), *The UN Convention on the Elimination of all Forms of Discrimination Against Women: A Commentary* (Oxford, Oxford University Press, 2012) 451. See the fascinating historical and analytical account the author provides of the development of this General Recommendation.

context, human rights bodies have reaffirmed the wider right of women and of girls to live free from violence.[62]

The interpretation of 2014 by the UN Human Rights Committee on the right to personal security under the International Covenant on Civil and Political Rights is interesting for both human security and VAW, as it stresses a double State obligation:

> States parties must take *both* measures to *prevent future injury* and retrospective measures, such as enforcement of criminal laws, in response to *past injury*. For example, States parties must respond appropriately to *patterns of violence* against categories of victims such as … *violence against women*, including domestic violence.[63] (emphasis added)

Mentioning for the first time economic injury as a form of gender violence, Article 1 of the 2003 Protocol to the African Charter on Human and Peoples' Rights on the Rights of Women in Africa also defines violence against women and spells out corresponding State obligations, as

> all acts perpetrated against women which cause or could cause them physical, sexual, psychological, and *economic harm*, including the *threat to take such acts;* or to undertake the imposition of arbitrary restrictions on or deprivation of fundamental freedoms in private or public life in peace time and during situations of armed conflicts or of war. (emphasis added)

It is also not a coincidence that inter-governmental bodies such as the Organisation for Security and Cooperation in Europe (OSCE), committed precisely to security and adopting a broad understanding of the idea, have emphasised the link between non-discrimination and gender equality in the socio-economic realm as a means of prevention of VAW. The OSCE calls on Member States

> to take measures to strengthen the *economic independence of women*, including ensuring *non-discriminatory* employment policies and practices, providing *equal access* to education and training, *equal remuneration* for equal work, *increased* work and educational opportunities, equal access to and control over economic resources with a view to *reducing women's vulnerability to all forms of violence*, including domestic violence and trafficking in human beings.[64] (emphasis added)

Against this setting, the convergences between the human security debate and that of women, peace and security have been analysed from a feminist perspective. At this crossroads the gendered forms of insecurity in

[62] See, eg UN Committee on the Rights of the Child, General Comment No 13, *The Right of the Child to Freedom from all Forms of Violence*, CRC/C/GC/13, 18 April 2011.

[63] UN Human Rights Committee, General Comment No 35, *Article 9 (Liberty and Security of Person)*, CCPR/C/GC/35, 16 December 2014, para 9.

[64] OSCE Ministerial Council Decision No 15/05, *Preventing and Combating Violence Against Women*, MC.DEC/15/05, 6 December 2005, OP 6.

women' and girls' lives, the broader contexts of gender inequality and discrimination, and the structural patterns of indirect violence that facilitate them are revealed. Such an analysis renders evident the need for a mutually reinforcing perspective that duly incorporates women and their views as a part of integral peace-building processes, as well as for these processes to tackle the structural violence at the root cause of women's human insecurity.[65]

On specifically legal conceptualisations of violence against women, promoting an integral view on its understanding, in 2011 the Council of Europe (CoE) adopted the Convention on Preventing and Combating Violence against Women and Domestic Violence (notably under the human security-related logo *safe from fear, safe from violence)*, which entered into force on 1 August 2014.[66] Distinctly, and linked to the issues dealt with in Chapter 6 of this book on female undocumented migrants, the Convention singles out 'migrant women' as a group in a specific state of vulnerability, in line with previous highlights of such risks by other institutions at the European level,[67] under the consideration that

> migrant women, with or without documents, and women asylum-seekers are *particularly vulnerable* to gender-based violence. Although their reasons for leaving their country vary, as does their legal status, both groups are at *increased risk of violence* and face similar difficulties in overcoming it. For this reason, the convention prohibits *discrimination* on the grounds of *migrant or refugee status* when it comes to implementing its provisions (article 4.3). It also requires that measures be taken to *prevent* such violence and *support victims* while taking into account the needs of vulnerable persons.[68] (emphasis added)

The CoE Convention also presents innovative features in the field of human rights and public policies, outlined in this book as a potential

[65] See McKay, Susan, 'Women, Human Security, and Peace-Building: A Feminist Analysis', Chapter 7, in IPSHU English Research Report Series No 19 *Conflict and Human Security: A Search for New Approaches of Peace-Building* (2004) 152–75; see especially Table 1: Women's and Girls' Human Security During and After Armed Conflicts: Indirect and Direct Violence/Unorganized and Organized Threat, at p 160. For the general study of structural violence and the coining of the term by Johan Galtung, see his 'Violence, Peace, and Peace Research' (1969) 6 *Journal of Peace Research* 3, 167–91. For a more recent account as related to human rights, see Ho, Kathleen, 'Structural Violence as a Human Rights Violation' (2007) 4 *Essex Human Rights Review* 2, 1–27.

[66] Convention on Preventing and Combating Violence against Women and Domestic Violence, adopted by the Committee of Ministers of the Council of Europe on 7 April 2011 and opened for signature in Istanbul, Turkey, on 11 May 2011; entered into force on 1 August 2014.

[67] For instance, OSCE Ministerial Council Decision No 15/05 (n 64), preambular para. 6, expresses concern over the 'particular targeting or vulnerability to violence' of migrant women, among other groups.

[68] See 'Migrant women, women asylum-seekers and women refugees', at www.coe.int/en/web/istanbul-convention/the-convention-in-brief. See in these same lines UN CEDAW Committee, General Recommendation No 33, *Women's Access to Justice*, CEDAW/C/GC/33, 3 August 2015, paras 9, 17f, 49, 52 and 53b.

avenue for addressing widespread vulnerabilities. Precisely because this is often the nature of VAW, apart from including the State obligation to adopt gender-sensitive policies 'of equality between women and men and the empowerment of women' (Article 6), it also includes a whole chapter on the obligation of States to adopt 'Integrated policies and data collection' to prevent and combat violence against women. Fortunately, other recent human rights instances have taken up the interrelation between the right to non-discrimination and the enjoyment of other human rights by women.[69]

Different efforts have been made to reaffirm the right of women and girls to live free from violence.[70] Due to sustained efforts by the women's movement, governments and other stakeholders, the issue of violence against women was also positioned as a priority on global human rights, health and development agendas. The elimination of all forms of violence against women and girls and the suppression of all harmful practices were encompassed as part of the 2030 Agenda for Sustainable Development, and included as specific targets (ie targets 5.2 and 5.3) in the Sustainable Development Goals adopted by the UNGA in 2015. Many of the responses to date to violence against women have focused primarily on intervening with affected individuals after the violence has occurred, which is of course a necessary response. At the same time, 'there is also an increasing need to address the broader factors that contribute to prevalence at a population level, and to implement programmes that prevent such violence from occurring in the first place'.[71] As such, the document *A framework to underpin action to prevent violence against women* was adopted in 2015 by UN Women and backed by several intra-UN institutions. The framework includes a preventive and human rights-based approach, and in portraying a human security lens, it also addresses 'root causes' of, and 'risk factors' for VAW, through identifying and listing those of a 'community/organisational' and 'societal' nature, a part from the 'individual/relationship' associated factors (amid the latter, 'food insecurity', 'socio-economic status' and 'poverty'). It also prioritises women and girls at 'higher risk' and those who are 'especially vulnerable' to suffering prevalent forms of VAW, notably among them irregular migrants/domestic workers.[72]

[69] See UN Committee Against Torture, General Comment No 3, *Implementation of Article 14 by States Parties*, CAT/C/GC/3, 19 November 2012, paras 32–34.

[70] On the right of children to live free from violence, particularly for girls, see UN Committee on the Rights of the Child, General Comment No 13 (n 62) 2011.

[71] See note by UN Women, ILO, UNDP, UNESCO, UNFPA, UNOHCHR, WHO on the document 'A Framework to Underpin Action to Prevent Violence against Women', 25 November 2015, available at www.unwomen.org/en/digital-library/publications/2015/11/prevention-framework.

[72] UN Women, *A Framework to Underpin Action to Prevent Violence against Women* (UN Women, ILO, UNDP, UNESCO, UNFPA, UNOHCHR, WHO, 2015) 16, 19 and Table 2 at p 26.

Although some national legal systems are starting to reflect in their internal legislation the broadly conceived notion of VAW,[73] we are still far from a sufficiently well asserted notion of human security which includes the right to live free from all forms of violence.

IV. HUMAN SECURITY AND VAW: SYNERGIES REINFORCING WOMEN'S HUMAN RIGHTS

In recent years, international human rights law has progressed significantly and has moved to affirm positive obligations of the State under the *due diligence standard*, now considered by some as 'emerging international customary law',[74] including in matters which were traditionally considered part of the private domain, such as domestic violence, in particular, against women and girls. In the World Plan of Action adopted by the Conference of the International Women's Year held in Mexico City in 1975, the need to address harms to the physical integrity of women was signalled and the 'Declaration of Mexico on the Equality of Women and their Contribution to Development and Peace' was adopted in 1975.[75] The UN treaty on the subject of discrimination against women, CEDAW, was adopted in 1979 and came into force in 1981. The UN CEDAW Committee, the treaty body in charge of monitoring state compliance and interpreting the Convention, adopted in 1992 its paradigmatic General Recommendation No 19 on VAW and in 1993 the UN

See also 'Agreed Conclusions of the Fifty-Seventh Session of the Commission on the Status of Women' (UN, 2013).

[73] The concepts of 'psychological violence', 'economic violence' and 'institutional violence' are taken into account by the Mexican General Law for the Access of Women to a Life Free of Violence, at the federal level (and similar laws at the state level), as types of violence it protects women against; *Ley General de Acceso de las Mujeres a una Vida Libre de Violencia*, published in *Diario Oficial de la Federación*, 1 February 2007, last reform published 20 January 2009. Other countries have also adopted positive changes, although challenges remain: see, eg, Human Rights Watch (HRW), *'The Law was Against Me': Migrant Women's Access to Protection for Family Violence in Belgium* (HRW, 2012).

[74] See Hasselbacher, Lee, 'State Obligations Regarding Domestic Violence: The European Court of Human Rights, Due Diligence, and International Legal Minimums of Protection' (2010) 8 *Northwestern University Journal of International Human Rights* 2, 198–200, available at www.law.northwestern.edu/journals/jihr/v8/n2/3. See also the conclusion of the UN Special Rapporteur on Violence Against Women, its Causes and Consequences, in her report of 2006, *Integration of the Human Rights of Women and the Gender Perspective: Violence Against Women. The Due Diligence Standard as a Tool for the Elimination of Violence Against Women* (para 29), 20 January 2006, report prepared by Yakin Ertürk in accordance with Commission on Human Rights Resolution 2005/41; and on the '*obligation* to exercise *due diligence* to prevent, investigate and punish' the perpetrators of VAW, see OSCE Ministerial Council Decision No 15/05 (n 64), preambular para 3.

[75] See the history analysed in Chinkin (n 61) 444.

Declaration on the Elimination of Violence against Women was adopted, as referred to above.

To start off with an illustrative example of the practical application of this understanding, in *A.T. v Hungary*,[76] the UN Committee of CEDAW in 2005 dealt with the case of a woman battered by her husband who was not prosecuted by the State. The Committee held that even though the damage to her right to physical integrity was done by a private party, the State knew and did not act with *due diligence*, whereby it was held responsible. These recent developments in human rights law have contributed in adequately conceptualising violence against women and girls as a State problem and a security concern.[77]

Much has been achieved since the adoption of the 1993 Vienna Declaration and Programme of Action, cited above, and by the famous 1995 Beijing Declaration and Platform for Action,[78] which both stressed the need to combat VAW; Beijing was actually pre-dated not only by the adoption of the 1993 UN Declaration on the Elimination of Violence Against Women in the universal arena, as described above, but also by the 1994 Inter-American Convention on the Prevention, Punishment and Eradication of Violence against Women (Convention of Belém do Pará) at the regional level. International criminal law has also advanced a great deal in the legal understanding of some of the most brutal forms of sexual violence affecting mainly—and in some cases exclusively—women and girls, notably through the categorisation as a crime against humanity of rape, sexual slavery, enforced prostitution, forced pregnancy and enforced sterilisation in the 1998 Rome Statute of the International Criminal Court.[79]

As will be examined, both the Inter-American Court of Human Rights (IACHR) and the European Court of Human Rights (ECHR) have concluded that, in terms of international human rights law, based on the

[76] UN CEDAW Committee, *A.T. v Hungary*, Communication No. 2/2003, UN Doc. CEDAW/C/32/D/2/2003, 26 January 2005.

[77] See Boerefijn, Ineke and Eva Naezer, 'Emerging Human Rights Obligations for Non-State Actors' in Benninger-Budel, Carin (ed), *Due Diligence and its Application to Protect Women from Violence* (The Netherlands, Martinus Nijhoff Publishers, 2008) 91–108; as well as Von Tigerstrom (n 34) 60. On academic and civil society activities concerning this issue, see http://www.duediligenceproject.org/.

[78] Beijing Declaration and Platform for Action adopted by the Fourth World Conference on Women: Action for Equality, Development and Peace, 15 September 1995, available at www1.umn.edu/humanrts/instree/e5dplw.htm.

[79] See Article 7.1g) of the Rome Statute of the International Criminal Court, adopted on 17 July 1998 and which entered into force on 1 July 2002. These legal categorisations of certain forms of gender-based violence as crimes against humanity or war crimes had also been advanced by the jurisprudence of the two *ad hoc* International Criminal Tribunals for Ex-Yugoslavia and for Rwanda, and have been further developed by both tribunals and by the case-law of the ICC itself; see Fries, Lorena, 'La Corte Penal Internacional y los avances en materia de justicia de género: una mirada retrospectiva' in Birgin, Haydée and Natalia Gherardi (coordinators), *Reflexiones jurídicas desde la perspectiva de género*, Colección 'Género, Derecho y Justicia' No 7 (Mexico, Suprema Corte de Justicia de la Nación, 2010) 211–38.

due diligence standard, States have an obligation to *prevent* this type of violence and to *take measures* in order to protect women facing situations of violence.[80]

Indeed, both regional Courts have applied the *due diligence standards* in cases concerning violence against women, be it domestic violence or broader forms of societal violence such as feminicide. Such *due diligence standards* have developed since the late 1980s mainly under Inter-American human rights law as a general criterion to evaluate State responsibility. These standards express the appropriate level of care and prevention measures that the State should take in order to protect and guarantee people's human rights from non-State actors, including the duty to investigate and punish such violations by non-State actors and properly redress the victims. Such understanding was proposed since the seminal *Case of Velásquez Rodríguez v Honduras* by the IACHR, in 1988, in which the Court dealt with an enforced disappearance alleged to have been carried out by official authorities. Under the argument that a widespread practice of enforced disappearances existed in Honduras at the time, and this could be adequately proved, the Court constructed an obligation of *due diligence of the State* and concluded that there was actually enough evidence to derive international State responsibility for the violation of the right to liberty and personal security. Years before the existence both of the Inter-American and the UN treaties on the subject of enforced disappearances—actually promoted at the UN level by Latin American countries following the regional legal development on the subject—the IACHR formulated such a principle of due diligence in terms of the obligation of the State to prevent such occurrences and guarantee in a reasonable measure the enjoyment of the rights of the American Convention on Human Rights to all persons under its jurisdiction (Article 1.1). It took this principle one step further than only looking at conducts by official authorities and was clear in concluding that

> An illegal act which violates human rights and which is initially not directly imputable to a State (for example, because it is the act of a *private person* or because the person responsible *has not been identified*) can lead to international responsibility of the State, not because of the act itself, but because of the *lack of due diligence to prevent* the violation or to *respond* to it as required by the Convention.[81] (emphasis added)

[80] Apart from the two cases of *Opuz v Turkey* (ECHR) and *Cotton Field v Mexico* (IACHR), which will be analysed in this text and which reaffirm those obligations, see the detailed analysis of the *obligation of prevention* carried out in the Concurring Opinion of Judge Diego Garcia-Sayán in relation to the Judgment of the Inter-American Court of Human Rights in the *Case of González et al ('Cotton Field') v Mexico*, of 16 November 2009, as well as the study of the international obligation of due diligence presented in Hasselbacher (n 72).

[81] *Case of Velásquez Rodríguez v Honduras*, IACHR, (Ser C) No 4, 172, Judgment of 29 July 1988, para 172. See also paras 169, 173–75.

Through applying the due diligence standard to cases of violence against women, the two regional courts have duly fleshed out the structural dimensions of the problem, and adjusted State obligations to reflect the situations of risk that women encounter, endorsing thereby what his text identifies as a 'human security-sensitive approach' to the interpretation of women's and girls' human rights.

The due diligence obligation of States has also recently been reaffirmed by CEDAW in 2010 in its General Recommendation No 28, *The Core Obligations of States Parties under Article 2 of the Convention on the Elimination of All Forms of Discrimination against Women*, which provides ways for States parties to implement domestically the substantive provisions of the Convention. CEDAW specifically clarifies that Article 2 'also imposes a *due diligence obligation* on States parties to *prevent discrimination* by *private* actors. In some cases, a private actor's acts or *omission of acts* may be attributed to the State under international law'. Consequently, CEDAW emphasises that States parties are obliged to ensure that private actors do not engage in discrimination against women as defined in the Convention.[82] (emphasis added)

At the same time, reflection may also come up concerning this point when viewed under the more general existing standards of State responsibility in international law that would probably not allow for a flexible or perhaps ambitious interpretation such as CEDAW's in considering that *omissions* by private parties could amount to State responsibility.[83] The *Draft Articles on Responsibility of States for Internationally Wrongful Acts* adopted in 2001 by the International Law Commission of the UNGA (ILC) indeed indicate that there is an internationally wrongful act when a conduct consisting of an *action* or *omission* meets two conditions: that it is attributable to the State under international law; and that it constitutes a breach of an international obligation of the State (Article 2 a and b). In its characterisation of conducts that can be attributed to the State, the Draft Articles do not leave much space for evaluating private action, by including basically State organs, persons or entities exercising governmental authority, or persons or groups 'in fact acting on the *instructions* of, or under the *direction* or *control* of, [the] State in carrying out the conduct' (Articles 3–10). This formulation requiring explicit State approval

[82] UN CEDAW Committee, General Recommendation No 28, *The Core Obligations of States Parties under Article 2 of the Convention on the Elimination of All Forms of Discrimination against Women*, CEDAW/C/GC/28, 16 December 2010, para 13.

[83] See International Law Commission, *Draft Articles on Responsibility of States for Internationally Wrongful Acts*, Supplement No 10, UN General Assembly A/56/10, November 2001. On a general discussion on the content of the Draft Articles, their status within international law and their impact in legal practice, see Crawford, James, 'The ILC's Articles on Responsibility of States for Internationally Wrongful Acts: A Retrospect' (2002) 96 *American Journal of International Law* 4, 874–90.

makes it virtually impossible to construct State responsibility arising from omissions by private actors when this explicit expression is not in place, a frequent situation when dealing with VAW. A plausible alternative construction in line with the Draft Articles could be that a State is responsible under international law for its own omissions, as well as when a situation amounting to discrimination results from the action or inaction of private parties.

However, it seems that the phrasing of CEDAW's interpretation in General Recommendation No 28 is opening up the possibility of concluding State responsibility for the omission of private parties 'in some cases', which could be defined and refined further according to criteria and the recent case-law on this subject, as analysed in this chapter. Apart from the State responsibility deriving from the conduct of private parties concerning VAW, one could in fact think of other practical examples of the conditions foreseen by CEDAW: if an individual or social pattern existed of repeatedly not paying a woman/women for their domestic work in a private households (conduct of *omission*) and the State had been advised of this situation or could have become aware that this was occurring (*knew or ought to have known*) and did not take action, then this could translate into State responsibility for not having a regulatory inspection system in place[84] or for not having carried out adequate supervision with knowledge of the specific circumstances. Thus, the State would be breaching its international obligations (to allude to the second element of the ILC's definition) of *prevention* for such harm to keep on happening, and of *protection* of the already affected woman/women, as articulated more clearly by recent case-law and normative standards. This position would seem to be confirmed by the recent International Labour Organisation (ILO) Convention Concerning Decent Work for Domestic Workers, of 2011, which lays down a State duty to protect domestic workers (many of them women) from abusive practices, including those carried out by *private employers* (Articles 8 and 15), as reviewed in the following chapters.

The acknowledgment of the impact of private actors on human rights has also increased in recent years and international State responsibility has been adjudicated in case-law and debated by scholarship. Examples may also be found in State responsibility for enforced disappearances by

[84] For instance, in the field of ESC Rights closely touched by private party action, the European Committee of Social Rights was critical towards Portugal's low number of inspectors dedicated to the supervision of employers in guaranteeing implementation of the prohibition of child labour, as not taking all necessary steps to comply with its obligations under the European Social Charter; ECSR, *ICJ v Portugal*, Complaint No 1/1998. See also Langford, Malcolm, 'Judging Resource Availability' in Squires, John, Malcolm Langford and Bret Thiele (eds), *The Road to a Remedy: Current Issues in the Litigation of Economic, Social and Cultural Rights* (Australia, Australian Human Rights Centre/The University of New South Wales in collaboration with Centre on Housing Rights and Evictions, 2005) 89–110.

private (or undetermined) parties, recognised by the IACHR since the late 1980s in *Velásquez Rodríguez v Honduras*, as referred to above, and now included since 2006 as a defined treaty obligation in the UN Convention on the subject. Indeed, the International Convention for the Protection of All Persons from Enforced Disappearance moves beyond *a priori* State authorisation, instruction, direction or control, as required by the non-binding Draft Articles on State Responsibility, and foresees that a State may be responsible for enforced disappearances carried out 'by persons or groups of persons acting with the authorization, support *or acquiescence* of the State', followed by a refusal to acknowledge such disappearance (Article 2).[85] In opening the door for international responsibility by reason of State acceptance or compliance and not explicit approval, the Convention has adopted a more protective person-centred stance. At the same time, it constitutes an international legal instrument that holds an acceptable record of consensus having been adopted in 2006 and having entered into force only a few years later in 2010.[86]

In this context, let us also recall the enormous struggle to gain recognition of 'private' violence against women as a human rights and a State concern, and the protection from it as a legally binding State obligation, as has been recounted in detail by feminist authors.[87] Keeping that in mind and tackling a field in constant evolution as discussed above, the 2001 Draft Articles would need to be updated and complemented with more gendered and protective interpretations that adequately promote and ensure women's human rights, as the ones developed recently by regional and UN human rights mechanisms. The point concerning the degree and scope of State responsibility regarding private party actions and omissions as related to women is open for discussion. Indeed, the former UN Special Rapporteur on VAW, Rashida Manjoo, actually dedicated her report of 2013 to this subject, creating a path for meaningful debate for the future of human security and the human rights of women and girls. The 2013 annual report of the UN Special Rapporteur on Violence against

[85] International Convention for the Protection of All Persons from Enforced Disappearance, UNGA A/61/488, adopted on 20 December 2006 in New York and entered into force on 23 December 2010.

[86] See http://treaties.un.org/Pages/ViewDetails.aspx?src=TREATY&mtdsg_no=IV-16&chapter=4&lang=en#EndDecv.

[87] See the account given by Hilary Charlesworth and Christine Chinkin, as mentioned above, on the difficulty of opening orthodox views concerning the (valid) sources of international law on the issue of VAW, in *The Boundaries of International Law. A Feminist Analysis* (Manchester University Press, Juris Publishing, 2000) 70–79. See also a feminist critique of the previous Draft Articles of 1979–1980 in which the ILC similarly did not widen imputability or State responsibility to cover State compliance with maintaining social and legal systems that allowed for endemic violations of physical and mental integrity such as VAW, in Charlesworth, Hilary, Christine Chinkin and Shelley Wright, *Feminist Approaches to International Law* (1991) 85 *The American Journal of International Law* 4, 629.

Women, its Causes and Consequences to the UN Human Rights Council was devoted to a study on the 'State responsibility for eliminating violence against women'. This analysis was carried out as a global study of the interpretation and implementation of the due diligence obligation by States,[88] and the report arrived at far-reaching conclusions. It seemed to overturn the question mark in this debate and replace it with a final period when it boldly affirmed that, as an exception to the general rules on State responsibility, on the issue of VAW:

> a State may incur responsibility where there is a failure to exercise due diligence to prevent or respond to certain acts *or omissions of non-State actors* … For due diligence to be satisfied, the formal framework established by the State must also be *effective in practice*.[89] (emphasis added)

Subsequent developments by the CEDAW Committee suggest a confirmation of this view. General Recommendation No 28 had already addressed VAW as a form of discrimination in clarifying that 'Gender-based violence may breach specific provisions of the Convention, *regardless of whether those provisions expressly mention violence*', an illuminating realisation when thinking of structural forms of discrimination against women, such as those related to socio-economic factors as developed in this book. The CEDAW Committee further underlined that 'States parties have a *due diligence obligation* to prevent, investigate, prosecute and punish such acts of gender-based violence',[90] (emphasis added) which may then also include structural forms of institutional violence or economic harm, as also confirmed in the Maputo Protocol on Women in Africa of the ACHPR, described above. In fact, in addition to VAW as a form of discrimination, in 2015 the CEDAW Committee also recognised a broader '*structural context of discrimination and inequality*'—owing to factors such as gender stereotyping, discriminatory laws, intersecting or compounded discrimination, procedural and evidentiary requirements and practices—as an obstacle to the realisation of women's right of access to justice.[91] (emphasis added)

Following along the same lines as General Recommendation No 28, quite recently, and in the context of the current migratory and refugee crisis, the CEDAW Committee in its General Recommendation No 32, *The Gender-Related Dimensions of Refugee Status, Asylum, Nationality and Statelessness of Women*, of 2014, also noted that the experiences of women during displacement are shaped by the *action or inaction* of various actors. As such, the Committee clarified that States parties bear the primary

[88] Report of the UN Special Rapporteur on Violence against Women, its Causes and Consequences, Rashida Manjoo, UNGA, A/HRC/23/49, 14 May 2013.

[89] *Ibid*, p 1.

[90] General Recommendation No 28 (n 82) para 19.

[91] CEDAW Committee, General Recommendation No 33, *Women's Access to Justice*, CEDAW/C/GC/33, 3 August 2015, para 3.

responsibility for ensuring that asylum-seeking women, refugee women, women nationality applicants and stateless women within their territory or under their effective control or jurisdiction, *even if not situated within their territory*, are not *exposed to violations* of their rights under the Convention, including when such violations are committed by *private persons and non-State actors*. Building on its previous interpretations, the Committee also affirms that in the context of asylum, refugee status, nationality and statelessness, 'States parties also have a *due-diligence* obligation to take the legislative and other measures necessary to prevent and investigate acts of *discrimination against women* that are perpetrated by *non-State actors*, to prosecute and adequately punish perpetrators of such acts and to provide *reparations* to women who are victims of discrimination'.[92] (emphasis added) Such interpretation is interesting in human security terms on three fronts. First, the type of actor it would cover. In the context of displacement, the State responsibility to oversee private party action and inaction would extend, eg, to human smugglers. Second, the interpretation also opens the door for a deeper study of extraterritorial/transnational human rights obligations. Third, in delivering a human security-sensitive approach, it also extends the due diligence obligation to the issue of reparations, although it does not expand on how exactly that would be achieved for the case of displaced/non-citizen women covered by the Recommendation.

Similarly, in the most recent recommendation by the CEDAW Committee at the time of writing, General Recommendation No 33, *Women's Access to Justice*, of 2015, the Committee confirms its position as a general stand in relation to all women, and recommends States parties to 'Exercise *due diligence* to prevent, investigate, punish and provide reparation for *all crimes* committed against women, whether by State or non-State actors'.[93] (emphasis added) Note that the due diligence obligation now adds to VAW and discrimination against women, the element of all crimes committed against women. With these developments, the due diligence obligation is further consolidated in international human rights law as an indispensable instrument to address VAW and other forms of discrimination against women. At the same time, the incorporation of this standard to the human security concept would contribute to properly consider VAW within its scope, delimit more precisely its boundaries, and construct tools that seek to address the widespread vulnerability and human insecurity of women.

In terms of seeking redress for structural conditions of vulnerability harming women, let us recall that in addition to the individual communications mechanism provided by CEDAW's Optional Protocol, the Protocol

[92] CEDAW Committee, General Recommendation No 32, *The Gender-Related Dimensions of Refugee Status, Asylum, Nationality and Statelessness of Women*, CEDAW/C/GC/32, 14 November 2014, paras 7 and 8.

[93] General Recommendation No 33 (n 91) para 51 a).

contains in Article 8 a mechanism of inquiry procedure. Such inquiry may be initiated by the CEDAW Committee upon receipt of reliable information on *grave or systematic violations* by a State party. Where warranted and with the consent of the State party, the inquiry may include a visit to its territory. The procedure foresees that after examining the findings of such an inquiry, the CEDAW Committee shall transmit these findings to the State party concerned, together with any comments and recommendations that should be addressed by the concerned State within a six-month period. Although the process is confidential, under certain circumstances the Committee may decide to make public its findings and recommendations, as well as the State's response, if such is the case.[94] This procedure may provide advantages over individual communications for tackling situations of structural human rights violations and broader needs of societal justice. In fact, the first time the mechanism of inquiry procedure was used by the CEDAW Committee was in the process carried out in 2004 to review the situation of the abduction, rape and murders of women and girls in Ciudad Juárez, Chihuahua, in Mexico, which will be studied below in the *Cotton Field v Mexico Case* by the IACHR. After that and up to the time of writing, the Committee had carried out another two inquiry procedures, in Canada and the Philippines. The CEDAW Committee report resulting from the inquiry procedure in Mexico and published in 2005, as well as the response by the Mexican Government, are publicly available.[95]

Considering other parallel mechanisms that address structural vulnerability in VAW, I now move on to exemplify the human security-sensitive approach through the in-depth study of two paradigmatic judicial decisions of 2009, one from the IACHR and one from the ECHR, to then spell out the doctrinal implications of this evolution.

A. ECHR and Domestic Violence

The ECHR decided *Opuz v Turkey* in 2009 building on some of its previous decisions notably that of *Bevacqua and S v Bulgaria* decided in 2008. In this last case, the applicant, Valentina Nickolaeva Bevacqua, argued that Bulgarian government officials had violated her right to respect for private and family life as guaranteed by Article 8 of the European

[94] See Optional Protocol to CEDAW, adopted by the UNGA on 6 October 1999, and entered into force on 22 December 2000, Articles 8 and 9. In either case—individual communications procedure or inquiry procedure—States must be party to CEDAW and to the Protocol. However, the Protocol includes an 'opt-out clause', allowing States upon ratification or accession to declare that they do not accept the inquiry procedure. Concerning general acceptance of the instrument, though, Article 17 explicitly provides that no reservations may be entered to the terms of the Protocol.

[95] CEDAW/C/2005/OP.8/MEXICO, 27 January 2015.

Convention by failing to take the necessary measures to provide an adequate legal framework that would protect her and her young son from the violent behaviour of her former husband, a view which was upheld by the Court.[96] It is also worth mentioning the two cases of *Kontrovà v Slovakia* and *Branko Tomašić and Others v Croatia*, which together with *Bevacqua* form a triad of cases previous to *Opuz* concerning domestic violence against women and their children, met by the State's lack of due diligence.[97]

The Court had also shown a human security-sensitive approach in previous cases involving violence against women, specifically in the expression of sexual violence. To give but an example, in *MC v Bulgaria*, of 2003,[98] the ECHR reviewed not only the situation of a 14-year-old girl who was raped in Bulgaria, but placed the lack of an adequate criminal investigation on the part of the Bulgarian authorities against the background of a broader *law and practice* in the field of rape criminalisation and its relationship to VAW. Through giving weight to the subjective element of human security in the need to consider 'the manner in which rape is experienced by the victim', as well as the 'particular vulnerability of young persons', and reaffirming the need for a 'context-specific assessment' of such cases, the Court analysed a wide array of sources, from comparative law at the European level, General Recommendation 19 of the CEDAW Committee on VAW, evidence provided by NGOs (Interights), to the jurisprudence of the International Criminal Tribunal for ex-Yugoslavia.[99] (emphasis added) This coordinated and interconnected approach to the analysis of human rights violations runs hand in hand with the focus and working methodology proposed by the human security idea.

In the case under analysis of *Opuz v Turkey* involving domestic violence,[100] possibly less clear-cut than cases involving sexual violence, the applicant Nahide Opuz, had been subjected by her husband over a period of years to different forms of physical and psychological mistreatment including death threats. The death threats had also been directed

[96] ECHR, *Case of Opuz v Turkey*, App No 33401/02, 9 June 2009; ECHR, *Case of Bevacqua and S v Bulgaria*, App No 71127/01, 12 June 2008.

[97] ECHR: *Kontrovà v Slovakia*, Appl No 7510/4, Judgment of 31 May 2007; and *Branko Tomašić and Others v Croatia*, Appl No 46598/06, Judgment of 15 January 2009.

[98] ECHR, *Case of MC v Bulgaria*, App No 39272/98, 4 December 2003 (Final 4 March 2004).

[99] *Ibid*. Framing its analysis in this interrelated examination, the Court reached the conclusion that 'any *rigid approach* to the prosecution of sexual offences, such as requiring proof of physical resistance in all circumstances, risks leaving certain types of rape unpunished and thus jeopardising the *effective protection* of the individual's sexual autonomy. In accordance with contemporary standards and trends in that area, the member States' *positive obligations* under Articles 3 [right to personal integrity/freedom from torture and ill-treatment] and 8 of the Convention [right to private life] must be seen as requiring the *penalisation and effective prosecution* of any non-consensual sexual act, including in the absence of physical resistance by the victim', *ibid*, para 166; see also paras 108, 126 and 164, 162, 163, 165, 171, 177 and 183.

[100] *Opuz v Turkey* (n 96).

against her mother who has eventually shot dead by him. For years the facts had been brought to the attention of State officials, but with no significant effect on the protection of Opuz and her mother. After the death of the applicant's mother, the actions were not duly prosecuted and punished by the criminal justice system of the State.

The ECHR held the State responsible for failing to exercise due diligence to adequately protect women from domestic violence, spelling out some of the practical obligations that such protection requires. In particular, the ECHR highlighted the need for enforceable measures of protection and a legislative framework that enables criminal prosecutions of domestic violence in the public interest, rendering the withdrawal of charges by the private party irrelevant in the worst cases. More concretely, looking at events not as isolated incidents but as part of a pattern amounting to a situation of risk (in view both of the recurrent actions concerning the specific victims but also the generalised impunity around violence against women in the region where the victims lived), the Court recognised that a State's failure to exercise due diligence to protect women against domestic violence, when it '*knows or ought to have known of the situation*',[101] (emphasis added) breached its positive obligation of taking '*preventive operational measures*'.[102] (emphasis added)

Thus, although the acts of violence had been carried out by a non-State actor, the applicant's husband, the Court found a State violation of the right to life of the applicant's mother and the right to physical and moral integrity of the applicant.[103] Tellingly, the decision relied also on CEDAW, the Inter-American Convention Belém do Pará, and reports from NGOs, to examine and characterise the situation of violence against women, including domestic violence, in Turkey.[104] In fact, based on the facts of the individual case and the analysed general context of discrimination against women, the ECHR concluded that the failure to exercise due diligence amounted to gender-based discrimination, violating women's right to non-discrimination and equal protection of the law (Art 14), in this case, in relation to the right to life (Art 2) and the right to physical and moral integrity (Art 3) of the European Convention.[105] For the first time, the Court concluded on a *State* violation of the right to non-discrimination in a case of *domestic* violence.

[101] *Ibid*, see para 130. The condition for the State to *know or ought to know* of a certain risk or threat as a parameter for international legal responsibility has also been used in other decisions by human rights bodies, for example, that of *Delgado Páez v Colombia* by the UN Human Rights Committee referred to in Chapter 3.

[102] *Opuz v Turkey* (n 96), see para 148.

[103] See Articles 2 and 3—which includes the prohibition of torture—of the European Convention for the Protection of Human Rights and Fundamental Freedoms.

[104] *Opuz v Turkey* (n 96) para 185.

[105] *Ibid*, paras 200 and 201.

The ECHR confirmed this basic doctrine of State responsibility for violence against women by non-State actors in later cases, such as *ES and Others v Slovakia* of 2009; *Rantsev v Cyprus and Russia*, *A v Croatia*, and *Hajudova v Slovakia* of 2010; and *Valiuliene v Lithuania* and *Eremia and Others v the Republic of Moldova*, both of 2013.[106] Unfortunately, the '*Opuz* line' of cases was swept aside in the recent judgment of *AA and Others v Sweden*,[107] which involved VAW affecting women from Yemen seeking asylum in Sweden, possibly giving leeway to the recent trend of increasingly restrictive immigration policy in Europe which often leaves vulnerable persons without due protection.

B. IACHR and Feminicide

Turning to a different regional context, another good example of legal analysis drawing connections between the 'building-blocks' of human security and human rights is provided by the 2009 *Cotton Field v Mexico* case resolved by the Inter-American Court of Human Rights.[108] A more in-depth examination is provided given the great significance of this case not only in affirming women's right to live free from violence but also their right to adequate reparations, including in aspects of structural vulnerability, and thus the implicit links revealed between these rights and the enjoyment of human security by women.[109]

The *Cotton Field* was the first case to reach the Court relating to the abductions and killings of more than 300 women and girls by non-State actors since 1993 in Ciudad Juárez (Chihuahua, Mexico). These cases

[106] *ES and Others v Slovakia*, App No 8227/04, 15 September 2009; *Rantsev v Cyprus and Russia*, App. No 25965/04, 7 January 2010; *A v Croatia*, App No 55164/08, 14 October 2010; *Hajudova v Slovakia*, App No 2660/03, 13 November 2010; *Valiuliene v Lithuania*, App No 33234/07, 26 March 2013; and *Eremia and Others v the Republic of Moldova*, App No 3564/11, 28 May 2013.

[107] See *AA v Sweden*, App No 14499/09, 28 June 2012 (Final 28 September 2012); see the Dissenting Opinion of Judge Ann Power-Forde, who laments the retreat in this case from 'the *Opuz* line' that she considered a positive development by the Court because of its recognition of gender-based violence as a form of discrimination against women (which she possibly thought necessary as the Court was not following the same line as in *N V Sweden*, App No 23505/09, 20 July 2010—an analogous case involving the possible deportation of a woman to Afghanistan entailing risk of violence—in which Judge Power-Forde was also sitting). See also *Irene Wilson v the United Kingdom*, App No 10601/0, 23 October 2012, involving domestic violence, a case which although declared inadmissible, contains an allusion by the Court of *Opuz* as the relevant standard for the State's obligation in giving attention to and investigating cases of such type of violence.

[108] Inter-American Court of Human Rights, *Case of González et al ('Cotton Field') v Mexico*, Judgment of 16 November 2009 (Preliminary Objection, Merits, Reparations, and Costs).

[109] See Rubio Marín, Ruth and Clara Sandoval, 'Engendering the Reparations Jurisprudence of the Inter-American Court of Human Rights: The Promise of the *Cotton Field* Judgment' (2011) 33 *Human Rights Quarterly* 1062–91.

have come to be known as the 'Ciudad Juárez Feminicides' because they represent a pattern of criminality targeting women and girls from 15 to 25-years-old who were abducted, usually then subjected to sexual violence and then killed, having often been tortured and mutilated. The *Cotton Field* decision dealt specifically with the abduction, sexual violence, and killing of a young woman, Claudia Ivette González (20-years-old), and two girls, Esmeralda Herrera Monreal (15-years-old) and Laura Berenice Ramos Monárrez (17-years-old) by non-State actors in 2001, and the subsequent failure of the State to act with due diligence in the investigation, prosecution and punishment of the perpetrators and to treat the next of kin of the deceased in a dignified way. Important for the effects of this book's argument on the links of insecurity to socio-economic precariousness, is the assessment that the three young women were of 'humble origins', 'underprivileged ... workers or students'. The remains of the three victims were found in a cotton field, where another five female bodies were also discovered; hence the name of the case.[110]

The case is extremely revealing for the purposes of this book because the Court based a significant part of its reasoning on the *severe, systemic and structural* threats and conditions of vulnerability experienced by victims, factors which the idea of human security contributes to underline. In assessing the Ciudad Juárez situation, the Court was willing to rely on reports produced by international bodies and actors such as the UN CEDAW Committee and the UN Special Rapporteur on Violence Against Women, its Causes and its Consequences, the Inter-American Commission on Human Rights and even Amnesty International, as well as on those produced by the autonomous human rights body of the National Human Rights Commission (Mexico) and those issued by different local NGOs.[111]

Basing its decision on the legal parameters offered by the American Convention on Human Rights—the Pact of San José—(ACoHR, also referred to as Inter-American Convention on Human Rights) as well as parts of the Belém do Pará Convention, the Court considered that the disappearances, killings and subsequent mistreatment and neglect of family members violated several rights, including the rights to life, personal integrity and liberty, the rights of the child, as well as access to justice and judicial protection.[112] Moreover, the killings and disappearances were considered to be gender-based, and thus amounting to a violation of the right not to be subjected to discrimination.[113] This was a result of both the fact that such crimes targeted women and girls specifically, as well as the fact that they

[110] *Cotton Field v Mexico* (n 108) paras 2, 165, 221, 230 and 391. Quotes from paras 168 and 230.

[111] *Ibid*, paras 140 and subsequent paras.

[112] See Articles 4(1), 5(1), 5(2), and 7(1), as well as Article 19, Articles 8(1) and 25(1) of the American Convention on Human Rights (ACoHR); and Articles 7(b) and 7(c) of the Convention of Belém do Pará.

[113] See Article 1(1) of the ACoHR.

took place in the context of a prevalent culture of discrimination against women.[114] The response of the Mexican authorities to these crimes was indeed plagued with irregularities, stereotypes, lack of adequate investigation and impunity.[115]

In the legal analysis, the IACHR highlighted the obligations of the State derived from the ACoHR and the Convention Belém do Pará, placing due emphasis on the need to take positive measures of prevention as a means to fight against impunity.[116] Literally,

> The Tribunal reiterates that the States should not merely abstain from violating rights, but must adopt *positive measures* to be determined based on the specific needs of protection of the subject of law, either because of his or her personal situation or because of the specific circumstances in which he or she finds himself.[117] (emphasis added)

For the Court, the determining factor in triggering the duty regarding *prevention* and attention of gender-based violence as an obligation of the State, including in relation to *third parties*, is the fact that the State '*knows, or ought to know*' of the situation. In this sense the case builds along the same lines of analysis initiated in the Inter-American System with *Maria da Penha Maia Fernandes v Brazil*, the first case of gender-based violence and State responsibility dealt with by the Inter-American Commission on Human Rights (IACoHR) in 2001. The case referred to a woman beaten by her husband, shot with the intention of killing her, and while in recovery, electrocuted by him while she was bathing. The IACoHR declared the State responsibility of Brazil and issued a series of recommendations including broad remedies in relation to systematic problems of violence against women.[118]

Returning to the *Cotton Field Case*, in particular, the Court focused on two separate moments, as occasions that ought to have prompted heightened preventive obligations: firstly, the moment in which the large scale violations in the region were duly documented, making the State authorities clearly *aware of the situation of structural vulnerability* that women and

[114] *Cotton Field v Mexico* (n 108) para 144.

[115] *Ibid*, para 146.

[116] *Ibid*, para 163.

[117] *Ibid*, para 243. In particular the Court interpreted that Article 5 of the American Convention entailed the State's duty to *prevent* and investigate possible acts of torture or other cruel, inhuman or degrading treatment (para 246) and that Article 7(1) of the Convention [right to personal liberty and security] entailed the obligation of the State to *prevent* the liberty of the individual being violated by the actions of public officials and private third parties, and to investigate and punish the acts that violate the right (para 247).

[118] IACoHR, *Maria da Penha Maia Fernandes v Brazil*, Case 12,051, Report No 54/01, Annual Report, OEA/Ser.L/V.II.111 Doc 20 rev, 2000, 16 April 2001.

girls encountered.[119] Second, was the moment of the first hours after the abduction and disappearance of the woman and two girls, given that the State *knew* that they could be subjected to sexual violence and be killed, which meant that it had a particularly strict due diligence obligation to prevent this from happening.[120]

The decision contains important insights as to how the duty to investigate and the consideration of what amounts to relevant evidence may be affected by a structural situation. In particular, the Court stressed the types of measures that should be taken in order to collect evidence of sexual violence during an autopsy of a person who has been killed violently, pointing out that when systematic human rights violations are taking place, not to consider such context during an investigation could jeopardise the investigation itself.[121] It then took into account the limited physical signs on the bodies of the victims, the pattern of criminal conduct in the killings of Ciudad Juárez and the failure by the Mexican authorities to gather proper evidence applying the required protocols, to consider that although the sexual violence had not been duly proven in the case of the victims, it could nevertheless be presumed.[122]

Far from limiting itself to a gender and human security-sensitive interpretation of the substantive and procedural aspects of the merits of the case, in the *Cotton Field* decision the Inter-American Court made a praiseworthy and only timidly precedented[123] effort to carry through those sensitivities to the domain of reparations. In particular, the Court explicitly endorsed the need to make sure that reparations were gender sensitive, meaning that they bear in mind the different impact that violence has on men and on women,[124] as well as duly transformative. Citing the Court:

> [B]earing in mind the context of *structural discrimination* in which the facts of this case occurred, which was acknowledged by the State…, the *reparations* must be designed to change this situation, so that their effect is not only of restitution,

[119] In interpreting the *duty of due diligence*, the Court was guided by Article 7(c) of the Belém do Pará Convention, which orders the state 'to prevent, investigate and impose penalties for violence against women' in connection with the American Convention. The Court considered that States have an obligation to establish an integral policy of prevention capable of adequately responding to the risk factors faced by women (as in Ciudad Juárez), strengthening the institutions in charge of addressing violence against women and setting up an adequate complaint mechanism; *Cotton Field v Mexico* (n 108), para 258 and 282.

[120] *Ibid*, para 283.

[121] *Ibid*, para 366.

[122] *Ibid*, para 220.

[123] See IACHR, *Case of Miguel Castro Castro Prison v Peru*, Merits, Reparations and Costs, Judgment of 25 November 2006, Series C, No 160.

[124] *Cotton Field v Mexico* (n 108) para 451.

> but also of rectification … [R]e-establishment of the same structural context of violence and discrimination is not acceptable.[125] (emphasis added)

In other words, the Court interpreted that when violations are expressions of situations of risk that women systematically encounter, it is those situations of risk and the vulnerabilities into which they translate that must be addressed to give victims due redress in the form of guarantees of non-repetition.

It was therefore not surprising to find that, among the concrete reparations measures that the Court ordered were not only monetary compensation measures for both material and moral harm, physical and mental rehabilitation measures, and measures of symbolic recognition, but also measures aimed at modifying the structural conditions so as to ensure non-recurrence.[126] As a concrete regional expression of the principles contained in the UN Basic Principles and Guidelines on Reparations adopted just a few years before,[127] the Court recognised that impunity generated suffering and hence non-material harm to the victims of the *Cotton Field* case[128] and ordered Mexico to investigate, prosecute and punish the perpetrators of the abduction, killing and inhuman treatment of the women and girls, not only as a primary obligation under the ACoHR but also as a reparation measure and as a guarantee of non-repetition. The Court specifically indicated that sexual violence should be investigated, taking into account internationally sanctioned guidelines such as those of the Istanbul and Minnesota Protocols.[129] The Court thus adopted a decided role in granting broad, detailed and structurally-directed reparations, as opposed to limiting itself to briefly ordering monetary compensation, as the tendency in the ECHR.[130]

Other important *guarantees of non-repetition* included the creation and updating of a national database with information of all missing women and girls and their genetic information,[131] a measure that could be

[125] *Ibid*, para 450. For an analysis of this case in relation to the evolution of VAW in human rights law and the related obligations under CEDAW, see Chinkin (n 61) 455 and subsequent pages.

[126] *Cotton Field v Mexico* (n 108) paras 446–601.

[127] See *Basic Principles and Guidelines on the Right to a Remedy and Reparation for Victims of Gross Violations of International Human Rights Law and Serious Violations of International Humanitarian Law*, adopted and proclaimed by UN General Assembly Resolution 60/147, 16 December 2005.

[128] *Cotton Field v Mexico* (n 108) para 454.

[129] *Ibid*, paras 497–502.

[130] For an analysis of the role of the IACHR regarding reparations as less deferential with the State party, and a comparison between its follow-up mechanism and that of the ECHR, see Huneeus, Alexandra, 'Courts Resisting Courts: Lessons from the Inter-American Court's Struggle to Enforce Human Rights' (2011) 44 *Cornell International Law Journal* 501–28, and specifically on the *Cotton Field Case*, see 496 and 501.

[131] *Cotton Field v Mexico* (n 108) para 512.

important for the investigations of such abductions and identification of the bodies found, as well as providing training to personnel directly or indirectly involved in the prevention, investigation and prosecution of VAW. For the Court, such training should place emphasis on women's rights, on engendering *due diligence* during different judicial proceedings and on overcoming social stereotypes.[132]

Indeed, the role played by the Court in embedding the due diligence duty as an international human rights obligation has been pivotal. In looking at the development of due diligence obligations, though, one must not leave aside the role of the Inter-American Commission on Human Rights. Let us recall the crucial stand by the Commission in 2001 through the first case affirming State obligations in this respect concerning VAW in *Maria da Penha Maia Fernandes v Brazil*, reviewed above. It should be also brought to light that the Commission has jurisdiction to review complaints against the United States on the basis of the American Declaration on the Rights and Duties of Man, and to issue relevant remedies, a legal competence that has recently displayed its potential in a case of VAW. In assessing US actions in light of the American Declaration, the Commission concluded in *Jessica Lenahan (Gonzales) et al v US*, of 2011, that the State had failed to act with *due diligence* to protect Jessica Lenahan and Leslie, Katheryn and Rebecca Gonzales from *domestic violence*, which violated the State's obligation *not to discriminate* and to *provide for equal protection before the law* under Article II of the American Declaration. It also found responsibility in the fact that the State failed to undertake *reasonable measures* to *prevent the death* of Leslie, Katheryn and Rebecca Gonzales in violation of their right to life under Article I of the American Declaration, in conjunction with their right to special protection as girl-children under Article VII of the American Declaration. Finally, in a similar position to the Court's in *Cotton Field*, the Commission concluded that the State violated the right to judicial protection of Jessica Lenahan and her next-of-kin, under Article XVIII of the American Declaration.[133] (emphasis added)

[132] *Ibid*, paras 451–52. Notice however, that the most far-reaching structural remedy asked by the victims was not granted by the Court only on procedural grounds: the Inter-American Commission and the victims' representatives requested the Court to order Mexico to design and implement a coordinated and long-term public policy to guarantee that cases of VAW would be prevented and investigated, the alleged perpetrators prosecuted and punished and the victims redressed; *ibid*, para 475. Mexico argued that it already had such a policy in place, substantiating its claim with evidence of legal and policy measures taken between 2001 and 2009; *ibid*, paras 476–77. The Court abstained from ordering the measures considering that the Commission and the victims' representatives had not provided the Court with sufficient arguments to prove that the measures adopted by Mexico did not amount to such a policy; *ibid*, para 493.

[133] See IACoHR, *Jessica Lenahan (Gonzales) et al v United States*, Case 12.626, Report No 80/11, OEA/Ser.L/V/II.142, 2011, para 199.

As a corollary, it should be noted that after the *Cotton Field Case*, the Inter-American Court resolved another two cases dealing with VAW, also against Mexico, the *Valentina Rosendo Cantú Case* and the *Inés Fernández Ortega Case*, both of August 2010, in which it reaffirmed the due diligence standards upheld in *Cotton Field*.[134] Both cases involved indigenous women of the Me'phaa people who had been tortured and raped by military officials in the southeast state of Guerrero in different circumstances in 2002, at the ages of 17 and 25, respectively, in a context marked by poverty, discrimination and what the IACHR called 'institutional military violence'.[135] Both Valentina (still a child of 17 at the time of the violations) and Inés lived in conditions of poverty and did not speak Spanish. The Court arrived at analogous conclusions in both sentences. To exemplify the Court's reasoning, let us take a closer look at the case of Valentina Rosendo, in which the Court observed that in Guerrero

> [i]ndigenous women continue to suffer the consequences of a patriarchal structure that is blind to gender equity, particularly within institutions such as the Armed Forces or the police, whose members are trained to defend the nation and to combat or attack criminals, but who are not sensitive to the human rights of the community and of women.[136]

Recounting the history of structural discrimination against indigenous women, violence and abuse against them (particularly in areas of intense militarisation), lack of due diligence and access to justice, as well as re-victimisation within the judicial system,[137] apart from the individual violations suffered by Valentina Rosendo and adjudicated under the American Convention on Human Rights and the Convention Belém do Pará,[138] the Court explicitly sustained that such context of vulnerability translated into *reinforced obligations of the State*.[139] (emphasis added)

The Inter-American Court ordered that the State must continue to implement permanent training programmes and courses on diligent investigation in cases of sexual VAW, which include an ethnic and gender-based perspective.[140] The Court considered, however (to the dismay of Judge

[134] IACHR, *Inés Fernández Ortega and Others v Mexico*, (Ser C) No 215, 30 August 2010; and *Valentina Rosendo Cantú et al v Mexico*, (Ser C) No 216, 31 August 2010.

[135] See more at Center for Justice and International Law, CEJIL, www.cejil.org/es/comunicados/sentencias-de-la-corte-interamericana-a-favor-de-ines-fernandez-y-valentina-rosendo-cump#sthash.eCCV5iK7.dpufis.

[136] *Rosendo Cantú v Mexico* (n 134) para 72. See also the similar case of *Ana, Beatriz and Celia González v México*, before the Inter-American Commission on Human Rights, in its Report No 53/01, Case 11,565, México, 4 April 2001.

[137] *Rosendo Cantú v Mexico* (n 134), paras 80, 124, 169, 225.

[138] *Ibid*, paras 3–8.

[139] *Ibid*, paras 175 and 182.

[140] *Ibid*, para 17.

Rhadys Abreu Blondet),[141] that it was not appropriate, on grounds of lack of sufficient evidence or reasoning, to rule on the more transformative collective reparation measures requested by the Inter-American Commission regarding: i) the design of a policy to guarantee indigenous women's access to justice through respect for their cultural identity, ii) the design and implementation of multidisciplinary health services for women who had been victims of rape, and iii) the design of participatory programmes which would contribute to the reinsertion into the community of indigenous women who had been victims of rape.[142]

Thus, although this case has been regarded as part of the triad of progressive cases which fully address women's human rights and illustratively unfold the implementation of Belém do Pará (the others being *Inés Fernández Ortega* and *Cotton Field* itself), in terms of reparations sadly the Court failed to address the more structural and long-term challenges before it, as it neglected to draw the logical conclusions of its prior doctrine regarding gender sensitive and transformative reparations.[143]

However, national decisions specifically resulting from the *Cotton Field* judgment suggest reasons for optimism on the local effect of international developments in women's human security and human rights. As an explicit measure of implementation of the IACHR's requirement to adapt the Mexican criminal investigation procedures to the Istanbul Protocol and consequently create a national database of missing women and related genetic information as referred to above, in October 2012 the Office of the Mexico City General Attorney (*Procuraduría General de Justicia del Distrito Federal*), issued a Protocol for the Immediate Search of Missing Persons, especially Women, Girls, Boys and Adolescents, which includes the obligation of creating a System of Genetic Data through the necessary inter-institutional cooperation and incorporated the *principle of due diligence* as one of the standards guiding State obligations in this matter.[144] Still, such normative advancements are a long way from practical application to social reality[145] and the whole potential of the Inter-American cases

[141] The dissenting view is expressed however in a Concurring Opinion to the full judgment; see *Concurring Opinion of Judge Rhadys Abreu Blondet Regarding the Judgment of the Inter-American Court of Human Rights in the Case of Rosendo Cantú et al v Mexico, of August 31, 2010*, paras 5–11.

[142] *Rosendo Cantú v Mexico* (n 134), paras 232, 235, 238.

[143] In this sense, see Rubio Marín and Sandoval (n 104) 1090.

[144] Procuraduría General de Justicia del Distrito Federal, 'Acuerdo A/015/2012 del C. Procurador General De Justicia Del Distrito Federal, por el que se emite el Protocolo Para La Búsqueda Inmediata de Personas en Situación de Extravío o Ausencia, en Especial de Mujeres, Niñas, Niños y Adolescentes', *Gaceta Oficial del Distrito Federal*, 4 October 2012; preambular para 1 (*Considerando*) and points *Segundo I; Decimotercero-Decimosexto* of the Protocol, at pp 5, 7 and 12–14.

[145] See eg, Human Rights Watch, *World Report 2014*, Mexico, available at www.hrw.org/world-report/2014/country-chapters/mexico; and CNDH assessment by the

has not been fully addressed by national judicial bodies, including the Mexican Supreme Court.[146]

One can only be confident that the Inter-American jurisprudence will revisit its opportunities of granting transformative reparations in cases of VAW involving structural vulnerability. A judgment issued at the time of review of this book seems to point in this direction. In the case of *Velásquez Paiz and Others v Guatemala*, of December 2015, involving the disappearance and murder of 19-year-old Claudina Isabel Velásquez Paiz, the IACHR concluded that the Government of Guatemala failed to implement the necessary *due diligence measures* to prevent the murder of Claudina Isabel in a *recognised context of violence against women* in the country. They also found that the investigation of Claudina's murder was plagued with serious irregularities which were the result of negative gender stereotypes. Apart from the individual reparation directly deriving from the violations to Claudina and her family's rights—to conduct a serious and thorough investigation of the facts surrounding the murder of Claudina Isabel and sanction the perpetrators—the Court also formulated reparations addressing the collective dimensions of the case, and ordered the State to organise a public act to apologise to the family for the violations committed; incorporate in the national education system and at all levels a permanent programme on the need to eliminate gender discrimination and VAW; strengthen the National Institute of Forensic Sciences; implement comprehensive training programmes on international standards for public officials involved in the investigation of women's homicides; and implement a strategy or mechanism for the effective search of women that have disappeared.[147] (emphasis added)

The examination of this chapter reveals parallels between the analysed human rights case-law and the human security literature, so much so that one wonders whether this may be pure coincidence or whether human

National Commission on Human Rights regarding the situation of indigenous women, at http://pulsoslp.com.mx/2014/06/21/mas-de-8-millones-de-mujeres-indigenas-en-mexico-sufren-violencia-cndh/#sthash.ELVj50go.dpuf.

[146] See, eg, the disappointed reaction of Tlachinollan, the NGO that litigated both cases of Valentina Rosendo Cantú and Inés Fernández Ortega, considering the Supreme Court's decision of May 2015 as lacking a full systematic analysis of the standards upheld in the Inter-American cases, at www.tlachinollan.org/comunicado-concluye-scjn-sin-un-analisis-profundo-en-materia-de-genero-y-etnicidad-la-revision-de-las-sentencias-de-la-coidh-en-los-casos-de-ines-y-valentina/.

[147] See IACHR, *Velásquez Paiz y Otros v Guatemala*, (Excepciones Preliminares, Fondo, Reparaciones y Costas), 19 November 2015, paras 136 and 169 (sentence not yet available in English at the time of writing); and http://rfkcenter.org/news/news/robert-f-kennedy-human-rights-wins-landmark-case-victims-femicide-guatemala/.

rights and human security communities instead are exercising reciprocal influences on each other.[148]

In other words, what we find are doors being opened for analysis and debate on the *interpretative synergies* that may arise between the concepts of human security and human rights. In particular, and in light of the mentioned cases, it seems that the human security approach, in placing emphasis on severe threats, situations of risk and structural vulnerabilities that individuals encounter as obstacles to the enjoyment of their most fundamental rights, underscores some of the insufficiencies of the classical doctrine of individual human rights, while theoretically grounding some of the more interesting and expansive recent evolutions on human rights violations and State responsibility.

As the analysed examples demonstrate, the evolution of human rights is moving along these lines, in a parallel and possibly interconnected way with the different uses and debates surrounding human security.[149] Regardless of whether this is being done in an intended or explicit manner, the fact is that both developments are synchronised in adopting a comprehensive view of human rights and human vulnerabilities, which as this chapter suggests, may be and should be usefully taken into account to promote a more effective realisation of the human rights of women and girls.

Change may indeed be in the air. In fact, to give but an example, in recent years the UN Human Rights Council adopted a resolution entitled 'Accelerating efforts to eliminate all forms of violence against women: *ensuring due diligence in prevention*', that closely links human rights and personal security concepts; duly underscores the notion of risk and vulnerability linked to the structural and pervasive dimension of the problem; and highlights the State obligation to enhance preventive measures in every domain of women's existence, as well as to fight against discrimination and to ensure the realisation of all human rights by women and girls,

[148] Regarding the relationship between (in)security and domestic violence, it is also interesting to note that the report by the Inter-American Commission of Human Rights on *Citizen Security and Human Rights*, dedicates a chapter precisely to gender-based violence, reviewing it from the perspective of *reinforced obligations of the State* in the area of VAW pursuant to the Convention of Belém do Pará. See OEA/Ser.L/V/II, Doc. 57, 31 December 2009, Chapter IV, A, 4.

[149] A good example in this respect is the *amicus curiae* presented by Carla Ferstman, Director of Redress—one of the main NGOs involved in the issue of reparations for human rights' violations—within the case of *Cotton Field v Mexico* (n 108), see para 14, fn 21. Carla Ferstman is, at the same time, one of the editors of the book *Human Security and Non-Citizens. Law, Policy and International Affairs*, published in 2010 a few months after this case, illustrating the possibilities of the 'human rights community' in engaging in dialogue with new global concepts and creating synergies in favour of the advancement of both the human security and the human rights of women and girls.

including those of a socio-economic nature, as key factors in preventing violence against them.[150] (emphasis added)

V. SOME CONCLUSIONS: GENDERED HUMAN SECURITY AND THE RIGHT TO LIVE FREE FROM VIOLENCE

Constructing human security from a strong gender and human rights-based approach, as suggested in this chapter, allows for the highlighting and reinforcement of State obligations in identified contexts and with regards to persons in situations of structural vulnerability, such as women and girls who are often subjected to multiple forms of discrimination and violence. Indeed, being broad and person-centred, the idea of human security opens a door to push forward a more comprehensive definition of violence that does not only comprise armed means of force and threatens or harms physical integrity, but also other means of coercion and deprivation that cause various types of harm. At the same time, an engendered human security may contribute to highlight the structural inequalities and discrimination that cause general conditions of vulnerability for women and girls at the collective level, a challenge that is hard to address when looking at the individual violations of human rights as isolated events.

In this sense, it is submitted that human security thus understood also provides criteria to assess the adequacy of measures taken by the State to protect the human security of women and girls, either at an individual or community level, in cases where the State knew or should have known of severe threats or risk situations thereby complementing the due diligence standard of human rights law. It is contended that this also promotes a proactive rather than a reactive or defensive approach, as it usually occurs in the analysis of individual cases of human rights violations.

Reviewing the mutual interconnections between human security and human rights, this chapter has argued that international human rights law helps make visible the ways in which VAW threatens and affects their human rights and general well-being. The human security concept should duly consider and make use of international human rights standards on the subject. Indeed, providing human security with a gender and human rights content is one of the possible ways to help give it a more precise scope, delineate its borders and spell out the State obligations

[150] UNGA, Human Rights Council, Resolution A/HRC/RES/14/12. 30 June 2010 (adopted without a vote). See in particular, P.P.5; P.P.9 and P.P.10; and O.P.6, O.P.10, and O.P.11. See also the similar resolution of the following year, UNGA, Human Rights Council, 'Accelerating efforts to eliminate all forms of violence against women: ensuring due diligence *in protection*', A/HRC/17/11, 14 July 2011; and UNGA, 'Intensification of efforts to eliminate all forms of violence against women', 67/144, 20 December 2012, OP 11.

in concrete cases involving persons in very wide-ranging conditions of vulnerability.

Inversely, the human security concept can also contribute to a 'managed expansion' of international human rights law.[151] As the recent case-law of the European and Inter-American Courts of Human Rights has reaffirmed, there exists a *causal link* between State negligence and human rights violations of the women and girls that constitute the direct victims of such violations, but also of women and girls in the society at large. In this sense, the focus that the human security concept places on risk situations would allow us to explicitly identify contexts that present systemic threats to women and girls. The express declaration of a risk situation would act as a 'detonator', activating and reinforcing the human rights obligations of the State, as I have argued above, especially in taking preventive measures, addressing the causes of the violations of human rights that have already taken place and granting reparations that redress individuals for the harm they have suffered while seeking to also redress the generalised conditions that facilitated such violations. More systemically, a human security 'red alarm' could act as a trigger for the design and implementation of public policies of prevention and attention to conditions of structural vulnerability tackled by women and girls, encouraging the State to meet its due diligence obligation and its general obligations to respect, protect and fulfil human rights of women and girls under its jurisdiction.

Fleshing out the intersections between human security and human rights, the chapter has suggested there are *synergies* which can generate a more comprehensive understanding of the human rights of women and girls, as well as more effective guarantees of their protection from the severe threats they confront. These synergies, if used further and in a more self-conscious way, may enrich judicial and quasi-judicial interpretations on the content of human rights and State responsibility, including in the domain of reparations, and duly inspire legal analyses on the structural conditions of vulnerability faced by women and girls potentially or actually affecting their human rights.

From the cases reviewed in this chapter, it can also be concluded that the wider definition of violence against women established in international human rights law and incorporated into the human security notion, would have to be taken into account not only in judicial interpretation, but also by the State and actors engaging in the construction of security norms and policies, as an issue worthy of concern in evaluating risks, as well as in facing and reducing situations of vulnerability of persons.

[151] In this sense, see Edwards, Alice and Carla Ferstman (eds), *Human Security and Non-Citizens: Law, Policy and International Affairs* (Cambridge, Cambridge University Press, 2010) p 9.

At the same time, and closing this circle, the idea of human security itself, which emphasises an expansive and inclusive view of risks and vulnerabilities, would gain conceptual precision by looking at international human rights law and therefore framing its proposals and agenda in terms of rights and the interpretation of these rights provided by international human rights mechanisms. This may render the human security agenda one that is useful to foster not only a 'rule of law' but also a 'rule of rights' culture. In light of the grave vulnerabilities faced by women and girls, and the serious human insecurity they confront, this would offer an especially timely tool to be used as a policy framework as well as an 'orienting concept' to better identify vulnerabilities and pave the route for more creative and integral legal analyses.

In these ways, a gendered and human rights-based approach to human security may actually serve as an engine for emancipation and a real challenging force to existing asymmetries in power and resources, deep injustices and, fundamentally, serious gender inequalities, which involve, allow and provoke so many of the violations of the human rights of women and girls throughout the world today.

5

Human Security and Rights of Undocumented Migrants and Other Non-Citizens

It is true that we have risked to die.
But we were born in the wrong part of the world.
If we do not risk, we get nothing from this life.
Youseff, an undocumented migrant in Italy

How our societies treat migrants will determine whether we will succeed in building societies based on justice, democracy, dignity and *human security* for all.

Navanethem Pillay, former UN High Commissioner for Human Rights[1] (emphasis added)

I. INTRODUCTION

IT IS COMMONLY said that lawyers love taxonomies. Human mobility, though, is a complex phenomenon that at times outruns the neat categories that international law has constructed to classify moving persons and render them rights accordingly. Indeed, human mobility can take several modalities from international and internal migration to forced and voluntary migration. Let us briefly explore the main modes of migration and the empirical data on migrant persons themselves to understand the human insecurities involved in these processes and how the legal framework interacts with them.

[1] Address by Ms Navanethem Pillay, former UN High Commissioner for Human Rights (2008–2014) at the Global Forum on Migration and Development/Civil Society Days, Puerto Vallarta, México, 10 November 2008. This and the previous quote is taken from International Commission of Jurists, *Migration and International Human Rights Law*, Practitioners Guide No 6 (Geneva, ICJ, 2011) 27.

According to existing data, it was estimated that as of 2013 there were about 232 million international migrants worldwide, that is, persons living and/or working in a country other than that of their birth or citizenship,[2] a number that increased to 244 million in 2015—the highest recorded up to date—although as a share of the world population, international migration has remained fairly constant over the past decades, at around 3 percent.[3] In most estimates, refugees are counted within international migrants; the latest figures available show that the number of refugees of concern to the UN High Commissioner for Refugees (UNHCR) in 2015 stood at over 15 million persons, including the dramatic increase in refugees due to those affected by the armed conflict in Syria, and that the great majority of refugees are distributed mainly among the developing world, most of them in Sub-Saharan Africa and Asia and the Pacific.[4]

Turning to international migrants more generally, the total number has increased over the last few years from an estimated 150 million in 2000 to 214 million persons in 2010, ie, as of 2010 it was calculated that migrants would constitute the fifth most populous country in the world.[5] During the period 2000–10, the global migrant population grew twice as fast than during the previous decade, accelerating to about 4.6 million migrants annually. In the aftermath of the global economic crisis, the annual increase in global migration slowed down and fell to about 3.6 million persons since 2010, but increased again due to the massive migration from 2014 to the time of writing.[6] Relevant facts to bear in mind are that almost half of the world's international migrants are women,[7] that according to data of 2015 migration has become increasingly urbanised—directed towards the main cities of destination countries, and that one out of every six international migrants (15% of the global migrant stock) is under the age of 20

[2] UN Department of Economic and Social Affairs (UN DESA)–OECD, *World Migration in Figures*, October 2013, p 1.

[3] See International Organization for Migration (IOM), 'Global Migration Trends 2015 Factsheet', IOM-Global Migration Analysis Centre, released 19 April 2016, available at www.iom.int/news/iom-releases-global-migration-trends-2015-factsheet.

[4] See UN High Commissioner for Refugees (UNHCR), 'Refugee Figures', at www.unhcr.org/pages/49c3646c1d.html. This figure of over 15 million refugees excludes the 5.1 million registered refugees that are looked after by United Nations Relief and Works Agency for Palestine Refugees in the Near East (UNRWA), which was set up in 1949 to care for displaced Palestinians; that is, counting Palestinian refugees, the total number of refugees worldwide is over 20 million persons. On counting of refugees within international migrants, see, eg The World Bank, *Migration and Remittances: Recent Developments and Outlook*, Migration and Development Brief 26, World Bank, 2016, pp 1–2.

[5] See International Organization for Migration, World Migration Report 2011: 'Communicating Effectively About Migration', 2011, p 49.

[6] UN DESA–OECD (n 2) p 1; and IOM (n 3) pp 4–5.

[7] *Ibid.*

and almost three-quarters of the total population of migrants (177 million) are of working-age between 20 and 64 years.[8]

The number of international migrants still represents a relatively low percentage of the world's population, and it is certainly much lower than the amount of internal migrants, that is, persons voluntarily moving or forcefully displaced within national borders. Indeed, contrary to commonly held beliefs, the 2009 *Human Development Report* by the UN Development Programme (UNDP) revealed that most migrants do not cross national borders, but instead move within their own country. Indeed, the UNDP's estimate was that 740 million people were internal migrants, almost 4 times the number of international migrants, according to 2007 data.[9] (emphasis added)

Despite the much higher number of migrants within national frontiers, human movement crossing international borders has become one of the most intractable and sensitive policy issues. Indeed, the political significance of international migration exceeds by far its numeric importance.[10]

International human movement has usually been considered as a highly controversial issue—*not only in 'rich' member countries* of the Organization for Economic Cooperation and Development (OECD), but also *in States that are comparatively wealthy*. Countries like South Africa and Malaysia attract significant numbers of migrants from within their regions, and face challenges that resemble those which confront the United States or the European Union (EU). Some societies, such as India, Mexico and Thailand, *both attract migrants and send many of their citizens abroad* in search of better opportunities. 'Expatriates' too, move across the globe, between countries of the North and to countries of the South, to manage business, conduct diplomacy or do humanitarian work. Very significant

[8] IOM, World Migration Report 2015: 'Migrants and Cities: New Partnerships to Manage Mobility' (IOM, 2015), particularly Chapter III, 'Urban Migrants, Vulnerability and Resilience'. On age of international migrants, see eg, IOM, 'Migration in the World', at www.iom.sk/en/about-migration/migration-in-the-world.

[9] UNDP, *Human Development Report 2009. Overcoming barriers: Human mobility and development* (New York, UNDP, 2009), pp. 1, 21, 24, and 25. See also the relevant graph at hdr.undp.org/en/content/challenging-common-misconception-many-more-people-move-within-borders-across-them. Taking simply the case of China, as recently as 2008, approximately 132 million migrant workers had moved from the country's rural regions to urban centres in search of work, usually performing low-paid jobs. Because of their status as 'temporary residents' (as opposed to 'permanent urban residents'), they were denied basic rights and services, as studied through *human security indicators*; see also Xu, Qingwen, 'Migrant Workers in China: Rights and Security' (2010) 31 *RDD. Regional Development Dialogue: Assessing Human Security* 1, 114–29.

[10] See International Council on Human Rights Policy (ICHRP), *Irregular Migration, Migrant Smuggling and Human Rights: Towards Coherence* (Geneva, 2010) p 8; and Oberoi, Pia, 'Empowering Migrants: Human Security, Human Rights and Policy' in Edwards, Alice and Carla Ferstman (eds), *Human Security and Non-Citizens: Law, Policy and International Affairs* (Cambridge, Cambridge University Press, 2010) 227.

movements of people also occur *within the South*, in numbers that surpass the more publicised South-North migration.[11]

Indeed, as of 2013, in terms of absolute numbers we find that the United States (US) had received 45.8 million migrant persons or 20 per cent of the global total; the Russian Federation, 11 million; Germany, 9.8 million; Saudi Arabia, 9.1 million; the United Arab Emirates and the United Kingdom, 7.8 million each; France, 7.5 million; Canada, 7.3 million; and Australia and Spain, 6.5 million each.[12] However, and possibly in contrast to the popular perception, the receiving countries with the highest percentages of migrants, in terms of proportion with respect to their total population, are not predominantly in the Global North. Actually, as of 2015, countries with a high percentage of migrants include Qatar (75.5 per cent), United Arab Emirates (88.4 per cent), Kuwait (73.6 per cent), and Singapore (over 45 per cent).[13]

In the European context, for example, figures of 2015 indicate that Liechtenstein is among the countries in Europe with the highest percentage quota of foreigners in comparison with its permanent population: 63 per cent of the overall population are foreigners. Within the EU, Luxembourg also presents a high percentage with a migrant population of 44.4 per cent.[14] Regarding the whole EU, however, the number of people residing in an EU Member State with citizenship of a non-member country on 1 January 2014 was 19.6 million, representing only 3.9% of the EU-28 population.[15] This last figure contrasts with the high percentage of migrants present in non-western societies and societies of the Global South.

As of 2013, six out of every 10 international migrants under the age of 20 resided in the developing regions of the world.[16] And in fact, in 2015, South-South migration exceeded South-North migration by two percentage points, representing 37% of the total international migrant stock. 90.2 million international migrants born in developing countries resided in developing countries in 2015, compared to 82.2 million in 2013.[17]

[11] ICHRP (n 8) p vi.

[12] UN DESA–OECD (n 2) p 2.

[13] IOM, 'Global Migration Trends 2015 Factsheet' (n 3) p. 5. See also The World Bank, *Migration and Remittances: Recent Developments and Outlook*, Migration and Development Brief 26 (Washington, D.C., The World Bank, 2016).

[14] See, eg IOM, 'Migration in the World' (n 8).

[15] See, eg Eurostat, 'Migration and migrant population statistics', at http://ec.europa.eu/eurostat/statistics-explained/index.php/Migration_and_migrant_population_statistics. Note also that France is the fifth top remittance-receiving country, India being the first, followed by China, Mexico and the Philippines (measured in absolute terms in billion USD); see World Bank, *Migration and Remittances Factbook*, 2011.

[16] UN DESA–OECD (n 2) p 1.

[17] IOM, 'Global Migration Trends 2015 Factsheet' (n 3) p. 7.

Concerning the universe of international migrants, it is hard to provide an exact number of undocumented migrants because of the clandestine situation they move and live in; there are, however, estimates that indicate that between 10 and 15 per cent of the world's international migrants are in an irregular or non-legal situation.[18] Other figures would suggest this percentage is higher: one of the global estimates of irregular migration suggests that there were at least 50 million irregular migrants worldwide in 2010, a large number of whom rely on smuggling services.[19]

This chapter analyses the human rights situation of undocumented migrants, applying the lens of human security. It will do so by reviewing, in section II, the distinct categories applicable to human mobility to recapitulate the differences between undocumented migrants and other persons on the move, and non-citizens. Then it will examine the relationship of undocumented migrants with State sovereignty and national borders under the proposed human security framework. In section III, it looks at international human rights law at the universal level of UN instruments addressing (undocumented) migrants, as well as the regional legal expressions concerning them. It will spell out in section IV the various conceptual interconnections between human security and the human rights of undocumented migrant persons, bringing some migrant voices to the fore through their testimonies, and analysing the different types of risks they confront, to then present some conclusions in section V on the current challenges migration law and policy pose to the fulfilment of universal human rights of undocumented migrants and their overall human security.

II. UNDOCUMENTED MIGRANTS, OTHER NON-CITIZENS, AND HUMAN SECURITY

Many undocumented migrants are 'migrant workers', who are specifically contemplated by the international legal framework, which covers both documented and undocumented migrant workers, as well as members of their families, as will be reviewed in the following section. Despite the difficulty in knowing the number of persons to which this legal regime is pertinent, as explained above, one must bear in mind as a starting point, that in principle all human rights are applicable to migrants (workers or not, documented or not) insofar as they are persons and, as such, entitled to basic universal protections. Let us consider, though, how

[18] International Labour Office, *International Labour Migration: A Rights-Based Approach* (Geneva, ILO, 2010) 32.

[19] IOM, 'Global Migration Trends 2015 Factsheet' (n 3) p. 11.

undocumented migration unfolds in concrete scenarios and the impact of the global and regional socio-economic and political context for migrants themselves.

Regarding some of the migration-receiving regions and countries of the developed world, civil society actors addressing this field in Europe, for example, estimate that the majority of undocumented migrants entered Europe legally but after a period of time, experienced difficulties and found themselves without the relevant permit for residence or employment, and stress that 'irregularity is caused by an administrative infringement and not a criminal offence. It is often a process fuelled by exploitation, redundancy, misinformation and administrative delays'.[20]

The lack of a documented legal status often shadows these persons' identity, labour conditions, enjoyment of rights and life experiences more generally. Undocumented migrants also face an increased and disproportionate risk of poverty and social exclusion.[21] This in turn causes undocumented migrants to be placed in conditions where they are vulnerable to abuse and violations of their human rights.

Undocumented migration takes place against a background of unequal global distribution of resources, services and opportunities. Although the focus of human rights has frequently been used as a critical approach to domestic and global inequalities, the framework of human rights itself, as has been argued, with its predominant emphasis on violations affecting individuals or on violations to be legally analysed as separate or isolated events, often provides a fragmented picture of phenomena that are in fact interconnected.

Taking this limitation into account, this chapter will explore whether the concept of human security, with its more comprehensive view of widespread threats and risks, may contribute to a more integrated approach, than that of human rights itself, towards the rights of undocumented migrants. The text focuses on undocumented migrants situated in critical and at times deadly conditions at State borders, or those living in vulnerable conditions within given national borders or in transit through different territorial jurisdictions. Thus, the present chapter addresses the question of whether international human rights law can be enriched through the concept of human security, to adapt to the national, transnational and global challenges posed by migrant persons in an undocumented situation.

[20] See http://picum.org/en/our-work/undocumented-migrants/. The Platform for International Cooperation on Undocumented Migrants (PICUM) leads a 'network of concerned individuals and organizations committed to ensuring real sustainable change for undocumented migrants by informing and influencing policy makers'.

[21] See, eg, PICUM, 'Undocumented Migrants and the Europe 2020 Strategy: Making Social Inclusion a Reality for all Migrants in Europe' (PICUM, 2015).

In addition to the economic crisis, in the midst of complex threats confronted or perceived by governments, increasingly restrictive immigration measures have been adopted, as well as fear-driven responses expressed in an often racialised 'othering' of individuals and populations on the move. This has led to a process of 'securitisation' of migration by certain States and political positions, a fact that has raised concerns over the possible pernicious effects of placing security and migration in the same box.[22] In this context, it must be stressed that this chapter proposes to explore this subject not as a path to securitise human mobility, but as an approach to humanise security for migrants.

Indeed, as this text shows, the existing geographical borders also draw the lines that shape the experience of the migrant in her journey through various physical spaces and jurisdictions. In some cases, these lines can signify the difference between life and death, on the one hand, or between a life with dignity or one filled with fear, on the other, as illustrated below. In this sense, regarding the human rights of undocumented migrants, two main situations can be distinguished: 1) undocumented migrants at the border and 'deaths at the fault-line'; and 2) risks to the human rights of undocumented migrants once in the territory of the receiving State. Both types of factual situation converge into another field worthy of separate consideration through a gendered human security lens: the particular risks faced by undocumented migrant women and girls.

The relationship between human security and the human rights of undocumented migrants in these scenarios will take into account that: a) migrants frequently face violations of their human rights; b) the sole state of legal irregularity is in itself a condition of vulnerability; and c) the international legal framework for the rights of migrants, in relation to their condition of migrants as such, and especially as undocumented migrants, is not fully nor coherently developed. There are gaps in existing international human rights law which only partially covers in its

[22] See Suhrke, Astri, 'Human Security and the Protection of Refugees' in Newman, Edward and Joanne van Selm (eds), *Refugees and Forced Displacement: International Security, Human Vulnerability, and the State*, (New York, United Nations University Press, 2003) 106–07. See also Benítez Manaut, Raúl and Daniel Hernández, 'Migración y Seguridad. Nueva clave en las relaciones Estados Unidos, México, Centroamérica' in Sepúlveda, Isidro (ed), *Seguridad Humana y nuevas políticas de defensa en Iberoamérica* (Madrid, Instituto Universitario General Gutiérrez Mellado, 2007) 269–90, who review post-9/11 transformations in US. and continental security policy to now cover migration, including for example measures such as the US proposal for the construction of a wall between the US and Mexico. See as well the analysis offered in Guild, Elspeth, *Security and Migration in the 21st Century* (Cambridge, Malden, MA, Polity, 2009); and Mitsilegas, Valsamis, *The Criminalisation of Migration in Europe: Challenges for Human Rights and the Rule of Law*, (Cham, Heidelberg, Springer, 2015).

provisions the condition of 'migrant workers'. Although migrants may hold overlapping identities, in their character of *only* migrants they fall outside other legal categories (indigenous peoples, internally displaced persons, refugees or stateless persons) and therefore they suffer from a serious lack of protection.[23]

The heightened condition of vulnerability of asylum-seekers and refugees against this background has been highlighted, emphasising that 'refugees are not a security threat, but rather *the first victims of insecurity*'.[24] (emphasis added) This state of vulnerability has also been analysed academically from the perspective of a protection crisis being facilitated by the economic crisis.[25] However, less scholarly work and especially scarcer judicial attention has focused on the general issue of the risks faced by undocumented migrants or persons with a temporary undefined legal status.

As reflected upon in the Introduction at the beginning of this book, the current challenges related to the millions of persons fleeing mainly from Syria, Afghanistan and Iraq, and their attempts to reach Europe, have resulted in life-threatening situations and in many cases have led to the shattering loss of thousands of lives, increasingly in 2015.[26] Many of these migrant deaths have not been documented or accounted for. Regarding those which have, recent figures indicate that in 2015, at least 5,400 migrants lost their lives or went missing during migration; 3,770 of these fatalities—including children—occurred in the Mediterranean[27] (see **Graph 1** below). This disastrously avoidable situation provokes deep moral, legal and political questions to Europe, and more concretely, to the EU: how authentic, firm and effectual is its commitment to humanitarianism, human rights and global justice in one of its greatest moments of truth and facing one of the most appalling tragedies of our time?

[23] In this sense, see Edwards and Ferstman (n 10) 4–5.

[24] 'Leaders Celebrate Anniversaries of Conventions on Refugees and Statelessness', *The Global Herald*, By News Desk; published on Wed, 07 Dec 2011, available at http://theglobalherald.com/leaders-celebrate-anniversaries-of-conventions-on-refugees-and-statelessness/26122/.

[25] See, eg, Chetail, Vincent and Celine Bauloz, *The European Union and the Challenges of Forced Migration: From Economic Crisis to Protection Crisis?*, EU-US Immigration Systems 2011/07, Robert Schuman Centre for Advanced Studies, European University Institute, San Domenico di Fiesole (FI), 2011.

[26] See, eg, IOM, 'Missing Migrants Project, Migrant Fatalities Worldwide', updated to 17 December 2015, available at http://missingmigrants.iom.int/; statements by UN Special Representative of the Secretary General on International Migration, concerning the EU reaction to the refugee situation, April 2015, at www.un.org/en/development/desa/population/migration/partners/srsg.shtml; and 'Refugee Crisis: National and Human Security Implications', a GCSP Public Discussion, Geneva Center for Security Policy, 2 November 2015, available at www.gcsp.ch/Events/Refugee-Crisis-National-and-Human-Security-Implications.

[27] IOM (n 3) p 15.

Graph 1

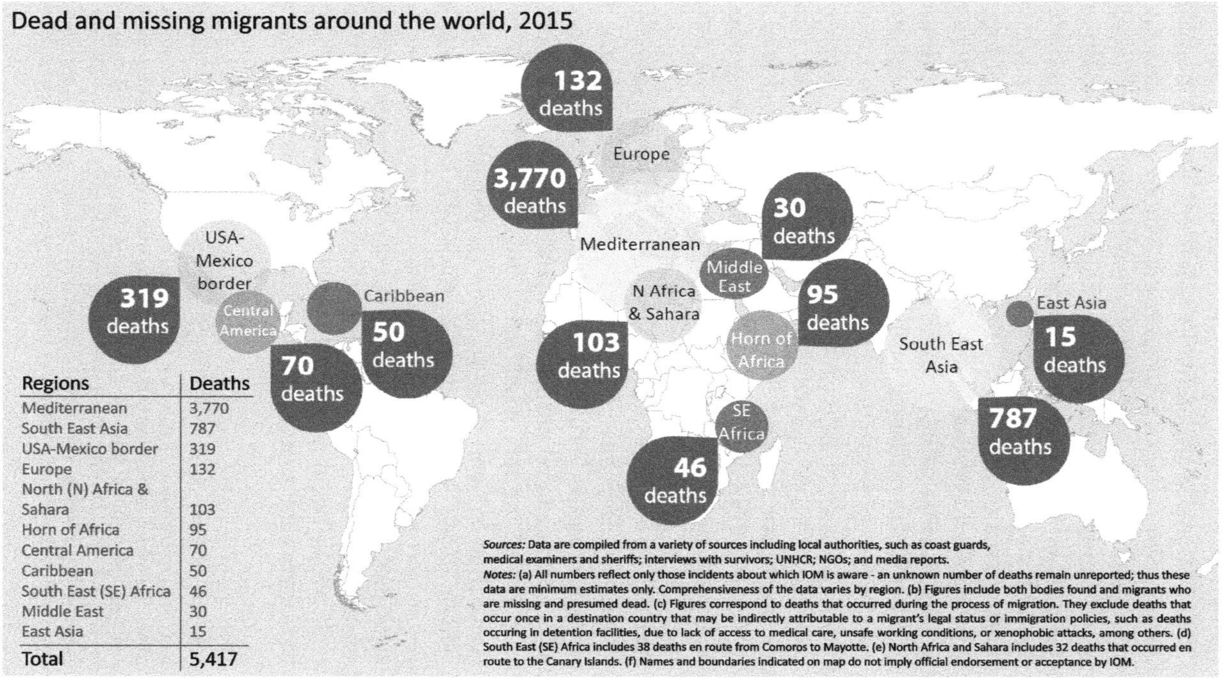

Regions	Deaths
Mediterranean	3,770
South East Asia	787
USA-Mexico border	319
Europe	132
North (N) Africa & Sahara	103
Horn of Africa	95
Central America	70
Caribbean	50
South East (SE) Africa	46
Middle East	30
East Asia	15
Total	**5,417**

Map provided by the International Organization for Migration's (IOM) Global Migration Data Analysis Centre (GMDAC). For more information, please see IOM's Missing Migrants Project—http://missingmigrants.iom.int/

To recapitulate from section I B of Chapter 2 on international refugee law, let us briefly recall that 'asylum-seekers' are the persons seeking protection—generically termed 'asylum'—from another State other than that of their nationality or habitual residence;[28] an asylum-seeker is someone who says she or he is a refugee, but whose claim has not yet been definitively evaluated. In mid-2015, there were more than 1.8 million asylum-seekers.[29] Refugees are the persons fulfilling this definition under the 1951 Convention on the Status of Refugees and its 1967 Protocol on the basis of the grounds mentioned therein, that is, as a person who is outside his or her country of nationality or habitual residence; has a well-founded fear of being persecuted because of his or her race, religion, nationality, membership of a particular social group or political opinion; and is unable or unwilling to avail him or herself of the protection of that country, or to return there, for fear of persecution. As mentioned in the Introduction to this chapter, at 2015 there were over 15 million refugees worldwide. However, concerning the process whereby an asylum-seeker may become a refugee, one must bear in mind that during mass movements of refugees (usually as a result of conflicts or generalized violence as opposed to individual persecution), there is not—and never will be—a capacity to conduct individual asylum interviews for everyone who has crossed the border. Nor is it usually necessary, since in such circumstances it is generally evident why they have fled. As a result, such groups are often declared *prima facie* refugees.[30] That being said, consider that by December 2015, the number of registered refugees from the Syrian Arab Republic in Turkey was almost 2.2 million, which grew to 2.7 million by the beginning of 2016, and that Syrians make up the vast majority of the refugee population within Turkey and Lebanon: by mid-2015, Lebanon was hosting 1.2 million Syrian refugees, Jordan 628,800, Iraq 251,300, and Egypt 131,900.[31] These figures contrast with the 1.1 million people—refugees, displaced persons and other migrants—that had made their way to the whole of the EU by the beginning of 2016 and the commitment of 2015 of the European Commission to relocate only 160,000 migrants in clear need

[28] See UNHCR, 'Asylum-Seekers', at www.unhcr.org/en-us/asylum-seekers.html. On the historical roots of asylum in State practice and the position of considering asylum as a general principle of international law, see Gil-Bazo, María Teresa, 'Asylum as a General Principle of International Law' (2015) 27 *International Journal of Refugee Law* 1, 3–28. Note that under this perspective, considering 'asylum' as a generic protection, potential refugees seeking asylum are only *one* of the possible sub-types of asylum-seekers and their condition may not necessarily result in (or legally deserve) the recognition of the status of refugee. Rather, other forms of asylum-granting are possible in addition to that of 'refugee status'.

[29] See IOM (n 3) p 8; and UNHCR, 'Asylum-Seekers', at www.unhcr.org/pages/49c3646c137.html.

[30] See UNHCR, 'Asylum-Seekers', at http://www.unhcr.org/pages/49c3646c137.html.

[31] IOM (n 3) p 8.

of protection to Member States,[32] a scheme that has not even been fully implemented yet.

As reviewed in Chapter 2, there are other expanded regional definitions of 'refugee' that allow for analogous protection. Internally displaced persons (IDPs), unlike refugees, have not crossed an international border to find sanctuary but have remained inside their home countries. Even if they have fled for similar reasons as refugees (armed conflict, generalised violence, human rights violations), IDPs legally remain under the protection of their own government—even though that government might be the cause of their flight.[33] Undocumented migrants, as will be reviewed below, become 'undocumented' or 'irregular' due to a variety of reasons. Indeed, the paths to irregularity are varied, including the case of rejected asylum-seekers. Still, a clarification is in place to flag that undocumented migrants are usually termed 'economic migrants' or 'survival migrants' given that a great number of them are on the move fleeing poverty and searching for endurance from extreme material deprivation and/or for better life opportunities, and are defined according to the criteria we will analyse below.

While it is academically, legally and politically important to keep these distinctions clear, let us not forget that frequently there are mixed migratory flows of people of different categories that are placed in the same boat—literally. In this context, the distinction between refugees and economic migrants has been signalled as legally necessary but artificial: people may be fleeing a situation based on a legally-endorsed cause for refuge (with the arbitrary character that the validation of torture and dictatorship as a basis for fleeing may have over poverty as a legitimate reason), and at the same time may wish to make the best of their situation and resettle in a place that allows for economic advancement.[34]

For the effect of this study, from the spectrum of persons in structural conditions of vulnerability related to human mobility, this chapter

[32] See, eg European Commission, 'Managing the refugee crisis: Immediate operational, budgetary and legal measures under the European Agenda on Migration', Press release, Brussels, 23 September 2015, at http://europa.eu/rapid/press-release_IP-15-5700_en.htm.

[33] See UNHCR, 'Internally Displaced People', at www.unhcr.org/pages/49c3646c146.html. See also the *World Disasters Report of 2012: Focus on Forced Migration and Displacement*, by the International Federation of Red Cross and Red Crescent Societies (IFRC) which indicates that there are 73 million forced migrants in the world, referring to 'people forced to flee their homes and communities because of many factors including conflicts, persecution, disasters and poverty'. Such figure may overlap with many of the IDPs, refugees and stateless people worldwide, but at the same time exceeds the number of people covered by such categories, indicating the need for a broader assessment of the complex phenomenon of human mobility. For a full analysis of these concerns, see Edwards and Ferstman (n 10).

[34] See the practical example of such a case in the Introduction of Takahashi, Saul (ed), *Human Rights, Human Security, and State Security: The Intersection*, (USA, Praeger Security International, 2014) Vol 1.

focuses mainly on undocumented migrants and to a certain extent on asylum-seekers. The reflections on the human insecurities regarding asylum-seekers are included throughout this chapter and the next, particularly in some of the illustrative case studies presented in section III of the following Chapter 6.

A. Who is an Undocumented Migrant?

While the international legal framework presents a definition of migrant as a worker—applicable both to documented and undocumented 'migrant workers'—it does not offer one for the 'migrant person' more generally. The lack of an international legal definition is particularly notorious regarding migrants in an irregular situation regarding their entry or residence to a given State. A notable exception is Advisory Opinion 18/03 of the Inter-American Court of Human Rights (IACHR), *Juridical Condition and Rights of Undocumented Migrants* (AO 18/03)[35] that deals with certain legal questions and principles applicable to all migrants insofar as persons (workers or not, documented or undocumented). Although this is an instrument of a non-binding nature, it has an authoritative power as a judicial opinion originating from the competent body to interpret the legal content of the human rights treaties at the Inter-American level. AO 18/03 defines 'migrant' as any person who emigrates (leaves a State in order to transfer to another and establish him/herself there) or immigrates (enters another State in order to reside there).[36]

Specifically by 'undocumented migrant', this text understands *those persons without a permit authorising them to enter, to stay or to engage in a remunerated activity in the State of destination pursuant to the law of that State and to international agreements to which it is a party*.[37] As this text evidences, they may have been unsuccessful in the asylum procedure, have overstayed their visa or have entered irregularly. The routes to becoming an undocumented migrant are complex and often the result of arbitrary policies and procedures over which the migrant has little or no control.

Some of the sources reviewed in this chapter address 'irregular' migration, a term which may also be used throughout this text under the same

[35] IACHR, *Juridical Condition and Rights of Undocumented Migrants*, Advisory Opinion OC-18/03 of 17 September 2003 requested by the United Mexican States (AO 18/03).

[36] AO 18/03, para 69, a) to e).

[37] Based on Article 5 of the International Convention on the Protection of the Rights of All Migrant Workers and Members of their Families adopted at the UN level (UN CRMW), and adapted to cover not only migrant workers but migrant persons in general; see also United Nations Committee on the Protection of the Rights of All Migrant Workers and Members of their Families (UN Committee on RMW), General Comment No 2, *The Rights of Migrant Workers in an Irregular Situation and Members of their Families*, 23 August 2013, point I.3.

meaning of 'undocumented' migration. On the other hand, in this book the use of the term 'illegal migration' or 'illegal migrants' is rejected, considering, as emphasised by Mary Robinson—former President of Ireland and UN High Commissioner for Human Rights—that 'there is no such thing as an illegal person…'[38]

Indeed, to qualify migrants as 'illegal' contributes to the criminalisation of migration, real or terminological, and feeds into the stereotyping of this sector of the population as persons who disregard the law and the social arrangements of the community they transit through or live in.[39] The categorisation of a person as illegal may violate the universal right to a legal personality that everyone is entitled to. Let us recall that Article 6 of the Universal Declaration of Human Rights (UDHR) clearly asserts that '*Everyone* has the right to recognition *everywhere* as a person before the law'. (emphasis added)

In my view, apart from these problematic aspects in terms of respect for human rights, the label 'illegal migration' also leads to confusion with actual criminal activities relating to human mobility and covered by their own international normative and regulatory framework, namely, human smuggling and human trafficking.[40] This book does not deal directly with the phenomena of human smuggling or human trafficking, and only addresses them insofar as they contribute to heightening the vulnerability faced by undocumented migrants and thus constitute human security concerns.

While the number of total undocumented migrants in the world is hard to calculate, as was mentioned above, there are some national and regional data available. For example in the US, the estimated number of irregular migrants in 2012 was of 11.4 million people, most of which are Hispanic, and many of them Mexican.[41] Against that background, civil society in the US has highlighted immigrant rights as a thermometer to test the condition of human rights in the society at large, by signalling that 'When the

[38] See Nelson Mandela Centre of Memory, 'Transcript of Mary Robinson's Nelson Mandela Annual Lecture. Freedom, Truth, Democracy: Citizenship and Common Purpose', 5 August 2012, available at www.nelsonmandela.org/news/entry/transcript-of-mary-robinsons-nelson-mandela-annual-lecture.

[39] See UN Committee on RMW, General Comment No 2 (n 37) point I.3.

[40] Such activities are covered by the Protocol to Prevent, Suppress and Punish Trafficking in Persons Especially Women and Children; and Protocol Against Smuggling by Land, Sea and Air, both supplementing the United Nations Convention against Transnational Organized Crime, 'Palermo Convention', all three instruments adopted and opened for signature, ratification and accession by UN General Assembly Resolution 55/25 of 15 November 2000. The Protocol Against Trafficking entered into force on 25 December 2003 and the Protocol Against Smuggling on 28 January 2004.

[41] See, eg, Migration Policy Institute, 'Unauthorized Immigrant Population Profiles', available at www.migrationpolicy.org/programs/us-immigration-policy-program-data-hub/unauthorized-immigrant-population-profiles.

government has the power to deny legal rights and due process to one vulnerable group, everyone's rights are at risk'.[42]

Other regional settings also have figures available. In the case of the EU, estimates suggest that in 2008 there were between 1.9 to 3.8 million persons residing irregularly in the EU, a figure which represents a decrease in the calculated number of irregular migrants residing in the EU in 2005 (3.1 to 5.3 million).[43] Other accounts may also be found in the Middle East and North Africa. To give but one example, recent studies estimate that between 2006 and 2012, at least 230,000 Ethiopians entered Yemen as irregular maritime migrants.[44]

However, for the effects of this book, I will concentrate on reviewing the human security and human rights of international undocumented migrants as a matter pertaining to the framework developed by international law and allowing for a novel examination under the human security lens.

Consequently, turning to definitions at the international level, in the realm of UN instruments, the International Convention on the Protection of the Rights of All Migrant Workers and Members of their Families (CRMW)[45] offers a definition of 'migrant worker', thus emphasising the global legal consideration of migration mainly as a situation related to labour. This Convention sets forth, in Article 2.1, that

> The term 'migrant worker' refers to a person who is to be engaged, is engaged or has been engaged in a remunerated activity in a State of which he or she is not a national.

As to the legal status of migrants, the CRMW clarifies in Article 5 that for the purposes of the Convention, migrant workers and members of their families:

> (a) Are considered as *documented or in a regular situation* if they are authorized to enter, to stay *and* to engage in a remunerated activity in the State of employment pursuant to the law of that State and to international agreements to which that State is a party;
> (b) Are considered as *non-documented or in an irregular situation* if they do not comply with the conditions provided for in subparagraph (a) of the present Article. (emphasis added)

[42] See American Civil Liberties Union (ACLU), 'ACLU's Immigrants' Rights Project', available at www.aclu.org/issues/immigrants-rights.

[43] Carrera, Sergio and Joanna Parkin, *Protecting and Delivering Fundamental Rights of Irregular Migrants at Local and Regional Levels in the European Union*, (Brussels, EU, Centre for European Policy Studies (CEPS)/European Union, 2011) 9.

[44] Danish Refugee Council (Regional Office for the Horn of Africa & Yemen)/Regional Mixed Migration Secretariat (RMMS), *Desperate Choices: Conditions, Risks & Protection Failures Affecting Ethiopian Migrants in Yemen* (European Commission/Swiss Agency for Development and Cooperation (SDC), October 2012) 8.

[45] International Convention on the Protection of the Rights of All Migrant Workers and Members of their Families (CRMW), adopted by General Assembly Resolution 45/158 of 18 December 1990 and entered into force on 1 July 2003.

What seems clear from the definition is that the reliance on the State—not any State, but the 'State of employment'—as the relevant actor to define regularity or the resulting irregularity 'by default' that the CRMW advances, is a given in this text, even within the only universal human rights instrument on the subject. There is no reference to a superior authoritative device to delimit admissible membership to the political community.[46] Notice, as well, in paragraph '(a)', the emphasised conjunctive *and* (not *or*) uniting the possibilities for being considered a documented migrant under the CRMW, that is, conditioning the character of regularity to the engagement in a remunerated activity, thus reinforcing only the labour dimension of migration.[47] Note also the requirement for an explicit and a formal authorisation ('pursuant to the law of that State') and not a *de facto* authorisation that could, under other interpretations, arise when the host State displays actions or omissions of toleration or even acknowledgment of the presence of migrants within its jurisdiction. Let us then turn to the specific modes of argumentation used to defend a legal and political regime that creates risks to the rights of persons and thus allows and constructs their exclusion from the rule of law.

B. A World without Borders? State Sovereignty and Undocumented Migrants

From the narrative described above, the picture of human rights of undocumented migrants and the risks confronting them provides a scene with many grey areas. It is also not a static image: the State's immigration and social protection measures may move from one side of the spectrum to another—from open to more restrictive, from rights' respecting to arbitrary—depending on different aims in public policy, economic constraints or electoral objectives.

In parallel to the definition of undocumented migrants provided above, it must not be overlooked that many undocumented migrants are not migrants anymore, at least not in the strict sense of the term, since they are not moving from one place of residence and/or work to another. More precisely, they are immigrants settled in the country of destination and often are fully-fledged members of the host political community and in some cases enjoy high levels of social integration. They pay taxes,

[46] See related analysis in Weissbrodt, David, *The Human Rights of Non-Citizens* (Oxford, Oxford University Press, 2008), Chapter 8 'Migrants'.

[47] In this last sense, concerning the consideration of migrant persons dominantly under an instrumental focus prioritising their utility for the functioning of the global economy, see the reflections in Dauvergne, Catherine, *Making People Illegal: What Globalization Means for Migration and Law*, Law in Context Series (Cambridge, Cambridge University Press, 2008) Chapter I.

contribute to the gross domestic product, are part of social and religious groups, and help shape their immediate collective environment and the cultural identity of their communities.

The other members of such communities, including authorities mostly at the national level, at times adopt a position of *quiet toleration* towards the presence of undocumented migrants for a series of reasons, ranging from the desire to preserve social cohesion to the convenience of having them perform certain jobs and social functions.[48] At the same time, it is local actors, including local authorities, who often work with limited resources to defend undocumented migrants' human rights and guarantee them a basic standard of living. These local actors are confronted on a daily basis with situations in which they witness that irregular legal status is an obstacle for a sizable part of the population in accessing basic social services. Professional groups, such as doctors and teachers, experience clashes between what their professional ethics tell them to do and the incriminatory discourse regarding undocumented migrants.[49]

To better assess the risks faced by migrants using a human security frame with human rights at its core, a starting point would be to analyse the dangers associated with exercising the human right to freedom of movement. Such a right has been approached by political theory, legal sociology and human rights law itself. Briefly mapping some of these points opens an introductory door for looking at migrants' human rights through a human security lens.

From the standpoint of political theory, it has been argued that in spite of their many disagreements, liberal theories of justice are committed to defending an ideal of open borders for immigration.[50] The argument has also been made in the sense that although States have a right to control their borders, the right to deport those who violate immigration laws is not absolute. Joseph Carens famously defended the view that with time, immigrants develop a moral claim to stay. Emphasising the moral importance of social membership, and drawing on principles widely recognised in liberal democracies, Carens calls for a rolling amnesty that gives unauthorised migrants a path to regularise their status once they have been settled for a significant period of time.[51] Recently, other authors have

[48] See, eg, Vonk, Gijsbert (ed), *Cross-Border Welfare State. Immigration, Social Security and Integration*, Social Europe Series (Antwerp, Intersentia, 2012) Vol 29.

[49] See http://picum.org/en/our-work/undocumented-migrants/.

[50] Political theorist Joseph H Carens famously defended this position in his 1987 article 'Aliens and Citizens: The Case for Open Borders' (1987) 49 *The Review of Politics* 2, 251–73. Although some of his arguments have changed over time, the central challenge to the legitimacy of border control from a normative standpoint is still valid. See also Pevnick, Ryan, *Immigration and the Constraints of Justice: Between Open Borders and Absolute Sovereignty* (Cambridge, New York, Cambridge University Press, 2011).

[51] Carens, Joseph, *Immigrants and the Right to Stay* (Boston, MIT Press, 2010). See also by the same autor, *The Ethics of Immigration* (New York, Oxford University Press, 2013), particularly Chapter 7 'Irregular Migrants'.

argued that the 'sovereignty book' or the 'exclusion book' are not strong enough to justify the denial of entrance to 'normal' migrants, that is, those who do not fall under other legally recognised categories, such as refugees or stateless persons. Under this position it is submitted that States are the actors who bear the burden of proof of arguing justified reasons for excluding migrants from entering their territory, and not migrants who have to present justified motives for claiming admission.[52] Apart from freedom of movement, a broader right to citizenship as members of a political community has been reviewed in the field of social analysis. For instance, recent modes of migrant activism that challenge formal understandings of membership have been explored, such as those of Latin American, especially Mexican migrants in the US, through what has been coined 'undocumented citizenship'.[53]

On the side of States, some of the concerns raised when human rights of undocumented migrants are brought forth are that this could restrict sovereign immigration powers or be interpreted as a defence of indiscriminate access into national territory. There is then a tension that must be acknowledged between the State's sovereign powers in immigration control and its obligation to ensure equality and non-discrimination in the respect and protection of human rights. As Linda Bosniak puts it, how far does sovereignty reach before it must give way to equality?[54] In this regard, Ruth Rubio Marín and Cristina María Rodríguez have argued that the human rights framework itself may offer the adequate balancing mechanisms to allow for the exercise of State faculties, while at the same time promoting a coherent standard of respect and protection of fundamental human entitlements, central to constitutional democracies—many of them receiving countries of migration. This 'human rights-sovereignty compromise' may shed light on ways of confronting the dilemma that anti-irregular immigration measures undoubtedly represent for the idea of universal personhood and human dignity.[55]

Against the background of the obligation of protection of universal human rights constructed in the post-World War II period as a State-based system, the current ambivalences we face with respect to 'the transformation of the international norm of sovereignty, already present in the early

[52] Schopel, Bas, *On the Right of Exclusion: Law, Ethics and Immigration Policy* (New York, Routledge, 2011). See also Pevnick (n 50).

[53] See McNevin, Anne, 'Undocumented Citizens? Shifting Grounds of Citizenship in Los Angeles' in Nyers, Peter and Kim Rygiel (eds), *Citizenship, Migrant Activism and the Politics of Movement* (New York, Routledge, 2012) 165–83.

[54] See Bosniak, Linda, 'Human Rights within One State. Dilemmas of Personhood in Liberal Constitutional Thought' in Dembour, Marie-Bénédicte and Tobias Kelly (eds), *Are Human Rights for Migrants? Critical Reflections on the Status of Irregular Migrants in Europe and the United States* (New York, Routledge, 2011) 201–21.

[55] See Rodríguez, Cristina María and Ruth Rubio-Marín, 'The Constitutional Status of Irregular Migrants: Testing the Boundaries of Human Rights Protection in Spain and the United States' in Dembour and Kelly (n 54) 73–98.

years of the establishment of the United Nations, pose a challenge to our contemporary world'.[56]

From the perspective of international human rights law, though, we will see throughout this chapter that as a general stand, this framework takes the power of sovereign States to decide who enters and remains in their territory as a given. However, it does at the same time reaffirm that it is not an absolute power and that it must meet a set of criteria in order to be considered legal and legitimate in terms of human rights.

And at this standpoint we encounter a certain paradox of the human rights paradigm: it is based on the will of sovereign States as a *sine qua non* requisite to build legal norms and mechanisms. But this to some extent ties its hands in making pronouncements to the validity and justification of the geographical restrictions of the State itself. Despite this, human rights law definitely does have a role to play, as it is submitted in this chapter, when international borders, entry or residence rules, become the cause of life-threatening conditions or serious injuries to human rights.[57] The rights to life, personal integrity, health, education, and access to justice, are some of the human rights most at risk in the everyday situations encountered by undocumented migrants, as portrayed in this chapter.

However, in order for human rights law to be able to meet this 'challenge of the contemporary world' in a much more effective way, it may need other notions to lean on, given the inherent limitations and blind spots that its own framework presents. Against the background of growing migration flows, a transnational phenomenon by nature that necessarily requires regional or global cooperation to be adequately approached, human security 'challenges us to revisit notions of territory and sovereignty as far as they inhibit global action'[58] in confronting such realities.

In that respect, this text will not deal at length with the question of the legitimacy of immigration control as such, but will challenge it insofar as it *severely* and *pervasively* affects or places at risk the human rights of persons and groups forming whole sectors of the population, namely undocumented migrants, and in some cases, particularly female undocumented migrants, constituting a double source of vulnerability. Because of immigration laws and practices, often increasingly restrictive and arbitrary, undocumented migrants frequently experience situations of structural

[56] On the political and legal dilemmas surrounding group membership and individual rights, and their analysis in the 1950s and 60s by Raphael Lemkin and Hannah Arendt against the background of the 1948 Genocide Convention, see Benhabib, Seyla, *Dignity in Adversity. Human Rights in Troubled Times* (Cambridge, Polity Press, 2011) 41–56, particularly 56.

[57] Such harms to the right to life have been characterised in some cases as a 'humanitarian crisis'; see the report by the ACLU and the National Human Rights Commission of Mexico, *Humanitarian Crisis: Migrant Deaths at the U.S.-Mexico Border*, 2009.

[58] Edwards, Alice, 'Human Security and the Rights of Refugees: Transcending Territorial and Disciplinary Borders' (2009) 30 *Michigan Journal of International Law* 3, 765.

vulnerability, thus meeting the threshold criteria to constitute a human security concern.

III. INTERNATIONAL HUMAN RIGHTS LAW ON MIGRANTS AND NON-CITIZENS

This section examines the UN normative framework as the central international parameter for evaluating the compatibility of State laws and policies with human rights standards. Regional positions are also studied as an important source of the development of international human rights law in this area.

Turning to UN standards, as was mentioned, the current legal framework presents gaps and shortcomings when it comes to migrants. However, important advancements have been made by UN human rights mechanisms in the last 15 years and some statements should be drawn as starting points to bear in mind and as a basis for further legal development in this arena:

1) According to international human rights law, based on the rules of *equality and non-discrimination*, in principle migrants have the same rights as any other person under the jurisdiction of the State, given that all human rights and fundamental freedoms should be universally promoted and respected by States without distinction as to race, sex, language or religion (arts 1, 3 and 55 of the UN Charter).[59] These general provisions were strengthened through the post-Cold War reaffirmation that 'all human rights are universal, indivisible and interdependent and interrelated' (Art 5 of the 1993 Vienna Declaration and Program of Action).[60] Let us also be reminded that the right to equality coupled with the right to non-discrimination, may translate into not only the negative obligation of the State to abstain from discrimination—either directly or indirectly—but also into positive obligations to take measures to achieve substantive equality, as explained in section IV A on economic, social and cultural rights (ESC Rights) in Chapter 1. In this sense, positive equality has also been distinguished from status-based non-discrimination as a separate obligation of the State.[61]

The character of universality of human rights, thus applicable to all persons, and the prohibition of discrimination, especially that which is based on race, would seem to relate directly to the situation of migrants and their

[59] Charter of the United Nations, signed on 26 June 1945 in San Francisco, USA.

[60] Vienna Declaration and Program of Action, UN General Assembly, World Conference on Human Rights, A/CONF.157/23, 12 July 1993.

[61] MacNaughton, Gillian, 'Untangling Equality and Non-Discrimination to Promote the Right to Health Care for All' (2009) 11 *Health and Human Rights: An International Journal* 2.

enjoyment of rights. The 1948 UDHR[62] went a step further than the UN Charter and specifically mentioned national origin as one of the prohibited reasons for discrimination when it set forth in Article 2 that '*Everyone* is entitled to all the rights and freedoms set forth in this Declaration, without distinction of any kind, such as race, colour, sex, language, religion, political or other opinion, *national or social origin*, property, birth or other status', thereby forbidding States from making differentiations in the recognition of rights on this basis. (emphasis added) Thus, nationality, race or ethnic origin, are explicitly prohibited as grounds for distinction. National origin differentiations have been considered 'first cousins' to those based on race; in consequence, they relate to areas where it is necessary to apply the principle of equality and equal protection.[63] This also resonates closely with the protection of the rights of undocumented migrants given that, as has been recognised recently by the EU Fundamental Rights Agency, the public reaffirmation and protection of these rights is central to the combat of racism.[64]

The UDHR is also clear in affirming in Article 6, as mentioned above, that '*Everyone* has the right to recognition *everywhere* as a person before the law'. (emphasis added) The right to legal personality seems strongly relevant for undocumented migrants when coupling it with the second part of the article which provides for this right in any place where the person might find her or himself. The situation of invisibility or in some cases, denial by the law—the condition of 'legal limbo'—often faced by undocumented migrants blatantly violates this provision.

In addition to the omnipresent right of legal personality to be respected and protected by the State of origin or nationality of the person, but also by the State where the person is physically situated, Article 7 foresees the right of equal protection of the law and non-discrimination when it asserts that '*All* are *equal before the law* and are entitled without any discrimination to *equal protection of the law*. *All* are entitled to *equal protection against any discrimination* in violation of this Declaration and against any incitement to such discrimination'. (emphasis added)

In a fascinating historical account of the UN law on migrants' human rights, Stefanie Grant leaves clear that the intention of the drafters of the UDHR was to cover *all persons*, including aliens. This seems to be

[62] Universal Declaration of Human Rights, proclaimed by the United Nations General Assembly in Paris on 10 December 1948, General Assembly Resolution 217 A (III).

[63] US Supreme Court, *Case of Trimble v Gordon*, referred to in the submission of Center for Justice and International Law (CEJIL) presented to the IACHR and quoted in the Court's *AO 18/03*, para 47, p 64.

[64] See the extensive work being done by the EU Fundamental Rights Agency on the issue of rights of irregular migrants, in particular the report *Fundamental Rights of Migrants in an Irregular Situation in the European Union*, 2011, available at http://fra.europa.eu/fraWebsite/research/publications/publications_per_year/pub-migrants-in-an-irregular-situation_en.htm.

confirmed when looking at the universalistic language employed by the UDHR in referring to 'everyone' and 'all' as the right holders of the entitlements comprised therein. She also traces back these legal developments to various moments, the most recent, and arguably the most important, being the shift in position by the UN Committee on the Elimination of Racial Discrimination (UN Committee on ERD), the treaty body in charge of legal interpretation and supervision of compliance with the International Convention on the Elimination of All Forms of Racial Discrimination (ICERD).[65] The Committee moved from its General Recommendation No 11 of 1993—which on the basis of exceptions allowed by Article 1.2 of ICERD left non-citizens generally outside the protection of the Committee[66]—to later adopt the interpretation of ICERD contained in its General Recommendation No 30, *Discrimination against Non-Citizens*, of 2004, which affirms the applicability of the Convention to acts of discrimination on the basis of citizenship or immigration status in certain circumstances, as will be analysed more in depth in point no 4 below. Grant suggests that this interpretation by the Committee was probably influenced by the Durban World Conference on Racism held a few years before in 2001, which signalled undocumented migrants and other non-citizens like asylum-seekers as some of the most targeted and affected groups by xenophobic expressions and racial discrimination. The fact is that through the position advanced by General Recommendation No 30, and defended by the referred author in light of UN history relating to migrants, a door has been opened to debate the need for more protective interpretations that legally cover undocumented migrants and shield them from unjustified differential treatment and abuse.[67]

2) A need to reaffirm the original prohibitions of discrimination of the UDHR was expressed in 1985 through the adoption by the UN of the *Declaration on the Human Rights of Individuals Who are not Nationals of the Country in which They Live*.[68] The text recognises the rights of the State to enact laws regarding nationality and citizenship. Article 2.1 makes clear that

> Nothing in this Declaration shall be interpreted as legitimizing the illegal entry into and presence in a State of any alien, nor shall any provision be interpreted as restricting the right of any State to promulgate laws and regulations

[65] International Convention on the Elimination of All Forms of Racial Discrimination (ICERD), adopted by UN General Assembly resolution 2106 (XX) of 21 December 1965 and entered into force 4 January 1969.

[66] UN Committee on the Elimination of Racial Discrimination (UN Committee on ERD), General Recommendation No 11, *Non-Citizens (Art 1), Gen Rec No 11 (General Comments)*, Contained in document A/46/18, 19 March 1993.

[67] See Grant, Stefanie, 'The Recognition of Migrants' Rights within the UN Human Rights System: The First 60 Years' in Dembour and Kelly (n 56) 25–47.

[68] *Declaration on the Human Rights of Individuals Who are not Nationals of the Country in which They Live*, adopted by UN General Assembly Resolution 40/144 of 13 December 1985.

concerning the entry of aliens and the terms and conditions of their stay or to establish differences between nationals and aliens.

However, the Declaration stresses in Article 1 that laws and regulations on nationality and citizenship 'shall not be incompatible with the international legal obligations of that State, including those in the field of human rights'. It confirms the human rights that should be accorded to all aliens, although admitting certain differentiation as to aliens legally in the territory of the host State with regards mainly to the right to property and the right of association and forming trade unions, which shall be regulated by domestic law. Several provisions of the Declaration also refer to aliens 'lawfully residing in the territory' (Articles 5.3 on freedom of movement; Article 5.4 on requirements for family reunification; notably Article 7 on right of non-expulsion except in limited circumstances and with respect to due judicial guarantees; and Article 8 on working conditions, health protection and social security).

Generally speaking, though, the standard set forth in this Declaration of 1985 was further developed in the instruments analysed below and has reached, as of this moment, a higher and more progressive level of protection.

3) The 1966 Covenants, the International Covenant on Civil and Political Rights (ICCPR), and the International Covenant on Economic, Social and Cultural Rights (ICESCR),[69] (all emphasis in subsequent quotes added) include relevant provisions for migrants. The ICCPR has been interpreted by its supervisory body, the UN Human Rights Committee (HRC), in different instances in relation to migrant persons. Although we may be far away from thinking of a world without borders, it is interesting to note that as early as 1986 the HRC clarified in paragraph 5 of its General Comment No 15 on *The Position of Aliens under ICCPR*, that

> The Covenant does not recognize the right of aliens to enter or reside in the territory of a State party … However, in certain circumstances an alien may enjoy the protection of the Covenant even in relation to entry or residence, for example, when considerations of non-discrimination, prohibition of inhuman treatment and respect for family life arise.[70]

In a right directly relevant for migrant persons usually not (fully) sharing the majority culture of the host State's population, the ICCPR, through Article 27, recognises the right of individuals belonging to minorities, in community with the other members of their group, to enjoy their own culture, to profess and practise their own religion, or to use their own

[69] Both instruments adopted and opened for signature, ratification and accession by UN General Assembly Resolution 2200A (XXI) of 16 December 1966 and entered into force on 23 March 1976.

[70] UN HRC, General Comment No 15, *The Position of Aliens under the Covenant*, CCPR General Comment No 15 (General Comments), 11 April 1986, para 5.

language. The same provision is included with regards to child members of these minorities in Article 30 of the Convention on the Rights of the Child.[71]

In interpreting Article 27, the UN Human Rights Committee adopted in 1994 an expansive interpretation and made clear in its General Comment No 23, *The Rights of Minorities (Article 27)*[72] that these rights also apply to migrant workers:

> Article 27 confers rights on persons belonging to minorities which 'exist' in a State party … it is not relevant to determine the degree of permanence that the term 'exist' connotes … Just as they need not be nationals or citizens, they need not be permanent residents. Thus, *migrant workers* or even visitors in a State party constituting such minorities are entitled not to be denied the exercise of those rights. As any other individual in the territory of the State party, they would, also for this purpose, have the general rights, for example, *to freedom of association, of assembly, and of expression.* The existence of an ethnic, religious or linguistic minority in a given State party does not depend upon a decision by that State party but requires to be established by objective criteria.

One must bear in mind, however, the fragile situation of millions of undocumented migrant workers living in States of all levels of development and income. Because of the vulnerability that legal irregularity entails, as well as the discrimination they frequently encounter, undocumented migrants often face difficulties to explicitly subscribe themselves as members of a community and enjoy their own culture freely and openly.

Under ICCPR, migrants enjoy specific guarantees of due process and review against expulsion measures, including the right to defence and right to legal representation. Article 13 of the ICCPR, though, only includes explicitly 'lawful aliens':

> An alien *lawfully* in the territory of a State Party to the present Covenant may be *expelled* therefrom only in pursuance of a decision reached in *accordance with law* and shall, except where compelling reasons of national security otherwise require, *be allowed to submit the reasons against his expulsion* and to have his case *reviewed* by, and be *represented* for the purpose before, the *competent authority* or a person or persons especially designated by the competent authority.

However, the obligation of protection towards undocumented migrants may be constructed under the more general ICCPR safeguards of the rights to non-discrimination (Article 2), liberty and security of the person (Article 9), due process of law (Article 14) and equality before the law (Article 26); understood as universal human rights as we have seen and, in

[71] UN Convention on the Rights of the Child, adopted and opened for signature, ratification and accession by General Assembly Resolution 44/25 of 20 November 1989, and entered into force on 2 September 1990, in accordance with Article 49.

[72] General Comment No 23, *The Rights of Minorities (Art 27)*, 08 April 1994, CCPR/C/21/Rev.1/Add.5, para 5.2.

terms of the Convention, applicable to *all* persons in the territory or under the jurisdiction of the State party (Article 2.1).

The UN HRC, in reviewing compliance with the ICCPR, has also pointed out that once the migrant person is inside the territory of a country, for example, retained within an administrative hostel, he or she deserves protection of the right to liberty and security of the person, especially if the individual is asking for refugee status and may be put at risk by returning to the country of origin.[73]

In 2014, the UN HRC in its General Comment No 35, *Article 9 (Liberty and Security of Person)*, clarified that the scope of the right of security of person under ICCPR did not cover *all risks* to physical or mental health. However, related to the conditions faced by undocumented migrants and asylum-seekers, the HRC did signal that 'Decisions regarding the detention of migrants must also take into account the effect of the detention on their physical or mental health', opening the door for challenging, among other State actions, prolonged detention, precarious and unsanitary conditions of migration detention centres, lack of judicial review of immigration and asylum procedures, and deprivation of liberty of children, particularly considering the extreme vulnerability and need for care of unaccompanied minors.[74]

As will be reviewed in the following chapter, especially in the section on illustrative legal cases, the fact that the European Convention for the Protection of Human Rights and Fundamental Freedoms (ECoHR) does not include a similar provision to Article 13 of the ICCPR may explain the limited jurisprudence of the European Court in protecting migrants against expulsion. Right to private and family life, in some cases coupled with the right to non-discrimination, have been argued as defence mechanisms, although they usually only cover regular migrants. Some recent interesting developments by the Court, nonetheless, can be found in the field of undocumented migrants and asylum-seekers, as will be reviewed in the present and following chapter.

Regarding the ICESCR, a specific provision allows for a tempering in the binding applicability of the Convention's 'economic rights' to non-nationals, in the case of developing countries. Article 2.3 indicates that 'Developing countries, with due regard to human rights and their national economy, may determine to what extent they would guarantee

[73] See UN HRC, *A. Australia*, Communication No 560/1993, CCPR/C/59/D/560/1993, 3 April 1997, paras 9.2 and 9.4 in relation to 7.2. See also the general evaluations by the UN Working Group on Arbitrary Detention: Deliberation No 5 concerning the situation regarding immigrants and asylum-seekers, E/CN.4/2000/4, 2000; Situation regarding immigrants and asylum seekers, E/CN.4/1999/63, 1999; and Situations regarding immigrants and asylum seekers, E/CN.4/1998/44, 1998.

[74] UN HRC, General Comment No 35, *Article 9 (Liberty and Security of person)*, CCPR/C/GC/35, 16 December 2014, paras 9 and 18.

the *economic rights* recognized in the present Covenant to *non-nationals*'. In this sense, it has been argued by some authors that if such a distinction is valid relating to non-nationals in general, then when addressing irregular migrants, more so, there is no clear legal human rights' obligation in the field of ESC Rights.[75]

Independently of the possible difficulties that the qualitative division between developed and developing countries may awaken, a counter-argument to discuss would be that the Covenant only mentions the distinction with relation to economic rights and not all the other social and cultural rights included in this instrument, which would thus remain applicable in all cases. At the same time, the logic behind this provision seems to be that the exception is allowed for developing countries in considering their particularly precarious economic resources and institutional structure, but such exemption is not applicable to developed countries, by reason of their (hypothetical) possibility to guarantee the economic rights foreseen in the Covenant. Of course, in a period like the current economic and financial crisis, developed States may also argue for holding justified reasons to deny or diminish these rights when considering undocumented migrants.[76] As was described above, though, the two general obligations of taking steps to fulfil the minimum core of all ESC Rights and of implementing the Convention observing the right of non-discrimination prevail despite economic downturns or resource constraints. In line with these general duties, as will be seen below, the European Committee on Social Rights (ECSR) and the UN Committee on RMW have concluded there are certain legal obligations in the field of ESC Rights when relating particularly to irregular migrants living in conditions of extreme poverty.

In 2014, the UN Office of the High Commissioner for Human Rights (OHCHR) published a report entitled 'The Economic, Social and Cultural Rights of Migrants in an Irregular Situation'. Explicitly using a reflection on 'human security' as the basis to point out that 'irregular migrants are disproportionately exposed to human rights violations',[77] the report seeks to challenge common assumptions about the entitlement of irregular migrants to fundamental ESC Rights, such as the right to health care, to education, to an adequate standard of living, to social security and to fair working conditions. The report also defines legal and practical barriers which prevent irregular migrants from enjoying their rights in each

[75] See Vonk, Gijsbert (n 48), for different positions on ESC Rights of undocumented migrants.

[76] In this respect, see the documentation presented concerning the backing away of Spain in 2012 and other European States from measures of social and health benefits in the case of undocumented migrants, when such schemes previously covered all persons, including persons residing irregularly in the country; available at www.picum.org.

[77] UN OHCHR, *The Economic, Social and Cultural Rights of Migrants in an Irregular Situation* (New York and Geneva, UN, 2014) 8–9.

of these areas and, in line with what was argued at the beginning of this chapter, stresses the importance of not labelling undocumented migrants as 'illegals' due to their migration status.[78]

4) There are other relevant interpretations, possibly influenced by the entry into force of the UN CRMW in 2003, which will be detailed below. They reaffirm that the rights to equality and non-discrimination should be understood to apply to migrants in relation to all human rights, and also provide criteria on how to realise these principles when exercising territorial sovereignty.

Under the ICERD, it is possible to make distinctions, exclusions, restrictions or preferences between citizens and non-citizens (Article 1.2), thus seemingly leaving non-citizens outside the protection under the definition of racial discrimination of the Convention (Article 1.1). However, while aware of this provision, the UN Committee on ERD, interpreted in General Recommendation No 30, *Discrimination against Non-Citizens*, of 2004,[79] that this distinction

> must be construed so as to avoid undermining the basic prohibition of discrimination; hence, it should not be interpreted to detract in any way from the rights and freedoms recognized and enunciated in particular in the Universal Declaration of Human Rights, the International Covenant on Economic, Social and Cultural Rights and the International Covenant on Civil and Political Rights (para 2).

With this General Recommendation, the Committee shifted from its first position expressed in General Recommendation No 11 of 1993, which had set forth that Article 1.2 of the ICERD, excepts from the definition of racial discrimination the actions by a State party which differentiate between citizens and non-citizens, and only allowing for the qualification included in Article 1.3 in the sense that among non-citizens, States parties may not discriminate against any particular nationality.[80]

In its most recent General Recommendation No 30 on the subject, though, the Committee demonstrates a less strict approach, more adapted to the exigencies posed by the twenty-first century reality of the progressively serious violations experienced by migrants and non-citizens. In its 2004 interpretation of a treaty adopted in 1965, the Committee specified that

[78] *Ibid*, 4–5.

[79] UN Committee on ERD, General Recommendation No 30, *Discrimination Against Non-Citizens*, (General Comments), available at Compilation of General Comments and General Recommendations adopted by Human Rights Treaty Bodies. Addendum, HRI/GEN/1/Rev.7/Add.1, 4 May 2005.

[80] General Recommendation No 11 (n 66) para 1.1. On a defence of the shift by the Committee's General Recommendation No 30 in light of the UN history relating to migrants, see also Grant (n 67).

its General Recommendation No 30 replaces General Recommendation No 11, and makes clear in paragraphs 3 and 4, that:

> although … some of these [human] rights, such as the right to participate in elections, to vote and to stand for election, may be confined to citizens, *human rights are, in principle, to be enjoyed by all persons.* States parties are under an obligation to guarantee *equality between citizens and non-citizens* in the enjoyment of these rights to the extent recognized under international law.
>
> Under the Convention, differential treatment based on *citizenship or immigration status* will constitute discrimination if the criteria for such differentiation, judged in the light of the objectives and purposes of the Convention, are *not applied pursuant to a legitimate aim, and are not proportional to the achievement of this aim.* (emphasis added)

It is true that under a literal interpretation of Article 1.2 of the ICERD, one could deem that it is not the most orthodox exercise of the Committee's faculties to determine racial discrimination in cases involving citizenship or immigration status alone, as it is not expressly competent to do so under the treaty. Indeed, in a partly dissenting Individual Opinion in a case before the sister treaty body of the UN HRC, Committee Members Nigel Rodley and Martin Scheinin, in the context of explaining the role of the HRC as regards the ICCPR, noted in 2002 that

> in its practice the Committee has not addressed distinctions based on *citizenship* from the perspective of race colour, ethnicity or similar notions but as a *self-standing issue* under article 26.2 [of ICCPR]. In our view distinctions based on citizenship fall under the notion of 'other status' in article 26 and *not* under any of the grounds of discrimination covered by *article 1, paragraph 1, of the CERD.*[81] (emphasis added)

At the same time, it is also true that the clear intention of the Committee on the ERD is to carry out a harmonic and integrated interpretation of the general human rights obligations of equality and non-discrimination contained in the other legal instruments it refers to and that embody principles that inspired the adoption of the ICERD in the first place. While upholding the normative spirit of the prohibitions of discrimination of the Convention and the permitted exceptions of Article 1.2, the Committee's interpretation does not create a blank check for *any* distinction between citizens and non-citizens/persons with a regular or irregular immigration status, to be considered as measures that would fall under the ICERD's definition of racial discrimination, but in fact only those *not applied pursuant to a legitimate aim and that are not proportional to the achievement of this*

[81] Individual Opinion by Committee Members Sir Nigel Rodley and Mr Martin Scheinin (partly dissenting), in UN Human Rights Committee, *Karakurt v Austria*, Communication No 965/2000, UN Doc CCPR/C/74/D/965/2000, 4 Apr 2002.

aim, in line with general criteria in the field of non-discrimination law, as reviewed above in this text. The Committee was then cautious enough to phrase the State's obligations in terms of a non-discrimination duty, not indicating at this point that such obligation would translate into the need to adopt positive measures for attaining full substantial equality between these different social groups.

Therefore, even when admittedly the Committee does exceed the literal sense of Article 1.2 in its interpretation, the overall importance of General Recommendation No 30 as a tool for an improved human rights defence may not be disregarded, especially in light of the fact that the current legal framework presents few normative mechanisms that allow for such protection and evidence demonstrates the increasing and critical human rights violations and human insecurity suffered by undocumented migrants and other non-citizens in recent years, as accounted for throughout this chapter. Indeed, this much needed advancement in the legal interpretation of the ICERD is especially relevant for migrants, given the often racialised discourse, policies and laws affecting them, and touches upon the intersectional or cumulative forms of discrimination they often face, more so in the case of undocumented female migrants, who confront heightened vulnerabilities on account of their gender, as will be studied in the following chapter.[82] The potential of this interaction between the general human rights of equality and non-discrimination and the recognition of the severe human insecurity undocumented migrants suffer, triggered by General Recommendation No 30, in turn uncovers one of the *interpretative synergies* relevant for legal analysis as proposed in Chapter 6 of this book.

The practical dimension of the Committee's interpretation is also revealed in recent facts: in 2008 the Committee concluded that the Dominican Republic's laws, policies and practices on nationality and birth registration were discriminatory against Haitians and Dominicans of Haitian origin.[83] Reaffirming not only the more obvious and abstract obligation of non-discrimination based on racial, ethnic or national origin, the Committee also drew the links between the right to nationality and equal access to *citizenship*, and determined that the Dominican Republic was in violation of the ICERD for not making this right accessible to

[82] On intersectional discrimination, see Crenshaw, Kimberley, 'Mapping the Margins: Intersectionality, Identity Politics, and Violence Against Women of Color' (1991) 43 *Stanford Law Review*. On the differences between sex as biological and gender as socially built, as well as the construction of gender roles in cultural context, see Charlesworth, Hilary and Christine Chinkin, *The Boundaries of International Law. A Feminist Analysis* (UK, Juris Publishing, Manchester University Press, 2000) 3–4.

[83] UN Committee on ERD, *Concluding Observations of the Committee on the Elimination of Racial Discrimination: Dominican Republic*, UN Doc CERD/C/DOM/CO/12, 16 May 2008; see para 14.

Haitians under its jurisdiction, many of them undocumented migrants, as well as harming the whole spectrum of their human rights from the civil and political arena to their ESC Rights. Such considerations pick up on the Committee's indication in General Recommendation No 30 that States parties '[t]ake into consideration that in some cases *denial of citizenship* for long-term or permanent residents could result in creating disadvantages for them in access to employment and social benefits, in violation of … anti-discrimination principles'.[84] The Committee's arguments also build upon the case of the *Yean and Bosico Girls v the Dominican Republic* by the IACHR, of 2005, dealing precisely with the daughters of undocumented migrants, and reviewed in different parts of this text and also commented upon by other UN treaty bodies, namely, the UN Committee on ESC Rights, as explored in Chapter 1 above and in the illustrative judicial cases at the end of the following chapter.

5) Another development—possibly triggered by the entry into force in 2003 of the UN Convention on the Protection of the Rights of All Migrant Workers and Members of their Families—may be found in General Comment No 6 of the Committee on the Rights of the Child, *Treatment of Unaccompanied and Separated Children Outside their Country of Origin*, of 2005,[85] (emphasis added) which placed special attention on the rights of migrant children and also provides criteria for the better understanding of the principle of non-discrimination. The Committee has indicated that State obligations under the Convention apply to each child within the State's territory and to all children subject to its jurisdiction. Moreover, it reaffirmed that State obligations under the Convention apply within the borders of a State, including with respect to *those children who come under the State's jurisdiction while attempting to enter the country's territory*. Therefore, it noted that the enjoyment of rights stipulated in the Convention is not limited to children who are citizens of a State party and must therefore, if not explicitly stated otherwise in the Convention, also be available to all children—including asylum-seeking, refugee and *migrant children*—irrespective of their nationality, *immigration status* or statelessness.

Issued only one year after General Recommendation No 30 of the Committee on ERD, the UN Committee on the Rights of the Child similarly interpreted that

> The principle of non-discrimination, in all its facets, applies in respect to all dealings with separated and unaccompanied children. In particular, it prohibits any discrimination on the basis of the *status of a child* as being unaccompanied or

[84] General Recommendation No 30 (n 79) paras 14–15.

[85] UN Committee on the Rights of the Child, General Comment No 6, *Treatment of Unaccompanied and Separated Children Outside their Country of Origin*, CRC/GC/2005/6, 1 September 2005, paras 12 and 18. Subsequent literal quote and references from para 18.

> separated, or as being a refugee, asylum-seeker or *migrant*. This principle, when properly understood, does not prevent, but may indeed call for, differentiation on the basis of *different protection needs such as those deriving from age and/or gender*. Measures should also be taken to address possible misperceptions and stigmatization of unaccompanied or separated children within the society. (emphasis added)

The Committee also clarified that policing or other measures concerning unaccompanied or separated children relating to public order are only permissible where such measures are based on the law; entail individual rather than collective assessment; comply with the principle of proportionality; and represent the least intrusive option. It reaffirmed that in order not to violate the prohibition on non-discrimination, such measures can, therefore, never be applied on a group or collective basis, an indication that has unfortunately found violations, for instance, in actions by the French Government in 2011 concerning collective expulsions of Roma people.

In the same vein as the position involving the rights of the child, the Committee on ERD had specified that under the Convention, States parties must 'Ensure that public educational institutions are open to non-citizens and *children of undocumented immigrants* residing in the territory of a State party'.[86] (emphasis added)

6) Similarly, the UN Committee monitoring compliance of the UN Convention on the Elimination of All Forms of Discrimination Against Women (CEDAW Committee) in its General Recommendation No 26 on *Women Migrant Workers*, of 2008, highlighted the possibility of certain categories of women migrant workers being at risk of abuse, one of such categories being undocumented women migrant workers. The Recommendation aimed 'to elaborate the circumstances that contribute to the specific vulnerability of many women migrant workers and their experiences of *sex- and gender-based discrimination* as a cause and consequence of the violations of their human rights'.[87] (emphasis added and equally in all subsequent quotes) The CEDAW Committee emphasised that

> While States are entitled to control their borders and regulate migration, they must do so in full compliance with their obligations as parties to the human rights treaties they have ratified or acceded to. That includes the promotion of *safe migration procedures* and the obligation to respect, protect and fulfil the human rights of women throughout the migration cycle. Those obligations must be undertaken in recognition of the social and economic contributions of women migrant workers to their own countries and countries of destination, including through *caregiving and domestic work*.[88]

[86] General Recommendation No 30 (n 79) para 30.

[87] UN CEDAW Committee, General Recommendation No 26, *Women Migrant Workers*, CEDAW/C/2009/WP.1/R, adopted on 5 December 2008, para 2.

[88] *Ibid*, para 3.

And in a clear echo of the *freedom from fear* and *freedom from want* aspiration of the human security idea, the CEDAW Committee underlined how

> *Undocumented women migrant workers* are particularly vulnerable to exploitation and abuse because of their irregular immigration status, which exacerbates their exclusion and the *risk of exploitation*. They may be exploited as forced labour, and their access to minimum labour rights may be limited by *fear of denouncement*. They may also face harassment by the police. If they are apprehended, they are usually prosecuted for violations of immigration laws and placed in detention centres, where they are *vulnerable to sexual abuse*, and then deported.[89]

In its General Recommendation No 28, *The Core Obligations of States Parties under Article 2 of the Convention on the Elimination of All Forms of Discrimination against Women*, of 2010, the CEDAW Committee also recognised that although States primarily exercise territorial jurisdiction,

> [t]he obligations of States parties apply, however, without discrimination both to citizens and non-citizens, including refugees, asylum-seekers, migrant workers and stateless persons, within their territory or effective control, even if not situated within the territory. States parties are responsible for all their actions affecting human rights, regardless of whether the affected persons are in their territory.[90]

The reaffirmation of such an obligation would also seem to be echoed by the case of *Hirsi v Italy*, of 2012, in which the European Court of Human Rights (ECHR) concluded that Italy's 'push-back' policy of migrants at sea trying to arrive in the country, was in violation of human rights law given that the State had to ensure the right of every migrant for her or his situation to be individually considered, and that this obligation extended to all spaces over which a State party exercises effective control, which may include vessels on the high seas.[91]

In the same General Recommendation No 28, the CEDAW Committee also highlighted the State's obligation of designing and implementing a *general policy* on elimination of discrimination against women, under Article 2 of the Convention, and specifically addressed migrant and refugee women in spelling out that

> The policy must identify women within the jurisdiction of the State party (*including non-citizen, migrant, refugee, asylum-seeking and stateless women*) as the rights-bearers, with particular emphasis on the groups of women who are most marginalized and who may suffer from various forms of *intersectional discrimination*.[92]

[89] *Ibid*, para 22.

[90] UN CEDAW Committee, General Recommendation No 28, *The Core Obligations of States Parties under Article 2 of the Convention on the Elimination of All Forms of Discrimination against Women*, CEDAW/C/GC/28, 16 December 2010, para 12.

[91] ECHR, *Hirsi Jamaa and Others v Italy*, Appl No 27765/09, 23 February 2012.

[92] General Recommendation No 28 (n 90) para 26.

Converging with the concerns of the two thematic cores of this book, the CEDAW Committee dedicated in 2014 its General Recommendation No 32 to the *Gender-Related Dimensions of Refugee Status, Asylum, Nationality and Statelessness of Women*. The Recommendation emphasised that women and girls can be especially vulnerable to abuse during mass displacement situations—as experienced presently with the largest numbers of asylum-seekers since World War II. As recounted in the previous chapter, the Committee reaffirmed the State's *due diligence obligation* regarding these categories of displaced women covered by the Recommendation, opening the door for determining State responsibility for actions and *omissions* of *private parties*, for instance, in this context, human smugglers.[93]

This recent reflection of the human security concerns in certain expressions of human rights law pertaining to migrants, more particularly in those directed to women and children, tells us of the potential value of utilising the concept for advancing broader and more protective interpretations of the scope of human rights and the State's obligations in relation to migrant persons.

Let us now turn to the human rights instruments specifically dedicated to universal human rights in the context of mobility and how such rights should be applied to persons living or working in countries other than that of their birth, nationality or citizenship.

A. CRMW and UN Special Rapporteur on the Human Rights of Migrants

Of the whole UN normative human rights structure, one of the nine core human rights treaties refers to migrants, specifically to migrant workers and their families, namely, the CRMW, adopted in 1990 and entered into force in 2003.[94]

As recounted at the beginning of the chapter, the CRMW considers within its scope both documented and undocumented migrant workers, contemplating different types of workers: 'frontier worker', 'seasonal worker', 'seafarer', 'worker on an offshore installation', 'itinerant worker', 'project-tied worker', 'specified-employment worker' and 'self-employed worker'.

[93] CEDAW Committee, General Recommendation No 32, *Gender-Related Dimensions of Refugee Status, Asylum, Nationality and Statelessness of Women*, CEDAW/C/GC/32, 14 November 2014, paras 3, 7 and 8.

[94] International Convention on the Protection of the Rights of All Migrant Workers and Members of Their Families (CRMW), adopted by General Assembly Resolution 45/158 of 18 December 1990, entered into force on 1 July 2003. All subsequent references to the CRMW refer to this instrument.

Regarding the monitoring of the CRMW in relation to both documented and undocumented migrant workers as defined above, the UN Committee on the Protection of the Rights of All Migrant Workers and Members of their Families (UN Committee on RMW) was established in Article 72.1 of the CRMW as the body of independent experts in charge of supervising the application of the Convention.

As can be observed, this instrument refers to the rights of *all* migrant workers, that is, documented and undocumented (Part III), on the general basis of the principle of non-discrimination with respect to rights (Part II). The Convention does, however, distinguish a set of additional rights to be recognised for documented migrant workers (Part IV). The UN Convention was drafted based on two prior instruments, the International Labour Organization (ILO) Migration for Employment Convention (Revised) of 1949 (No 97) and the ILO Migrant Workers (Supplementary Provisions) Convention of 1975 (No 143), and the three instruments together constitute what has been called the *international charter on migration*, providing a broad normative framework covering the treatment and rights of migrants, as well as inter-State cooperation on regulating migration.[95]

The CRMW does not create new rights for migrants, but rather in a similar way to what has been done through human rights treaties referring to other groups (for example, the UN Convention on the Rights of Persons with Disabilities), it specifies how such rights should be understood and applied to migrant workers and members of their families. Indeed, it is the only human rights treaty with universal aspiration that places existing human rights standards in the specific context of migration.

Interesting for the transnational phenomena this instrument deals with, the CRMW provides for a mechanism of inter-State complaints for the effect that a State party claims that another party is not fulfilling its obligations. It will become operative when 10 States parties have made the necessary declaration under Article 76.2 (at the time of writing in 2015, only Guatemala and El Salvador had accepted such competence).[96] In any case, until the time of writing this text, according to information of the UN OHCHR, inter-State complaints had never been applied in the history of human rights treaty bodies' procedures.[97]

[95] Taran, Patrick A, 'Clashing Worlds: Imperative for a Rights-Based approach to labour migration in the age of globalization' in *Mondialisation, migration et droits de l'homme: le droit international en question/Globalization, Migration and Human Rights: International Law under Review*, under the supervision of Vincent Chetail (Collection of the Geneva Academy of International Humanitarian Law and Human Rights, Bruylant, 2007) Vol II, 421. See also the accompanying Recommendations Nos 86 and 151 to the ILO Conventions.

[96] See http://treaties.un.org/Pages/ViewDetails.aspx?src=TREATY&mtdsg_no=IV-13&chapter=4&lang=en#2.

[97] See www.ohchr.org/EN/HRBodies/TBPetitions/Pages/HRTBPetitions.aspx#interstate.

Similarly to other human rights treaty bodies, such as the ICCPR, the CRMW also contains in Article 77 a provision allowing for individual communications to be considered by the CRMW upon express consent of the State party of such competence of the Committee. In the same way as the inter-State complaints mechanism, these provisions will become operative when 10 States parties have made the necessary declaration under Article 77.8. At the time of writing, four States, Guatemala, El Salvador, Mexico and Uruguay, had accepted the competence of the Committee in this respect, although Turkey, upon its ratification in 2004, made a declaration indicating that it would accept the Committee's competence under both Articles 76 and 77 'at a later time'.[98]

Following the general principles of equality and non-discrimination, the CRMW sets forth in Article 7 an *umbrella obligation* of non-discrimination with regards to all human rights:

> States Parties undertake, in accordance with the international instruments concerning human rights, to respect and to ensure to all migrant workers and members of their families within their territory or subject to their jurisdiction the rights provided for in the present Convention without distinction of any kind such as to sex, race, colour, language, religion or conviction, political or other opinion, national, ethnic or social origin, nationality, age, economic position, property, marital status, birth or other status.

This confirms the position sustained by UN bodies in the previous years to the CRMW, in reaffirming the duty to respect the human rights of all migrant workers, regardless of their legal status. Apart from a strict non-discrimination obligation, the UN Committee on the RMW also affirmed the need for reinforced protective measures when it considered that in cases of extreme poverty and vulnerability, States parties are under a duty to provide emergency social assistance to irregular migrant workers and members of their families for as long as they might require it.[99]

At the same time, it goes without saying that migrant persons hold the general duties that any other citizen does, a general obligation that notwithstanding was specified in the CRMW itself. Article 34 of the Convention states that nothing in Part III of the Convention shall have the effect of relieving migrant workers and members of their families from either the obligation to comply with the laws and regulations of the State of employment and any State of transit or the obligation to respect the cultural identity of the inhabitants of those States. The obligation to comply with the laws and regulations of the State of employment or any State of transit

[98] See Turkey's Declaration E) regarding Articles 76 and 77 upon its ratification of the CRMW on 27 September, 2004, available at http://treaties.un.org/Pages/ViewDetails.aspx?src=TREATY&mtdsg_no=IV-13&chapter=4&lang=en#2.

[99] See the Committee's concluding observations, Argentina, 2011 (CRMW/C/ARG/CO/1), para 30.

comprises a duty to refrain from any hostile act directed against national security, public order or the rights and freedom of others.

Of course, multicultural, multi-ethnic and multi-religious States present different challenges of their own, independently of, and in some cases including, undocumented migrants. These questions are, however, to be answered within the debate of human rights and democracy, more than within the discussion on multiculturalism, similarity and diversity, inclusion and exclusion of the political community. To place the reflection on migration only on this last framework, risks the often easy passage from what Javier de Lucas calls the 'society of indifference' to the 'society of disdain' (*sociedad del menosprecio*) and in the more extreme cases to the 'society of hatred'.[100] Indeed, the indifference of the law towards undocumented migrants or their specific legal exclusion from rights, situates them in a 'legal limbo' as portrayed in this book, and carries with it a deeper danger. The normalisation in everyday life of such legal exclusion leads to social, economic and political segregation of undocumented migrants endorsed or facilitated by the law. It allows for the construction of a group of 'second-class' persons, also termed as an 'underclass'.[101] This inflated emphasis on the 'otherness' of migrants and especially of their 'otherness in rights' may ultimately channel racial or xenophobic discourse, conducts and policies towards irregular migrants, as duly highlighted by human rights bodies.

To adequately situate the reflection of undocumented migration in the broader field of human rights, let us recall the role of human rights treaties and other rights-based approaches to migration. As the embodiment of the UN human rights standard for migrants and one of the nine core universal human rights instruments, the CRMW is the strongest existing legal parameter to assess the norms and policies adopted by States on the issue of migration. As of the time of writing, the CRMW has been ratified by 48 States, the most recent one being Madagascar on 13 May 2015. The CRMW is of course open for further accessions, which could signal movement in a positive direction, if we are to take into account that before 1998 only nine States had ratified the Convention, while from 1998 to 2004 another 18 did,[102] and in the last few years the number of State

[100] De Lucas, Javier (ed), *Inmigración e integración en la UE: dos retos para el s. XXI* (Eurobask, 2012) 11–13.

[101] On the creation of an 'underclass' of Third Country Nationals in EU countries caused by the construction and application of EU Law on migration and the inadequacy of anti-discrimination law and policy, as well as insufficient human rights protection by the ECHR, see Jesse, Moritz, 'Missing in Action: Effective Protection for Third-Country Nationals from Discrimination under Community Law' in Guild, Elspeth, Kees Groenendijk and Sergio Carrera (eds), *Illiberal Liberal States. Immigration, Citizenship and Integration in the EU* (England/USA, Ashgate, 2009) 198–203.

[102] Office of the United Nations High Commissioner for Human Rights, 'The International Convention on Migrant Workers and its Committee', Fact Sheet No 24 (Rev 1), United Nations, New York and Geneva, 2005, p 3.

ratifications and accessions has been steadily increasing to reach 48 ratifications at the end of 2015.[103] Still, the CRMW is the human rights treaty with the lowest membership and is far from reaching its goal of universal coverage.

In this respect, the UN OHCHR signalled in its Management Plan 2012–2013 that thelow level of ratification reflects persistent fears or misunderstandings held by States, particularly destination States, about losing control of migration management. In many countries, these concerns have resulted in and been exacerbated by, an alarming and visible rise in xenophobic rhetoric in national political discourse.

Within the Member States of the CRMW, one may find mostly countries of origin but also some countries of transit and/or hosting of large numbers of migrants, such as Mexico and Turkey. Among ratifying States, there are countries from almost all regions of the world, except for the EU. However, 11 Member States of the EU have ratified one or both ILO Conventions which served as a basis for the CRMW (Nos 97 and 143, indicated above) and, at the time of writing, two non-EU European States, Turkey and Albania, are parties to the CRMW;[104] an interesting fact if one considers Turkey is at the time of writing the host country of the majority of migrants derived from the armed conflict in Syria. While most of these persons are refugees, others will foreseeably find themselves in the condition of undocumented migrants and/or will possibly deserve overlapping protection from different legal instruments, including the CRMW.

The European Parliament has called on EU Member States to ratify the CRMW[105] and the former Secretary General Kofi Annan in 2004 *urged* EU States to become Parties to the CRMW.[106] Nevertheless, until now no EU Member State has ratified nor signed the CRMW. However, it must be noted that Italy, for example, based much of its comprehensive national migration law of 1998 on the provisions of the CRMW. In addition, a legal study concluded that Belgian law is almost entirely in conformity with the main provisions of this Convention, which would mean few obstacles to ratification. It should also be noted that Belgium, together with Italy, Spain and Portugal ratified both ILO migrant workers Conventions, which could offer potential roads to ratification of the CRMW.[107] This should be countered, though, with the many human rights' concerns raised in

[103] See http://treaties.un.org/Pages/ViewDetails.aspx?src=TREATY&mtdsg_no=IV-13&chapter=4&lang=en#2.

[104] *Ibid.*

[105] European Parliament. 2006. *Resolution on Development and Migration*, Doc P6_TA (2006) 0319, 6 July 2006.

[106] United Nations Secretary-General Kofi Annan's Address to the European Parliament upon receipt of the Andrei Sakharov Prize for Freedom of Thought (Brussels), 29 January 2004, at www.europa-eu-un.org/articles/en/article_3178_en.htm.

[107] See references in Taran (n 95) 423.

relation to the EU Return Directive of 2008,[108] concerning the return of migrants 'illegally staying' in the territory of the Member States, and the legislative and policy amendments it has brought about at the national level by means of the transposition and practical application of the Directive's provisions.[109]

Thus, the prospects for EU States ratifying the CRMW seem dim at a time of concentrated regional economic integration within the EU; although it remains to be seen what doors may be opened with the entry into force of the EU Charter of Fundamental Rights through the 2009 Lisbon Treaty and its remission to the jurisprudence of the ECHR. This and the heightened political priority granted by the recently founded EU Fundamental Rights Agency to the human rights of irregular migrants, might point towards interesting approaches that could integrate in one way or another a full understanding of the universal human rights and the overall human security of migrants.[110]

Meanwhile, the current UN Special Rapporteur on the Human Rights of Migrants, Francois Crépeau, presented in 2015 his follow-up report to the thematic study he had submitted to the Human Rights Council in June 2013. This last study analysed EU migration management in the context of border management, not only in light of the programmes and policies of the individual States visited, but also considering the overarching EU migration policy framework, focusing on their impact on the human rights of migrants.[111] In the 2015 report, in a human security-oriented stand, and in light of the current refugee crisis, he recommended that the EU fully recognise the push and pull factors of irregular migration, including that undertaken by sea, and the EU's responsibility in *managing* and *mitigating* them. In prioritising regular migration channels—an issue not explicitly demanded by human rights law but clearly called for under a human security lens—he recommended for the EU to take a global leadership role in relation to the Syrian civil war and other humanitarian crises and reduce

[108] Directive 2008/115/EC of the European Parliament and of the Council of 16 December 2008 on common standards and procedures in Member States for returning illegally staying third-country nationals [2008] OJ L348/98–107. On a critical analysis from the perspective of cases by the CJEU involving the application of the Directive, see Vavoula, Niovi, 'Detention of Irregular Migrants—The Returns Directive Shows its True Colours In Mahdi (C-146/14 PPU)' in European Law Blog, 15 September 2014, available at http://europeanlawblog.eu/?p=2501.

[109] See IACHR, Resolution 03/08, 'Human Rights of Migrants, International Standards and the Return Directive of the EU', June 2008. Personal notes taken at the Workshop 'Irregular Migration in Europe: Legal and Judicial Problems Raised by the Implementation of the Return Directive', EUI, 19 October 2012, also give an account of such concerns.

[110] For a critical analysis, see Guild, Elspeth, Kees Groenendijk and Sergio Carrera, 'Understanding the Contest of Community: Illiberal Practices in the EU?' in Guild, Groenendijk and Carrera (n 101) 1–25.

[111] UN Special Rapporteur on the Rights of Migrants, 'Report on the Regional Study on the Management of the External Borders of the European Union and its Impact on the Human Rights of Migrants', A/HRC/23/46, 2013.

the market for smugglers by developing, in cooperation with other States in the global North, *resettlement opportunities* so that the EU can accommodate over one million of the world's refugees (0.2 per cent of the total population of the EU) over a number of years.[112] The EU reaction to such recommendation has been far off the mark: the predominant EU response to human smugglers has been to participate in the approval of UN Security Council Resolution 2240 of 9 October 2015 authorising Member States, under Chapter VII of the UN Charter, to seize vessels that were confirmed as being used for migrant smuggling or human trafficking from Libya.[113] Such response may be criticised in light of the parameter framed by the UN Special Rapporteur, which allows pointing out that using Chapter VII to address a humanitarian crisis is erroneous in view of the alternative human security-guided paths of action already recommended from the standpoint of international human rights law. The adoption of Resolution 2240 does not cease to be paradoxical if one considers that it took more than four years to reach a UN Security Council resolution on the armed conflict in Syria (Resolution 2254, adopted on 18 December 2015), while the decision on migrant smugglers was adopted at record speed with no strong parallel measures to tackle the human insecurities faced by migrants—considering both the insecurities they are running away from and the ones caused by smugglers. A more long-term, strategic and positively ambitious position in terms of human rights would be to consider the concrete recommendations of human rights bodies as a blueprint for action and as the minimum essential to address the human rights of migrants and uphold the EU's democratic and universalist commitment.

At the same time, recognising the complexity of the upholding of human rights standards in situations of migratory pressures at State borders and in a world divided by State territorial jurisdictions, human rights bodies have carried out an effort to provide clearer criteria on how to confront such challenges. The UN OHCHR issued in 2014 the *Recommended Principles and Guidelines on Human Rights at International Borders*, resulting from consultations with a broad range of experts and stakeholders. The Principles reiterate, though, that the starting point is 'the belief that respecting the human rights of all migrants, regardless of their nationality, migration status or other circumstances, facilitates effective border governance'. Based on three principles consisting of the primacy of human rights; non-discrimination; and assistance and protection from harm, the instrument contains 10 concrete guidelines on international border

[112] Report of the UN Special Rapporteur on the human rights of migrants, François Crépeau, 'Banking on Mobility over a Generation: Follow-up to the Regional Study on the Management of the External Borders of the European Union and its Impact on the Human Rights of Migrants", A/HRC/29/36, 8 May 2015, paras 98 and 100.

[113] UN Security Council (UNSC), Resolution 2240, S/RES/2240(2015), 9 October 2015.

governance that, adopting a human security-friendly approach, 'establish accountability between duty-bearers and rights holders, emphasise participation and empowerment, and focus on vulnerability, marginalization and exclusion'.[114] As such, the document recognises empirical realities of suffering and intends to orient State action and adapt human rights implementation to contemporary migrant situations.

B. Regional Human Rights' Systems and Undocumented Migrants

Non-discrimination, equality before the law and equal protection of the law are basic and general principles of law relating to the protection of human rights. The IACHR's AO 18/03 reaffirms the highest status of the principle of equality and non-discrimination in concluding that

> the principle of equality before the law, equal protection before the law and non-discrimination belongs to *jus cogens*, because the whole legal structure of national and international public order rests on it and it is a fundamental principle that permeates all laws.[115]

Thus, the principle of non-discrimination implies that any differences in the treatment meted out to migrants must conform to international law and must not breach migrants' internationally recognised human rights. As an entrance point to analyse the human security–human rights relationship in the context of undocumented migration, let us first review the existing legal framework to determine its limitations and possibilities for pushing forward alternative interpretations.

There have been important regional developments relating to the human rights of migrants at the Inter-American level, and in the African and European landscapes.[116] This section briefly reviews such regional approaches. A specific mention is warranted, though, of the Inter-American framework in this subject, as the only regional standard which examines specifically and in depth the status of undocumented migrants with relation to human rights. Although at the universal level, as has been signalled, the existing legal category for the protection of human rights in the context of migration is that of 'migrant worker', at the Inter-American

[114] UN OHCHR, *Recommended Principles and Guidelines on Human Rights at International Borders* (Geneva, OHCHR, 2014) 2.

[115] AO 18/03 of the IACHR, para 101.

[116] For an analytical comparison between UN and European instruments, both at the level of European human rights law and in EU Law, see Kapuy, Klaus, 'European and International Law in Relation to the Social Security of Irregular Migrant Workers' in Pieters, Danny and Paul Schoukens (eds), *The Social Security Co-ordination between the EU and Non-EU Countries* (Antwerp, Intersentia, 2009) 115–55. On the African developments related to human mobility and human rights, think eg, of the Kampala Convention for the Protection and Assistance of Internally Displaced Persons in Africa, which entered into force on 6 December 2012.

level, AO 18/03 constitutes a legal instrument that protects all undocumented migrants as such in their condition of 'structural vulnerability'.[117] This position is also confirmed by the IACHR in its more recent Advisory Opinion OC-21/14, of 2014, *Rights and Guarantees of Children in the Context of Migration and/or in Need of International Protection*, in reference to the heightened exposure to real or potential violations of human rights by the children of undocumented migrants.[118]

Indeed, the IACHR's AO 18/03 should be deemed as an authoritative legal source insofar as it interprets the Inter-American human rights legal framework, basically the 1948 American Declaration on the Rights and Duties of Man and the 1969 American Convention on Human Rights,[119] but also as it analyses European human rights law as a comparative resource, as well as UN human rights law and international law more generally as binding sources for States in the Americas.

In AO 18/03 the Inter-American Court emphasised, as was briefly mentioned above, that

> the fundamental principle of equality and non-discrimination forms part of general international law, because it is applicable to all States, regardless of whether or not they are a party to a specific international treaty. At the current stage of the development of international law, the fundamental principle of equality and non-discrimination has entered the domain of *jus cogens*.

This in turn provides for a set of relevant consequences, among others, that 'the general obligation to respect and guarantee human rights binds States, regardless of any circumstance or consideration, including the migratory status of a person'. It further concluded that the *migratory status* of a person cannot constitute a justification to deprive him or her of the enjoyment and exercise of human rights, including those of a labour-related nature. When assuming an employment relationship, the migrant acquires rights that must be recognised and ensured because he or she is an employee, irrespective of regular or irregular status in the State where the person is employed. As the Court clarifies, 'these rights are a result of the employment relationship'.[120] (emphasis added)

[117] AO 18/03, paras 112, 113, 130, 131, 149 and 160; see also para 9 of Reasoned Concurring Opinion of Judge Sergio García Ramírez to AO 18/03, as well as the *amicus curiae* presented by Jorge Bustamante from *Universidad Nacional Autónoma de México* (later appointed UN Special Rapporteur on the Human Rights of Migrants from 2005 to 2011) at p 81.

[118] See IACHR, Advisory Opinion OC-21/14 of 19 August 2014, Requested by the Argentine Republic, The Federative Republic of Brazil, The Republic of Paraguay and The Oriental Republic of Uruguay, *Rights and Guarantees of Children in the Context of Migration and/or in Need of International Protection*, paras 59, 61 and following.

[119] American Declaration on the Rights and Duties of Man (ADRDM), Organization of American States (OAS) Res XXX 1948; American Convention on Human Rights (ACoHR or Pact of San José), OAS Treaty Series No 36, adopted on 22 November 1969 and entered into force on 18 July 1978.

[120] AO 18/03, at concluding paras 4, 6 and 8.

Notably, there is a specific reference to the human security framework as one of the considerations around this AO 18/03, in Concurring Opinion of Judge Sergio García Ramírez (point 5), who quoted the report *Human Security Now* in referring to the motivations for migratory movements:

> In a recent publication, it is recalled that 'most individuals migrate in order to improve their living conditions, seek new opportunities or escape poverty'; although we should not overlook other reasons, such as: family reunion, war and other conflicts, human rights violations, expulsion, and discrimination. At the 'end of the 20th century, there were an estimated 175 million international migrants, nearly 3% of the world's people and twice the number in 1975. Some 60% of the international migrants, about 104 million, are in developing countries
>
> (Commission on Human Security, *Human Security (sic)*, New York, 2003, p 41).

It must also be signalled that AO 18/03 is an expression of a previous regional trend of concern towards migrants' and other non-citizens' human rights. Since its early years, the Inter-American Commission on Human Rights (IACoHR) had given particular attention to the situation of refugees in the western hemisphere, such as the mass exodus of refugees from the Caribbean in the 1960s, especially after the Cuban Revolution of 1959. Subsequently, the human rights challenges that military dictatorships created in the 1970s throughout the Southern Cone tested the responsiveness of the IACoHR regarding the protection of refugees. During the 1980s, civil wars in Central America posed similar challenges for the Commission. As was referred to above in Chapter 2, in section I on international law, risk and structural vulnerability, the 1984 Cartagena Declaration on Refugees was adopted by several Inter-American States as a result of such challenges, and confirmed by the reassessments of the 1994 San José Declaration and the 2004 Mexico Declaration.[121]

Relating directly to migrants' rights, in 1996 the IACoHR decided to appoint one of its seven Commissioners as Special Rapporteur on Migrant Workers and their Families as a group experiencing 'extreme vulnerability'. The Special Rapporteur also participated in the discussion surrounding the request of AO 18/03, as part of a coordinated approach to migrants' human rights between the Inter-American Commission and the Court. In 2012, in order to respond to the multiple challenges of human mobility in the region from international and internal migration to forced and voluntary migration, the Commission decided to amend the mandate of the Rapporteurship on Migrant Workers and Members of their Families, renaming it as Rapporteurship on the Rights of Migrants. As such, the broadened mandate of the Rapporteur (at the

[121] For an account of this development, see Cançado Trindade, Antônio Augusto, *A humanizaçao do direito internacional* (Brazil, Editora del Rey, 2006) 281–86.

time of writing, Commissioner Enrique Gil Botero, from Colombia), also covers 'asylum seekers, refugees, complementary protection seekers and beneficiaries, stateless persons, victims of human trafficking, internally displaced persons and other vulnerable groups in the context of human mobility', thereby institutionalising a tacit practice that in previous years had become part of the Rapporteurship's work on individual petitions, cases, precautionary and provisional measures and thematic and country reports involving such groups.[122] This decision also responds to the recognition of the tests posed by internal migration, much higher in number than international migration, as referred to in the introduction to this chapter, but presenting similar conditions of vulnerability within the specific reality of the Americas. The legal recognition of such vulnerability is also reflected in another regional setting by the adoption of the Kampala Convention for the Protection and Assistance of Internally Displaced Persons in Africa, which entered into force on 6 December 2012. This is the only legally binding instrument in the field of IDPs, and as such, it may provoke interesting interpretative standards, and be potentially enlightening for future analysis on international migration.

It is also important to recall that regional human rights instruments contain a substantive protection covering all migrants against *refoulment*[123] and collective expulsion.[124] However, most procedural safeguards in individual expulsion proceedings in regional human rights treaties only explicitly apply to 'aliens' who are 'lawfully' within the territory of a State party.[125] In comparison to instruments at the UN level reviewed above, we find a similar provision regarding the right to defence and the right to legal representation foreseen for 'lawful aliens' within expulsion proceedings, in Article 13 of ICCPR. These rights may be expanded, though, to also cover undocumented migrants subject to expulsion procedures, through a harmonious interpretation of the universal rights to non-discrimination, equality before the law, liberty and security of the

[122] During its first period (1997–2000), Colombian historian Álvaro Tirado was in charge of the Special Rapporteurship. Subsequently, in 2000, the IACoHR appointed Argentine jurist and Professor Juan E Méndez as Special Rapporteur (later appointed by the UN Secretary General in 2004 as Special Adviser on the Prevention of Genocide). In 2004, the IACoHR appointed Freddy Gutiérrez Trejo, a Venezuelan attorney and professor, as Special Rapporteur. In 2008, the IACoHR appointed Commissioner Felipe González, from Chile, to a four-year term, who covered these additional groups deemed in need of protection; see www.cidh.org/Migrantes/migrants.background.htm.

[123] See European Convention on Human Rights, Art 3; American Convention on Human Rights, Art 22, para 8; African Charter on Human and Peoples' Rights, Art 5.

[124] See Protocol No 4 to the European Convention on Human Rights, Art 4; American Convention on Human Rights, Art 22, para 9; African Charter on Human and Peoples' Rights, Art 12, para 5; Arab Charter on Human Rights, Art 26, para 1.

[125] Protocol No 7 to the European Convention on Human Rights, Art 1; American Convention on Human Rights, Art 22, para 6; Arab Charter on Human Rights, Art 26, para 2; African Charter on Human and Peoples' Rights, Art 12, para 4.

person, and due process of law, all included in regional instruments, as previously examined.

At the European level, the rights protected in the European Social Charter apply to 'foreigners only insofar as they are nationals of other Contracting Parties lawfully resident or working regularly within the territory of the Contracting Party concerned',[126] or to migrant workers and their families 'lawfully within their territories'.[127] A relevant exception is the right to education, which is guaranteed to *all* migrant children, regardless of their migration status, in all regional human rights systems.[128]

Generally, the European response to undocumented migrants has been less categorical than the Inter-American. At the normative level, the 1950 European Convention on the Protection of Human Rights and Fundamental Freedoms, although not referring specifically to migrants, protects them insofar as it is applicable to all persons under the State's jurisdiction.[129] The 1961 European Social Charter (ESC) and the 1996 Revised European Social Charter (RESC), afford some degree of protection to undocumented migrants mainly through the right to non-discrimination in relation to different rights such as labour rights and, as was indicated, guarantees of non-expulsion.[130] Also, through the supervision bodies of both instruments, the ECHR and the ECSR, respectively, the rights of migrants have to a certain extent been reaffirmed and protected. However, again, the usual approach of the ECHR has been to underline the obligation of States to ensure the right to private and family life (Art 8) and to non-discrimination (Art 14) with respect to other rights in relation to non-nationals who are *lawfully* residing in their territory.[131]

There are some important exceptions, though, to the general stand of only considering lawfully residing migrants under the umbrella of European human rights protection. The ECSR, in monitoring Luxembourg's compliance, for instance, has interpreted Article 13, paragraph 4, of the ESC as requiring Member States to ensure that all migrant workers, independently of their migration status, are able to access emergency

[126] See European Social Charter, Appendix.

[127] European Social Charter, Art 19, paras 4–9.

[128] African Charter on Human and Peoples' Rights, Art 17.1; African Charter on the Rights and Welfare of the Child, Art 11; Protocol No 1 to the European Convention on Human Rights, Art 2 (read in conjunction with Art 14 of the ECoHR). See also the jurisprudence of the European Committee on Social Rights at Art 17, para 2, of the Revised European Social Charter and that of the Inter-American Court of Human Rights at Art 19 of the American Convention on Human Rights.

[129] European Convention for the Protection of Human Rights and Fundamental Freedoms (ECoHR), Art 1.

[130] European Social Charter (ESC); and Revised European Social Charter (RESC); see Arts 18 and 19 of both instruments.

[131] See for example the cases by the ECHR of *Gaygusuz v Austria*, Appl No 173/71/90, Judgment of 19 September 1996, and *Poirrez v France*, Appl No 40892/98, Judgment of 30 September 2003.

social assistance for as long as they might require it,[132] an obligation that was also reaffirmed by the Committee on RMW, as described above.

Let us recall, though, that the ESC was adopted in 1961 with a nationality-based reciprocity structure as a foundational feature, and not with the primary aspiration of constituting an instrument embodying universal human rights. In this respect, the interpretations by the ECSR may respond at least partly to the logic of guaranteeing the functioning of a system of mutual benefits, exchanges and trade-offs and not necessarily or as a priority goal to upholding human rights standards. The ECSR has evolved, though, and has moved towards less instrumental and more protective interpretations with a general significance for human rights law, such as that referred to above in reviewing Luxembourg's compliance and explicitly addressing undocumented migrants.[133]

To give but another example of hopeful avenues to more protective positions, reciprocity arguments requiring the conditionality of analogous benefits in place in a first State party to legitimate compliance with the recognition of rights in a second State party, have been rejected by dissenting members of the ECSR itself, reflecting that 'the importance of the Charter lies in its multilateral nature, *with no reciprocity condition*. If this principle is breached, its articles concerned with social protection might just as well be repealed'.[134] (emphasis added) Specifically regarding children of migrant workers addressed in the revision of compliance of the UK, one of the dissenting members expressed concern over the majority's interpretation that 'States cannot be required to pay child allowances to nationals of States party when there is no corresponding entitlement'; and added that this view was 'incompatible with the principle that equal treatment cannot be made subject to exceptions or *reciprocity conditions*'. Further preoccupation was expressed for not moving in line with the more progressive case-law of the ECHR (*Gaygusuz v Austria* and *Poirrez v France*, referred to above, were quoted) and for considering that the majority interpretation disregarded cases 'where dependent children of migrant workers do not live on their territory or have a minimum period of residence or employment requirement which places non-nationals at a disadvantage'.[135] In reviewing compliance of the Russian Federation with equal

[132] See ECSR, Conclusions XIX-2 (Luxembourg), 22 December 2009.

[133] For an analysis of the ECSR, see Khaliq, Urfan and Robin Churchill, 'The European Committee of Social Rights' in Langford, Malcolm (ed), *Social Rights Jurisprudence. Emerging Trends in International and Comparative Law* (Cambridge, Cambridge University Press, 2008) 428–52.

[134] ECSR, Conclusions XVIII-1 (UK), Articles 1, 5, 6, 12, 13, 16 and 19 of the Charter, 2006; Dissenting Opinion by Mr Jean-Michel Belorgey, joined by Mr Nikitas Aliprantis, Mrs Csilla Kollonay-Lehoczky and Mr Lucien Francois; at first page of the Opinion.

[135] *Ibid*; Dissenting Opinion of Mr Tekin Akillioğlu with Conclusion relating to Article 12, para 4; see last two paragraphs of the Opinion.

treatment of non-nationals regarding the right to vocational guidance and to vocational training accorded by the Charter (Articles 9 and 10), the ECSR *unanimously* affirmed that 'length of residence requirements or employment requirements and/or the application of the *reciprocity clause* are contrary to the provisions of the Charter'.[136] (emphasis added) It must be remembered, though, that most of these developments refer to *documented* non-nationals.

In this context, and recalling the standards reviewed in the section on ESC Rights in Chapter 1 of this book, it is important to keep in mind that even if many migrant workers in an *undocumented* situation do not participate in contributory schemes of social security, they contribute to financing social protection arrangements and programmes by paying indirect taxes.[137]

The cases of alleged human rights violations deriving from expulsion of non-citizens, and for our effects of undocumented migrants, as well as the rules applicable to such expulsions, have usually been reviewed by the European Court in terms of violations of the *non-refoulment* principle under Article 3 of the ECoHR (prohibition of torture), or under Article 2 (right to life), on the one hand; or in the framework of violations of the right to private and family life on the other (Article 8), but not in more general terms of respect to the right of due process of law and fair trial. This can possibly also be explained in light of the fact that the ECoHR does not include a mirror provision to that of Article 13 of the ICCPR described above (rights of aliens to legal certainty, due process and fair trial when confronting an expulsion decision). The lack of such a provision has left the Court somewhat tied, given it confronts obstacles to review generalised situations of risk and actual violations faced by undocumented migrants in the host State, and when they reach the situation where an order of expulsion is made against them or are actually expelled, the Court can only verify if a few minimum standards were observed, such as those contained in Articles 2 or 3 mentioned above.

Even within this parameter, the Court has shown variations in its interpretation of the scope of 'family' in the protection of family life, the relevance of language and social ties, and the gravity of the individual's conduct when weighed against the *broader need for public order as a legally justified basis for expulsion.*[138] (emphasis added) Regarding

[136] ECSR, Conclusions 2012, (Russian Federation), Articles 1, 9, 10, 15, 18, 20 and 24 of the Revised Charter, January 2013, pp 12–13.

[137] See *Report of the United Nations High Commissioner for Human Rights to the Economic and Social Council*, E/2010/89, 1 June 2010, para 46.

[138] See for example *Dalia v France*, Appl No 26102/954, Judgment of 19 February 1998; *Slivenko et al v Latvia*, Appl No 48321/99, Judgment of 9 October 2003 (GC); *Maslov v Austria*, Appl No 1638/03, Judgment of 28 May 2008 (GC); *Trabelsi v Germany*, Appl No 41548/06, Judgment of 13 October 2011 (available only in French), para 23.

concretely undocumented migrants, there are a few cases in which the non-citizen was first residing regularly and then denied renewal of his or her residence permit and was thus undocumented when having experienced the alleged violation. For example, in *Trabelsi v Germany*, involving a man of Tunisian origin at risk of deportation from Germany and analysed under Article 8 of private and family life, the subjective element of human security shows its face, in an account included in the judgment describing the applicant's 'lack of perspective and *insecurity* regarding his future fate and right of residence' when confronting the threat of expulsion to Tunisia.[139] However, the Court shifted from the position adopted in the previous similar case of *Maslov v Austria*, of 2008, and concluded in 2011 that in *Trabelsi* there had been no violation by the State, seemingly being supportive or at least permissive of the State's increasingly restrictive immigration policies, in parallel to similar positions adopted in recent years in all of Western Europe. The case of *Kiyutin v Russia* presents however an interesting turn in terms of migrants' rights and the possibility of suspending or supressing an expulsion order on the basis of health reasons (although always argued under Article 8 of private and family life), as will be studied in the following chapter.[140]

IV. A HUMAN SECURITY LENS TO MIGRANT HUMAN RIGHTS: LEGAL IRREGULARITY AS A SOURCE OF RISK

> No man in his right senses would voluntarily choose such a life in preference to the one of normal, family, social life which exists in every civilized community.
>
> But there comes a time, as it came in my life, when a man is denied the right to live a normal life, when he can only live the life of an outlaw because the government has so decreed to use the law to impose a state of outlawry upon him.
>
> *Nelson Mandela*[141]

A. The Human Security–Human Rights Synergy as Challenging Existing Boundaries

The spatial and political frontiers that condition respect and enjoyment of people's human rights seem to be put into question when dealing with situations affecting the rights of irregular migrants. The life-threatening and life-supressing conditions, as well as the determinants of fear and

[139] *Trabelsi v Germany* (n 138) para 23.
[140] *Kiyutin v Russia*, Appl No 2700/10, Judgment of 10 March 2011.
[141] Excerpt from Mandela, Nelson, *Long Walk to Freedom* (Boston, Little, Brown & Co, 1994).

misery dominating the daily existence of most irregular migrants, indeed seem to challenge the boundaries of the political community as constrained to territorial Nation-States as we know them. If we take a step back and refrain from taking for granted existing territorial limitations as defining the content of community and the realisation of rights, then certain legal and political concepts such as 'citizenship' start to become blurred, and possibly we can begin to envision notions such as that of 'undocumented citizenship'.[142]

The invisibility affecting irregular migrants—identified as being in a situation of 'legal limbo' in this book—when perpetuated and experienced in a systematic manner, presents an even greater risk to social cohesion and the upholding of the principles of the rule of law. This initial expression of indifference may in turn lead to what Javier de Lucas calls the 'society of disdain' (*sociedad del menosprecio*), as referred to above. But even more seriously, it has been demonstrated how it may later open the way for mistreatment and ultimately heighten the risk of a 'society of hatred' affecting undocumented migrants and other distinct social or ethnic groups.

When looking at the transnational phenomenon of migration, one must also bear in mind the reaffirmation by the human rights bodies at the UN level as well as by ECHR jurisprudence, in the sense that in legal terms each State is individually responsible for its own actions, even if it carries them out as part of a joint partnership with other States or as a result of an implementation measure of a resolution of another international body, for example, the UN Security Council.[143] In this sense, in the case of *Hirsi v Italy*, the ECHR condemned the practice of 'push-backs' at sea by Italy mainly of migrants arriving from Libya, even when such a practice was partly based on a bilateral agreement between the two countries that allowed for this.[144]

However, one wonders if this is sufficient in dealing with the protection and guarantee of the rights of irregular migrants. This would seem to bring us back to the debate on the duty of international cooperation wrapped into Article 28 of the UDHR, on the right of everyone to a social and international order in which human rights can be fully realised, as

[142] McNevin (n 53).

[143] In the recent case of *Nada v Switzerland* the ECHR found—taking into account the previous decision of the UN Human Rights Committee in *Sayadi and Vinck v Belgium*—that while the applicant's listing by the Sanctions Committee of the UNSC was attributable to the UN, the implementation of the sanctions by Switzerland was attributable to Switzerland itself; see paras 88–92 and 121–22 of *Nada v Switzerland (GC)*, Appl No 10593/08, 12 September 2012, as well as UN Human Rights Committee, *Sayadi and Vinck v Belgium*, Communication No 1472/200622, October 2008; both cases concerning measures—transit or travel bans, among others—imposed or applied by States (Switzerland and Italy on the one hand, and Belgium in the second case), pursuant to the implementation of UNSC resolutions based on the listing made by its Sanction Committee and legal provisions adopted thereby domestically.

[144] See *Hirsi v Italy* (n 91).

discussed in Chapter 2, section II B on Human Security and Human Rights in Public International Law, as well as in Chapter 3. As I argued there, human security can be said to embody a modern materialisation of such right, complementing existing proposals on the contemporary realisation of the right to development and other forms of assessment of broader and contextual global economic inequalities and the legal, political and procedural structures that render them possible.[145]

To place migrants' human rights within such discussion, we can summarise by recalling that various human rights' treaty bodies have increasingly and also consistently (especially considering the last 10 years) reaffirmed the applicability of human rights standards to migrant persons and the prohibition of discrimination based on national origin or immigration status. They have paid particular attention to the situation of migrant women and children and have emphasised the obligation of States, unless specified otherwise in the treaties, to facilitate the accession and enjoyment by all migrants—documented and undocumented—to all human rights—civil, political, economic, social and cultural.

Indeed, as Pia Oberoi puts it,

> in placing primary emphasis on the individual, both the human rights and the human security framework challenge the dominant discourse prevalent in migration policy-making today, which asserts that the principle of sovereignty accords states an ascendant position, able ultimately to privilege state security over the 'human security' of migrants.[146]

Thus, in speaking of the rights of migrants, the departing point in the debate is not—as it is often purported—the national sovereignty of States and their ability to regulate territorial borders, but rather what the law, or different legal systems, have to say about such rights and the principles that ground them. Indeed, the UN Special Rapporteur on the Human Rights of Migrants, Mr François Crépeau, has very recently highlighted the tendency observed in some declarations by public officials and the mass media to consider that migrants who arrive in States where they have not been invited to come or to enter, somehow do not enjoy the same rights as the rest of the people. Such pattern has led to the creation of spaces of administrative discretion based on an underlying belief that two kinds of human rights exist, those held by citizens and those of *a second-class category*, deserved by non-citizens. It must be underlined though, as he clarified, that international law is firm in stipulating that all human rights are to be enjoyed by all human beings, with the only exceptions

[145] See Curtis, Josh and Shane Darcy, 'The Right to a Social and International Order for the Realisation of Human Rights: Article 28 of the Universal Declaration and International Cooperation' in Keane, David and Yvonne McDermott (eds), *The Challenge of Human Rights. Past, Present and Future* (USA/UK, Edward Elgar, 2012) 34–35.

[146] Oberoi (n 10) 270.

allowed by international human rights law itself.[147] International law has been constructed, at least partly, precisely through the progressive understanding of State sovereignty as involving the responsibility of ensuring a series of values and living conditions for the persons under the State's jurisdiction, *qua* persons with dignity, as a sufficient reason for the legal recognition and enjoyment of a set of rights, a process that could be considered, as Judge Cançado Trindade does, 'the humanization of International Law'.[148] In that sense, the first affirmation that would have to be signalled is that universal human rights are, in principle, and with few exceptions, applicable to *all migrants*, regular and irregular.

At the same time, though, universal human rights of migrants are met with some barriers within international law itself and with numerous obstacles at the domestic level, as will be evidenced in the following sections. As Ryszard Cholewinski puts it, the difficult plight of migrant workers in many countries of the world to secure their basic human and labour rights, 'and their limited access to legal remedies both in law and in practice, often exacerbated by their non-citizen and/or unauthorized status, reveals a substantive gulf between "rhetoric and reality" in guaranteeing these rights to all persons'.[149]

Facing the existing gaps in international and domestic law, the human security approach may in fact contribute to reinforcing the central starting point in thinking about undocumented migrants: 'You do not need a visa or a residence permit to qualify for human rights. Simply being born is your passport to human rights protection'.[150]

[147] Statements by F Crépeau at the debate *The Management of the External Borders of the EU and its Impact on the Human Rights of Migrants: The Italian Experience. A Consultation between the UN Special Rapporteur on the Human Rights of Migrants, Mr François Crépeau, Civil Society, and Academia,* organised by the Migration Policy Centre, Robert Schuman Centre for Advanced Studies of the European University Institute (EUI), with the support of the Open Society Foundations, EUI, Florence, Italy, 3 October 2012. Personal record taken. See also press release 'UN Special Rapporteur on the Human Rights of Migrants Concludes his Third Country Visit in his Regional Study on the Human Rights of Migrants at the Borders of the European Union: Italy', Rome, 8 October 2012, at www.ohchr.org/EN/NewsEvents/Pages/DisplayNews.aspx?NewsID=12640&LangID=E.

[148] See Cançado Trindade (n 121), who calls this construction the 'new *ius gentium* of the twenty-first century', 320 and subsequent pages. See also Cassese, Antonio, *International Law*, 2nd edn (Oxford, Oxford University Press, 2005) 45; and Teitel, Ruti G, *Humanity's Law* (Oxford, Oxford University Press, 2011) 192; and her analysis of the 'human security turn' to global justice at 139–64. For a discussion that can also be applied to undocumented migrants, see Teitel's reference to Hannah Arendt's right to have access to rights and thus to belonging to an organised community as a basis for emphasising the tendency towards global solidarity by current international law, 209.

[149] Cholewinski, Ryszard, 'Labour Migration Management and the Rights of Migrant Workers' in Edwards and Ferstman (n 10) 275.

[150] Speech by Morten Kjaerum, Director, European Union Agency for Fundamental Rights (FRA), 'Dignity and Rights of Irregular Migrants', 4th Fundamental Rights Conference, Warsaw, Poland, 21–22 November 2011, p 2, underlined in original. Available at http://fra.europa.eu/fraWebsite/attachments/MK-Speech-FRC-NOV2011.pdf.

B. Immigration Measures and Testimonies by Undocumented Migrants

At the level of empirical evidence, multiple sources provide for shocking accounts of the extreme vulnerability experienced by undocumented migrants at the border and more generally as the 'uninvited' members of society.[151] The factual accounts of the human insecurity suffered by undocumented migrants are numerous and frequently reveal racial prejudice and xenophobic expression. To draw a representative picture, this text looks at some symbolic cases. These cases reveal government responses of many of the receiving countries that are otherwise defensive of the human rights discourse and practice—including EU Member States such as Italy and Greece—as well as policy positions at the European level more generally, that signal preoccupying tendencies of being 'deeply corrosive of respect for universal human rights'.[152]

Of course, responsibility is also to be set on sending and transit countries in contributing to the human insecurity that drives people away in the first place or not adequately protecting them from risks during the migration journey. At the level of bilateral, regional and international understandings that are necessarily called for when facing a transnational phenomenon, surely these challenges are best met through an outlook and strategy of 'shared responsibility'. However, this text focuses mainly on the constructed vulnerability and human insecurity that the lack of a legal immigration status produces for migrant persons, who often suffer human rights violations as a result. On the productive and more creative side, the book also proposes ways in which the human security conception can work together with human rights law to identify these risks and formulate approaches to better prevent, confront and alleviate them.

In looking at the human security–human rights relationship on this subject, two main situations can be distinguished: 1) undocumented migrants at the border: deaths at the 'fault-line'; 2) the risks to human rights of undocumented migrants once in the territory of the receiving State. Specific threats stemming from the gender dimension of undocumented migration can also be identified in both settings. Particular risks are also associated to the situation of undocumented women migrant domestic workers. Because of the differentiated and disproportionate impact that the risks affecting undocumented persons represents for women and

[151] See Harding, Jeremy, *Border Vigils: Keeping Migrants out of the Rich World* (London, New York, Verso Books, 2012), where he revisits and updates his previous book *The Uninvited: Refugees at the Rich Man's Gate* (London, Profile Books, London Review of Books, 2000).

[152] See Human Rights Watch, *World Report 2012. Events of 2011*, p 44.

girls, and especially considering their vulnerability to different forms of violence (see Chapter 4) this issue merits separate consideration, also in line with the approach adopted by human rights bodies. As such, the following Chapter 6 of this book will analyse the distinctive human security situation of undocumented migrant women and girls.

i. Undocumented Migrants at the Border: Deaths at the 'Fault Line'[153]

The empirical accounts of the human insecurity experienced by undocumented migrants are varied and this section provides some examples of the magnitude of the human dimension of the risks experienced throughout the migration journey.

To start with the North American region comprised of Canada, the US and Mexico, let us highlight that the border-crossing of persons from Mexico to the US—the largest migration corridor in the world—and the risks associated with it are so critical that they have been categorised as 'a humanitarian crisis'.[154] People often lose their lives through drowning in the Mexico–U.S. bordering river, the Río Grande; die from dehydration or hypothermia when crossing the Arizona desert; or as a result of different types of abuse at the hands of human smugglers—risks that have increased over the last few years.[155] Estimates indicate that almost 400 persons die each year trying to cross the Mexican–US border,[156]

[153] The term 'migratory fault lines' has been used to describe migratory flows triggered by economic disparities between neighbouring States; see UN Commission on Human Rights, 'Report on the Human Rights of Migrants submitted by the Special Rapporteur of the Commission on Human Rights', A/59/377, 22 September 2004, para 7. The flows occur across land and sea borders where migratory pressures are most acute because they divide States with very different standards of living. Stefanie Grant proposes this concept as a useful way of thinking about individual protection needs and also about 'the wider asymmetries in human development, *human security* and human rights which drive irregular migration'. She identifies three fault lines: the land border between Mexico and the US, the maritime borders between North Africa and Southern Europe, and those between the Horn of Africa and the Southern Arabian Peninsula, the first two of which I mainly examine. I follow her in the use of this term to frame the analysis of the reviewed migrant risks; Grant, Stefanie, 'Irregular Migration and Frontier Deaths. Acknowledging a Right to Identity', in Dembour and Kelly (n 54) 49. Emphasis added.

[154] See the report by the ACLU and the independent public body, the National Human Rights Commission of Mexico, *Humanitarian Crisis: Migrant Deaths at the U.S.-Mexico Border*, 2009. On the largest migration corridors in the world, see World Bank (n 4) p 1.

[155] Peña, Alex, 'Migrants Face Higher Risks Illegally Crossing the Border' in NBC Latino, 20 September 2012, http://nbclatino.com/2012/09/20/migrants-face-higher-risks-illegally-crossing-the-border/. The author bases his account on the study by Isacson, Adam and Maureen Meyer, *Beyond the Border Buildup: Security and Migrants Along the U.S.–Mexico Border* (Washington Office on Latin America (WOLA)/*El Colegio de la Frontera Norte,* April 2012).

[156] Figures from the Mexican Ministry of Foreign Affairs and US Border Patrol authorities, quoted in Isacson and Meyer report (n 155) 40.

placing the figure at 2,219 deaths between January 2006 and March 2012.[157] Notably, while immigration from Mexico to the US registered a decrease between 2005 and 2011—particularly since 2008, which is possibly due to the economic crisis in the US—because of increasingly harsh US immigration and security policies and growing violence at the border, the number of deaths has remained the same and the search for new crossing routes and the dangers associated with the crossing itself have intensified. Indeed, 'while overall migration has decreased, for those who attempt the trip, the *probability of death* from exposure on U.S. soil has *increased sharply*'.[158] (emphasis added)

Since before this situation had reached its current gravity for crossing migrants, a historical account describing the social attitudes and official policies towards immigrants in general in the late nineteenth and twentieth century US, had revealed their political construction as 'unwelcome strangers'.[159] Moreover, the conditions experienced by undocumented migrants had already seen them being termed as 'strangers to the Constitution', in referring to their exclusion from the enjoyment of fundamental rights.[160]

On the southern side of the Mexican border, the circumstances are no more favourable. Central American migrants mainly from Guatemala, Nicaragua, El Salvador and Honduras, who attempt to cross the Mexican border usually by train to transit through the country in their path towards the US, confront severe life-threatening conditions throughout their journey. There are myriad accounts of their vulnerability to accidents on the train at the southern border, popularly referred to as '*La Bestia*' ('The Beast') that has caused mutilations and death.[161] The attempts of migrants to cross the border and the subsequent travel have been

[157] Isacson and Meyer report (n 155). See also García, Judith, 'Cada 24 horas muere un mexicano al querer pasar a EU ilegalmente: SRE' in *El Sol de México*, 5 August 2012, available at www.oem.com.mx/elsoldemexico/notas/n2645139.htm.

[158] Isacson and Meyer report (n 155) 9–13. Quote from 41. The report explains the link between the National Strategy of the Border Patrol and its 'prevention through deterrence' approach that worked insofar as migrants were pushed towards more remote and inhospitable areas of the border and thus many decided not to cross, but at the expense of the migrants who did: because of the increased risks of crossing, the number of deaths has not diminished, 14 and 40.

[159] See Reimners, David M, *Unwelcome Strangers. American Identity and the Turn against Immigration*, (New York, Columbia University Press, 1998).

[160] See Neuman, Gerald L, *Strangers to the Constitution: Immigrants, Borders, and Fundamental Law* (Princeton, New Jersey, Princeton University Press, 1996).

[161] See, eg, *La Bestia*, the documentary on the plight of Central American migrants trying to enter Mexico by train through the southern border usually with the aim of transiting through the country in their path to the US, available at www.eluniversal.com.mx/notas/736080.html; the web-documentary by PICUM on irregular migrants, *Undocumentary*, available at www.undocumentary.org; and the film *Terraferma*, on the situation faced by North African migrants attempting to reach Italy by sea and the conditions of detention centres.

categorised as 'hell',[162] a 'route of danger',[163] an experience of 'terror'[164] and a 'death trap'.[165] Civil society reports, UN and Inter-American sources and the independent public body of the Mexican National Human Rights Commission highlight how migrants have also recently become victims of various crimes, including kidnapping, extortion, rape and murder, at the hands of smugglers or organised crime, mainly drug-trafficking, during their crossing and transit in Mexico, at times with complicity or participation of State officials,[166] a situation that has increased dramatically in the last few years, placing the figure of kidnapped migrants in Mexico at over a shocking 20,000 between 2008 and 2011.[167] Paradoxically, this has come to being partly due to a transformation of criminal organisations as a response to the Government's hard stance against drug cartels (adopted since 2006), which have then resorted to targeting migrants as a source of blackmail and income, or penetrated the business of human smuggling or human trafficking.[168] At the same time, due to the lack of

[162] Vega, Arturo, 'El infierno de los inmigrantes centroamericanos', *Periódico El Universal*, lunes 10 de enero de 2011, Ciudad de México, available at www.eluniversal.com.mx/notas/736080.html.

[163] Dudley, Stephen, 'Parte III: La Ruta del Peligro' in *Insight Crime. Crimen Organizado en las Américas*, 28 November 2012, available at http://es.insightcrime.org/investigaciones/migrantes-centroamerica-mexico.

[164] Godoy, Emilio, 'México, escala de terror para inmigrantes centroamericanos', 28 abril 2012, available at http://ipsnoticias.net/nota.asp?idnews=95272.

[165] Amnesty International, 'Mexico must Investigate Shocking Spike of Attacks and Killings of Migrants', 18 June 2015, available at www.amnesty.org/en/latest/news/2015/06/mexico-must-investigate-shocking-spike-of-attacks-and-killings-of-migrants/.

[166] National Human Rights Commission of Mexico (CNDH): *Informe Especial sobre los Casos de Secuestro en Contra de Migrantes*, 2009, and the follow-up *Informe Especial sobre Secuestro de Migrantes en México*, February 2011, available at www.cndh.org.mx/node/35; Jorge Bustamante, Report of the UN Special Rapporteur on the Human Rights of Migrants to the UN Human Rights Council, A/HRC/7/12, 25 February 2008; Meyer, Maureen with contributions from Stephanie Brewer, *A Dangerous Journey through Mexico: Human Rights Violations against Migrants in Transit*, WOLA and Centro Prodh, December 2010, available at www.wola.org/publications/a_dangerous_journey_through_mexico_human_rights_violations_against_migrants_in_transit. See also IACoHR, *Human Rights of Migrants and Other Persons in the Context of Human Mobility In Mexico*, OEA/Ser.L/V/II. Doc. 48/13, IACoHR, Organization of American States, 30 December 2013, particularly on 'structural vulnerability' of undocumented migrants, paras 82 and 83.

[167] The two CNDH reports account for 9,758 migrants kidnapped in Mexico between September 2008 and February 2009, of which 9,194 were kidnapped by organised gangs; and for 11,333 migrants kidnapped between April and September 2010. Of these, 76 percent were from Central America and 10.6 percent were from Mexico. See also Amnesty International, *Culpables conocidos, víctimas ignoradas. Tortura y maltrato en México* (Índice: AMR 41/063/2012) 2012, 'Abusos Contra Migrantes', p 11, cases at p 13.

[168] One of the gravest cases that provides evidence of this shift is the kidnapping in August 2010 by the organised criminal gang *Los Zetas* of 72 undocumented migrants in the northeast Mexican State of Tamaulipas, who were later found killed in a clandestine grave; see IACoHR, Annex to Press Release 82/11, 'Preliminary Observations of the IACHR's Rapporteurship on the Rights of Migrant Workers on its Visit to Mexico', 2 August 2011, available at www.cidh.oas.org/pdf%20files/IACHRPreliminaryObservations%20Mexico2011.pdf.

or inadequacy of an institutional response in the face of such situations, and the consequent obstacles to the right of access to justice of abused migrants and their families, their vulnerability to violence and crime and the resulting impunity has been categorised as leaving 'invisible victims'[169] in a situation of double victimisation: the violation of one of their human rights (eg to life, to personal integrity, or the right of women to live free from violence), and the subsequent violation of their right of access to justice.

Similarly, the mass influx of undocumented Cuban migrants arriving in Costa Rica during 2015 in their attempt to cross to Nicaragua as part of their journey to the US—in many cases to reunite with relatives—has awakened 'deep concern' in the IACoHR, due to their 'extreme vulnerability'. In November 2015, upon the massive arrival of 4,500 migrants on the Costa Rican side of the border, the Nicaraguan military security forces barred their passage to Nicaragua and were reported to have committed several human rights abuses.[170]

On the other side of the Atlantic, regarding the attempts of people to reach Europe from Northern Africa and the Middle East, the account is no less critical. Several versions from non-governmental organisations (NGOs) have documented in the last few years high numbers of migrant deaths in the Mediterranean, a sea with many busy shipping lanes where international law and centuries of custom oblige ships to assist those in need. Political upheaval and armed conflict in the Middle East and North Africa since 2011 created particular circumstances that may have led to more people embarking on even more dangerous crossings. Yet, migration to Europe by those fleeing persecution or just seeking a better life is a regular, yearly phenomenon, and so too are deaths at sea. According to the NGO Fortress Europe, over 13,500 people died attempting these crossings between 1998 and 2010.[171] The current refugee crisis of millions of people primarily fleeing armed conflict in Syria, migrating mostly to Turkey, Lebanon and Jordan, and to a much lesser extent to Europe, as recounted in the figures provided above, has also translated into their heightened

[169] See Amnesty International, *Víctimas invisibles. Migrantes en movimiento en México*, 28 April 2010. See also Instituto Tecnológico Autónomo de México (ITAM), *Migración centroamericana en tránsito por México hacia Estados Unidos: Diagnóstico y recomendaciones-Hacia una visión integral, regional y de responsabilidad compartida*, ITAM, Mexico City, 2014, urging for a human security view in the Mexican migratory regime, 34.

[170] IACoHR, 'IACHR Expresses Deep Concern regarding Situation of Cuban Migrants on the Costa Rica-Nicaragua Border', Press Release, 8 December 2015.

[171] See Human Rights Watch, *Hidden Emergency: Migrant Deaths in the Mediterranean*, by Judith Sunderland, Human Rights in Europe, August 2012. See also the analysis in Scheinin, Martin, in collaboration with Ciaran Burke and Alexandre Skander Galand, *Rescue at Sea: Human Rights Obligations of States and Private Actors, with a Focus on the EU's External Borders*, RSCAS Policy Paper 2012/05, Robert Schuman Centre for Advanced Studies, Global Governance Program, European University Institute, Florence, 2012.

vulnerability. The death tolls of people trying to reach European coasts by the Mediterranean Sea have increased tragically during 2015, costing the lives of more than 3700 persons, including children.[172]

Sadly, the perils of those who survive do not end upon arrival to the territory of the country of destination.

ii. Risks to Human Rights of Undocumented Migrants in the Territory of the Receiving State

The risks and actual human rights violations that undocumented migrants encounter in the receiving States in the realms of access to health, personal integrity, social protection measures, labour conditions, housing and food, are myriad and often particularly heightened in the case of women and girls,[173] as will be studied in detail in the following chapter.

Apart from policies, there are also restrictive laws which have enhanced the vulnerability of migrants and deepened their human insecurity—in the case of a federal system even in an asymmetric manner within one same country. An example is the recent Alabama Immigrant Act, or 'Beason-Hammon Act', in the USA, which entered into force on 28 September 2011. A Human Rights Watch report noted that in the first two months that the law was in effect,

> local officials have used it to deny unauthorized immigrants access to everyday necessities such as water and housing in violation of their basic rights. The law also denies all unauthorized immigrants fundamental rights protections that should apply to everyone, not just citizens, making them *more susceptible to discriminatory harassment* and abuse by local authorities and ordinary people. They live in a *climate of fear and uncertainty*, which has had a particularly severe impact on children.[174] (emphasis added)

Similarly, the Support Our Law Enforcement and Safe Neighborhoods Act, referred to as 'Arizona SB 1070', which was analysed recently by the US Supreme Court, has been accused of facilitating racist profiling. The SB 1070 is considered to be the strictest anti-irregular immigration measure in US legislative history. The US Supreme Court considered the constitutionality of the law, widely denounced as being racist, and its judgment is likely to set the direction of immigration law in America for years to come. In Arizona, where the Hispanic population reaches 41 per cent, tensions between residents and the police increase a little more each day. Indeed,

[172] IOM, 'Missing Migrants Project, Migrant Fatalities Worldwide', updated to 17 December 2015, available at http://missingmigrants.iom.int/latest-global-figures.

[173] See the 2011 *Report of the UN Special Rapporteur on Violence Against Women*, UNGA A/66/215, 2011; and Vonk (n 48).

[174] Human Rights Watch, *No Way to Live. Alabama's Immigrant Law* (United States, Human Rights Watch, 2011), quote from back cover.

two specific clauses of the law encourage the police to be more proactive. They can for example, control the identity of anyone coming their way, should they suspect this person of being irregularly on the territory. As a result, the number of Hispanics sent to jail because they were unable to produce their driver's license is constantly on the rise. With more than 30 men and women deported each day, the city of Phoenix has one of the highest deportation rates in the country.[175]

Indeed, these cases have not been left without judicial review, although the outcomes have not always been supportive of immigrants' rights. On 25 June 2012, the US Supreme Court overturned three out of four provisions of the anti-immigration law Arizona SB 1070, arguing that such powers rested with the Federal Government. The Justices blocked parts of Arizona's SB 1070 that would have made it a state crime for irregular immigrants to seek work or not to carry documents. The Court's decision appears to give States such as Arizona quite a limited role in enforcing laws against irregular immigrants. Police departments can notify federal agents if they have a suspect in custody, but they cannot keep the suspect in a county jail simply on State immigration charges. However, the Supreme Court upheld the contentious section 2B, better known as 'show me your papers'. This provision requires the police to check the immigration status of anyone they stop before releasing them. This law and five other similar laws in other States in the US are at present being legally challenged by civil rights' organisations. Taking into account the gender dimension of applying this type of law, several women's rights organisations highlight that women immigrants are making enormous social and economic contributions in US communities and consider that laws like Arizona SB 1070 ignore this reality and reflect 'a broken system that leaves women in the shadows'.

In the United States, risks of violations of human rights of migrants, especially undocumented migrants and asylum-seekers, and the abuses themselves (including rape, trafficking and other forms of serious violence) have revealed such a severe nature that Human Rights Watch conducted extensive research and analysis on the subject, and issued 11 in-depth reports from 2009 to 2011 alone.[176] Against this background,

[175] *The Guardian*, 24 April 2012, referred to in PICUM Bulletin of 9 May 2012.

[176] Those Human Rights Watch reports most related to our subject are: *No Way to Live: Alabama's Immigrant Law*, 14 December 2011; *Detained and at Risk: Sexual Abuse and Harassment in United States Immigration Detention*, 25 August 2010; *Deportation by Default: Mental Disability, Unfair Hearings, and Indefinite Detention in the US Immigration System*, 25 July 2010; *'Tough, Fair, and Practical': A Human Rights Framework for Immigration Reform in the United States*, 8 July 2010; Human Rights Watch, et al, *Returned to Risk: Deportation of HIV Positive Migrants*, 29 September 2009; *United States—Forced Apart (By the Numbers): Non-Citizens Deported*

migrants have not remained passive and have carried out different actions and strategies to claim their rights and gain empowerment.[177] Still, the clandestine situation of undocumented migrants shadows their experiences and often deters their approach to formal mechanisms of justice and redress.

In the case of North Africa, similar accounts may be found. The report *'We Are Foreigners, We Have No Rights': The Plight of Refugees, Asylum-Seekers and Migrants in Libya* gives testimony to the atmosphere of lawlessness, racism and xenophobia, faced by undocumented foreign nationals, and worsened in the post-Gaddafi era. Undocumented non-citizens are at *continuous risk* of exploitation, arbitrary and indefinite detention in harsh conditions, as well as beatings, sometimes amounting to torture.[178] (emphasis added) Analogous conditions met by Ethiopian irregular migrants in Yemen are also accounted for as 'desperate choices' between staying in their country of origin in a situation of poverty and lack of opportunity, or taking the journey to attempt a better life facing serious risks to their physical integrity and basic labour rights.[179]

Similarly, in another African case involving undocumented migrants but with a clearly differentiated gender impact, a report by Human Rights Watch describes an alarming pattern of human rights violations by members of Angolan security forces against Congolese migrants. Women and girls, who are often detained with their children, have been victims of sexual abuse including gang rape, sexual exploitation, and being forced to witness the sexual abuse of other women and girls.[180]

In terms of legally-created risks, many European States have adopted provisions in recent years that criminalise certain aspects of irregular immigration, not clearly differentiating clandestine entrance and residency, with the internationally recognised crimes of people smuggling and human trafficking. In any case, what does seem clear is that, partly due to pressure by EU institutions, we are in the presence of what

Mostly for Nonviolent Offenses, 15 April 2009; *Detained and Dismissed: Women's Struggles to Obtain Health Care in United States Immigration Detention*, 17 March 2009.

[177] See for example Gordon, Jennifer, *Suburban Sweatshops: The Fight for Immigrant Rights* (USA, Belknap/Harvard University Press, 2005), a fascinating work that reconstructs the legal plight of undocumented Mexican migrant workers in New York City in the struggle to claim their rights.

[178] Amnesty International, *"We Are Foreigners, We Have No Rights": The Plight of Refugees, Asylum-Seekers and Migrants in Libya*, November 2012, based on fact-finding visits to Libya between May and September 2012.

[179] See Danish Refugee Council (Regional Office for the Horn of Africa &Yemen)/Regional Mixed Migration Secretariat (RMMS), *Desperate Choices: Conditions, Risks & Protection Failures affecting Ethiopian Migrants in Yemen*, 2012.

[180] Human Rights Watch, *'If You Come Back We Will Kill You': Sexual Violence and Other Abuses Against Congolese Migrants During Expulsions from Angola*, 2012.

some authors have critically called 'the administrativisation of criminal law',[181] referring to the surrender of a juridical-criminal institution to administrative goals external to criminal law. In this case, migration policy goals seem to have crept into criminal law which has traditionally been regarded as *ultima ratio* and not as an instrument to reach public policy objectives.

All these conditions, politically, socially, and legally crafted, place undocumented migrants and their rights at risk, and reiterate, reinforce and enhance their vulnerability. Indeed, their defencelessness and heightened exposure to human rights violations reach levels of structural vulnerability that the human security perspective contributes to make visible.

V. SOME CONCLUSIONS: MIGRATORY REGIMES AS THE ULTIMATE TEST TO HUMAN SECURITY AND HUMAN RIGHTS

Migration across borders is an archetypical transnational phenomenon open to human security scrutiny. Looking at the international legal framework, in a world in which we now have constructed a sufficiently solid legal architecture reaffirming the human rights of all persons mainly through State obligations, it would seem that the rights of migrant persons ought to be made operational according to certain criteria—physical proximity, residence, or degrees of social integration—but that in any case the question is more about the distribution of obligations than about the existence and applicability of such rights.

Still, assuring the human rights of undocumented migrants and other non-citizens has become one of the most challenging situations for contemporary international law. In theoretical terms it places a test on the applicability of the principle of universality of human rights to undocumented migrant persons: the cosmopolitan promise of international human rights law is put to trial. And in practical terms it is a challenge as well because the condition of undocumented migrant is one of the gravest sources of vulnerability today.

Human security allows to make visible the detrimental effect on human rights of the increasingly severe application of immigration restrictions, which may and does leave persons outside the law or invisible to the

[181] Cancio Meliá, Manuel and Mario Maraver Gómez, 'El derecho penal español ante la inmigración: un estudio político-criminal' in Bacigalupo/Cancio Meliá (eds), *Derecho penal y política transnacional* (Barcelona, Atelier, 2005) 343–415 (reference from 398; all translations are my own), signalling the contradictions of the Spanish legal system and arguing that they can be better explained through a logic of 'criminal law of the enemy' (*derecho penal del enemigo*) that focuses on the author as member of a group, rather than on the criminal action as such.

law,[182] and therefore in a situation of State-constructed vulnerability. Paradoxically, the strict and often arbitrary application of certain laws, in the form of administrative (and increasingly criminal) immigration regulations, seems to be hindering the effective implementation of human rights law, with respect to sizeable sectors of the population, namely undocumented migrants.

The irregular character of their entry or residence in a given State would seem to extend at times to the whole realm of the human experience of undocumented migrants. In addition, the perceived threat posed by increased migration and population mobility, both within and across borders, is often presented as a critical situation where respect for human rights is seen as an additional luxury because undocumented migrants are considered to enjoy or deserve diminished human rights protection. These conditions tend to place undocumented migrants in a certain '*legal limbo*', void of rights or the possibility of accessing them. This is particularly true of detention centres where migrants are forced to reside while their legal situation is determined. In this respect, human security has been defended as a relevant tool for arguing in favour of moving 'from rights-free zones to rights-fulfilling States'.[183]

Let us now turn to analyse how both types of the studied risks, at the fault line and once in the territory of the receiving State, particularly affect the human security and human rights of undocumented migrant women and girls. In doing so, we will connect the two main thematic cores of this book—violence against women and conditions faced by undocumented migrants—under the encompassing lens of human security.

[182] See for example Düvell, Franck and Bastian Vollmer, *European Security Challenges*, EU-US Immigration Systems 2011/07, Robert Schuman Centre for Advanced Studies, San Domenico di Fiesole (FI): European University Institute, 2011.

[183] Human Rights Ahead, 'What Next for Human Rights?', Working Paper, A Reflection on the 60th Anniversary of the Universal Declaration of Human Rights, Human Rights Ahead, Spain, December 2008, available at www.hrahead.org/our-agenda/promoting-human-security.

6

Undocumented Female Migrants and Illustrative Migrant Cases

I. INTRODUCTION

THE ANALYSIS PRESENTED regarding the thematic cores of Chapters 4 and 5, violence against women, and the rights of undocumented migrants, converge in the present chapter to examine, under the human security–human rights synergy, the aggravated vulnerability and violence experienced by undocumented migrant women and girls. Indeed, some of the limits and lacunae of international law addressing undocumented migrants are especially identifiable when applying a gendered human security focus.[1] Some of these shortcomings have fortunately been placed as a priority consideration by the UN Committee on the Rights of Migrant Workers and Members of their Families, as well as by other human rights bodies, as will be described below.

Thus, section II will apply a gendered human security lens, as articulated in Chapter 4, to study the different gendered implications of migration reflected in the various forms of violence against undocumented female migrants and undocumented domestic workers.

In section III the text will reflect on some general illustrative quasi-judicial and judicial cases concerning migrants in general, which intend to exemplify how a human security-sensitive perspective may orientate the interpretation of human rights when put to work in practice, as well as the consequences that may unfold when it is overlooked.

Concluding section IV presents some reflections applicable both to the previous and the present chapter, on the necessity of undocumented

[1] On these gaps and flaws, see Mullally, Siobhán, 'Domestic Violence Asylum Claims and Recent Developments in International Human Rights Law: A Progress Narrative? (2011) *International and* 60, 459–484; Fudge, Judy, 'Decent Work for Migrant Care Workers'at 'Gender and Migration: Workers at the Interface of Migration and Development', UN Women, International Labour Organization (ILO), at the Fourth United Nations Conference on the Least Developed Countries (LDC-IV), May 2011, available at www.ilo.org/global/meetings-and-events/events/conference-on-least-developed-countries/WCMS_155339/lang--en/index.htm. See also Resnik, Judith, *Migrations and Mobilities: Citizenship, Borders, and Gender* (co-edited with Seyla Benhabib) (New York, New York University Press, 2009).

migrants, particularly female migrants, to realise their 'right to have access to rights' as an essential human security requirement to thereby achieve the fulfilment of their universally recognised human rights.

II. UNDOCUMENTED FEMALE MIGRANTS: WORKERS AND WOMEN AT RISK

In adopting a gendered human security approach to the condition of women migrant workers, the most vulnerable being domestic workers, it has to be noted that the spectrum of discrimination, exploitation and human rights violations experienced by such workers is at times promoted by international law itself. The architecture of international human rights law, allowing exceptions in the application of labour and social security standards, partly supporting the traditional private/public divide, and permitting the imposition of migration restrictions, as reviewed in section III of the previous chapter, do not deeply challenge this continuum.

Similarly, the recently adopted ILO Convention Concerning Decent Work for Domestic Workers, otherwise an important advancement, excludes from the applicability of the Convention persons who perform domestic work only occasionally or sporadically and not on an occupational basis (Article 1.c)) and permits States parties to exclude wholly or partly from its scope 'limited categories of workers in respect of which special problems of a substantial nature arise' (Article 2.2.b)).[2] In this context, the recourse to private means to meet the demand for certain lines of work, and the recruitment of migrant domestic workers to meet 'care deficits', not only evidence a retreat from the Welfare State, but also fail to pose broader questions on how to value and maintain care work.

In this context, the care deficit experienced in several European Welfare States, especially in Southern Europe, is particularly relevant for migrant female workers. Indeed, the demand for domestic and other workers to carry out care functions, often finds the side of supply in migrant women. Although there is an identifiable demand–supply relationship, due to economic austerity and frequent fears for social and political cohesion running along (often post-colonial) ethnic and racial lines, the claims for a harsher State immigration policy have become stronger, shaping the

[2] ILO Convention 189, *Convention Concerning Decent Work For Domestic Workers*, adopted by the General Conference of the ILO at its 100th session, 16 June 2011. See also Robinson, Fiona, 'The Importance of Care in the Theory and Practice of Human Security' (2008) 4 *Journal of International Political Theory* 2, 167–88. The author argues however that a human rights-based approach to human security does not sufficiently take into account the relevance of relations of care, caring values and care activities for the maintenance of long-term human security.

'transnational political economy of care'.[3] As a result, European State policy has recently overlooked or denied the existence of such an economic relationship, closing the legal channels for safe migration routes to access the territory of demanding States and the care labour market, and thus impacting on the entrance of migrants, especially women, through irregular means to the host State and on the creation of spaces for them to live and work in an undocumented manner.[4]

Again, this 'legal limbo' in turn places migrant women in an exposed position to labour exploitation, abuse and violence, with the differentiated gender dimension this involves. As many of the rest of the so called 'low-skilled' migrants, as well as the broad category of undocumented migrants, most women leave a State where they experience poverty and exclusion, to move within a market that wants and needs migrants, but doesn't welcome them, in turn facing a State that offers few avenues to defend, protect and guarantee their rights. Indeed, human insecurity is the cause and consequence of their condition. Within the realm of migrants in general, though, the vulnerability constructed by the law is at the heart of *undocumented* migrant women's human insecurity.

Several civil society organisations have also documented the effects of the lack of access to justice of undocumented women abused and living in EU countries.[5] For example, a recent Human Rights Watch report tellingly entitled *'The Law was Against Me': Migrant Women's Access to Protection for Family Violence in Belgium*, found major protection gaps for migrant women who experience domestic violence in Belgium. Women who migrate to Belgium to join a husband or partner may face deportation if they report the violence during the period when their status is being confirmed, as do undocumented migrant women. Domestic violence victims, especially undocumented women, also lack adequate access to shelters. These shelters often require women to contribute to the cost. Undocumented women who cannot do so are not eligible for financial support

[3] See Williams, Fiona, 'Towards a Transnational Analysis of the Political Economy of Care', SULCIS Working Papers, Stockholm University Linnaeus Center for Integration Studies—SULCIS / Scandinavian Working Papers on Economics, WP No 2011:6, 9 August 2011.

[4] Summary presented by Siobhán Mullaly as part of an on-going research project on Migrant Domestic Workers and EU Law, Workshop on Gender and Migration held at the EUI on June 19–21 2012. Personal notes taken. See also UN OHCHR, Europe Regional Office, *Rights of Migrant Domestic Workers in Europe*, 2011, available at www.europe.ohchr.org/Documents/Publications/Study_Domestic_Migrant_webversion.pdf. See also Triandafyllidou, Anna, 'Irregular Migration and Domestic Work in Europe: Who Cares?' in Triandafyllidou, Anna (ed), *Irregular Migrant Domestic Workers in Europe: Who Cares?* (Burlington, Farnham, Research in Migration and Ethnic Relations Series, Ashgate, 2013) 1–15.

[5] See Human Rights Watch (HRW), 'Belgium: Abused Migrant Women Fear Deportation. Legal Loopholes, Inadequate Shelter Access Send Women Back to Abusers', 8 November 2012, available at www.hrw.org/news/2012/11/08/belgium-abused-migrant-women-fear-deportation.

from local authorities available to other victims of domestic violence. Some women end up living on the streets after escaping very violent partners, who on occasions have threatened to kill them.[6]

Indeed, undocumented women are particularly vulnerable. Unauthorised stay in several EU countries is a criminal offence and police are required to report anyone who they suspect is in the country illegally to immigration authorities, such as in Belgium, for example. Women who do come forward have few avenues to obtaining legal status, especially if they do not have children. Other women endure years of abuse at the hands of their partner, coming forward only when they obtain permanent residence through their children: only when they 'have papers'.[7] One of the civil society logos of 'sans papiers, mais pas sans droits'[8] seems to crudely come to mind.

Undocumented migrant women, including those who lost residency rights as a result of escaping violence, may risk deportation when they seek help from the police, and even if they are entitled to receive protection, many do not know this and continue to fear deportation. Indeed, 'the real or perceived risk of deportation may create almost insurmountable barriers for undocumented victims of domestic violence to seek help and protection and can expose them to further abuse and exploitation. It also leads to impunity for perpetrators'.[9] In the case of the US, as was mentioned above, through the application of certain laws such as Arizona's SB 1070, the fact that women immigrants are making enormous social and economic contributions in US communities is overlooked and such laws reflect 'a broken system that leaves women in the shadows'.

A. Responses by Human Rights Actors

Migrants' precarious situation in the US has merited a strong response by academia and civil society. In a similar exercise to the 2011 *Maastricht Principles on Extraterritorial Obligations of States in the area of Economic, Social and Cultural Rights*, referred to in Chapter 3, section I on Article 28 of the UDHR, members of academia and social and human rights

[6] See HRW, *'The Law was Against Me': Migrant Women's Access to Protection for Family Violence in Belgium*, November 2012. Belgium signed the Council of Europe Convention on Preventing and Combating Violence against Women and Domestic Violence on 11 September 2012, but has yet to ratify it.

[7] HRW, *'The Law was Against Me'*, *ibid*, Executive Summary. See also the web-documentary by PICUM www.undocumentary.org for accounts on immigration legislation in several European countries.

[8] See GISTI, Groupe d' Information et de Soutien des Immigrés, 'Les notes pratiques. Sans-papiers mais pas sans droits', 5e édition, juin 2009, available at www.gisti.org/publication_pres.php?id_article=1615.

[9] HRW, *'The Law was Against Me'* (n 6) p 39.

organisations also adopted in 2011 a set of principles—in this case specifically addressing non-citizens—the *Boston Principles on the Economic, Social and Cultural Rights of Noncitizens*.[10] Focusing attention on ESC Rights, rather than on the dominant US tradition of civil and political rights, the Boston Principles are 30 standards drawn from international human rights, humanitarian, and migration-related treaties, guidelines, and other statements of best practice, as well as recommendations by US-based civil society. Specifically based on challenging the invocation of 'national security' as a legitimation by US federal, state and local officials to tighten immigration measures and limit immigrants' rights, the Principles include many articulations of rights which are interesting for the purposes of this book.

Applying a cross-cutting and integrated perspective, the Boston Principles build on recent developments in international human rights law and reaffirm the general principles of equality and non-discrimination towards all non-citizens regardless of immigration status (Principles 1 and 2), combining them with specific State obligations regarding the rights of non-citizens, particularly children (Principles 22, 23 and 25), *women at risk of gender-based discrimination and violence* (Principle 26), members of minorities or indigenous peoples (Principle 24), persons with disabilities (Principles 27 and 28), and asylum-seekers or refugees (Principle 29).[11] In a similar vein to the position of this book, the Principles reaffirm the rights of access to justice and accountability (Principles 7 and 8), and the rights to an adequate standard of living, decent work, education, health, social security and family life of all non-citizens, documented and undocumented (Principles 9, 10, 19, 20–22). (emphasis added)

As standards especially affecting the situation of undocumented migrants, the Principles signal State obligations to respect core human rights at stake in immigration proceedings and enforcement actions. Recognising deportation as one of the most severe sanctions a government can carry out, it calls for residence in the US and family ties to be given due consideration in any proceeding that may result in such measure (Principle 5). In a principle echoing the Inter-American Court of Human Rights' (IACHR) Advisory Opinion 18/03, *Juridical Condition and Rights*

[10] *The Boston Principles on the Economic, Social and Cultural Rights of Noncitizens* ('The Boston Principles'), 1 May 2011, Annotated Version, available at www.northeastern.edu/law/pdfs/academics/phrge-principles-long.pdf; see also Lewis, Hope and Rachel E Rosenbloom, 'The Boston Principles: An Introduction' (2011) *Notre Dame Journal of International, Comparative and Human Rights Law* 1, 145–56.

[11] The Principles were discussed within the Institute of Human Rights 'Beyond National Security: Immigrant Communities and Economic, Social and Cultural Rights' held at Northeastern University School of Law on 14–15 October 2010; see the resulting Report with the same name published by the Program on Global Economy and Human Rights of Northeastern University School of Law, 15 May 2012.

of Undocumented Migrants (AO 18/03), of 2003, studied in the previous chapter, the Boston Principles also remind us that deportation shall not be resorted to for the purpose of depriving a non-citizen worker of the employment rights arising out of the authorisation of residence and the work permit, nor in retaliation for the exercise of workers' rights or for seeking the protection of other human rights (Principle 18).

In adopting a human security-sensitive lens, the Principles include 'the right to access public benefits *without fear*' (Principle 6). Notably, they also set forth the right of non-citizens to seek asylum and enlist an additional criterion to the traditional ones in laying down their right to be protected against forcible return to or resettlement in any place where the non-citizen's life, safety, liberty *and/or health* would be at risk, which seems to direct us towards the reflections on the gender-relevant *Case of N v UK* by the ECHR, presented below and in Chapter 7 of this text. In a standard that would reduce undocumented migrants' human insecurity and sense of fear, the Principles go one step further and recognise a right of all non-citizens and members of their families, *including those who entered the country irregularly*, to pursue citizenship according to due process of law and in accordance with their human rights (Principle 29).

The Principles are also clear in stating that 'Immigration laws, policy and enforcement must not be discriminatory in *intent or effect*. Measures taken for *national security* must be *free of discrimination* and must *ensure* that noncitizens are *not subjected* to racial, ethnic, or religious profiling or stereotyping' (Principle 30). Cognisant of the interrelated risks that such justifications entail for overall human security, the annotated version of Principle 30 clarifies that 'The *systematic* violation of human rights undermines national security and public order and *itself jeopardizes international and domestic peace and security*'.[12]

More generally, the UN Committee on the Protection of the Rights of All Migrant Workers and Members of their Families (UN Committee on RMW) plays a fundamental role in shedding light on the vulnerabilities faced by migrants, particularly female migrants, and clarifying the concrete ways in which human rights of all migrant workers, documented and undocumented, and members of their families should be understood and applied.

Indeed, in its General Comment No 1, *Migrant Domestic Workers*, of 2011, the UN Committee on RMW noted that

> migrant domestic workers are at *heightened risk* of certain forms of exploitation and abuse … These *risks and vulnerabilities* are further aggravated for migrant domestic workers who are *non-documented or in an irregular situation*, not least

[12] The Boston Principles, Understanding C of Principle 30, 'Impact of Human Rights Violations on Security'.

> because they often risk deportation if they contact State authorities to seek protection from an abusive employer.[13] (emphasis added)

In this sense, undocumented migrants often face a *double victimisation* given that on the one hand, their irregular status places them at higher risk of violations of their human rights, and on the other, their human right of *access to justice* is also affected because of their fear of deportation. The Committee also highlights a similar exposure and a correlated fear which aggravates such risk, when it analyses 'women migrant domestic workers with irregular status, who are *especially vulnerable* during pregnancy, as they are often *afraid* to contact public health services out of *fear of deportation*'.[14] Similarly, the CEDAW Committee has recently recognised how migrant women are also *disproportionately criminalised* owing to their status, and the impact of this as an obstacle to their right of access to justice.[15]

Turning to the regional reality in Europe, one possible way to fully address the gaps for migrant women described in the present section, is to promote State ratification of the Council of Europe Convention on Preventing and Combating Violence against Women and Domestic Violence, the Istanbul Convention, described in Chapter 4, which requires countries to ensure protection irrespective of migrant status (Article 4.3). It also singles out 'migrant women' as a group in a specific state of vulnerability, under the consideration that

> migrant women, with or without documents, and women asylum-seekers are *particularly vulnerable* to gender-based violence. Although their reasons for leaving their country vary, as does their legal status, both groups are at *increased risk of violence* and face similar difficulties in overcoming it. It also requires that measures be taken to *prevent* such violence and *support victims* while taking into account the needs of vulnerable persons.[16] (emphasis added)

As mentioned above, though, at the time of writing only some European countries have ratified the Convention and the Convention only entered into force in 2014. As an on-going complementary position to strengthen legally binding provisions, I argue for a human security-based approach that can fill gaps requiring non-Party States to act under a *due diligence obligation* to prevent and take measures to address such violence against women, independently of the existence (or not) of a strict, fully developed legal obligation to do so.

[13] UN Committee on the Protection of the Rights of all Migrant Workers and Members of their Families, General Comment No 1, *Migrant Domestic Workers*, CRMW/C/GC/1, 23 February 2011, para 7.

[14] *Ibid*, para. 43.

[15] CEDAW Committee, General Recommendation No 33, *Women's Access to Justice*, CEDAW/C/GC/33, 3 August 2015, para 49.

[16] See 'Migrant women, women asylum-seekers and women refugees', at www.coe.int/en/web/istanbul-convention/the-convention-in-brief

Addressing the conditions of undocumented migrants at the global level, in its account of State obligations towards undocumented migrant domestic workers, especially women and children, the UN Committee qualifies the vulnerabilities they face as 'extreme' and based on Article 69 of the International Convention on the Protection of the Rights of All Migrant Workers and Members of their Families (CRMW) calls for States to take appropriate measures to address such vulnerabilities and 'consider policies, including regularization programmes, to avoid or resolve situations in which migrant domestic workers are undocumented or are at risk of falling into irregular status'.[17]

The intersectional discrimination[18] suffered as an undocumented migrant worker and as a woman, had also been signalled by the UN CEDAW Committee in its General Recommendation No 26 on *Women Migrant Workers*, of 2008, as was mentioned in Chapter 5.

Similarly, the recent International Labour Organization (ILO) Convention Concerning Decent Work for Domestic Workers refers in Articles 8 and 15 to the State obligation to also apply the provisions of the Convention to domestic migrant workers and the duty to protect them from abusive practices, including those carried out by private employers.[19]

Because of the pervasive risks detected in relation to the rights of undocumented migrants and the recognition that 'migrant workers and members of their families in an irregular situation often *live in fear*', the UN Committee on RMW dedicated its General Comment No 2, of 2013, to the broad questions regarding precisely *The rights of migrant workers in an irregular situation and members of their families*. Migrant women and girls within this group are unable or unwilling to turn to institutional mechanisms to seek redress for such violations. Due to the clandestine nature of their existence as undocumented workers, they fear denial of their rights or deportation if they dare come forward, for they often face serious substantive or procedural obstacles when they do.[20]

The cumulative and multiple forms of risk and discrimination identified by the UN Committee and to a certain extent by the ILO, are also confirmed by cases of the last few years in the US, reflected in the

[17] General Comment No 1 (n 13) para 52.

[18] On intersectional discrimination, see Crenshaw, Kimberley, 'Mapping the Margins: Intersectionality, Identity Politics, and Violence Against Women of Color' (1991) 43 *Stanford Law Review*. See also Lewis, Hope, 'Between Irua and "Female Genital Mutilation": Feminist Human Rights Discourse and the Cultural Divide' (1995) 8 *Harvard Human Rights Journal* 1; and Banks, Taunya Lovell, 'Toward a Global Critical Feminist Vision: Domestic Work and the Nanny Tax Debate' (1999) 3 *Journal of Gender Race & Justice* 1, 1–44.

[19] ILO Convention 189, Convention Concerning Decent Work For Domestic Workers, adopted by the General Conference of the International Labour Organization at its 100th session, 16 June 2011.

[20] UN Committee on RMW, General Comment No 2 *on the Rights of Migrant Workers in an Irregular Situation and Members of their Families*, 23 August 2013, point I.2.

report by Human Rights Watch issued in May 2012, *Cultivating Fear: The Vulnerability of Immigrant Farmworkers in the US to Sexual Violence and Sexual Harassment*. The report reveals that hundreds of thousands of immigrant farmworker women and girls in the United States face a *high risk of sexual violence and sexual harassment* in their workplaces because, according to the report, US authorities and employers fail to protect them adequately. The report describes rape, stalking, unwanted touching, exhibitionism, or vulgar and obscene language by supervisors, employers, and others in positions of power. Most farmworkers interviewed said they had not reported these or other workplace abuses, due to *fear* of reprisals, job loss or deportation. The report emphasises the way in which immigrant farmworkers are subject to a dysfunctional immigration system and labour laws that exclude them from basic protections that many workers take for granted.[21]

As an illustration of the practical application of the gendered human security framework proposed in this book, one can find that the risk of human rights violations in these conditions in the United States had already been highlighted some months before by the UN Special Rapporteur on Violence against Women. The Special Rapporteur, Rashida Manjoo, reported that her visit in 2011 to the US revealed the *particular vulnerability of undocumented immigrant women to violence, including sexual harassment and abuse, in the workplace*.[22] (emphasis added)

In the face of this 'red alarm', that is, *knowing* of the existence of actual abuses and *risks* of further violations, according to the criteria already analysed before in this text, the State's obligations of protection had been triggered. The US or any State in the same situation, had an obligation to prevent and protect women farmworkers, especially immigrant women as particularly vulnerable, from the human rights violations they had already suffered or were likely to encounter. If a human security approach had been taken by US authorities in the light of the UN Special Rapporteur's report, and the evidence documented thereby, probably some of these human rights violations would have been prevented. As it has been shown above in Chapter 4, the use of non-governmental sources of information, like this NGO report, is one of the human security tools used recently in judicial analysis to shape the courts' view on the level of State responsibility.

Although not explicitly referring to undocumented migrant women, General Comment No 3 of the UN Committee against Torture, of 2012, seems to perfectly fit the conditions faced by such women and the need for States to guarantee their human security in relation to their right of

[21] Available at www.hrw.org/node/107044.

[22] Report of the UN Special Rapporteur on Violence against Women, UN General Assembly Resolution A/66/215, 2011, paras 43–46.

access to justice. The General Comment devotes significant attention to the duty for States to ensure that women and also victims of torture or inhuman or degrading treatment who are members of other marginalised or vulnerable groups (a category applicable to undocumented migrants, for example) are not denied access to justice or mechanisms for seeking and obtaining redress on a discriminatory basis, and also stresses that States must ensure that procedures to determine redress do not pose *obstacles* to members of vulnerable groups that could *prevent or discourage them from pursuing their claims*.[23] (emphasis added)

The way legal irregularity interacts with the susceptibility of women migrant workers as exposed in the above-mentioned documents, allows for a deeper understanding of their 'constructed vulnerability'.[24]

When confronted with the violation of a particular human right, undocumented migrants, and especially women and girls within this group, are unable or unwilling to turn to the institutional mechanisms to seek redress for such violation. Due to the clandestinity derived from their irregular legal status, they fear denial of their rights or deportation if they dare come forward, or they often face serious substantive or procedural obstacles when they do. This violation of both a certain human right and to their right to access to justice, translates into a double victimisation as explained above, and constitutes a grave source of human insecurity.

Indeed, access to justice is one of the most indicative rights of a generalised state of societal human security. As emphasised above, the inability to seek and obtain a remedy for breaches of domestic and international human rights law, exacerbates the *vulnerability, insecurity and isolation* of persons living in poverty and *perpetuates* their impoverishment.[25] Certain groups as ethnic and racial minorities, contemporarily coupled with migrants, especially women, have been recognised as suffering *structural discrimination and exclusion, disproportionately* represented among the *poor*, and therefore encountering *additional barriers to access justice*.[26] (emphasis added)

[23] UN Committee against Torture, General Comment No 3, *Implementation of Article 14 by States Parties*, CAT/C/GC/3, 19 November 2012, paras 32–34.

[24] On the role of the State in constructing vulnerability, see Anderson, Bridget, 'Mobilizing Migrants, Making Citizens: Migrant Domestic Workers as Political Agents' (2010) 33 *Ethnic and Racial Studies* 1, 69. See also Scrinzi, Francesca, 'The Globalisation of Domestic Work: Women Migrants and Neodomesticity' in Freedman, Jane (ed), *Gender and Insecurity: Migrant Women in Europe* (Aldershot, Ashgate, 2003) 77–90.

[25] See *Guiding Principles on Extreme Poverty and Human Rights* (contained in the Final Draft submitted by the Special Rapporteur on extreme poverty and human rights, Magdalena Sepúlveda Carmona, UN General Assembly Resolution A/HC/21/39, 18 July 2012), endorsed by UN Human Rights Council in Resolution 21/11 of 27 September 2012, para 67.

[26] *Report by the UN Special Rapporteur on extreme poverty and human rights on the obstacles to access to justice for persons living in poverty*, UN General Assembly Resolution A/67/278, 9 August 2012, para 18.

For some authors such as Judge Cançado Trindade, the right of individuals to access the international system of justice has even reached the status of *ius cogens*.[27]

The debate on the status in international law of the right of access to justice, or more specifically to international justice, as part of *ius cogens*, exceeds the main focus of this book. The relevant fact for our purposes is to note that this debate reflects the high significance of this human right in international law and that, in any case, the human right of access to justice is a 'key' right, which serves as guarantee of the general functioning of a legal system as a means not only for proper individual redress but also as an indicator of the social and political legitimacy of a legal system as a whole. An effective realisation of the right of access to justice at a generalised level, through the path of reparations, also gives way to the re-composing of the system where it has been unwilling or unable to duly prevent the violation or properly protect the person from certain risk factors. Contrarily, this chapter's examples of the systemic obstacles faced by undocumented migrant persons, particularly women and girls, for this right to be fulfilled, reveal serious protection gaps in the national and international legal framework and/or its implementation and such barriers place them in a situation of structural vulnerability.

III. ILLUSTRATIVE LEGAL CASES OF A HUMAN SECURITY APPROACH TO MIGRANTS' HUMAN RIGHTS

This section intends to exemplify how a human security-sensitive perspective may orient the interpretation of human rights when put to work in practice in regards to the situation of migrants, as well as the consequences that may unfold when it is overlooked. The selected case-law is not exhaustive and rather intends to illustrate the concrete forms in which a 'human security approach' is embedded in these normative legal expressions and where there is room for creative construction and alternative interpretations. Thus, the section will draw the picture of how some of the identified normative tools of Chapter 5 and this chapter, may be utilised to enhance human rights protection when applied through a human security-based approach or reduce such protection when disregarded.

[27] See Cançado Trindade, Antônio Augusto, *The Access of Individuals to International Justice* (Oxford, New York, Oxford University Press, 2011). Let us also recall in this instance the precedent set by the decisions of the ICJ in the *Avena Case* (*Mexico v United States*, Judgment of 31 March 2004) and the *LaGrand Case* (*Germany v United States*, Judgment of 27 June 2001). In these cases, the ICJ called for the US to remedy, in its domestic law, a violation of a fundamental right of the individual, specifically Article 36 of the Vienna Convention on Consular Relations, setting forth the right of foreigners arrested in one of the States parties to be advised of their right to consular assistance, a right of which Mexican and German detainees, respectively, had not been informed of by US authorities.

A. 'Human Security-Sensitive' Cases

With its call to view widespread and systematic threats that are often overlooked in traditional individualistic human rights analysis, the idea of a human security-sensitive outlook seems to have found its way as a useful tool for judicial interpretation, of which those with a more direct bearing on the identification of structural vulnerabilities under the human security-human rights synergy will be discussed in further detail in the following subsections.

i. MSS v Belgium and Greece

The ECHR in the case of *MSS v Belgium and Greece*, precisely in the realm of non-citizens, considered the transfer of an Afghan asylum-seeker from Belgium to Greece—where he had been living on the streets with no access to minimum means of subsistence—to be a violation by Belgium of Article 3 (on obligation of *non-refoulment*) and of such Article in conjunction with Article 13 (right to an effective remedy) of the European Convention on Human Rights and Fundamental Freedoms (ECoHR). It also concluded that Greece violated Article 3 because the living conditions experienced by the applicant as part of the group of asylum-seekers more generally, amounted to a violation of the right to be free from torture and inhuman or degrading treatment. Notably, it did so arguing that MSS was in a vulnerable situation by taking into account his individual distress but against the background of *systemic conditions of material deprivation* faced in Greece by asylum-seekers as a 'vulnerable population group in need of special protection'.[28] In this respect, one may recall that the analysis of systemic risk situations is considered as a general stand in the 1984 Cartagena Declaration on Refugees, explained in Chapter 2.

Based on considerations of existing systemic risks for asylum-seekers in Greece, the ECHR found that the decision by Belgium to return the applicant to Greece (the country where he had first entered the EU), violated Article 3 because it exposed him to treatment prohibited in such Article, such prohibition being of an absolute nature and regarded by international case-law and legal analysis to constitute *ius cogens*.[29]

It is true that the ECHR had for many years maintained that an expulsion or deportation of an individual to a country where she or he may

[28] ECHR, *MSS v Belgium and Greece*, App No 30696/09, 21 January 2011, para 251; see also paras 232 and 233.

[29] On *ius cogens*, see, eg, ICJ, *Application of the Convention on the Prevention and Punishment of the Crime of Genocide, Preliminary Objections*, Judgment, ICJ Reports 1996, p 595; and *Reservations to the Convention on Genocide*, Advisory Opinion, ICJ Reports 1951, p 15; *Case Concerning The Barcelona Traction, Light and Power Company, Limited, Belgium v Spain*, Judgment 5 February 1970, para 33.

be subjected to treatment in violation of Article 3 incurs the responsibility of the deporting State under the Convention.[30] It had also constrained asylum-seeker and refugee removals by reliance on the prohibition of exposure to torture or to inhuman or degrading treatment or punishment, requiring a verification by the State of a real risk under Article 3 through an examination of the foreseeable consequences of the expulsion that took into account (1) the general situation in the country of destination and (2) the personal circumstances of the asylum-seeker.[31] But the decision in *MSS* is original in the sense of insisting that *subjection to severe precarious economic conditions abroad* may meet that test.[32] Emphasising objective as well as subjective elements of human insecurity, the Court noted MSS's indigence in Greece due to official inaction, the 'prolonged uncertainty' of his situation, and the 'total lack of any prospects of his situation improving', and considered such conditions to also give rise to a violation by Greece of the absolute prohibition of torture and inhuman treatment contained in Article 3.[33]

In what would seem to be a connection between policy considerations and judicial adjudication, the UN Millennium Development Goals (MDG) Report 2010 had warned that

> Conflicts are a major threat to *human security* and to hard-won MDG gains. Years after a conflict has ended, large populations of refugees remain in camps with limited employment and education opportunities and inadequate health services. Not surprisingly, refugees often become dependent on subsistence-level assistance and *lead lives of poverty and unrealized potential*.[34] (emphasis added)

In recognising material deprivation as amounting to inhuman treatment and, in consequence, to a possible basis for violation of the *non-refoulment*

[30] As the first in a line of cases in this sense, see *Soering v United Kingdom*, 7 July 1989, Series A No 161, paras 90–91, where the US sought the extradition from the UK of a fugitive who faced murder charges in the state of Virginia. The applicant sought to have the extradition halted on the grounds that should he be convicted of murder in the US, he would face the death penalty. See also *Chahal v the United Kingdom*, 15 November 1996, para 96.

[31] See the ECHR cases of *Y v Russia*, Appl No 20113/07, 4 December 2008, see note 88, para 78; *Saadi v Italy*, Appl No 37201/06, 28 February 2008, paras 128–29; *N v Finland*, 38885/02, Appl No 38885/02, 26 July 2005, see note 87, para 167; *Vilvarajah and Others v The United Kingdom*, Appl Nos 13163/87, 13164/87, 13165/87, 13447/87, 13448/87, 30 October 1991, para 108.

[32] See the analysis in Hesselman, Marlies, 'Sharing International Responsibility for Poor Migrants? An Analysis of Extra-Territorial Socio-Economic Human Rights Law' (2013) 15 *European Journal of Social Security* 2, 187–208.

[33] *MSS v Belgium and Greece* (n 28) paras 260–63. See also paras 238 and 239, and concluding paras 5, 10 and 13. In this sense, see also United Nations High Commissioner for Refugees (UNHCR), 'Submission by the Office of the United Nations High Commissioner for Refugees in the case of *M.S.S. v. Belgium and Greece*', June 2010, available at www.unhcr.org/4d4bfebe9.pdf.

[34] UN, *The Millennium Development Goals Report 2010* (MDG Report 2010) p 15. See also O'Sullivan, Maria, 'Human Security and the Protection of Refugees in Africa' in Abass, Ademola (ed), *Protecting Human Security in Africa* (Oxford, Oxford University Press, 2010).

principle, the ECHR upheld the right of MSS—an Afghan national—under Article 3 of the European Convention, not to be expelled by Belgium due to the risk of suffering torture or inhuman or degrading treatment because of the systemic precarious socio-economic conditions of asylum-seekers in the country of return, and the risk of not being able to access an adequate remedy in case of violations given the particularly appalling living conditions of asylum-seekers in Greece.[35] Thus, the Court concluded, among other violations, that Belgium had violated the principle of *non-refoulment*, and that Greece had also violated Article 3 on the account of the living conditions of MSS which amounted to inhuman or degrading treatment.

Through the decision, the Court also endorsed MSS's entitlement to exist within a context of social conditions that allowed him to enjoy the broader freedom to live in dignity, in line with the idea of human security *as an enabling environment for human rights*, as argued in Chapter 3 of this book. In turn, this individual decision seems to find a shared link with the prevalent more generalised concern at the global level expressed in the MDG Report regarding the hardship confronted by refugees and asylum-seekers as a collective.

To put this case in its proper context, as the human security emphasis pushes us to do, one must also consider that Afghans and Iraqis were at the time of the Court's consideration, the largest refugee populations under the UNHCR mandate (currently outnumbered by Syrians), totalling 2.9 million and 1.8 million people, respectively, according to data from the end of 2009. Together they accounted for nearly half of all refugees under UNHCR care.[36] In light of this, the case of *MSS v Belgium and Greece* acquires special relevance and raises acute questions as to the role of developed countries in the global refugee system and, more importantly, in upholding the humanitarian principles that gave way to its creation.

ii. NS and Others v SSHD

The possible influence of human security ideas at the European level may be adventured into even further in looking at the more reduced

[35] *MSS v Belgium and Greec* (n 28) paras 357–59. For other ECHR cases involving non-nationals, see *Gaygusuz v Austria*, Judgment of 16 September 1996, para 42; *Koua Poirrez v France*, Judgment of 30 September 2003, para 46. In both of these judgments, Article 1 of the First Protocol to the ECHR, 1952, concerned with the protection of property, was interpreted as encompassing access to social security benefits for the non-nationals concerned. See also UN Human Rights Committee (HRC), Communication No 965/2000 concerning the case *Karakurt v Austria*, 4 Apr 2002, UN Doc CCPR/C/74/D/965/2000, para 8.4, relating to a regularly working Turkish citizen in Austria and the limitation to his right to stand for election to the relevant work-council, on the basis of his citizenship. The UN HRC decided there had actually been a violation of Art 26 of the International Covenant on Civil and Political Rights on non-discrimination.

[36] MDG Report 2010 (n 34) p 15. For updates, see http://data.unhcr.org/mediterranean/regional.php

geographic area of competence of the EU, through a recent case by the Court of Justice of the European Union (CJEU), *NS and Others v SSHD*, of 2011, which was similar to the ECHR case of *MSS v Belgium and Greece*, but occurred 11 months later, in England rather than in Belgium. The case concerned an Afghan asylum-seeker in the United Kingdom who first entered the EU through Greece. Ordinarily the applicant would have been sent to Greece to have his asylum claim considered there. However, he challenged his transfer to Greece, claiming that his human rights would be infringed by such a transfer as Greece would be unable to process his application. There also seems to be a human security perspective at work in the interpretation of EU law in this case in the way the Court considered collective conditions and systemic obstacles for the enjoyment of human rights, when it declared that

> Member States, including the national courts, may not transfer an asylum seeker to the "Member State responsible" … where they cannot be unaware that *systemic deficiencies* in the asylum procedure and in the reception conditions of asylum seekers in that Member State amount to substantial grounds for believing that the asylum seeker would face a *real risk* of being subjected to inhuman or degrading treatment.[37] (emphasis added)

The CJEU, in studying the applicable EU Dublin regulation on asylum-seekers and refugees against 'fundamental rights', concluded that 'the presumption underlying the relevant [Dublin] legislation, … that asylum seekers [in another EU Member State] will be treated in a way which complies with fundamental rights, must be regarded as rebuttable'. Therefore, 'European Union law precludes the application of a conclusive presumption that the Member State which Article 3(1) of Regulation No 343/2003 indicates as responsible observes the fundamental rights of the European Union'.[38]

iii. IM v France

Similarly, the case of *IM v France*, decided by the ECHR in February 2012,[39] involved a Sudanese man from Darfur who was arrested upon

[37] Court of Justice of the European Union, Judgment of the Court (Grand Chamber) of 21 December 2011 (references for a preliminary ruling from the Court of Appeal (England & Wales) (Civil Division) and from the High Court of Ireland—United Kingdom, Ireland)—NS (C-411/10) v Secretary of State for the Home Department and ME (C-493/10), ASM, MT, K.P, EH v Refugee Applications Commissioner, Minister for Justice, Equality and Law Reform: *NS and Others v SSHD*, Judgment of the Court (Grand Chamber), 21 December 2011 in Joined Cases C-411/10 and C-493/10, paras 94 and 106; para 2 of the Operative Part of the Judgment.

[38] *NS and Others v SSHD*, *ibid*, paras. 104 and 105. See also the review presented in Buckley, Joanna, 'NS v Secretary of State for the Home Department (C-411/10)' (2012) *European Human Rights Law Review* 208–10.

[39] ECHR, *IM v France*, Appl No 9152/09, 2 February 2012, see paras 145 and 155.

arrival in France and sentenced to one month in prison for an immigration infraction. At the end of his sentence, IM was placed in immigration detention pending deportation to Sudan. His application for asylum, submitted while in detention and processed under the accelerated procedure, was rejected. Because his appeal to the National Court of Asylum did not have suspensive effect, he risked being returned to Sudan before the Court had examined his appeal.

In its ruling the ECHR underlined that the effectiveness of an appeal depends on the requirements of quality, speed and its suspensive effect, considering in particular the importance the Court attaches to Article 3 of the ECoHR and the irreversible nature of the harm likely to be caused if the risk of torture or ill-treatment should be realised. In finding fault with the 'fast track' procedure, the Court emphasised that the individual did not in practice have the means to appeal, and concluded there had been a violation of the right to an effective remedy (Article 13). For at least five years, ACAT France, Amnesty International France and Human Rights Watch had advocated to French authorities the need to bring France's asylum procedure in line with international human rights law. In this sense, the State *knew or ought to have known* of the risk this type of procedure posed for asylum-seekers' rights, and thus had room to apply its preventive duty and protect IM's human rights and security.

iv. Kuric and Others v Slovenia

In another recent illustrative case, *Kuric and Others v Slovenia*—this one involving statelessness—the ECHR analysed the situation of people who had been left without a nationality for years due to a lack of fulfilment of an administrative procedure after the partition of former Yugoslavia. Thus, the applicants in this case were left stateless after the dissolution of Yugoslavia and later had their records removed from the civil registry, losing their right to residence. The Grand Chamber of the Court ruled in 2012 that the Slovenian authorities' treatment of the so-called 'erased' was in violation of Article 8 (right to private and family life) of the European Convention, as well as Article 14 (prohibition of discrimination) in relation to Article 13 (right to an effective remedy). The Court found that the prolonged refusal to resolve the applicants' residence status constituted an interference with their right to private and/or family life, and that they had been discriminated against because they were in a disadvantaged situation compared to other foreigners in Slovenia.[40] Under a human security lens, the sentence also enhances the victims' freedom from fear of deportability and their *de facto* situation of lack of access to rights due to their condition of statelessness.

[40] See ECHR, *Kuric and Others v Slovenia* (GC), Appl No 26828/06, 26 June 2012.

v. Kiyutin v Russia

The ECHR case of *Kiyutin v Russia*, of 2011, despite its similarities with the case of *N v UK* which will be reviewed below as a 'non-human security-sensitive' case may offer hope in leading the way for future, more protective interpretations that could also incorporate a much needed gendered perspective. In *Kiyutin v Russia*, the case involved an Uzbekistan national married to a Russian woman with whom he had a daughter and who had resided in Russia since 2003. He was denied a residence permit by Russia and subsequently received an expulsion order from such country on the basis that he was HIV-positive. The Court specifically recognised that

> Admittedly, not all settled migrants, no matter how long they have been residing in the country from which they are to be expelled, necessarily enjoy 'family life' there within the meaning of Article 8 … However, the concept of 'family life' must at any rate include the relationships that arise from a lawful and genuine marriage…, such as that contracted by the applicant with his Russian spouse and in which their child was born.

The Court concluded that Russia had actually violated Art 8 in conjunction with Art 14 (non-discrimination) by denying the residence permit to the applicant and ordering his expulsion in a discriminatory manner on account of his health status, given that people with HIV status are considered 'a vulnerable group'. Interestingly, the Court used General Comment No 20 of the UN Committee on Economic, Social and Cultural Rights, *The Right to Non-Discrimination*, in its interpretation of the scope and content of discrimination.[41]

vi. Case of the Yean and Bosico Children v Dominican Republic

Within the jurisprudence of the IACHR, there is a significant case that considers the dimensions of gender and children's rights in the context of undocumented migration, in which the Court revisited the same line adopted in its AO 18/03, already examined. In the *Case of the Yean and Bosico Children v Dominican Republic*, of 2005, the Court concluded that the Dominican Republic violated the right to nationality of two girls of Haitian origin, Dilcia Yean and Violeta Bosico, daughters of undocumented migrants, since the Civil Registration Office refused to issue their birth certificates, even when they enjoyed this right according to Dominican legislation itself.[42]

Drawing the implicit links between the human security approach and the enjoyment of human rights by persons in vulnerable conditions, the

[41] ECHR, *Kiyutin v Russia*, Appl No 2700/10, 10 March 2011, paras. 55, 74, 64 and 30.

[42] IACHR, *Case of The Yean and Bosico Children v Dominican Republic*, Judgment of 8 September 2005.

Court analysed this case considering the whole social setting in which the girls were placed and underlined that

> the discriminatory treatment imposed by the State on the Yean and Bosico children is situated *within the context of the vulnerable situation* of the Haitian population and Dominicans of Haitian origin in the Dominican Republic, to which the alleged victims belong. (emphasis added)

Looking at the widespread character of these threats through the study of the individual experience of the girls, the Court emphasised the double situation of vulnerability of the victims, because of their lack of nationality and the fact they were girls. The Court held that racial discrimination in access to nationality breaches the American Convention on Human Rights and concluded that the discriminatory application of nationality and birth registration laws rendered children of Haitian-descent stateless. This violated the recognition of their juridical personality, and was an affront to their dignity. They were unable to access other critical rights to education, to a lawfully registered name, and to equal protection before the law. The expulsion of Violeta Bosico from school violated her right to special protection as a child.[43]

As part of the subsequent impact of this case, it should be noted that in response to the Court's order to halt discrimination against Dominicans of Haitian descent, the Government began its 'retroactive policy' of withdrawing citizenship from people who were once recognised as citizens of the Dominican Republic. As a result, in June 2010, a petition was filed before the Inter-American Commission on Human Rights (IACoHR) in the case of *Emildo Bueno v Dominican Republic,* concerning the case of a man who used to hold Dominican citizenship and was deprived of it. Despite the fact that he was born, raised and had previously held identification documents in the Dominican Republic, he was later denied an identity document on the basis of his Haitian descent. This retroactive application of the law and the revocation of nationality in the Dominican Republic left Emildo Bueno stateless and it was contended that it violated his rights to family life. At the time of writing, the case was under consideration within the Inter-American human rights system.[44]

The systemic character of these risks was taken up some years later by the UN Committee on ESC Rights when it regretted that regardless of the *Yean and Bosico* judgment, discrimination against Haitian children persisted in the Dominican Republic. It voiced its concern that such discrimination had even transcended the realm of practice and had been incorporated not

[43] *Ibid*, paras 168, 142 and 134.

[44] See Summary of the Initial Petition in the case of *Emildo Bueno Oguis v Dominican Republic*, presented to the IACoHR, 1 June 2010; Open Society Justice Initiative and Center for Justice and International Law (CEJIL), available at www.soros.org/sites/default/files/Petition%20Summary-20100601.pdf.

only into migration laws but also into the 2010 Dominican Constitution, illustrating the circular relationship between discriminatory laws and the reinforcement of harmful practices. Adopting the language of human security concerns, the Committee noted that the generalised situation of revocation of identity documents or non-renewal of residency documents based on such legal provisions had '*increased the exposure* of Haitian children and Dominican children of Haitian descent, especially, to *discriminatory practices*'.[45] (emphasis added) In fact, this position is coherent with Article 29 of the CRMW which specifically sets forth the right of a child of a migrant worker (documented or not) to a name, registration of birth and nationality.

vii. Nadege Dorzema et al v Dominican Republic

The environment of structural discrimination assessed in the *Yean and Bosico Case*, and its practical consequences, have been revisited by the IACHR several times, given that such situation was later extended to a great number of Haitians. As a result, the case of *Nadege Dorzema et al v Dominican Republic* was presented.

The case involves events that took place along the Dominican Republic's border with Haiti on 18 June 2000, when members of the Dominican army opened fire on a vehicle that was transporting a group of Haitians. Seven individuals lost their lives, and several others were wounded. The acts were prosecuted in military courts, even though family members of those executed had requested that the case be subject to the jurisdiction of the regular courts. After several years of proceedings, the military courts acquitted the soldiers involved. The case also covers the fact that some of the victims who survived suffered a violation to their personal liberty and violations to their right to a fair trial and their right to judicial protection, given that they were expelled from the Dominican Republic without having received due guarantees based on their status as migrants. Finally, the case falls within a *context of structural discrimination* against Haitians or persons of Haitian origin at the hands of Dominican agents.[46]

In October 2012, the Court ruled against the Dominican Republic for its responsibility in the existing general pattern of discrimination against migrants. The Court concluded there was a violation of the right to equality and non-discrimination and, for the first time in its jurisprudence, of the prohibition of collective expulsions of foreigners contained in Article 22 of the American Convention. It also constitutes a landmark

[45] UN Committee on Economic, Social and Cultural Rights, Concluding Observations of the report submitted by the Dominican Republic, E/C.12/DOM/CO/3, 19 November 2010, para 11.

[46] See IACHR Press Release (Case 12.688), available at www.oas.org/en/iachr/media_center/PReleases/2011/012.asp.

case in regards to the standards of due process of law in migration matters (as a continuation of the jurisprudential evolution deriving from a previous case, *Vélez Loor v Panama*, of 2010).[47] In *Nadege* the Court used the concept of indirect discrimination and discussed the burden of proof in the context of discrimination within a State, lowering such burden for the petitioners and shifting the procedural weight to the State to give evidence that such discriminatory environment did not exist.[48]

viii. Benito Tide Méndez et al v Dominican Republic

Also in 2012, in July, the IACoHR filed an application with the Inter-American Court in the case of *Benito Tide Méndez et al v Dominican Republic*. The facts of this case refer to the arbitrary detention and summary expulsion from the territory of the Dominican Republic into Haiti of Benito Tide Méndez and another nine adults and 17 children.

The summary expulsions occurred in a context of *collective* and mass expulsions of individuals, affecting both Dominicans and foreigners and *both documented and undocumented persons* who had their permanent residence in the country and strong employment and familial ties with the Dominican Republic. Claims have been made that phenotypical characteristics and a darker skin colour were decisive factors when individuals were selected for detention and subsequent expulsion, indicating a *pattern* of discrimination. All the victims of the case were expelled to Haiti.[49] At the end of 2013, the IACoHR carried out a visit *in loco* to the Dominican Republic and expressed grave concern with the situation which risked leaving dozens of persons in a condition of statelessness.

In August 2014, the IACHR issued another historical judgment in *Benito Tide Méndez et al*, renamed as *Case of Expelled Dominican and Haitian Persons v Dominican Republic*.[50] The Court accumulated the cases of several

[47] IACHR, *Case of Vélez Loor v Panama. Preliminary objections, merits, reparations and costs.* Judgment of 23 November 2010.

[48] IACHR, *Case of Nadege Dorzema et al v Dominican Republic*, Judgment of 24 October 2012 (Merits, Reparations and Costs), paras 38–40, 220, 222, 227, 228, 230, 234, 235, 237 and 238. See also Pelletier Quiñones, Paola, 'Análisis Sentencia Nadege Dorzema y Otros v República Dominicana, Corte Interamericana De Derechos Humanos' (2013) *Revue québécoise de droit international*, Hors-série 385–410. See also the subsequent case of *Pacheco Tineo v Bolivia*, upholding the principles of equality and non-discrimination, in this case in the context of asylum-seekers, regarding a Peruvian family rejected in their petition of asylum by Bolivia; IACHR, *Case of the Pacheco Tineo Family v Bolivia, Preliminary objections, merits, reparations and costs*, Judgment of 25 November 2013.

[49] See IACHR Press Release, 'IACHR Takes Case Involving Dominican Republic to the IA Court HR', 18 July 2012 (Case No 12.271), available at www.oas.org/en/iachr/media_center/PReleases/2012/091.asp. For a full analysis, see González Morales, Felipe, *Sistema Interamericano de Derechos Humanos. Transformaciones y Desafíos* (Valencia, Tirant lo Blanch, 2013).

[50] IACHR, *Case of Expelled Dominican and Haitian Persons v Dominican Republic*, Judgment of 28 August 2014. (Preliminary Objections, Merits, Reparations and Costs).

expelled persons, clearly explained the differences between nationality and immigration procedures, and in a bold decision stepping on the traditional limits of State sovereignty, ordered the Dominican Republic to issue documents of nationality and identity/regular immigration status, to all the affected persons. It thus determined an obligation of protection in cases of structural discrimination, be it towards undocumented migrants or non-nationals, and reaffirmed the principles of equality and non-discrimination as applied to undocumented migrants developed since its AO 18/03. As of 2015, the implementation of the sentence has, however, met with numerous practical obstacles such as the lack of reliable statistical data on the number of persons enjoying a right to reside in the Dominican Republic, as well as political obstacles regarding political will to implement necessary administrative procedures to fully execute the decision.[51]

ix. BS v Spain

Another relevant case, also dealing with the intersecting points of discrimination against women and migration, as approached in this book, is that of *BS v Spain*, resolved by the ECHR in July 2012.[52] The case concerned a woman of Nigerian origin, legally residing in Spain, who was stopped by the police while working as a prostitute on the outskirts of Palma de Mallorca. The Court found that the State had not conducted an adequate and effective investigation into her allegations of ill-treatment on two occasions when she was stopped and questioned in the street. Using the human security language, the Court considered that the domestic courts had not taken into account BS's *special vulnerability* to discriminatory attacks inherent in her situation as an *African woman working as a prostitute*.[53] (emphasis added) The Court concluded there had been a violation of Article 3 (prohibition of inhuman and degrading treatment, in its procedural arm relating to the lack of an effective investigation), as well as of Article 14 (prohibition of discrimination) in conjunction with Article 3.

However, in looking at the further human security dimensions of this case, it is interesting to note that the applicant had sought for *structural problems of discrimination* against prostitutes of African origin to be addressed by the Court, transcending her own individual situation. Such structural discrimination, also of an intersectional character—on the basis of race and gender—was reflected both in the fact that prostitutes of a 'European phenotype' were not routinely stopped by police forces, as well as in the prejudiced approach displayed by the Spanish judiciary system

[51] See CEJIL, Center for Justice and International Law, 'República Dominicana debe cumplir obligaciones en materia de nacionalidad y migración', 29 July 2015, available at http://cejil.org/en/node/7426.

[52] ECHR, *BS v Spain*, Appl No 47159/08, 24 July 2012.

[53] *Ibid*, para 71.

in this type of cases affecting black women. In fact, in her request for reparations, apart from her individual petition of monetary compensation, the applicant asked for the procedure regarding the investigation of ill-treatment to be reopened as a measure of *restitutio in integrum*, and for the broader measure of a protocol to be adopted by Spanish authorities to set adequate standards for official responses to discrimination cases of this kind.[54] (emphasis added) The Court rejected these structural measures of reparation based on the argument of the State's discretion in the measures of executing the judgment and implementing reparations (under the jurisprudential interpretation of Article 46 of the ECoHR) and settled with the traditional individual monetary redress—in this case 30,000 euros for moral damage—thus missing out on exploring the deeper and more far-reaching human security implications of the case.

x. KAB v Spain

In the case *KAB v Spain*, also of 2012,[55] the European Court of Human Rights held, by a majority of six to one, that there had been a violation of Article 8 (right for respect to private and family life) of the European Convention on Human Rights. The case concerned the adoption—despite the father's opposition—of a child who was declared abandoned after his mother's deportation. The applicant, KAB, was a Nigerian national who was born in 1976 and lived in Barcelona. In 2001 he entered Spain irregularly with his partner, C, a Nigerian national, and their son O, who had been born in 2000, and settled in Murcia. He regularised his residence and work authorisations between May and September 2001. On 17 October 2001 C was deported from Spain without being allowed to return for 10 years. Her lawyer had pleaded that she was the mother of a one-year-old baby but the order was nevertheless enforced. O was taken in by friends of the couple, as the applicant (the father) was in Barcelona for work-related reasons. On 1 November 2001 an investigation was opened by the prosecutor responsible for minors. As the Child Protection Department had not succeeded in reuniting the child with its mother, O was declared abandoned on 16 November 2001 and placed in a children's home. On 30 November 2001 the applicant went to the Child Protection Department and, claiming to be the child's biological father, said that he disagreed with the placement. He expressed his intention to undergo a paternity test. In January 2002 the director of the children's home took O for the test but it did not take place as the applicant *had not paid for it*. In the absence of further news of KAB the child was placed in a foster family. The family initiated an adoption procedure in respect of O, but it was suspended when

[54] *Ibid*, paras 61–64; 70 and 78–81.
[55] ECHR, *KAB v Spain*, Appl No 59819/08, 10 April 2012 (final 10 July 2012).

KAB brought an action to establish paternity on 20 November 2004. After obtaining recognition of his paternity in November 2005, he started proceedings to challenge the adoption but was unsuccessful.

The Family Court took the view that KAB's agreement to the adoption was not required because, as the applicant had not discharged the duties inherent in parental authority, a hearing was sufficient. That decision was upheld by the *Audiencia Provincial*, which pointed to the applicant's lack of interest and found in particular that he had confined himself to seeking the paternity test, 'without conviction', before giving up on encountering the first difficulty and remaining passive for two years. The applicant's *amparo* appeal was declared inadmissible as being devoid of constitutional content. On 25 April 2007, O's adoption by his foster family was authorised by the Family Court. On an appeal by KAB that decision was upheld by the Supreme Court. Relying on Articles 6 (right to a fair hearing) and 8 (right to respect for private and family life), the applicant complained that he had been deprived of all contact with his son and that neither he nor the child's mother had been informed of the proposal to adopt the child. He also complained that the authorities had remained inactive regarding C's deportation and his attempts to prove his paternity.

The Court found, in particular, that the *authorities' inaction*, the deportation of the mother without prior verification, the failure to assist the applicant with his formalities, in spite of his *vulnerability* and *precarious social and economic situation*,[56] and the exclusive attribution of responsibility to the applicant for the child's abandonment, had decisively contributed to preventing any possibility of reunion between father and son, in breach of the applicant's right to respect for his private life. The Court also noted the State's obligation to duly take into account *in a realistic manner*, not only the procedural routes available *in theory* in a given legal system, but also the *political and legal context* in which they develop, as well as the *personal circumstances of the applicants*.[57] (emphasis added) These considerations seem to reflect two main human security components. First, the need for State bodies to assess the structural context underlying the formality of the law and its practical implementation, when ruling on or adjudicating a case. Second, the judgment emphasises the State's duty to consider conditions of vulnerability and precariousness of a person, and his or her relationship to a broader disadvantaged group (in this case undocumented/poor migrants), as a part of its human rights' obligation to prevent further violations and reinforce protection towards such persons.

On the other hand, under a human security perspective, and especially comparing this judgment with the previous one of *BS v Spain* issued in the same year, the reparations granted by the Court in *KAB* seem grossly

[56] *Ibid*, paras 113 and 114; see also paras 93 and 110–11.
[57] *Ibid*, para 74.

inadequate considering the gravity of this case: only 8000 euros of monetary compensation for moral damage (compared to 30,000 euros in the previous case), and nothing to improve generalised adoption procedures in Spain, especially those regarding non-national children and/or parents, to provide them with safeguards for human rights protection. Given that the sentence was delivered 11 years after the facts (and three after its first acknowledgement by the ECHR), when the child has already been living for several years with a foster family, it can be clearly concluded that the main aspects of this situation will not change and have irreparably affected the applicant and child's (as well as the mother's) lives.

xi. Sonko v Spain

In the case of *Sonko v Spain* resolved by the UN Committee Against Torture (CAT), on 27 January 2012,[58] the Committee looked at the conditions faced by undocumented migrants from Senegal trying to arrive by boat to the autonomous Spanish city of Ceuta in September of 2007, which was intercepted by the Civil Guard at sea and left near the coast of Morocco. Due to police negligence in not leaving them close enough to the coast (and presumably perforating their life-jackets), one of the Senegalese nationals, Mr Sonko, died by drowning. Thus, the Committee concluded that Spain had violated Articles 12 and 16 of the UN Convention Against Torture and Other Cruel, Inhuman or Degrading Treatment for not having adequately protected Mr Sonko's right to life and personal integrity, which amounted to ill-treatment under the Convention, as well as his family's right to due process, for not having properly investigated the circumstances of presumable ill-treatment surrounding Mr Sonko's death.[59]

The fact that Mr Sonko was alive and well when intercepted by the Civil Guard and dead when he arrived on the Moroccan coast under the control of the same authority, brought the Committee to consider that there was a causal link between these two facts, given that these undocumented migrants were under Spain's jurisdiction—understood as effective control under international law (para 10.3)—when these events took place.

Applying a similar criteria to the one used by the ECHR and the IACHR in *Opuz v Turkey* and *Cotton Field v Mexico*, analysed above in Chapter 4, the UN CAT shifts the burden of proof to the State, and asserts that because of the absolute nature of the legal prohibition of ill-treatment, it is for Spain to prove that it protected the victim's personal integrity, and not inversely, for the victim's family to prove that the State was responsible for Mr Sonko's death by drowning. Indeed, the failure of the Spanish State to guarantee the safety and integrity of the persons under its jurisdiction

[58] UN CAT, *Sonko v Spain*, CAT/C/47/D/368/2008, 27 January 2012.
[59] *Ibid*, paras 10.6–10.8.

amounted, according to the Committee, to a violation of its obligation to duly protect them from ill-treatment under the CAT, a reinforced obligation in view of the fact of Mr Sonko's *particular vulnerability as a migrant* (para 10.4). (emphasis added)

This level of vulnerability and the corresponding State obligations concluded in this case remind us of the position adopted by the UN Committee on ESC Rights reviewed in Chapter 1, which details the circumstances in which a *reversal of the burden of proof* is allowed or even called for regarding the most vulnerable groups and those with the most urgent needs. On the other hand, as Gerardo Pisarello has signalled referring precisely to the case of migrants and in line with the Committee on ESC Rights, the existence of an asymmetric relationship of subordination and defencelessness between two subjects, individual or collective, authorises the reversal of the burden of proof in the case of a presumed violation of a right. In this sense, he has considered ESC Rights as freedom rights, borrowing partly from Amartya Sen's idea of development as freedom, insofar as the lack of their enjoyment to an extreme degree leads to the annulment of freedom.[60] Thus, the importance of prioritising attention to the most vulnerable persons, who are placed at a higher risk of violation of their human rights. The notion of human security helps to highlight this condition of risk and vulnerability in a way that is relevant for the law, as revealed through the analysis of the cases above.

B. 'Non-Human Security-Sensitive' Cases

Other examples can be given as to what the consequences are of disregarding a human security perspective to the legal analysis of human rights violations in the area of human rights of migrants, as shown in the following subsections.

i. N v United Kingdom

The case of *N v United Kingdom*,[61] decided by the ECHR, involved a Ugandan woman who had arrived in the UK on a false passport and, although she did not know it at the time, was HIV-positive. In the UK she had received life-sustaining medical treatment that would purportedly allow her to live 'for decades'. N had been rejected as an asylum-seeker and if she were to be deported back to Uganda, there was strong evidence

[60] Pisarello, Gerardo, 'Los derechos humanos de los migrantes' in Añón, María José (ed), *La universalidad de los derechos sociales: el reto de la inmigración* (Valencia, Tirant lo Blanch, 2004) 58 and 70.

[61] ECHR, *N v United Kingdom* (GC), Appl No 26565/05, 27 May 2008, paras 18 and 19.

to suggest, due to the lack of her anti-retroviral drugs in the Ugandan health system, that she would die within two years of her return. The Court concluded that the removal of N to Uganda would not be a violation of the *non-refoulment* obligation contained in Article 3 of the European Convention, prohibiting the removal of a person at risk of torture or cruel, inhuman or degrading treatment.[62]

Some of the criticisms against this sentence have been countered, stating rather dismissively that

> Disappointing to many as this case may seem, it is in line with earlier case law to a great extent. In fact, the Court has held only once in a health case context, in a case of an applicant with HIV/AIDS who would be sent back to the tiny island of St. Kitts (*D. v. the United Kingdom*), that Article 3 would be violated if the applicant would be expulsed.[63]

However, the Joint Dissenting Opinion of Judges Tulkens, Bonello and Spielmann in the case of *N v UK* expressed its concern with the Court taking a different stand in this case than in the analogous judgment of *D v United Kingdom*, issued more than 10 years before. In that case involving an applicant with HIV/AIDS who would be sent back to St Kitts where he would be left deprived of health care and moral support, the Court declared that Article 3 would be violated if he was expulsed given that he was at a 'critical stage' of illness.[64] The Dissenting Judges argued that the case of *N v UK*—in which the applicant 'with no doubt' would face 'an early death' on return to Uganda—was no different in its extreme circumstances to *D v UK*. In a view in line with the human security-sensitive perspective, they concluded that

> finding a potential violation of Article 3 in this case would not have been an extension of the exceptional category of cases which is represented by *D. v. the United Kingdom* … The distinguishing of the present case from that of *D. v. the United Kingdom* is thus, in our opinion, misconceived.[65]

They also emphasised their grave preoccupation with the Court's balancing exercise when dealing with Article 3, a non-derogable right containing

[62] See the analysis of *N v UK* in Barak-Erez, Daphne and Aeyal M Gross (eds), *Exploring Social Rights: Between Theory and Practice* (Oxford, Hart Publishing, 2007) 192; and in Langford, Malcolm (ed), *Social Rights Jurisprudence. Emerging Trends in International and Comparative Law* (Cambridge, Cambridge University Press, 2008) 288.

[63] ECHR Blog, Grand Chamber Judgment in *N v UK*, Wednesday 28 May 2008, available at http://echrblog.blogspot.com.es/2008/05/grand-chamber-judgment-in-n-v-uk_28.html. For a more detailed overview of the Court's case-law on the issue of expulsions of persons with health problems under Article 3 ECHR, see: Veelke, Derckx, 'Expulsion of Illegal Residents (Aliens) with Medical Problems and Article 3 of the European Convention of Human Rights' (2006) 13 *European Journal of Health Law* 313–19 (electronic access eg through Ingenta Connect).

[64] ECHR, *D v the United Kingdom*, Appl No 30240/96, 2 May 1997.

[65] Joint Dissenting Opinion of Judges Tulkens, Bonello and Spielmann in ECHR, *N v United Kingdom* (n 61) paras 23 and 24.

a prohibition of an absolute nature and, thus, not subject to 'a fair balance between the demands of the general interest of the community and the requirements of the protection of the individual's fundamental rights', as the Court had carried out with respect to N's case;[66] a balancing that the same Court had actually explicitly prohibited three months before in *Saadi v Italy*.

In analysing the validity of returning very ill persons to countries with poor health care facilities under a (gendered) human security-human rights lens that highlights the transnational dimensions of the issue, several reflections may be spelled out. As Eva Brems puts it, this type of case

> reveals an uncomfortable truth about the limits of the human rights commitment of European states. Like other rich states with long democratic traditions, they like to insist on the universality of human rights vis-à-vis less democratic (and often poorer) other states. Yet in transnational situations, their formal commitment to universal human rights is upheld only thanks to barely credible legal wriggling … [and] a legal reasoning that allows them to wash their hands in innocence. The dissenters brilliantly pierce through this legal fiction.[67]

Indeed, the Dissenting Judges brilliantly uncovered the real fear of the majority when they clarified that the claim had not been articulated that Article 3 places 'an obligation on the Contracting State to alleviate … disparities through the provision of free and unlimited health care to all aliens without a right to stay within its jurisdiction', as the majority had affirmed. The Judges highlight that

> the view expressed by the majority that such a finding 'would place too great a burden on the Contracting States' … reflects the *real concern* that they had in mind: if the applicant were allowed to remain in the United Kingdom to benefit from the care that her survival requires, then the *resources of the State* would be overstretched. (emphasis added)

They firmly rebut by emphasising that such a consideration

> runs counter to the absolute nature of Article 3 … and the very nature of the rights guaranteed by the Convention that would be completely negated if their enjoyment were to be restricted on the basis of *policy considerations* such as budgetary constraints. (emphasis added)

In addition, they also reaffirm the absolute nature of the protective status of Article 3 when countering the underlying belief of the majority that 'the implicit acceptance … of the allegation that finding a breach of Article 3

[66] *Ibid*, para 7. See also para 44 of the judgment. See also a comparative examination of the two cases in this sense in Dauvergne, Catherine, *Making People Illegal: What Globalization Means for Migration and Law*, Series The Law in Context (Cambridge, Cambridge University Press, 2008) 164–67.

[67] Brems, Eva, 'Thank you, Justice Tulkens: A Comment on the Dissent in N v UK' in *The Strasbourg Observers*, 14 August 2012, available at http://strasbourgobservers.com/2012/08/14/thank-you-justice-tulkens-a-comment-on-the-dissent-in-n-v-uk/.

in the present case would open up the *floodgates to medical immigration* and make Europe vulnerable to becoming the "sick-bay" of the world'. In adopting an evidence-based approach, the Dissenting Judges underline that 'the so-called "floodgate" argument is totally misconceived'.[68]

It may be added that in viewing the two cases with similar conditions under a gendered perspective, one may note that both in the previous case of *D v UK* and the latter one of *Kiyutin v Russia* (reviewed above in the previous line of illustrative cases), the individuals that received protective judgments were both men, whereas in this case N, a woman, was denied the Court's safeguard. It must also be noted that she had escaped Uganda on the account of having been ill-treated and raped.[69] Under a gendered and human security lens, not only were the structural implications of HIV/AIDS in the African context overlooked, but also the differentiated impact the virus and its manifestations hold for women specifically within a context of discrimination and violence against women,[70] as viewed in Chapter 4 of this book.

As the human security framework invites us to do, let us duly recall the broader structural issue at stake, in this case affecting N as an individual but derived from a global challenge. Indeed, emphasis must be made on the fact that HIV/AIDS has become not only a global health problem, but also an economic development crisis because of the vast socio-economic impact HIV/AIDS has had and continues to present in developing countries, especially those in sub-Saharan Africa. Since 2001, the UN Secretary-General had argued that

> acquired immunodeficiency syndrome (AIDS) has become a major development crisis … In the hardest hit regions, AIDS is now reversing decades of development … By eventually impairing economic growth, the epidemic has an impact on investment, trade and national security, leading to still more widespread and extreme poverty. In short, AIDS has become a major challenge for *human security*.[71] (emphasis added)

[68] Joint Dissenting Opinion of Judges Tulkens, and Spielmann in ECHR, *N v United Kingdom* (n 61), para 8.

[69] *N v the United Kingdom* (n 61) para 10.

[70] See Ssenyonjo, Manisuli, 'Human Rights of Women in Africa: A Prerequisite for Human Security' in Abass, Ademola (ed), *Protecting Human Security in Africa* (Oxford, Oxford University Press, 2010), taken from OXFORD SCHOLARSHIP ONLINE (www.oxfordscholarship.com). See also Statement by the African Union Chairperson, Professor Alpha Oumar Konare, in Celebration of the International Women's Day of 8 March 2007.

[71] *Special Session of the General Assembly on HIV/AIDS: Report of the Secretary-General*, UN GAOR, 55th Sess, Agenda Item 179, A/55/779, 2001, pp 4 and 6. Along these lines, for an analysis of whether placebo-controlled trials violate international human rights law within the context of the relationship between developed and developing countries, see Fidler, David P, '"Geographical Morality" Revisited: International Relations, International Law, and the Controversy over Placebo-Controlled HIV Clinical Trials in Developing Countries (2001) 42 *Harvard International Law Journal* 299, available at http://0-www.lexisnexis.com.biblio.eui.eu/hottopics/lnacademic/?verb=sr&csi=143840.

Relating this global context to the legal analysis of this case, Eve Lester has argued that a different result could have been reached by the Court had it applied a 'human security approach' that emphasised the critical life-threatening risk N faced, viewed in the light of complementing Article 3 in light of the core content of the human right to the highest attainable standard of health.[72] Moreover,

> judicial decisions that integrate human security into their analysis may compel states to translate their rhetoric into real deliverables which would increase accessibility and availability of anti-retroviral drugs in the developing world where the full burden of the HIV/AIDS pandemic is yet to be felt.[73]

Maybe such an outlook by the Court would have truly lived up to the commitment of guaranteeing N's human right to health and ultimately her right to life in the face of an imminent risk of losing it.

The more humanitarian jurisprudential line of *D v UK* may possibly be recovered at some point. In the case of *SJ v Belgium*, concerning the threatened expulsion from Belgium of a Nigerian mother suffering from AIDS, the applicant alleged an Article 3 violation in regards to being returned to Nigeria. In the end, the parties reached a friendly settlement in August 2014, which the State agreed to on the basis of the 'strong humanitarian considerations weighing in favour of regularising [the applicant's] residence status and that of her children'. On 6 January 2015, the applicant and her children were issued with residence permits granting them indefinite leave to remain.[74]

ii. Nacic and Others v Sweden

An issue involving some common denominators with *N v UK* was resolved similarly by the ECHR in *Nacic and Others v Sweden*, in May 2012. The case refers to the situation of a family of Roma ethnicity from Serbia (in the Kosovar region) who migrated to Sweden as a result of the armed conflict and at the time of the case, some of its members faced possible deportation. One of the family members was a young man in need of mental health care with a previous history of attempted suicide.

[72] The concrete aspects of the right to health considered part of the 'Core Obligations' of States, have been laid out by the UN Committee on ESC Rights in its General Comment No 14, *The Right to the Highest Attainable Standard of Health (Article 12 of the International Covenant on Economic, Social and Cultural Rights)*, E/C.12/2000/4, 11 August 2000, paras 43–45.

[73] Lester, Eve, 'Socio-Economic Rights, Human Security and Survival Migrants: Whose Rights? Whose Security?' in Edwards, Alice and Carla Ferstman (eds), *Human Security and Non-Citizens: Law, Policy and International Affairs* (Cambridge, Cambridge University Press, 2010) 354. For the detailed analysis of this case, as well as the similar case of *D v United Kingdom* under the human security notion, see the whole chapter, 314–56.

[74] ECHR, *SJ v Belgium*, Appl 70055/10. Friendly settlement: 26 August 2014.

In this respect, the Court evaluated their situation first under Article 3 on the right to be free from inhuman or degrading treatment and the right of *non-refoulment* in the face of a risk of encountering such treatment. In following the previous judgment of *N v UK*, the Court not only analysed the situation of the individual applicants, but actually laid down the 'general principles' governing expulsion of aliens in cases of risk based only on that sole case. The ECHR considered that

> *Aliens* who are subject to *expulsion* cannot, in principle, claim any entitlement to remain in the territory of a Contracting State in order to continue to *benefit from medical, social or other forms of assistance* and services provided by the expelling State. The fact that the applicant's circumstances, including his *life expectancy*, would be *significantly reduced* if he were to be removed from the Contracting State is *not sufficient* in itself to give rise to a breach of Article 3. The decision to remove an alien who is suffering from a *serious* mental or physical illness to a country where the facilities for the treatment of that illness are *inferior* to those available in the Contracting State may raise an issue under Article 3, but only in a *very exceptional case*, where the *humanitarian grounds* against the removal are *compelling*.[75] (emphasis added)

One wonders if the grounds evaluated in the present case were not compelling enough, or how grave the circumstances would have to be for the Court to consider protecting persons previously recognised in its case-law as 'vulnerable' when placed in an even more 'serious' situation of precariousness.

The Court also analysed the case under Article 8 considering that a measure interfering with rights guaranteed by Article 8.1 of the Convention (right to private and family life) could be regarded as being 'necessary in a democratic society' if it is taken

> in order to respond to a pressing social need and if the means employed are proportionate to the aims pursued. The national authorities enjoy a certain margin of appreciation in this matter. The Court's task consists of ascertaining whether the impugned measures struck a fair balance between the *relevant interests*, namely the individual's *rights* protected by the Convention on the one hand and the community's *interests* on the other. (emphasis added)

The Court further noted that both the Swedish Migration Court and the Migration Court of Appeal came to the conclusion that the third applicant (the young man of 21 years of age at the time of the case) could receive adequate medical care in Kosovo and Serbia. In this connection, the Court observed that mental health care is available in Kosovo and Serbia; albeit still under reconstruction and not of the same standard as in Sweden.[76]

[75] ECHR, *Nacic and Others v Sweden*, Appl No 16567/10, 15 May 2012 (Final 24 September 2012), para 49.

[76] *Ibid*, paras 80 and 83.

Referring to the young man's condition, the Court observed that he had lived in Sweden with the other applicants since 2006 and that according to the most recent medical certificate, dated June 2011, he had begun to feel better since being granted a residence permit. He had left the treatment centre and moved to an apartment. He had also begun studies at a college for adults. However, his positive development had been halted by the *threat of disruption of the family* and he had showed signs of falling back into *depression*. While acknowledging that this information is worrying, the Court found that it had to be taken into account that the medical certificate mainly contained a description of how the applicant himself feels and that it neither suggests that he currently had a medical condition, nor that he was undergoing psychiatric or other treatment. In the Court's opinion, the medical certificate also indicated that his state of health was connected to a large extent to the situation he was in at the time of the case and deemed there had been no further deterioration of his health since June 2011,[77] although this fact was precisely connected to having been granted the residence permit, as the medical certificate itself indicated, and presumably to the possibility of thus living *free from fear*, to employ human security language.

After noting that the applicants would be confronted with general difficulties as Roma people in Kosovo and Serbia, including their access to medical care, the Court surprisingly finds that the general situation in Kosovo and Serbia is not sufficient to conclude that people of Roma ethnicity cannot be sent there. In a very unfortunate move, in my understanding, the Court reached an outcome that left the applicants completely unprotected, by concluding that

> having regard to all the circumstances and taking into account the margin of appreciation afforded to States under Article 8.2 of the Convention, the Court considers that the Swedish authorities did not fail to strike a *fair balance* between the *personal interests* [note that it does not say the 'rights'] *of the applicants as regards their family life* on the one hand and to ensure an *effective implementation of immigration control* and *hence* to preserve the *economic well-being of Sweden* on the other.

It thus concluded that there was no violation of Articles 3 and 8 of the Convention.[78] (emphasis added)

The Court's reasoning is, in my view, deeply problematic. First, the judgment seems to equate or to confuse 'interests' with 'rights' in some instances, or to openly only speak of interests when referring to individual rights. The text of the Convention in Article 8 protects the 'right' to

[77] *Ibid*, para 84.
[78] *Ibid*, paras 87–88.

private and family life, to be weighed by the State against certain 'interests'. In this respect, the interest of the economic well-being of the country is a legitimate aim that may be considered necessary in a democratic society (Article 8.2). However, the assumption of the Court of unquestionably establishing a causal link between effective immigration control and the economic well-being of a State presents many doubts as to its empirical grounding, or at least, none is provided to support this argument. This 'flood-gate' argument fearing for the economic sufficiency of the State seems to be completely out of place in a judicial body that is evaluating if a human rights violation has taken place or is at risk of occurring, as in this case.

At the same time, it is true that immigration norms are 'prescribed by law' in Sweden, and in that sense under a very broad view the formal requirement for a justified interference with family life is met, as also prescribed by Article 8.2. When applying a human security lens, though, the links between immigration law and possible human rights violations become evident, as signalled above. What is precisely sought for from the Court is for it to be the adjudicator of individual human rights put at risk by such immigration law and policy. This is so especially in facing persons in *vulnerable conditions* such as Roma people and persons with mental health problems (two groups previously recognised as particularly vulnerable by the Court),[79] and more particularly against the background of *systemic risks* to be confronted by persons upon return to their country of origin, in this case, in access to the health system in Kosovo or Serbia.

If a human security lens had been applied to this case, the Court would have, on the one hand, given a different weight to the fact that the applicants 'under tremendously difficult circumstances, managed to maintain their essential bond as a family unit', as the Partially Dissenting Judges Spielmann and Power-Forde did. The Judges also argued that the applicants were 'of Roma ethnicity and have the *added vulnerability* of mental health problems'.[80] And on the other hand, it would have also given due consideration to the potential risk of violation of the right to be free from inhuman or degrading treatment (in ideal thinking viewed also in its relationship to the right to health, even if only as a persuasive argument),

[79] See, eg, Möschel, Mathias, 'Is the European Court of Human Rights' Case Law on Anti-Roma Violence "Beyond Reasonable Doubt"?' (2012) 12 *Human Rights Law Review* 3, 479–507; and Peroni, Lourdes and Alexandra Timmer, 'Vulnerable Groups: The Promise of an Emergent Concept in European Human Rights Convention Law' (2013) 11 *International Journal of Constitutional Law* 1056–85.

[80] *Nacic and Others v Sweden* (n 75), Partially Dissenting Opinion of Judges Spielmann and Power-Forde, para 2.

analysed on its own or coupled with the right to non-discrimination, to be suffered by the applicants upon return. In any event, in my understanding, the validity of a State decision to deny a residence permit and consequently to deport the applicants, should have been evaluated in light of the possible violations of Articles 3 and 8 on their own footing, and not under the argument of 'effective implementation of immigration control'.

In this respect, the IACHR's AO 18/03 comes to mind, with the point emphasised since 2003 that 'States may not *subordinate* or condition observance of the principle of equality before the law and non-discrimination to achieving their *public policy goals*, whatever these may be, including those of a *migratory character*'.[81] (emphasis added) Of course, the views of the IACHR are not binding for the ECHR, but it is suggested that this last Court could possibly benefit from reviewing such arguments which hold an authoritative character given they are based on one of the few comprehensive studies done at the judicial level on the legal obligations of States regarding the human rights of migrants, and in that sense, a useful source of legal analysis and one of the modern developments of international human rights law more generally.

Turning back to the ECHR, it should be noted that the Court, in analysing the case of *Nacic and Others v Sweden*, while relying on reports by the World Health Organisation to assess the country's situation relating to human rights' respect and protection, did not pay any attention to reports by human rights monitoring bodies (as it had done in other cases of evaluation of general country situations),[82] or to reports by civil society

[81] IACHR, AO 18/03, *Juridical Condition and Rights of Undocumented Migrants*, requested by the United Mexican States, 17 September 2003, concluding para 11. For argumentation see para 172. This point of the AO 18/03 on the legitimacy of public policy objectives measured in the light of the principle of equality and non-discrimination was used as a source of analysis of the controversial Bossi-Fini Law on migration measures in Italy; see Tramontano, Mario Umberto, 'Is the Bossi-Fini Law (L.189/2002) in Compliance with Arts. 2 and 26 of the International Covenant on Civil and Political Rights?', p 8, available at http://es.scribd.com/doc/63794132/.

[82] See for example ECHR, *N v Finland*, Appl No 38885/02, Judgment, 26 July 2005 (Final 30 November 2005), where the Court refers to the existence of 'credible and objective human rights reports' as a necessary source for proper evaluation, para A.1.136. In a previous case, the Court also considered the general human rights situation of Colombia; see ECHR, *HLR v France (GC)*, Appl No 24573/94, Judgment, 29 April 1997, although in that case, as was reviewed in Chapter 2, it concluded that there had been no violation by France of Article 3. In the case of *Sufi and Elmi v the United Kingdom*, Appl Nos 8319/07 and 11449/07, 28 June 2011, the ECHR dedicated more than 100 paragraphs of its judgment to carefully carry out a detailed, evidence-based assessment of the country situation of Somalia, including threats to 'food security', to analyse the risk of suffering torture or ill-treatment alleged by the applicants.

organisations in Kosovo or Serbia (as it had done in previous cases relating to violence against women studied in Chapter 4 above), in order to properly evaluate the problems faced in relation to the human rights of persons with mental disabilities in the health system of such countries. Thus, the human rights and human security of the applicants were left unprotected, and what does seem most likely is that they returned to face critical conditions of vulnerability.

As a corollary to this section on 'non-human security-sensitive' cases concerning migrants, it should be pointed out that there are other recent cases that seem to point to a certain harshening of the ECHR's position towards the rights of potential refugees that could possibly, and unfortunately, be explained within the recent trend of increasingly restrictive immigration policy in the EU and Member States, for instance, a 2012 case also against Sweden regarding violence against women.

iii. AA and Others v Sweden

In *AA and Others v Sweden*, the case involved women from Yemen who had already been victims of family violence in their country and were seeking asylum in Sweden, being denied such protection by the ECHR—surprisingly so in the context of the Arab Spring and to the dismay of Judge Ann Power-Forde as expressed in her Dissenting Opinion.[83] As a different feature to *Opuz v Turkey*, this case would also demonstrate an added 'intersectional vulnerability' of these women on account of their gender, coupled with their condition of non-citizens, particularly of asylum-seekers previously recognised as a vulnerable group by the Court, as reviewed above; an element of intersectionality that was overlooked by the Court. Indeed, it comes off as quite striking in and of itself that these Yemeni women were left without due protection, and considering as well the broader context of the recent adoption in 2011 of the Council of Europe Convention on Preventing and Combating Violence Against Women and Domestic Violence, specifically directed, among other goals, at protecting migrant women as one of the most vulnerable groups in Europe, as reviewed in Chapter 4 above and in the present chapter.

Let us now draw some conclusions under the human security–human rights synergy, applicable to both undocumented migrants in general, and to the particular case of female undocumented migrants.

[83] ECHR, *AA and Others v Sweden*, Appl No 14499/09, 28 June 2012 (Final 28 September 2012). In relation to the recent seemingly harshening position of the Court, see also *Trabelsi v Germany*, Appl No 41548/06, judgment of 13 October 2011, analysed in Chapter 5.

IV. SOME CONCLUSIONS ON UNDOCUMENTED MIGRANTS AND WOMEN: HUMAN SECURITY AS THE 'RIGHT TO HAVE ACCESS TO RIGHTS'

Being an undocumented migrant woman or girl constitutes one of the greatest sources of vulnerability and human insecurity in our world today. I have argued that assuring the principle of universality of all human rights towards undocumented migrants and other non-citizens, is one of the most challenging situations for contemporary international law. In the case of female undocumented migrants another legal and political principle is put to the test: gender equality as a human rights axiom and a commitment of democratic societies. Indeed, the right to equality is materialised in the case of undocumented migrant women in their right to be free from discrimination. Understanding violence against women as a form of discrimination against women, as reviewed above, allows us to reinforce migrant women's right to live free from violence. The human security-human rights call obliges the State and other actors to prioritise the protection of such women and their right to live free from violence over irregular migratory status.

The empirical realities of constant risks, deportability and lack of access to justice faced by undocumented migrants and migrant domestic workers, coupled with existing legal gaps including those in international human rights and labour law, impact directly and disproportionately on irregular migrant women and girls, as analysed in the present chapter, placing them in conditions of heightened vulnerability to different forms of violence, including sexual violence, which human security contributes to evidence. It also exposes other forms of violence against migrant women and girls, such as those of an institutional or economic nature, and the intersectional forms of discrimination, deprivation and poverty experienced by female undocumented migrants on account both of their gender and of their irregular migratory status.

From the analysis of the previous and the present chapters, we can observe that an enhanced and integrated approach to the State's positive obligations would follow when applying a gendered human security-human rights perspective to the rights of migrants. This may be done, firstly, through utilising the human security lens to review collective threats that facilitate human rights violations of individual undocumented migrants and to identify particular heightened risks structurally affecting female migrants. Secondly, it also involves a procedural shift for human rights courts in opening up to new and non-traditional means of evidence such as reports of non-governmental organisations, UN and regional bodies, UN and regional human rights mechanisms, national/local human rights institutions, and even news reports, and it also translates into closer dialogue and cross-referencing between them, in a more fluid and attentive way of documenting the widespread and systemic character of vulnerabilities placing human rights at risk or actually violating them.

At the same time, the human security-sensitive cases, and their contrast to those not adopting a human security-based approach, bring to light an array of *interpretative synergies* that the human security-human rights interaction may allow for when assessing, in this case, the rights of undocumented migrants and other non-citizens, and particularly those of female undocumented migrants. Those synergies, to be developed more in detail in the following chapter, may also represent a parameter of reference for evaluating when an administrative, legal or judicial decision—or even a legally relevant action or omission of non-State actors and powerful entities more generally—is embodying a 'non-human security-sensitive' perspective.

The cases, coupled with the empirical realities faced by undocumented migrants, particularly women and girls, and depicted throughout the previous and present chapters, reveal an extreme collective vulnerability to human rights violations of undocumented migrants that is insufficiently addressed by international human rights law. On the other hand, the reflection may be made that asylum-seekers enjoy a legal construction allowing them to be in the territory of the host State that would theoretically render them more protected than undocumented migrants. However, with the growing mixed flows of migrants in the midst of an economic crisis, particularly in the case of the US and Western Europe, and persons fleeing from armed conflict in Syria, the cases also reveal an increasing vulnerability affecting asylum-seekers in analogous ways to that placing undocumented migrants at risk. As an afterthought having examined the cases, it may also be paradoxically true that undocumented migrants, by remaining in clandestinity, are actually achieving a self-preservation objective, whereas asylum-seekers by actually requesting refuge ignite their visibility and position themselves in the hands of the State, which, as is frequently revealed, adopts an indifferent or harmful position towards their human rights and human security.

An insight stemming from this chapter is to critically assess the current globalised political economy that promotes the free movement of goods and services but constrains the free movement of persons, especially of a certain type of persons based on racialised and socio-economic terms, submitting them to the economic and labour needs of the market. In several democratic settings, irregular migratory status is the one exclusionary category left almost untouched. These exclusionary categories created by the State's immigration laws and policies, those deriving from regional normative systems such as the EU, and some of the provisions of international law itself, permit and shape the experience of human insecurity of migrant persons and non-citizens. It often ranges from the weak status of enjoyment of human rights, to suffering their violation, and finally to fearing or in fact confronting the lack of a political and legal framework to exercise the right of access to justice to seek redress.

This constructed vulnerability and the 'legal limbo' it entails also bring the spotlight to the rights of the 'other', the most diverse 'other' today being the non-citizen, more concretely the undocumented migrant, as her difference is not only in gender, ethnic, cultural, and social, but rather it is an 'otherness in rights'. Because of the increasing legally institutionalised articulation of distinction through irregular migratory status, the right to have rights, to paraphrase Hannah Arendt,[84] still remains a door to be opened for millions of migrant persons worldwide—half of them with the face of a woman.

[84] Arendt, Hannah, *The Origins of Totalitarianism* (San Diego, New York, London, A Harvest Book, 1951) 296–97.

7

Conclusions on the Human Security–Human Rights Synergy and Prospective Routes

IF WE ENVISION the law as a living phenomenon and—especially in democratic regimes—as a dialectic process potentially embodying values towards the common good, the prospective of the human security–human rights intersection becomes clear. The possibilities of the law in this field, particularly through international human rights law, to address structural problems or to tackle 'small-scale' injustices, emerge as a very real and tangible path. Some guidelines on how to do so are suggested in the following sections.

I. SOME CONCEPTUAL CONCLUSIONS

It has been argued in this text that the interaction between human security and human rights holds promise for more expansive and integrated legal interpretations that result in increased protection for persons and groups in their everyday lives, especially those in conditions of vulnerability. Through the research a framework with doctrinal and practical implications was constructed, the 'human security–human rights synergy'. The main content and arguments of such a framework were presented in Chapter 3. I thus turn to some general reflections bringing together the two parts of this book, the conceptual framework and its application to the legal analysis of the thematic cores of examination, violence against women (VAW), the risks to the human rights of undocumented migrants, and the converging review of the heightened vulnerability faced by undocumented female migrants, emphasising throughout socio-economic vulnerability as a human security concern.

I have proposed to unleash human security's potential as an avenue for challenging traditional notions of violence and broadening security concerns related to specific human rights or rights of marginalised groups, such as economic, social and cultural rights (ESC Rights), women's rights and rights of undocumented migrants, and particularly undocumented female migrants, through the threshold-based consideration of structural vulnerability that, theoretically and practically, may touch upon any human right in a given context.

Concerning the added value of human security to human rights law, it has been argued that human security contributes to make visible risks to human rights that would otherwise remain shadowed. Supplementing this role, human security has also been signalled as an orienting notion for a better understanding of the *interconnectedness* in the phenomena of risks posed to human rights enjoyment and to actual human rights' violations. It is true that human rights law already provides for conditions of vulnerability to be examined as affecting an identifiable individual's or group's rights; human security, however, adds value in accentuating the contextual and structural elements that facilitate or present obstacles to the enjoyment of human rights, even when such rights may not be connected to a traceable specific group with determined boundaries of membership. In underlining the severity of the threat, and not its source, human security offers more flexible paths to analyse the role of non-State actors in causing and maintaining vulnerability and exploitation, in ways which the predominantly State-based architecture of human rights law finds hard to address. Human security also contributes to recognising the 'seamless web' of the law, to use Rebecca Cook's terms, in which legal concepts and decisions in seemingly unrelated areas can be made to reinforce or confound each other.[1]

At the same time, the critical engagement with human security has revealed its weak areas in the need for a strong normative grounding that can be provided, I have claimed, by international human rights law, as a general standard of fulfilment—and the relevant aspects of international refugee, humanitarian and criminal law. The research has also dealt with the double human security strategies of 'protection' and 'empowerment'. While the reviewed human rights legal framework and case-law expose avenues for implementing reinforced protection on a human security basis, the pillar of 'empowerment' calling for agency and involvement of the persons targeted by human security measures, has yet to be developed much further. I have also defended the idea that the construction of human security on the basis of human rights law and indicators as objective normative references points, limits the possibility of it being co-opted to justify or conceptually underpin abusive or oppressive aims through processes of securitisation of different subjects.

[1] Cook, Rebecca J, 'Human Rights Dimensions of Health Security' (2003) 97 *American Society of International Law Proceedings* 106.

The human security–human rights synergy thus holds normative, methodological, and epistemological implications. It leads us to consider threats to persons and groups that would otherwise remain invisible or marginalised and translate them into considerations of justice and the language of rights; it orientates us in asking different questions and approaching them from the angle of structural vulnerability; and it invites us to acquire knowledge through the dialogue with and the empowerment of those who are silenced and those who yearn to be heard, by constructing 'an epistemology of the excluded', as put by Siobhán Mullaly,[2] or for our effects, an 'epistemology of the vulnerable'.

I have also proposed that human security can constitute an *enabling environment* for the realisation of human rights. I have thus submitted that the result of looking at the connection between the *core content* of human rights and viewing them integrally may be considered *human security*. From this perspective, human security refers not only to the protection from severe threats and risks, but in a *positive sense*, also becomes a *guarantee* at the collective level, a general condition which is necessary to allow the full enjoyment of *all* human rights by all persons. According to this understanding, human security may act as the modern materialisation of the right to an *enabling social and international environment* foreseen in Article 28 of the *Universal Declaration of Human Rights* (UDHR), and thus complement the primarily individualist basis of human rights and reinforce the collective expressions of human rights where they exist.

The study of the issues under analysis through the human security–human rights synergy has revealed and proposed ways in which human security is and can be relevant to the law of human rights, and how human rights can inform and deliver a more precise and operational conception of human security. These identified *interpretative synergies* may work together towards the enhanced protection of the rights of people in their daily reality, in particular, those who do not only confront isolated moments of risk or human rights violations, but rather those in conditions of structural vulnerability, specifically women and girls suffering or at risk of violence, as analysed in Chapter 4, undocumented migrants and other non-citizens, as reviewed in Chapter 5, and undocumented female migrants, as examined in Chapter 6.

Indeed, such topics present legal challenges in terms of bringing to life and making effective the human rights of the people (un)covered by such norms. At the factual level, VAW is still widespread and pervasive and apart from constituting a form of discrimination and a human rights

[2] Mullaly, Siobhán, 'Attending to Method in *Feminist Approaches*' in *IntLawGrrls. Voices on international law, policy, practice*, Friday 19 October 2012, available at www.intlawgrrls.com/2012/10/attending-to-method-in-feminist.html.

violation in itself, it is also an obstacle for the enjoyment of other human rights. The migratory phenomenon is, by its very nature, transnational and thus relates to human security's concerns for a new paradigm that adequately responds in a coordinated way to situations affecting people and transcending national borders.

Human security may then act as the 'missing link' between the individual and the collective dimension of human rights violations. The focus of this book has been on 'structural' vulnerability, formed by the conjunction of the underlying, systemic societal conditions that place rights at risk or openly harm them. Structural vulnerability thus has been understood in this text as *the heightened and endemic degree of exposure to experiencing human rights violations.*

What human security can do, as has been demonstrated in this research, is act as the bridge between different collective or societal conditions that threaten individual (or group) human rights, that is, the *structural risks to rights*. These risks, or their compounded combination, may be so critical or severe so as to create a disruptive environment for human rights that facilitates their violation, openly acting against Article 28 of the UDHR. Human security may then function as a heuristic tool to identify circumstances where the State is compelled to take additional measures regarding concrete human rights as foreseen in normative instruments, standards and indicators.

It does not, however, only reinforce the statist dimension of the risks to rights, but actually also carries consequences for the horizontalisation or transnationalisation of responsibilities. True, there is not even consensus on the level and scope of State responsibility in certain matters of human rights violations within international law. This does not however imply that the need to discuss and think creatively about alternative legal avenues is not urgently called for, as the depicted situations of structural vulnerability of women, girls and undocumented migrants worldwide, among others, make blatantly evident. Indeed, the obligations attached to non-State actors such as persons perpetrating VAW, abusive employers, transnational corporations, or regional organisations, become more visible through a human security lens. The conceptual interaction of a gendered human security with human rights renders clear the risks and vulnerabilities affecting persons and groups and calls for a stronger and more protective legal response, which is only starting to be displayed by UN human rights mechanisms such as the Committee on the Elimination of Discrimination against Women (CEDAW Committee), the UN Committee on ESC Rights and the UN Committee on the Protection of the Rights of All Migrant Workers and Members of their Families, as well as regional judicial bodies, as will be detailed below.

This fortunate, although timid and somewhat inconsistent, reply would be much better complemented with a preventive rather than a reactive stand by States and other actors, such as regional organisations, civil society and the business sector, and would serve a critical and mainstreaming function within the UN and regional organisations themselves.

The legal implications of the human security–human rights juxtaposition point at the very least to reinforcing State obligations of protection in the context of structural vulnerability regarding its own actions or omissions. It also would orientate towards defining State responsibility concerning the actors under its jurisdiction that commit human security-threatening actions or inactions when such situations amount to discrimination or such private parties act with the State's acquiescence, that is, a determination of responsibility always through the filter of the State.

At the most, the synergies between human security and human rights could eventually lead us, first, to the direct international legal responsibility of such non-State actors. Second, a gendered human security–human rights lens also holds hermeneutic relevance for evaluating the political coherence of the State's foreign policy with democratic and human rights standards, and ultimately it may support the possibility of adjudicating State responsibility for its actions in this field.

The book constructed the human security–human rights synergy by looking more distinctly at the reflection of human security principles in judicial and quasi-judicial decisions, through the human rights bodies at the UN level, as well as the European, Inter-American and African systems of human rights. Evidence indicates that at these three regional levels, as well as within their human rights' systems, human security is indeed embedded to different degrees in the historical traditions influencing understandings of security in each of these regional contexts, thus revealing a strong grounding to relate human security to human rights and further advance the legal implications of such a connection in the ways specified in the following concluding section.

II. LEGAL INTERACTION: INTERPRETATIVE SYNERGIES BETWEEN HUMAN SECURITY AND HUMAN RIGHTS

In Part **II** of this work, the human security–human rights synergy, constructed in Part I, was applied in relation specifically to two thematic cores under human rights instruments and case-law: VAW and girls, on the one hand; and on the other, the human rights of undocumented migrants and other non-citizens; and analysed in a subsequent chapter of convergence between the two, studying undocumented migrant women and girls. The implications of the human security–human rights synergy for the understanding of socio-economic risks to rights was reflected throughout the whole text. From this analysis, a series of considerations can be extrapolated and systematised.

A. General Considerations

In addition to the selected thematic cores of this book, of course many others could be viewed under the proposed framework and generate innovative legal questions. To name some, global public health, landmines, small arms and light weapons, collective security in the UN Security Council and the African Union have been analysed through the human security lens.[3] The two selected thematic cores, though, are jointly representative insofar as the two themes, VAW and violations to the human rights of undocumented migrants, enter the realm of structural vulnerabilities which are faced by considerable sectors of the population and in all parts of the world. They also find a common denominator in being present in liberal democratic polities holding generally acceptable records in respect to human rights. They are not confined to or limited by armed conflict and the consequent legal order of international humanitarian law. They hold academic value and speak to a broad audience as issues that allow for novel questions on human rights and revisit others in a new light.

The structural vulnerabilities experienced both by women and girls at risk of or suffering violence, and by undocumented migrants, are analogous in that they confront gaps in international law, in human rights law and/or its implementation, that have rendered these tools insufficient in addressing concerns on both topics. These cracks in the system allow thousands of persons to fall between norms, to remain unprotected and in some cases, to confront life-threatening situations. Threats to human security in the form of socio-economic deprivation and inequality, as evidenced in section IV A of Chapter 1, on human security and ESC Rights, are a *cross-cutting issue* placing both women and girls facing violence as well as undocumented migrants—often poor and socially marginalised—in heightened conditions of vulnerability. It is not a coincidence that legal, philosophical, political and sociological scholarship, international and inter-governmental organisations' reports, human rights universal and regional mechanisms and multiple civil society activities have recently focused their attention on prioritising both issues on their agenda.

Thus, the present text analysed whether human rights law has something more to offer in the face of these challenges and, if so, how it may do so effectively in order to deliver some of the promises envisioned by the universalist human rights spirit and the legal architecture constructed around it.

Both themes are dissonant in the fact that although VAW and girls is still widespread, protection from it has found its way into specific legal

[3] See for instance the thematic division presented in Von Tigerstrom, Barbara, *Human Security and International Law. Prospects and Problems* (Studies in International Law) (Oxford and Portland, Hart Publishing, 2007).

instruments and growing public awareness places it on the political agenda as a matter of discrimination and thus a violation to equality; but undocumented migrants have generally not engaged in—and much less won—the political battle given their clandestine situation, as signalled above in the references by the UN Special Rapporteur on the Human Rights of Migrants, Francois Crépeau. A possible exception to this are some groups of Latin American undocumented migrants, mostly Mexican, in the US that have gained political power and carved out a space for 'undocumented citizenship' to present social and legal claims.[4] Still, in general terms, as Luigi Ferrajoli has also highlighted in analysing inclusion/exclusion, foreignness is precisely the only exclusive category left alive today in many legal systems.[5]

At the UN level, the number of ratifications of the only legal instrument with universal aspiration dealing explicitly with undocumented migrants, the UN *International Convention on the Protection of the Rights of All Migrant Workers and Members of their Families* (CRMW), is relatively low, in comparison to CEDAW and the additional regional instruments at the Inter-American, African and European levels that also tackle several forms of VAW, including psychological and economic harm. Hope is to be found, though, in the position by the UN Committee on the Elimination of Racial Discrimination, which in 2004 interpreted in its General Recommendation No 30 *Discrimination Against Non-Citizens*, that the prohibition of racial discrimination of the *International Convention on the Elimination of All Forms of Racial Discrimination* (ICERD) also covered illegitimate distinctions based on immigration status, thus explicitly incorporating undocumented migrants into the scope of protection of the Convention.

The human security paradigm is highly useful for a deeper understanding of the rights of both groups, though perhaps for fairly different reasons: for women and girls, half the world's population, it may shed light on the myriad forms of violence and discrimination they suffer and thus incorporate the 'missing half' of security conceptions. For undocumented migrants situated in the context of a global and transnational political economy of free (or thinly regulated) movement of goods and services but not of persons, and affected by a strongly statist discourse and practice of border control, the shift of the security focus from the State to the individual is a breath of fresh air. This is particularly the case in considering the specific group of undocumented female migrants and the varied

[4] See McNevin, Anne, 'Undocumented Citizens? Shifting Grounds of Citizenship in Los Angeles' in Nyers, Peter and Kim Rygiel (eds), *Citizenship, Migrant Activism and the Politics of Movement* (London, Routledge, 2012) 165–83.

[5] See Ferrajoli, Luigi, *Derechos y garantías. La ley del más débil*, Italian-Spanish translation by P Andrés Ibañez and A Greppi, (Barcelona, Editorial Trotta, 1999), especially Chapter 4. See also Brown, Garret W, 'The Laws of Hospitality, Asylum Seekers and Cosmopolitan Right: A Kantian Response to Derrida' (2010) 9 (3) *European Journal of Political Theory*.

and compounded forms of discrimination, exploitation and violence they confront, and that are made visible by the human security light regardless of whether these risks are State-created. The human security–human rights call also obliges the State and other actors to prioritise the protection of such women and their right to live free from violence over irregular migratory status.

Then again, the two themes, VAW and girls, and violations to the rights of undocumented migrants, re-connect in their presence in and relevance to developed and developing countries, liberal democracies and authoritarian regimes, the context of peace or armed conflict, to different degrees and intensities, but with the common denominator of representing structural vulnerabilities worldwide. The definitions and standards developed by human rights law, for example, the due diligence standard within the human rights law understanding of VAW, may contribute to the better characterisation of this threat as a genuine human security concern and the design of new mechanisms to tackle it. On the other hand, the human security proposal of *freedom from fear, freedom from want and freedom to live in dignity* seems to hold promise in adding value to identifying and addressing such collective vulnerabilities through offering an integrative approach to fill the relevant legal gaps and fulfil the human rights of affected women and girls, and undocumented migrants and other non-citizens.

The 'legal limbo' and the lack of enjoyment of human rights of undocumented migrants, pose legal questions at the conceptual level in terms of the universality of human rights when considered in light of legal status. Other challenges also emerge in the practical sphere, while the lack of protection towards undocumented migrants has been aggravated in the last few years with the economic crises in the US and Europe, and currently with the situation of millions of migrants and refugees fleeing from armed conflict mainly in Syria, and also Iraq and Afghanistan. The terrorist attacks by ISIS in Paris, Lebanon and Mali in November 2015, and in Turkey, Pakistan and Brussels in 2016, among many others, have also contributed to creating a hostile environment for the recognition and protection of migrants' rights. The issue of undocumented migration today also connects with most countries of the world, whether as sending, transit or host societies. It has steadily increased worldwide (although slowing down in recent years with the economic crisis), thus requiring us to question whether the current legal framework is up to date and adequate to meet the challenges undocumented migration presents, and those related to the protection of the human rights of undocumented migrants themselves. Migrants without documents are placed in an indeterminate midpoint, economically and socially marginalised and politically disempowered. They face critical human insecurities: daily uncertainty, fear of deportability, precarious access to health and housing, and fragile labour conditions. Due to clandestinity, they confront numerous difficulties in being able to exercise their right of access to justice when another human right has been violated, thus facing a double victimisation. Indeed, for some, the most important distinction in the contemporary era is the one between those with legal migration status and those without it.[6] As referred to above, Hannah Arendt's 'right to have access to rights' comes to mind when grasping the legal exclusion and invisibility experienced by undocumented migrants.

B. Violence against Women

Chapter 4 highlighted that although the concept of VAW and girls has been strongly developed by international human rights law, it has seldom been taken into account explicitly in human security concerns relating to violence. Thus, in the last part, the chapter examined the consequences of the interaction of applying a human security lens to the legal analysis of VAW and their human rights, and of including the human rights definition of VAW within the human security sphere, and fleshed out the added value of this dialogue. The concrete synergies deriving from this relationship and the reviewed case-law will be specified below.

As a general stand, a gendered human security which duly incorporates the legal grounding of the right of women and girls to live free from violence, it has been argued, would confront reasoned criticisms of the notion of human security as being too broad by giving it a more precise delimitation supported by existing normative legal standards in human rights law. At the same time, it would enhance its legitimacy and practical applicability. To consider the concept of violence against women and the standard of due diligence as developed in international human rights law, as part of the definition of violence worthy of protection under the human security proposal, would render its scope clearer and duly address one of the most pervasive large-scale threats as a real security concern.

C. Undocumented Migrants, Asylum-Seekers and Female Migrants

In Chapter 5 of this book, the human security approach contributed to making visible the empirical interconnected threats faced by undocumented migrants and identifying risks to several of their human rights, quite notably that of access to justice. Similarly, it reflected throughout the chapter some of the specific risks confronted by asylum-seekers at a

[6] See Sassen, Saskia, *Losing Control? Sovereignty in an Age of Globalisation* (New York, Columbia University Press, 1996).

time when the economic crisis and mixed flows of migration allow for the weakening protection of this group of non-citizens.

Chapter 6 of this book addressed the application of the gendered human security lens as proposed in Chapter 4 to spell out the particular risks and types of violence faced by undocumented migrant girls and women, as well as the vulnerabilities experienced more specifically by female undocumented migrant domestic workers. It also analysed illustrative quasi-judicial and judicial cases referring to migrants more generally, taken from the UN and regional systems of human rights in order to exemplify how a human security-sensitive perspective could guide human rights interpretation, as well as the consequences that evolved when it was disregarded. The analysis presented here interconnects and compares the cases, systematises the findings and draws conclusions of general significance for this study.

From these analysed 'human security-sensitive' and 'non-human security-sensitive' cases at the end of Chapter 6, it would seem at first glance that the tendency both in the Inter-American Court of Human Rights (IACHR) and the European Court of Human Rights (ECHR) has been protective of the rights of undocumented migrants and asylum-seekers. Given the higher number of the first type of 'human security-sensitive' cases, this might easily be presumed. Taking a closer look, though, at the judicial cases coupled with the EU normative instruments in the field, the low level of ratifications by European countries of the UN CRMW, and the national and local legal, judicial and institutional responses within the US, the EU and its Member States, dismissive of the human rights of undocumented migrants, as revealed in Chapters 5 and 6, the evidence points to a growing racialisation of the migration discourse and an eroded regime of protection of the universal human rights of vulnerable migrants and other non-citizens. Reactions by other host or transit States—both regarding the chapter's accounts of 'deaths at the fault line' and that of the situation of migrants once in the territory of the receiving State—are not more encouraging, such as those in Libya, the Dominican Republic and Mexico, for example.

There is also an optimistic prospect when extracting lessons from the examined judicial responses. The line of Inter-American cases of the *Yean and Bosico Girls*, of 2005; *Nadege Dorzema et al ('Guayubín Massacre')*, of 2012; and *Benito Tido Méndez and Others*, of 2014, (renamed as the *Case of Expelled Dominican and Haitian Persons)*, all against the Dominican Republic, provide testimonies of the collective harm suffered by undocumented migrant adults and children of Haitian origin. Under a human security-sensitive approach, the IACHR addressed such conditions of 'structural vulnerability and discrimination' and concluded on the State's responsibility in violations to the rights to nationality and to equal protection before the law, to a name and to juridical personality in detriment of the affected persons, confirming the principles of equality and non-discrimination as applicable to undocumented migrants/non-nationals, as it had developed originally in its Advisory Opinion (AO) 18/03, *Juridical Condition and Rights of Undocumented Migrants*, of 2003.

The interpretations in the case of *MSS v Belgium and Greece* by the ECHR extend the scope of the right to be free from torture or ill-treatment and apply the *non-refoulment* principle (Article 3 European Convention on Human Rights and Fundamental Freedoms (ECoHR)), to cover conditions of extreme material deprivation, thus constituting an original and promising avenue to render this right more easily justiciable in cases of severe socio-economic precariousness.

In light of the human security blueprint and the global and interrelated challenges it makes visible (for the purpose of these cases: the impact of HIV/AIDS, poverty and the world distribution of migrants and refugees) one would want to see, however, an expansion of ESC Rights as well, such as the right to health, for instance. Had due weight been given in *N v UK* to the structural vulnerability caused by having AIDS, and being N, a female undocumented migrant at risk of returning to the struggling country of Uganda, the ECHR would have possibly been driven to reach a different conclusion in the case, and grant N a much needed protection, similar to the one it did actually offer in the previous case of *D v UK*, involving a foreign male individual from St Kitts and Nevis affected by HIV/AIDS and at risk of expulsion.

The danger of employing a balancing exercise in relation to the non-derogable right of Article 3, as signalled with concern in the Dissenting Opinion of *N v UK*, could also be applied to *Nacic and Others v Sweden*. A human security-sensitive perspective would have pointed to the inadequacy of prioritising migration policy over the individual rights of the applicants. This policy-rights equilibrium is out of place when dealing with persons in a situation of vulnerability. On the contrary, in such conditions, the human security–human rights synergy makes visible the duty to reinforce protection in the context of the 'added vulnerability' faced in that case by persons of Roma ethnicity and at the same time suffering mental health problems; a protective interpretation called for in the Partially Dissenting Opinion of this judgment by Judges Spielmann and Power-Forde.

Another observable tendency which is revealed from an examination of the cases is that it would seem that the ECHR has engaged more with cases of asylum-seekers as in *MSS v Belgium and Greece, IM v France, Nacic v Sweden* and *AA v Sweden* (the first two favourable to the applicants and the latter two not finding a violation) and the IACHR has been more open to analysing the conditions of undocumented migrants, first through the Advisory Opinion (AO) 18/03 of the IACHR, *Juridical Condition and Rights of Undocumented Migrants*, of 2003, and then through the *Yean and*

Bosico Girls v Dominican Republic in 2005 and the subsequent related cases. This is possibly so due to, among other reasons, the recent harmonisation attempts of a common EU migration policy and apparently the resulting deference by the ECHR to individual States in cases involving undocumented migrants that do not enjoy any other overlapping legal status, such as that of 'asylum-seeker'.

The 2011 case of *Kiyutin v Russia* by the ECHR presents however an interesting turn in terms of migrants' rights and the possibility of suspending or supressing an expulsion order on the basis of health reasons (although always argued under Article 8 of ECoHR on private and family life). Similarly, in *SJ v Belgium*, of 2014, the ECHR prompted protection of an AIDS-affected undocumented immigrant mother, but based only on 'humanitarian grounds' and not on the jurisprudential consideration of certain rights. It is to be hoped for that under a gendered human security lens an integrated interpretation of the right of being protected from the risk of torture or ill-treatment, coupled with the right of women to live free from violence, and the human rights to life and health as related to the rights of equality and non-discrimination, may render diverse outcomes in future cases.

Regarding the threats faced by undocumented migrants and other non-citizens, as an overall conclusion from the analysed case-law, it seems that the principle (and at the same time rule) of due diligence in relation to VAW, triggered when the State *knew or ought to have known* of a risk situation or an actual violation, could well be exported to the cases of undocumented migrants. Such principle requiring State prevention and protection from [actions and omissions of] private parties, which was originally understood in relation to VAW, was later expanded to discrimination against women in general, and through the CEDAW Committee's General Recommendation No 33 on women's access to justice, is now amplified to also cover 'all crimes' committed against women. This could be applied in order to argue through a human security lens that when the State was aware of the situation of vulnerability of a certain person or group, including when caused by a private actor such as companies or private employers, its duty to prevent and to take measures is activated. This would pertain, as any other human rights norm, to the persons and actors under the State's jurisdiction or its effective control, and would involve a reinforced obligation of protection towards those experiencing particular vulnerability, such as undocumented migrants. The door still remains open as to how exactly the transnational dimensions of migration could be confronted through Statist logic, as that still prevailing in public international law, and shared by the human rights legal architecture.

It seems, though, that the human security conception with its emphasis on risk factors regardless of the source (State actor or otherwise) and on the transboundary phenomena placing persons at risk, may offer further promising paths to explore its potential as a catalyst for the realisation of human rights in the contemporary world. These risk situations in the least grave scenario translate into *de iure* or *de facto* denial or limitation of access to rights, and in the worst-case scenario, not at all unusual, they amount to 'humanitarian crises', 'life-threatening situations' or actual harm to physical integrity and loss of life.

The vocation of a binding character attached to human rights law would also serve the purpose of placing the human rights of undocumented migrants at the top of the human security agenda. The universality of the human rights of migrants, confirmed by the existing international legal framework and the principle of *ius cogens* of equality and non-discrimination, may also be used as a tool for human security to reaffirm the need to address the vulnerabilities faced by undocumented migrants, not only as an issue of moral claim but as *an issue of law*. Indeed, the human security of undocumented migrants constitutes an intersection point where several of the deep-seated roots of liberal democratic societies seem to meet head on: principles and institutions such as equality, citizenship and universal human rights seem to collide with the evidence of discrimination, vulnerability and risk which people on the move and persons with an irregular migratory status frequently find themselves facing.

D. Conclusions Concerning Women and Migrants: The Interpretative Synergies

On the basis of the research on both topics, it is submitted that there are identifiable parallels between the analysed normative standards of the regional human rights systems in Africa, Europe and the Americas and, more specifically, between the studied human rights case-law of the European and Inter-American Courts of Human Rights, and the set of concerns posted in the literature around human security, so much so that one wonders whether this may be pure coincidence or whether human rights and human security communities are instead exercising reciprocal influences on each other. What we find are doors being opened for analysis and debate on the *interpretative synergies* that may arise between the concepts of human security and human rights. In particular, and in light of the mentioned cases, it seems that the human security approach, in placing emphasis on severe threats, situations of risk and structural vulnerabilities that persons encounter as obstacles to the enjoyment of their most fundamental human rights, underscores some of the insufficiencies of the classical doctrine of individual human rights, while theoretically grounding some of the more interesting and expansive recent evolutions on human rights violations and State responsibility.

The *interpretative synergies* identified in the book suggest that the evolution of human rights is moving along these lines, in a parallel and possibly interconnected way with the different uses and debates surrounding human security. Regardless of whether this is being done in an intended or explicit manner, the fact is that both developments are synchronised in adopting a comprehensive view of human rights and human vulnerabilities, which as this book suggests, may be and should be usefully taken advantage of for the effective realisation of the human rights of women and girls, and of undocumented migrants and other non-citizens in need of protection such as asylum-seekers, refugees and stateless persons. The proposed analytical framework could, of course, be extrapolated and enriched to review conditions of vulnerability of other persons, groups and rights at risk. This set of interpretative tools would, however, hopefully constitute the starting point of approaching these empirical situations from a human rights–security perspective, which may expand the ways in which we think about them in international law.

This book proposes that the legal inferences and implications arising from the normative and case-law analysis carried out in chapters 2 (on risk and vulnerability), 4 (on VAW), 5 (on undocumented migrants), and 6 (on undocumented female migrants) are complementary to such a degree that their comparison produces results of general significance. Based on the examined scholarship, international and regional human rights instruments, and case-law, the potentials of the human security-human rights interaction may be summarised in what the book advanced in Chapter 3 has termed *interpretative synergies* which also refer to some illustrative legal expressions in each point:

Interpretative Synergies between Human Security and Human Rights

a) **The inadequacy of limiting the understanding of violations of human rights to only those that represent vertical threats to individuals (coming from the State), usually leaving discrimination and violence from non-State actors (horizontal violence) as belonging outside the sphere of primary human rights concerns.**

   On this point, the cases of *Opuz v Turkey* by the ECHR and *Cotton Field v Mexico* by the IACHR, both of 2009, studied in depth in Chapter 4, give clear evidence of the potential of having brought VAW, regardless of its non-State source, into the realm of human rights concerns and, thus, within the scope of State responsibility.

b) **The identification of threats to human rights enjoyment in order to establish thresholds and therefore criteria for a 'red alarm' as a trigger to activate the State's obligations of prevention and protection in compliance with the due diligence standard.**

   The cases of VAW in *Cotton Field v Mexico* by the IACHR and *Opuz v Turkey* by the ECHR are a reflection of the possibilities of rendering the State internationally responsible for the actions of private parties based on the *due diligence standard,* when the State *knew or ought to have known* of such actions which, in these cases, amounted to a risk against women or girls. In relation to VAW, the due diligence standard has been interpreted by human rights bodies as including prevention against VAW and discrimination against women. The due diligence obligation of States was reaffirmed and taken a step further by the CEDAW Committee in 2010 in its General Recommendation No 28, *The Core Obligations of States Parties under Article 2 of the Convention on the Elimination of All Forms of Discrimination against Women,* in which it clarified that according to this obligation States parties must *prevent discrimination* by *private* actors and emphasised that in some cases, a private actor's acts or *omission of acts* may be attributed to the State under international law. Consequently, the CEDAW Committee emphasises that States parties are obliged to ensure that private actors do not engage in discrimination against women as defined in the Convention. Based on the CEDAW Committee's General Recommendation No 33 on *Women's access to justice,* of 2015, the due diligence obligation would also cover a State obligation to 'prevent, investigate, punish and provide reparation for *all crimes* committed against women, whether by *State or non-State actors*'. (emphasis added)

The reliance on the due diligence standard by the ECHR to expand the scope of the right to life is also observable, whilst not named as such, in the case of *Oneryldiz v Turkey*, of 2004, by the ECHR, as well as in the case of *Delgado Páez v Colombia* by the UN HRC, of 1990, to broaden the understanding of the right to liberty and security of the person, as analysed in section I of Chapter 2 on international law, risk and structural vulnerability. The case of *Xákmok Kásek v Paraguay* by the IACHR, of 2010, also reaffirms the State's obligation of prevention when facing a *known risk* that could materialise into human rights violations, in this case of the rights to life and personal integrity due to extreme socio-economic vulnerability.

This book has identified the legal irregularity of migrants as a source of risk. Thus, the call for safe migratory routes included in General Recommendation No 26 of the UN CEDAW Committee on *Migrant Women Workers,* of 2008, reflects this point of the human security–human rights cooperation and calls for preventive measures to confront life-threatening situations for undocumented migrants and protective action to ensure their rights.

Eventually, the due diligence obligation as a preventive stance translated into *strengthened protection* could be expanded to directly cover other non-State actors—for the purposes of this book, family members or any person or group who poses a threat of discrimination and/or violence against women or girls, as signalled by CEDAW; but also abusive employers, companies, recruitment agencies, smugglers, or other actors involved in the migration process. The 'exporting' of the due diligence standard developed in VAW to the vulnerability experienced by undocumented migrants finds a natural convergence when addressing undocumented migrant women and girls at risk of or suffering compounded forms of discrimination and violence.

c) **The insufficiency of understanding the fulfillment of human rights as the equivalent to the non-violation of rights and, thus, the need to underline *positive obligations*, that is, active measures by the State, to prevent violations of human rights and to guarantee their realisation.**
Such active measures also extend to the realm of *prevention* in order to not only maintain conditions of non-violation, but also to avoid violations from occurring in risk situations and thus creating a human security environment conducive to the respect of human rights, as analysed in relation to Article 28 of the UDHR. This insight also moves beyond a strict negative/positive conception of obligations and rather illustrates the *continuum* of obligations involved in the respect and protection of all human rights.
The various instruments and cases reviewed in section I of Chapter 2 are paradigmatic in this sense. The IACHR cases of the '*Street Children' v Guatemala* of 1999 and *Xákmok Kásek v Paraguay* of 2010, as well as those of *DH and Others v Czech Republic* of 2007 and recently *Horváth and Kiss v Hungary* of 2013, both by the ECHR, give testimony to this position. Normative instruments like the 2003 Maputo Protocol on the Rights of Women in Africa, also contain steps forward in the creation and reaffirmation of legally binding obligations in the field of positive measures directed at prevention.
In the broader field of active measures directed to guarantee not only the non-violation but also the realisation of human rights, the cases of *DH and Others* and *Horváth and Kiss* point to more ample consequences of human rights responsibility in the field of designing and implementing national education policies that are respective of human rights standards and ensure equality and non-discrimination.

d) **The need to identify *structural failures* in the protection of human rights standards in a given society and to flesh out the implications that this may have when it comes to general State (or non-State) action, or to deciding concrete allegations of individual human rights violations.**
These implications include three aspects: substantive; procedural; and collective harm:

1. On the *substantive* front, the possibility to understand that certain conducts with disparate impact on vulnerable groups may also amount to a phenomenon of discrimination and a consequent violation of the rights to equality and non-discrimination.

Here we find General Comment No 20 on *The Right to Non-Discrimination* by the UN Committee on ESC Rights, of 2009, as well as the cases of *DH and Others v Czech Republic* and *Horváth and Kiss v Hungary* by the ECHR, which concluded a violation of the right to education on the basis of indirect discrimination. The IACHR in *Xákmok Kásek v Paraguay* also derived State responsibility from an unattended situation of 'structural discrimination' manifested in conditions of extreme poverty and 'acute vulnerability'.

On the other hand, *MSS v Belgium and Greece* by the ECHR identified the systemic failures of the EU Dublin regime as affecting impoverished asylum-seekers to the point of amounting to a violation of the rights of an absolute nature contained in Article 3 (freedom from torture or ill-treatment and the principle of *non-refoulment*). The case by the Court of Justice of the EU of *NS and Others v SSHD*, of 2011, echoed such terms and addressed the issue of 'systemic deficiencies' in the asylum process.

The *Guidelines on Extreme Poverty and Human Rights* adopted by the UN Human Rights Council, in 2012, as well as the positions of the UN Committee on ESC Rights on forced evictions and the right to social security also identify systemic conditions of vulnerability that must be addressed by the State and relevant actors in order to make the enjoyment of human rights by the persons affected by such conditions possible.

The *substantive* implications of this synergy may also point to addressing the structural failures in the protection of human rights once identified, and especially when recognising systemic vulnerability, through prioritising a *protective* stance independently of a verifiable phenomenon of State discrimination or direct human rights violations or the full articulation of a specific legal standard requiring State action.

On this point, the 1984 Cartagena Declaration of Refugees at the Inter-American level, complemented by the reassessments of the 1994 San José Declaration and the 2004 Mexico Declaration on Refugees, is an example of the recognition of the existence of systemic conditions creating vulnerability, which in that instance affecting Central and South America, motivated a broadening of the definition of 'refugee' to cover persons whose 'lives, safety or freedom have been threatened by generalized violence, foreign aggression, internal conflicts, massive violation of human rights or other circumstances which have seriously disturbed public order', and thus expanded State obligations of protection.

Transcending the traditional refugee law requirement of individual and personalised risk as the basis for State obligations, this enlarged definition opened the door for the effective State safeguard of a great number of persons in need. While the existence of such structural risk situation in a given national setting—eg think of circumstances in the 1980s stemming from private actors that seriously disturbed the public order—would possibly not have amounted to a human rights violation under traditional standards of State responsibility, the Cartagena Declaration recognised the social and political reality severely harming people's human rights. Consequently, addressing this reality through what we could call today a human security perspective, it built on existing instruments to advance a State obligation to address such harms—independently of a previous human rights infringement or not by the State. In parallel to, or possible even before, focusing on the determination of legal responsibility, it prioritised the urgency of a legal tool to cooperatively and effectively protect people. This human security-sensitive position further translates into the generation of reinforced, increased or even new State obligations once 'soft-law' instruments such as the Declaration become entrenched in legal practice, as described in Chapter 2, section I on international law, risk and structural vulnerability.

This substantive implication of addressing structural failures in the protection of human rights on a more general basis, independently from State responsibility in individual cases, could be understood today through a broader and more constructive approach concerning State action to formulate laws and public policies—in conjunction with other social actors in participatory processes—that eliminate the systemic obstacles that hinder human rights' realisation and rather adopt adequate measures for their protection and fulfillment, particularly addressing persons or groups in vulnerable conditions, as is further signalled below in the last section of this Chapter on prospective routes.

2. On the *procedural front*, the implications of this synergy may include the need to duly contextualise the cases and to rely on non-traditional sources of evidence—such as reports by UN or regional bodies and human rights mechanisms, national or local human rights institutions, non-governmental organisations (NGOs), reports of country visits or concluding observations on specific countries by relevant human rights bodies—in order to better understand the background conditions of such cases.

These implications may also involve taking into account on a persuasive or authoritative basis the sources produced by international legal practice, such as declarations, resolutions or guidelines resulting from UN, regional or inter-State decision-making bodies, when such instruments tackle structural factors affecting human rights and set forth standards or principles to orientate State conduct, or that of other relevant actors. Guidelines formulated by academics and civil society actors could also constitute examples of these influential sources, such as the *Maastricht Principles on Extraterritorial Obligations of States in the area of Economic, Social and Cultural Rights*, and the *Boston Principles on the Economic, Social and Cultural Rights of Noncitizens*, both adopted in 2011, as studied in Chapters 3 and 6 above.

Other non-traditional sources to be considered in human rights interpretation may include expert legal interpretations carried out by UN or regional human rights mechanisms and courts, such as Advisory Opinions or General Comments and Recommendations by UN treaty bodies, as well as jurisprudence from individual cases resolved by UN or regional quasi-judicial bodies, or by judicial bodies different from that issuing the judgment (for instance, through modes of cross-reference and 'judicial dialogue').

As reviewed in detail above, the IACHR referred to a rich array of sources in its AO 18/03, *Juridical Condition and Human Rights of Undocumented Migrants*, of 2003; the analysed cases on VAW provide multiple examples in this sense; and the ECHR has accepted non-traditional sources of evidence to evaluate contextual elements of the countries of origin of migrants or asylum-seekers, in cases such as *N v Finland* and *HLR v France, Sufi and Elmi v the United Kingdom*, notably in the latter addressing 'food security' concerns expressed in UN and NGO reports, and even relying on news reports and including a map of Somalia within the judgment.

Similarly, taking into account existing patterns of conduct in a certain society and the State's systematic failure to prevent them, courts may reverse or lighten the *burden of proof* for individual victims in specific cases.

The expressions of this synergy are multiple and varied. The mention of General Comments No 3, *The Nature of States Parties Obligations*, of 1990, and No 9 *The Domestic Application of the Covenant*, of 1998, by the UN Committee on ESC Rights, is in line here. Under these interpretations of the *International Covenant on Economic, Social and Cultural Rights*, the burden of proof as to taking adequate and sufficient measures to fulfill the rights of the Covenant guaranteeing non-discrimination, and respecting the principles of progressivity and non-regressivity, falls on the State party. The burden of proof of non-violation was also required regarding another right, in this case civil and political, the right to be free from torture or ill-treatment, in the case of *Sonko v Spain* before the UN Committee Against Torture (UN CAT), of 2012, and in its procedural aspect, in the ECHR case of *BS v Spain*, of 2012 as well, regarding the duty of investigation into an allegation of ill-treatment by an African woman prostitute in Spain who suffered police harassment.

Another *procedural* implication that comes to the fore by using this lens would involve accepting third-party submissions in the form of *amicus curiae*, for example, in legal proceedings affecting human rights, both before formal human rights bodies, as well as in other international bodies not formally engaged in human rights adjudication but actually impacting on the enjoyment of any given human right(s). To give but an illustrative example, think of investment disputes before arbitration bodies that concern human rights, as will be further detailed below in the proposals of prospective routes of engagement.

3. On the aspect of *collective harm* (precisely in terms of increased structural vulnerability), it is necessary to duly reflect on the damage that derives from individual violations which contribute to a pattern of systematic violations in generating an insecure environment or vulnerable condition. The synergy thus signals the need for *systemic redress* through transformative reparations, meaning reparations able to help individual victims but also help subvert previous structures of discrimination prevalent in society.

   The most illustrative case in this regard is undoubtedly *Cotton Field v Mexico* by the IACHR, of 2009. This judgment also reflects a gendered human security as proposed in this book and takes its structural approach all the way to the last step of granting reparations for the individual victims and at the same time broader social remedies.

   Another highly representative case is *Xákmok Kásek v Paraguay* by the IACHR, of 2010, which explicitly included within its order of reparations to the State the duty to guarantee 'food security', 'health security' and water and sanitation infrastructure for the concerned indigenous community within a two-year period. Making explicit the human security-human rights symbiosis that had been at play implicitly in previous cases, the Court in this instance provided a very significant testimony of how the human security lens may work in practice as applied to human rights. First, the conceptual consideration by the Court of a *known risk* to the State, as an element at the centre of the human security notion. Second, the expansive and integrated interpretation of human rights permeating this case also reached out to the realm of reparations. The violations found involved the rights to equality and non-discrimination and mainly focused on civil and political rights (rights to life, personal integrity and judicial protection).

In the reparations part, however, the Court took into consideration the *causal links* between the lack of timely State action regarding the socio-economic vulnerability of the community and the death of some of its members. Consequently, it granted structural and interrelated reparations that also impact on ESC Rights such as food, health and access to water, independently of the findings of specific State responsibility in violating such rights.

Other instances evaluating context beyond individual conditions and recognising structural vulnerability or discrimination, thus employing a human security-sensitive lens, include AO 18/03 of the IACHR, *Juridical Condition and Rights of Undocumented Migrants*, of 2003, and the IACHR case of *Yean and Bosico Girls v Dominican Republic*, of 2005. The ECHR cases of *BS v Spain* and *KAB Spain*, of 2012, involving African migrants, woman and man, respectively, also reflect consideration of vulnerability as related to gender and socio-economic condition. Similarly, in *Kiyutin v Russia*, of 2011. The ECHR considered the applicant who was HIV positive as part of a 'vulnerable group' and thus, worthy to be protected against expulsion. However, in all these contentious cases, the conclusion on the violation was the final 'structural' step that the Court was ready to take. It stopped at that point and the subsequent reparations provided were only individual.

e) **The need to surpass the division or hierarchical placing of human rights and to better conceptualise *all* of them—civil, political, economic, social and cultural—in terms of *interdependence*, for it is the interaction of different deprivations of rights, including denial of legal personality or conditions of poverty and material destitution, which generates the structural situation of vulnerability and human insecurity which call for *reinforced positive obligations* of the State and other parties.**

In line with this synergy is the International Court of Justice Advisory Opinion of 2004, *Legal Consequences of the Construction of a Wall in the Occupied Palestinian Territory*, studied in section IV A of Chapter 1, on ESC Rights, for its reaffirmation that such rights are an essential part of human rights law to be complied with by States, even in the context of armed conflict. Also AO 18/03 of the IACHR, *Juridical Condition and Rights of Undocumented Migrants*, reviewed above, approached the whole spectrum of their human rights on the basis of the *ius cogens* principle of equality and non-discrimination, and viewed such rights directly through the lens of structural vulnerability.

In *Rosendo Cantú v Mexico*, on violence against an impoverished indigenous woman, the IACHR explicitly sustained that the due diligence obligation translated into *reinforced obligations of the State*.

f) **To provide a managed expansion of international human rights law, contributing to an integrated and enhanced interpretation towards the protection of human rights.**

The protective interpretation of human rights could also refer to the non-derogable elements of rights or their minimum core, as reviewed in the text (see also Figure 1 in Chapter 3). This would not substitute the set of rights to be upheld in each given context, including those of armed conflict, generalised conflict situation or state of emergency. It would, however, allow for the consideration of risk situations, particularly structural ones, affecting the core content of *all* human rights—civil, political, economic, social and cultural—which the State *knew* or *ought to have known* about and, consequently, to provide more extensive criteria to trigger its obligations of prevention, attention and/or granting reparations.

An example of this type of interpretation can be found in General Comment No 29, *States of Emergency (Article 4)*, by the UN HRC, of 2001, in which the Committee considered the requirement of court review over the lawfulness of detention to constitute a *non-derogable element* of the right to personal liberty and security, even when this right is not referred to in Article 4 of ICCPR as one of the non-derogable rights in a state of emergency.

In analysing the non-compliance of the State with *positive obligations* of taking measures directed to *risk prevention and attention*, the proposed framework may provide guidance with regard to the causes of violations of rights, through *actions* or through *omissions*, especially concerning these positive obligations. For instance, in the famous *Case of the Mayagna (Sumo) Awas Tingni Community v Nicaragua*, by the IACHR, of 2001, regarding State action damaging to the collective property of an indigenous community, the IACHR indicated that according to 'the rules of law pertaining to the international responsibility of the State and applicable under International human rights law, *actions or omissions* by any public authority, whatever its hierarchic position, are chargeable to the State' (emphasis added). This is reinforced by General Recommendation No 28 of the CEDAW Committee, reviewed above, issued almost ten years later, in 2010. The CEDAW Committee considered that 'in some cases', a *private actor's* acts or *omission of acts* may be attributed to the State under international law. Given this interpretation already renders possible the attribution of State responsibility for a *private actor's omissions*, so much more so when we are facing a *State omission*. Indeed, the human security-human rights synergy makes visible the way in which a State failure to act and take preventive and protective measures in cases of VAW and risks to undocumented migrants, particularly female migrants, deeply affects individual human rights and further creates a generalised state of insecurity, a 'disabling environment' for the realisation of all human rights.

g) **The provision of tools to transcend the conceptual danger of viewing *non-citizens*, particularly undocumented migrants, as *non-persons*, and thus reaffirming the universality of all their human rights.**

Because migratory law, discourse and policy tends to contribute to the construction of the 'other' through the 'us/them' dichotomy, this synergy acts as a counter-balance to strengthen the theoretical and legal foundation of migrants' equality in dignity and rights.

It may be concluded from the analysis of the illustrative legal cases that there is a mixed picture which gives way to a critical account and, at the same time, offers reason for hope. Some of the problems addressed, though, are so generalised, critical and severe, that I have proposed that an alternative analytical framework is in place for such beneficial prospects to be materialised. This book has argued that human security with its accent on acute and widespread threats, and therefore on the collective dimension of risks, should be seen as a pre-condition and at times a necessary complement to the exercise and enjoyment of individual human rights which, when viewing each one on its own footing, may tell us an incomplete story of the realities that people are facing on the ground.

Since I have already condensed the interpretative synergies of what human security and human rights can do by working together, now a comparison is called for. What would a non-human security case look like and how does it contrast with cases where the human security elements were actually taken into account?

The ECHR cases of *N v UK*, of 2008, and *Nacic and Others v Sweden*, of 2012, analysed in detail at the end of Chapter 6 and reviewed above, demonstrate how a non-human security sensitive approach resulted in leaving without protection, respectively, a Ugandan HIV-positive woman and a Kosovar family (one of their members with a mental condition of depression) who had migrated to Sweden in the midst of the war of the former Yugoslavia and was struggling to build a better life, and allowed for the expulsion of both, to the dismay of the Dissenting Opinions in the two cases which signalled their disagreement with the majority's legal interpretation and conclusions.

As a way of recapitulating only some of the normative expressions of the human security–human rights synergy contained in representative authoritative and judicial analyses of those presented in Chapters 1 to 6 above, and summarised in the proposed *interpretative synergies*, the following Table 1 presents the central elements of the synergy and some illustrative cases in which such elements were absent. The cases/instruments presented are grouped firstly on the basis of subject matter and then chronologically in relation to each issuing body:

Table 1: Practical implications of the human security-human rights synergy for legal analysis[7]

	Obligation to apply due diligence standards in cases of 'known risk' (Obligations of prevention/actively taking measures of reinforced protection), including non-State actors	Consideration of systemic/ structural risks or vulnerabilities	Reversal of burden of proof on the State	Use of non-traditional evidence (reports by UN and regional HR mechanisms, NGOs, national or local HR institutions)	Consideration of material deprivation/ relation to ESCR, as an element of discrimination or risk of torture or inhuman treatment	Remedies addressing collective measures/ dimensions
Opuz v. Turkey, ECHR, 2009 (VAW)	✓	✓	✓	✓		
Cotton Field v. Mexico, IACHR, 2009 (VAW)	✓	✓	✓	✓		✓
N. v. Finland, ECHR, 2005 (Asylum seeker)		✓		✓		
M.S.S. v. Belgium & Greece, ECHR, (Asylum seeker)	✓	✓ (Qualified)	✓ (Qualified)	✓	✓	
Yean and Bosico Girls v. Dominican Republic, IACHR, 2005 (Undocumented migrants)	✓		✓		✓	✓

(continued)

[7] The referred cases and instruments are only quoted by way of example. As such, they are not exhaustive of the proposed human security-human rights synergy or of the full range of cases/instruments explored in this book, but rather are included to provide an illustrative categorisation of the elements of this synergy.

Table 1: *(Continued)*

	Obligation to apply due diligence standards in cases of 'known risk' (Obligations of prevention/actively taking measures of reinforced protection), including non-State actors	Consideration of systemic/ structural risks or vulnerabilities	Reversal of burden of proof on the State	Use of non-traditional evidence (reports by UN and regional HR mechanisms, NGOs, national or local HR institutions)	Consideration of material deprivation/ relation to ESCR, as an element of discrimination or risk of torture or inhuman treatment	Remedies addressing collective measures/ dimensions
Nadege Dorzema et. al. v. Dominican Republic, IACHR, 2012 (Undocumented migrants)	✓	✓	✓	✓	✓	✓
Nacic and Others v. Sweden, ECHR, 2012 (Undocumented migrants)	X	X	X	✓	X	X (Rejects)
N. v. UK, ECHR, 2008 (Undocumented migrant)	X	X	X	✓	X	X (Rejects)
Sonko v. Spain, UNCAT, 2012 (Undocumented migrant)	✓	✓	✓			
B.S. v. Spain, ECHR, 2012 (Migrant woman)		✓	✓			X (Rejects)

(continued)

Table 1: *(Continued)*

	Obligation to apply due diligence standards in cases of 'known risk' (Obligations of prevention/actively taking measures of reinforced protection), including non-State actors	Consideration of systemic/ structural risks or vulnerabilities	Reversal of burden of proof on the State	Use of non-traditional evidence (reports by UN and regional HR mechanisms, NGOs, national or local HR institutions)	Consideration of material deprivation/ relation to ESCR, as an element of discrimination or risk of torture or inhuman treatment	Remedies addressing collective measures/ dimensions
Xákmok Kásek Indigenous Community v. Paraguay, IACHR, 2010 (ESC Rights)	✓	✓	✓	✓	✓	✓
General recommendation No. 32, *The gender-related dimensions of refugee status, asylum, nationality and statelessness of women*, CEDAW, 2014	✓	✓	✓			
General Recommendation No. 33, *Women's access to justice*, CEDAW, 2015	✓	✓	✓	✓		✓

III. PROSPECTIVE ROUTES

In the case of this research, concrete ways have been identified in which human security and human rights can be mutually supportive. This synergy can provide for a language, a fabric, and a frame in which the legal interpretation of human rights can be rendered more protective and integrated in covering interrelated risk factors, and weaving connections between the core contents of the human rights in question concerning each particular situation. Human security also underlines the interdependence and equal hierarchy of all human rights—civil, political, economic, social and cultural—in supporting or undermining the human security of persons and communities, especially those living in conditions of vulnerability.

It can also constitute a tool for *prioritisation* that can further elements to assess and evaluate levels of human need and vulnerability and can add value to existing human rights-based approaches (HRBA) and indicators of different fields that already deal with such needs (think of development for example, and the importance for HRBA as stressed by Mary Robinson and Philip Alston).[8]

Apart from being consonant with current HRBA, human security seems to also hold potential to provide criteria for resolving situations of *conflicts between rights*. Although the classical human rights' position is that the utmost effort should be carried out for all rights to be protected in a harmonic way, which this text aligns with, it is also true that there are challenges that come up in practice which actually do require privileging one right of a certain person or group above another such right.[9] This does not lead to establishing an *a priori* list of which rights are more 'fundamental' than others, a position that is not shared in this book, as has been argued throughout. Neither does it mean cancelling out completely the second right in the case of conflict: as it has been portrayed above, human rights bodies and literature have affirmed that the core content of each right should always be maintained, even in the case of rights susceptible to temporary suspension or derogation.

[8] See the analysis made by Gasper, Des, 'Human Rights, Human Needs, Human Development, Human Security: Relationships between Four International "Human" Discourses' (Institute of Social Studies, The Hague, GARNET Working Paper: No 20/07, July 2007) 10 and following. See also the useful comparative overview of current conceptions related to rights, needs and dangers, contained in Table 4, 32.

[9] For an analysis of conflicts between rights, see Brems, Eva (ed), *Conflicts between Fundamental Rights* (Antwerp, Intersentia, 2008), particularly De Schutter, Olivier and Francoise Tulkens, 'Rights in Conflict: The European Court of Human Rights as a Pragmatic Institution' at 169–216.

However, human rights scholars and lawyers, judges, policy-makers and activists could benefit from relying on richer criteria based on *levels of risk and vulnerability* in the ways suggested in this book, to assess what Mary Robinson has also recognised as the need for more defined standards for making adequate differentiations between 'ordinary' human rights circumstances, and life-threatening situations.[10] Providing criteria doesn't only operate in the case of 'conflicting' rights, but more importantly also for *positive dialogues* between rights, such as facilitating a closer and mutually reinforcing relationship between civil and political, economic, social and cultural rights. In giving their genuine dimension to threats of a socio-economic nature and emphasising the indivisibility of physical and material survival, human security also contributes in placing related rights to such threats in their due hierarchy.

This task of *criteria provider* would be fulfilled through the concept of risk and vulnerability as a condition for urgent action to protect specific rights of those persons or collectives in such a situation. When the threat amounts to a *structural vulnerability*, a reinforced obligation of protection by the State is triggered, as the judicial decisions studied in this book have recently started to acknowledge. The existence of such a collective threat cannot be easily perceived and documented through human rights standards alone, even when using non-discrimination principles, as human rights in the legal sense focus generally on *individual* rights, on the one hand, and *actual enjoyment*, on the other. Thus, the existence of a *risk situation*, that is, a situation of *potential* violation of the human rights of a *group* of persons with shared characteristics—think of gender, ethnicity, class, religion, national origin or legal status, to name some—becomes a bit vague and difficult to construct. Thus, leaning on the elements provided by the human security concept, opens the door for broader and more protective human rights interpretations that duly consider interconnected conditions of structural vulnerability that place a person or a whole collective at risk of experiencing a human rights violation and, in some cases, may conclude that the sole existence of such vulnerability in itself already constitutes a violation, as analysed throughout this book.

From the account displayed in the book, other conditions have been categorised by scholarship and human rights bodies both as the cause and the consequence of human rights violations. Think of poverty or discrimination, for instance, as reviewed in the text. The empirical evidence addressed and the case-law examined demonstrates how human insecurity, too, plays this double role: it is at the heart of risk situations that lead to the violation of rights, and once such potential harms are concretised,

[10] Robinson, Mary, 'What Rights Can Add to Good Development Practice' in Alston, Philip and Mary Robinson (eds), *Human Rights and Development: Towards Mutual Reinforcement* (New York, Oxford University Press, 2005) 25–41.

they result in further human insecurity. This reinforcing cycle is provoked and perpetuated most notably in the context of underlying structural vulnerability, in some cases constructed by the law itself, more outstandingly in that of undocumented migrants. It can only be broken with an active reaffirmation and implementation of human rights-based policies, laws and judicial decisions. This book has raised a voice in favour of such actions to be taken as part of a broader project of building interrelated conditions of human security understood as a facilitating environment to make possible the full realisation of all human rights, a modern materialisation of Article 28 of the UDHR. There are of course other valuable initiatives sharing these common objectives. Human security, I have argued, holds the potential of complementing such efforts and debates and of bringing them together under a common language, doctrinal analysis and practical implementation.

To give an example of how such potentials could work, let us think of the assessment of foreign policy and external action referred to in the previous section through the lens offered by the human security-human rights symbiosis. Such an evaluation would apply not only to the State's position in formal human rights issues and bodies, but also concerning its activity in bilateral or multilateral investment treaties and arbitration procedures, for instance, before the International Center for the Settlement of Investment Disputes (ICSID), and within inter-governmental bodies such as the World Intellectual Property Organisation, the World Trade Organisation or the International Monetary Fund.[11] For instance, under a human security sensitive approach, could business corporations involved in the provision of public services such as water or electricity be charged with international legal responsibility in the field of human rights for their actions? Does the State hold a legal obligation to align its actions with human rights principles and norms in the investment or arbitration treaties and procedures it engages in? In both cases, independently of or as a complement to the existence of strict legal obligations or the finding of legally verifiable violations, could we evaluate State or non-State actor conduct or omission *placing rights at risk,* on the one hand, or *disregarding persons or groups in vulnerability* on the other, eg women in conditions of discrimination or violence, people in poverty, undocumented migrants? If so, are these actions or abstentions relevant for human rights law?[12]

[11] For a specific 'human security approach' to international trade and the right to work, see Howse, Robert and Ruti G Teitel, *Beyond the Divide: The Covenant on Economic, Social and Cultural Rights and the World Trade Organization*, Dialogue on Globalization, Occasional Paper No 30, Friedrich-Ebert-Stiftung, Geneva Office, April 2007, 14–19.

[12] Think of *Case of Aguas del Tunari SA v. The Republic of Bolivia* (ICSID Case No ARB/03/02). For a full account, see Thielbörger, Pierre, 'The Human Right to Water Versus Investor Rights: Double-Dilemma Or Pseudo-Conflict?' in Dupuy, Pierre-Marie, Francesco Francioni and Ernst-Ulrich Petersmann (eds), *Human Rights in International Investment Law and Arbitration* (Oxford, Oxford University Press, 2009) 487–510.

This line of reflection would thus complement ongoing debate on human rights and transnational corporations, extra-territorial obligations in the field of ESC Rights, or the human rights obligations surrounding extreme poverty, as detailed in preceding reflections.

Human security also adds up to other 'humanising' discourses, such as human rights, human development, and human needs, as Des Gasper notes.[13] It is submitted that human security can thus serve a certain *mapping function* of diverse fields that are frequently carried out in a disconnected and non-communicated manner, despite being constructed on similar foundations and principles, and holding shared practical implications. One must only recall Alston's 'ships passing in the night' analogy referring to the relationship between human rights and development.[14] Thus, human security is not only useful in pushing for a more humanised security agenda, opposing or expanding State-centered or reductionist views of security. It is also helpful as a *working alliance*[15] between these different humanised discourses and can give way to constructive partnerships with the development and human rights worlds, if not with other fields, such as climate change and environmental protection. Especially in the realm of human rights law these potentials have not been explored much or deeply, whereby this book has proposed that one of such added values lies in providing for *interpretative synergies* between human security and human rights analysis that can work for the benefit of both the rights and the security of people.

To further develop these working alliances, I highlight some possible routes. While the book touches at many instances on UN, African, European and Inter-American instruments, it reflects a more intense dialogue between the European and Inter-American experiences, partly because of the dominant presence of Latin American cases in the regional human rights system. The research reveals how this exchange is usually absent. Hopefully this book can contribute in building one of the necessary bridges to give way to this dialogue, that of the English and Spanish language legal and political scholarship and case-law, particularly the Latin American expressions of international law.

In this context, as a prospective route for future analysis, I signal the issue of the Inter-American practice related to human security and consolidated over the past few years, through its political bodies and through its human rights system, as a possible emerging customary norm viewed from the perspective of the sources of public international law.

13 Gasper (n 11) 30.

14 Alston, Philip, 'Ships Passing in the Night: The Current State of the Human Rights and Development Debate Seen through the Lens of the Millennium Development Goals' (2005) 27 *Human Rights Quarterly* 3 755–58.

15 *Ibid*, 1.

On the other hand, the analysis of illustrative cases provided evidence that judicial decisions, even when aligning with human security and human rights standards, often arrive late, or as responses to individual cases; they are insufficient in addressing widespread challenges. Human security helps emphasise the need for *prevention*, a goal that could also be achieved through legal reform and/or public policy. In this sense, the human security–human rights framework can also be policy-prescriptive. Similar potentials have started to be explored and applied in the Latin American and Inter-American context more generally, and constitute an issue for further research.[16]

Under the reviewed light of human security in its positive sense as an *enabling environment for human rights* embodying Article 28 of the UDHR, human security may also contribute to constructing a 'rule of rights' (*Estado de derechos)* complementing and transcending the 'rule of law' (*Estado de Derecho*). As this text has attempted to demonstrate, it is through the protection of human rights, particularly of those most vulnerable, that any political regime, State model or international arrangement, acquires its legitimacy and fosters the greatest possibilities of creating conditions for a peaceful and just social and international order, especially for the silenced and marginalised, as feminist scholars Charlesworth, Chinkin and Wright remind us in duly relocating the priorities of international law.

I have argued that in this ongoing debate legal scholarship should be present and add a voice to a dialogue which touches the heart of human rights advancement and the protection of people in all societies, developed and developing alike, in particular the most vulnerable, so many of whom still await for a humane answer from international law. Through a gendered human security and by deepening the potentials of the human security–human rights synergy, international law may well complement current person-centred efforts and offer alternative ways to confront and alleviate severe and critical vulnerability and human suffering. In taking issues of everyday structural injustice seriously, international law might acquire the human face so many persons desperately call for.

[16] See, eg Vázquez, Daniel and Domitille Delaplace, 'Public Policies from a Human Rights Perspective: A Developing Field' (2011) 8 *Sur—International Journal on Human Rights* 14 (Biannual, English Edition); and Abramovich, Víctor, 'De las Violaciones Masivas a los Patrones Estructurales: Nuevos Enfoques y Clásicas Tensiones en el Sistema Interamericano de Derechos Humanos", (2009) 6 *Sur, Revista Internacional de Derechos Humanos* 11 (also available in English).; Dulitzky, Ariel, 'The Inter-American Human Rights System Fifty Years Later: Time for Changes' (2011) *Quebec Journal of International Law.* See also National Human Rights Programs of Mexico and Guatemala; and for a gendered human security/human rights policy, note the example of The Regional Program in Latin America of UNIFEM (today incorporated into UN Women), 'Ciudades Seguras: Violencia hacia las Mujeres y Políticas Públicas' ('Safe Cities: Violence Against Women and Public Policies').

Bibliography

ACADEMIC SOURCES

Abramovich, Víctor, *Los estándares interamericanos de derechos humanos como marco para la formulación y el control de las políticas sociales* (Buenos Aires, Anuario de Derechos Humanos, 2006).

——, 'De las Violaciones Masivas a los Patrones Estructurales: Nuevos Enfoques y Clásicas Tensiones en el Sistema Interamericano de Derechos Humanos' (2009) 6 *Sur, Revista Internacional de Derechos Humanos* 11 (also available in English).

—— and Christian Courtis, *Los derechos sociales como derechos exigibles* (Prologue by Luigi Ferrajoli) (Spain, Editorial Trotta, 2002).

Acharya, Arabinda and Amitav Acharya, 'Human Security in Asia: Conceptual Ambiguity and Common Understandings', Centre for Peace and Development Studies, 2001, available at York University, Toronto, at www.yorku.ca/robarts/archives/chandigarth/S.

Alcalde Villacampa, Javier, 'The Mine Ban Treaty, New Diplomacy and Human Security Ten Years Later', Book review of Williams, Jody, Mary Wareham and Stephen Goose (eds), *Banning Landmines: Disarmament, Citizen Diplomacy, and Human Security*, (New York, Roeman and Littlefield, 2008) in (2008) *European Political Science* 7:4.

Alkire, Sabine, 'Concepts of Human Security' in Chen, Lincoln, Sakiko Fukuda-Parr and Ellen Seidensticker (eds), *Human Insecurity in a Global World* (Harvard, Harvard University Press, 2003).

Alston Philip, 'A Human Rights Perspective on the Millennium Development Goals', Paper prepared as a contribution to the work of the Millennium Project Task Force on Poverty and Economic Development (NYU Law School, Center for Human Rights and Global Justice, 2004).

——, 'Ships Passing in the Night: The Current State of the Human Rights and Development Debate Seen through the Lens of the Millennium Development Goals' (2005) 27 *Human Rights Quarterly* 3.

—— and Mary Robinson (eds), *Human Rights and Development: Towards a Mutual Reinforcement* (New York, Oxford University Press, 2006).

Anderson, Bridget, 'Mobilizing Migrants, Making Citizens: Migrant Domestic Workers as Political Agents' (2010) 33 *Ethnic and Racial Studies* 1.

Anderson, Kenneth, 'The Ottawa Convention Banning Landmines, the Role of International Non-Governmental Organizations, and the Idea of International Civil Society' (2000) 11 *European Journal of International Law* 1.

Añón, María José (ed), *La universalidad de los derechos sociales: el reto de la inmigración* (Valencia, Spain, Tirant lo Blanch, 2004)

Aubin, Louise, 'UNHCR and Human Security' in Devin, Guillaume (ed), *Making Peace: The Contribution of International Institutions*, translated by Roger Leverdier, Basingstoke (New York, Palgrave Macmillan, 2011).

Banks, Taunya Lovell, 'Toward a Global Critical Feminist Vision: Domestic Work and the Nanny Tax Debate' (1999) 3 *Journal of Gender, Race & Justice* 1.

Barak-Erez, Daphne and Aeyal M Gross (eds), *Exploring Social Rights: Between Theory and Practice* (Oxford, Hart Publishing, 2007).

Basch, Linda, 'Human Security, Globalization, and Feminist Visions' (2004) 16 *Peace Review* 1.

Beck, Ulrich, *Risk Society: Towards a New Modernity* (London, Sage, 1992).

Behringer, Ronald M, *The Human Security Agenda: How Middle Power Leadership Defied U.S. Hegemony* (London, New York, Continuum, 2012).

Benedek, Wolfgang, 'Human Rights and Human Security: Challenges and Prospects' in Ferrándiz, Francisco and Antonius CGM Robben (eds), *Multidisciplinary Perspectives on Peace and Conflict Research: A View from Europe* (Bilbao, University of Deusto, 2007).

——, 'Human Security and Human Rights Interaction' in Goucha, Moufida and John Crowley (eds), *Rethinking Human Security* UK, Wiley-Blackwell and UNESCO, 2008).

——, 'Mainstreaming Human Security in United Nations and European Union Peace and Crisis Management Operations: Policies and Practice', in Benedek, Wolfgang, Matthias C Kettemann and Markus Möstl (eds), *Mainstreaming Human Security in Peace Operations and Crisis Management: Policies, Problems, Potentials*, (Abingdon, Oxon, New York, Routledge, 2011).

Beneyto, José María and David Kennedy (eds), *New Approaches to International Law. The European and the American Experiences* (The Hague, TMC Asser Press, Springer, 2013)

Benhabib, Seyla, *Dignity in Adversity: Human Rights in Troubled Times* (Cambridge, Polity Press, 2011).

Benítez Manaut, Raúl and Daniel Hernández, 'Migración y Seguridad. Nueva clave en las relaciones Estados Unidos, México, Centroamérica' in Sepúlveda, Isidro (ed), *Seguridad humana y nuevas políticas de defensa en Iberoamérica* (Madrid, Instituto Universitario General Gutiérrez Mellado, 2007).

Blainey, Geoffrey, *The Causes of War* (London, Macmillan, 1983).

Boerefijn, Ineke and Eva Naezer, 'Emerging Human Rights Obligations for Non-State Actors' in Benninger-Budel, Carin (ed), *Due Diligence and its Application to Protect Women from Violence* (The Netherlands, Martinus Nijhoff Publishers, 2008).

Bosniak, Linda, 'Human Rights within One State. Dilemmas of Personhood in Liberal Constitutional Thought' in Dembour, Marie-Bénédicte and Tobias Kelly (eds), *Are Human Rights for Migrants? Critical Reflections on the Status of Irregular Migrants in Europe and the United States* (New York, Routledge, 2011).

Bradford, Anu and Eric A Posner, 'Universal Exceptionalism in International Law' (2011) 52 *Harvard International Law Journal* 1.

Breau, Susan and Indira Carr, 'Humanitarian Aid, Human Rights and Corruption' in Odello, Marco and Sofia Cavandoli (eds), *Emerging Areas of Human Rights in the 21st Century: The Role of the Universal Declaration of Human Rights* (USA and Canada, Routledge, 2011).

Brems, Eva, 'Thank You, Justice Tulkens: A Comment on the Dissent in N v UK' in *The Strasbourg Observers*, 14 August 2012, available at http://strasbourgobservers.com/2012/08/14/thank-you-justice-tulkens-a-comment-on-the-dissent-in-n-v-uk/.

Buckley, Joanna, 'NS v Secretary of State for the Home Department (C-411/10)' (2012) *European Human Rights Law Review*.

Bunch, Charlotte, 'A Feminist Human Rights Lens on Human Security' (2004) 16 *Peace Review* 1.

Burke, Ciarán, *An Equitable Framework for Humanitarian Intervention* (Studies in International Law) (Oxford and Portland, Oregon, Hart Publishing, 2013).

Cançado Trindade, Antônio Augusto, *A humanizaçao do direito internacional* (Brazil, Editora del Rey, 2006).

——, *International Law for Humankind: Towards a New Jus Gentium* (The Netherlands, Martinus Nijhoff Publishers, 2010).

——, *State Responsibility in Cases of Massacres: Contemporary Advances in International Justice*, Inaugural address as Honorary Professor to the Chair in 'International and Regional Human Rights Courts', delivered on 10 November 2011 at Utrecht University.

——, *The Access of Individuals to International Justice* (Oxford, New York, Oxford University Press, 2011).

Cancio Meliá, Manuel and Mario Maraver Gómez, Universidad Autónoma de Madrid, 'El derecho penal español ante la inmigración: un estudio político-criminal' in Bacigalupo/Cancio Meliá (eds), *Derecho penal y política transnacional* (Barcelona, Editorial Atelier, 2005).

Carens, Joseph H, 'Aliens and Citizens: The Case for Open Borders' (1987) 49 *The Review of Politics* 2.

——, *Immigrants and the Right to Stay* (Boston, MIT Press, 2010).

——, *The Ethics of Immigration* (New York, Oxford University Press, 2013).

Carrera, Sergio and Joanna Parkin, *Protecting and Delivering Fundamental Rights of Irregular Migrants at Local and Regional Levels in the European Union* (EU, Brussels, Centre for European Policy Studies (CEPS)/EU, 2011).

Cassese, Antonio, *International Law*, 2nd edn (Oxford, Oxford University Press) 2005.

Chandler, David, 'Review Essay: Human Security: The Dog That Didn't Bark' (2008) *Security Dialogue* 39.

——, 'Resilience and Human Security: The Post-Interventionist Paradigm' (2012) *Security Dialogue* 43 (3).

Chapman, Audrey R and Benjamin Carbonetti, 'Human Rights Protections for Vulnerable and Disadvantaged Groups: The Contributions of the UN Committee on Economic, Social and Cultural Rights' (2011) *Human Rights Quarterly* 2011.

Charlesworth, Hilary, 'International Law: A Discipline of Crisis' (2002) 65 *Modern Law* 3.

—— and Christine Chinkin, *The Boundaries of International Law. A Feminist Analysis* (Manchester, Juris Publishing, Manchester University Press, 2000).

——, —— and Shelley Wright, 'Feminist Approaches to International Law' (1991) 85 *The American Journal of International Law* 4.

Cherubin-Doumbia, Giliane, 'African Commitments to Human Rights. A Review of Eight NEPAD Countries', *A Monograph for the African Human Security Initiative*, www.africanreview.org, available at www.issafrica.org/pubs/Other/ahsi/ChrubinMono/Contents.html.

Chetail, Vincent, 'Are Refugee Rights Human Rights? An Unorthodox Questioning of the Relations between Refugee Law and Human Rights Law' in Rubio Marín,

Ruth (ed), *Human Rights and Immigration* (Oxford, Oxford University Press, 2014).
—— and Celine Bauloz, *The European Union and the Challenges of Forced Migration: From Economic Crisis to Protection Crisis?*, EU-US Immigration Systems 2011/07 (San Domenico di Fiesole (FI), Robert Schuman Centre for Advanced Studies, European University Institute, 2011).
Chinedu Okafor, Obiora, 'The African Commission on Human and Peoples' Rights as a Collective Human Security Resource: Promise, Performance, and Prospects' in Abass, Ademola (ed), *Protecting Human Security in Africa* (Oxford, Oxford University Press, 2010).
Chinkin, Christine, 'Violence Against Women' in Freeman, Marsha, E, Christine Chinkin and Beate Rudolf (eds), *The UN Convention on the Elimination of all Forms of Discrimination Against Women: A Commentary* (Oxford, Oxford University Press, 2012).
Cholewinski, Ryszard, 'Labour Migration Management and the Rights of Migrant Workers' in Edwards, Alice and Carla Ferstman (eds), *Human Security and Non-Citizens: Law, Policy and International Affairs* (Cambridge, Cambridge University Press, 2010).
Chuang, Janie, 'Beyond a Snapshot: Preventing Human Trafficking in the Global Economy' (2006) 13 *Indiana Journal of Global Legal Studies* 137.
Conte, Alex and Richard Burchill, *Defining Civil and Political Rights: The Jurisprudence of the United Nations Human Rights Committee*, 2nd edn (Aldershot, England, Ashgate, 2004).
Cook, Rebecca J, 'Human Rights Dimensions of Health Security' (2003) 97 *American Society of International Law Proceedings* 101–06.
Coomaraswamy, Radihka, 'Human Security and Gender Violence' (2005) 40 *Economic and Political Weekly* 44/45.
Cooper, Michael D, 'Migration and Disaster-Induced Displacement: European Policy, Practice, and Perspective', CGD Working Paper 308 (Washington DC, Center for Global Development, October 2012).
Costello, Cathryn, 'Courting Access to Asylum in Europe: Recent Supranational Jurisprudence Explored' (2012) *Human Rights Law Review* 12 (2).
Courtis, Christian, 'La prohibición de regresividad en materia de derechos sociales: apuntes introductorios' in Courtis, Christian (compilador), *Ni un paso atrás: La prohibición de regresividad en materia de derechos sociales* (Buenos Aires, Del Puerto, 2006).
Crenshaw, Kimberley, 'Mapping the Margins: Intersectionality, Identity Politics, and Violence Against Women of Color' (1991) 43 *Stanford Law Review*.
Curtis, Josh and Shane Darcy, 'The Right to a Social and International Order for the Realisation of Human Rights: Article 28 of the Universal Declaration and International Cooperation' in Keane, David and Yvonne McDermott (eds), *The Challenge of Human Rights. Past, Present and Future* (USA/UK, Edward Elgar, 2012).
Dalby, Simon, *Environmental Security* (USA, University of Minnesota Press, 2002).
——, *Security and Environmental Change* (Cambridge, UK, Polity Press, 2009).
Darkwa, Linda, 'The Challenge of Sub-Regional Security in West Africa. The Case of the 2006 ECOWAS Convention on Small Arms and Light Weapons', Discussion Paper 69 (Uppsala, Nordiska Afrikainstitutet, 2011).

Dauvergne, Catherine, *Making People Illegal: What Globalization Means for Migration and Law*, Law in Context Series (Cambridge, Cambridge University Press, 2008).
Davis, Kevin E, Benedict Kingsbury and Sally Engle Merry, 'Indicators as a Technology of Global Governance', IILJ Working Paper 2010/2 Rev, Finalized 08/02/2011, International Law and Justice Working Papers, Institute for International Law and Justice, New York University School of Law.
De Lucas, Javier (ed), *Inmigración e integración en la UE: dos retos para el s. XXI* (Spain, Eurobask, 2012).
De Schutter, Olivier, UN Special Rapporteur on the Right to Food, 'Reshaping Global Governance: The Case of the Right to Food' (2012) 3 *Global Policy* 4.
—— and Francoise Tulkens, 'Rights in Conflict: The European Court of Human Rights as a Pragmatic Institution' in Brems, Eva (ed), *Conflicts between Fundamental Rights* (Antwerp, Intersentia, 2008).
Den Boer, Monica, 'Preventive Empires: Security Dynamics at Multiple Levels of Governance' (2011) 3 *Amsterdam Law Forum* 3.
Dersso, Solomon A (ed), *Promotion of Human Security in Africa. The Role of African Human Rights Institutions*, ISS Monograph Series, No 145, June 2008.
Doswald-Beck, Louise, 'Human Security: Can it be Attained?' (2003) 97 *American Society of International Law Proceedings*.
Duffy, Aiofe, 'Expulsion to Face Torture? *Non-Refoulment* in International Law' (2008) 20 *International Journal of Refugee Law* 3.
Dulitzky, Ariel, 'The Inter-American Human Rights System Fifty Years Later: Time for Changes' (2011) *Quebec Journal of International Law* (Special Edition).
Dupuy, Pierre-Marie, Francesco Francioni and Ernst-Ulrich Petersmann (eds), *Human Rights in International Investment Law and Arbitration* (Oxford, Oxford University Press, 2009).
Düvell, Franck and Bastian Vollmer, *European Security Challenges*, EU-US Immigration Systems 2011/07 (San Domenico di Fiesole, Robert Schuman Centre for Advanced Studies, European University Institute, 2011).
Edwards, Alice, 'Human Security and the Rights of Refugees: Transcending Territorial and Disciplinary Borders' (2009) 30 *Michigan Journal of International Law* 3.
—— and Carla Ferstman (eds), *Human Security and Non-Citizens: Law, Policy and International Affairs* (Cambridge, Cambridge University Press, 2010).
El Baradei, Mohamed, *The Age of Deception: Nuclear Diplomacy in Treacherous Times* (New York, Metropolitan Books/Henry Holt and Co, 2011).
Elmadmad, Khadija, *Femmes, Migrations et Droits au Maroc*, CARIM Notes d'analyse et de synthèse 2011/01, Série sur genre et migration/Module juridique (Florence, Italy, Institut Universitaire Européen, Robert Schuman Center for Advanced Studies, 2011).
Engle, Karen, 'The Grip of Sexual Violence: Reading UN Security Council Resolutions on Human Security' in Heathcote, Gina and Dianne Otto (eds), *Rethinking Peacekeeping, Gender Equality and Collective Security*, Series Thinking Gender in Transnational Times (UK, Palgrave Macmillan, 2014).
Estrada Tanck, E Dorothy, *Régimen jurídico internacional de las empresas transnacionales en la esfera de los derechos humanos*, Breviarios Jurídicos 36 (Mexico, Editorial Porrúa, 2005).

Falk, Richard A, 'Global Climate Change, Human Security, and the Future of Democracy' in Gill, Stephen (ed), *Global Crises and the Crisis of Global Leadership* (Cambridge, New York, Cambridge University Press, 2011).

Farer, Thomas, 'Human Security: Defining the Elephant and Imagining its Tasks' (2011) 1 *Asian Journal of International Law* 01.

Farmer, Paul, *Pathologies of Power: Health, Human Rights, and the New War on the Poor* (Berkeley, University of California Press, 2005).

Fernández Pereira, Juan Pablo, *La seguridad humana: un derecho emergente* (Barcelona, Ariel, 2006).

Ferrajoli, Luigi, *Derechos y garantías. La ley del más débil* (Italian-Spanish translation by P Andrés Ibañez and A Greppi) (Barcelona, Editorial Trotta, 1999).

Ferstman, Carla, 'The Human Security Framework and Counter Terrorism: Examining the Rhetoric Relating to Extraordinary Renditions' in Edwards, Alice and Carla Ferstman (eds), *Human Security and Non-Citizens: Law, Policy and International Affairs* (Cambridge, Cambridge University Press, 2010).

Fidler, David P, '"Geographical Morality" Revisited: International Relations, International Law, and the Controversy over Placebo-Controlled HIV Clinical Trials in Developing Countries' (2001) 42 *Harvard International Law Journal*, available at 0-www.lexisnexis.com.biblio.eui.eu/hottopics/lnacademic/?verb=sr&csi=143840.

Fineman, Martha Albertson, 'The Vulnerable Subject: Anchoring Equality in the Human Condition' (2008) 20 *Yale Journal of Law and Feminism* 1.

Florea Hudson, Natalie, *Gender, Human Security and the United Nations: Security Language as a Political Framework for Women* (New York, Routledge, 2010).

Freeman, Michael, 'Beyond Capitalism and Socialism' in Dine, Janet and Andrew Fagan (eds), *Human Rights and Capitalism. A Multidisciplinary Perspective on Globalisation* (UK, Edward Elgar, 2006).

Freitas, Raquel, 'Human Security and Refugee Protection after September 11: A Reassessment' (2002) 20 *Refugee: Canada's Periodical on Refugees* 4.

Fries, Lorena, 'La Corte Penal Internacional y los avances en materia de justicia de género: una mirada retrospectiva' in Birgin, Haydée and Natalia Gherardi (coordinators), *Reflexiones jurídicas desde la perspectiva de género*, Colección 'Género, Derecho y Justicia' No 7 (Mexico, Suprema Corte de Justicia de la Nación, 2010).

Fudge, Judy, 'Decent Work for Migrant Care Workers', at 'Gender and Migration: Workers at the Interface of Migration and Development', a special panel event by the United Nations Entity for Gender Equality and Women's Empowerment (UN Women) and the International Labour Organization (ILO) at the Fourth United Nations Conference on the Least Developed Countries (LDC-IV), May 2011, available at www.ilo.org/global/meetings-and-events/events/conference-on-least-developed-countries/WCMS_155339/lang--en/index.htm.

Fuentes, Claudia F and Francisco Rojas Aravena, *Promover la Seguridad Humana: Marcos Éticos, Normativos y Educacionales en América Latina y el Caribe*, Facultad Latinoamericana de Ciencias Sociales (Paris, FLACSO, UNESCO, 2005).

Fukuda-Parr, Sakiko, 'New Threats to Human Security in the Era of Globalization' in Chen, Lincoln, Sakiko Fukuda-Parr and Ellen Seidensticker (eds), *Human Insecurity in a Global World* (Harvard, Harvard University Press, 2003).

Gallagher, Anne, 'Human Rights and the New UN Protocols on Trafficking and Migrant Smuggling: A Preliminary Analysis' (2001) 23 *Human Rights Quarterly* 4.
Galtung, Irene, *Lawyers or Liars? Is World Hunger Suable in Court?*, PhD Thesis in Law (Florence, European University Institute, 2011).
Galtung, Johan, 'Violence, Peace, and Peace Research' (1969) 6 *Journal of Peace Research* 3.
——, *Peace: Research, Education, Action* (Copenhagen, Ejilers, 1975).
Garcia, Denise, *Disarmament Diplomacy and Human Security: Regimes, Norms, and Moral Progress in International Relations* (New York, Routledge, 2011).
García-Mora, Manuel R, 'The Law of the Inter-American Treaty of Reciprocal Assistance' (1951) 20 *Fordham Law Review* 1, available at http://ir.lawnet.fordham.edu/flr/vol20/iss1/1.
Gasper, Des, 'Human Rights, Human Needs, Human Development, Human Security: Relationships between Four International "Human" Discourses', GARNET Working Paper: No 20/07 (The Hague, Institute of Social Studies, 2007).
Gil-Bazo, María Teresa, 'Refugee Status, Subsidiary Protection, and the Right to be Granted Asylum under EC Law', Research Paper No 136, Refugee Studies Centre, Oxford University, UK-UNHCHR Policy Development and Evaluation Service, November 2006.
——, 'Asylum as a General Principle of International Law' (2015) 27 *International Journal of Refugee Law* 1.
Glasius, Marlies, 'Human Security from Paradigm Shift to Operationalization: Job Description for a Human Security Worker' (2008) 39 *Security Dialogue* 1.
——, 'Human Security: A Shifting and Bridging Concept that can be Operationalized' in Boerefijn, Ineke, Laura Henderson, Ronald Janse, and Robert Weaver (eds), *Human Rights and Conflict: Essays in Honour of Bas de Gaay Fortman* (Cambridge, Antwerp, Intersentia, 2012).
Glusac, Luka, 'Humanitarian Interventions in the Concept of Human Security' (2010) *Western Balkans Security Observer* 16.
González, Felipe, 'The Experience of the Inter-American Human Rights System' (2009–10) 40 *Victoria University Wellington Law Review* 1.
Goodwin-Gill, Guy S and Jane McAdam, *The Refugee in International Law*, 3rd edn (Oxford, Oxford University Press, 2007).
Gordon, Jennifer, *Suburban Sweatshops: The Fight for Immigrant Rights* (USA, Belknap/Harvard University Press, 2005).
Gowlland-Debbas, Vera, 'An Emerging International Public Policy?' in Fastenrath, Ulrich, Rudolf Geiger, Daniel-Erasmus Khan, Andreas Paulus, Sabine von Schorlemer and Christoph Vedder (eds), *From Bilateralism to Community Interest, Essays in Honour of Judge Bruno Simma* (New York, Oxford University Press, 2011).
Graham, David T and Nana K Poku (eds), *Migration, Globalisation, and Human Security* (London/New York, Routledge, 2000).
Grant, Stefanie, 'The Recognition of Migrants' Rights within the UN Human Rights System: The First 60 Years' in Dembour, Marie-Bénédicte and Tobias Kelly (eds), *Are Human Rights for Migrants? Critical Reflections on the Status of Irregular Migrants in Europe and the United States* (London/New York, Routledge, 2011).

——, 'Irregular Migration and Frontier Deaths. Acknowledging a Right to Identity' in Dembour and Kelly, *ibid*.

Guild, Elspeth, *Security and Migration in the 21st Century* (Cambridge, Malden, MA, Polity, 2009).

——, Kees Groenendijk and Sergio Carrera, 'Understanding the Contest of Community: Illiberal Practices in the EU?' in *Illiberal Liberal States. Immigration, Citizenship and Integration in the EU* (England/USA, Ashgate, 2009)

Harding, Jeremy, *The Uninvited: Refugees at the Rich Man's Gate* (London, Profile Books, London Review of Books, 2000).

——, *Border Vigils: Keeping Migrants out of the Rich World* (London/New York, Verso Books, 2012).

Hasselbacher, Lee, 'State Obligations Regarding Domestic Violence: The European Court of Human Rights, Due Diligence, and International Legal Minimums of Protection' (2010) 8 *Northwestern University Journal of International Human Rights* 2, available at www.law.northwestern.edu/journals/jihr/v8/n2/3.

Hastings, David A, 'Describing the Human Condition—from Human Development to Human Security', GIS-IDEAS 2008 Conference 'Towards a Sustainable and Creative Humanosphere', 2008, available at http://wgrass.media.osaka-cu.ac.jp/gisideas08/viewabstract.php?id=299.

——, 'Filling Gaps in the Human Development Index'. UNESCAP, Working Paper WP/09/02, 2009, available at www.unescap.org/publications/detail.asp?id=1308.

——, 'The Human Security Index: An Update and a New Release', Human SecurityIndex.org, 2012, available at www.humansecurityindex.org/wordpress/wp-content/uploads/2012/02/hsiv2-documentation-report1_1.pdf.

Hathaway, James C, 'EU Accountability to International Law: The Case of Asylum' (2011) 33 *Michigan Journal of International Law* 1.

Helgesen, Jan, 'Between Helsinkis—and Beyond? Human Rights in the CSCE (Conference on Security and Cooperation in Europe) Process' in Rosas, Allan and Jan Hegelsen (eds, with the collaboration of Donna Gomien), *Human Rights in a Changing East-West Perspective* (London and New York, Pinter Publishers, 1990).

Hesselman, Marlies, 'Sharing International Responsibility for Poor Migrants? An Analysis of Extra-Territorial Socio-Economic Human Rights Law' (2013) 15 *European Journal of Social Security* 2.

Heyzer, Noeleen, 'Combating Trafficking in Women and Children. A Gender and Human Rights Framework' in Truong, Thanh-Dam, Saskia Wieringa and Amrita Chhachhi (eds), *Engendering Human Security. Feminist Perspectives* (USA, Women Unlimited, India/Zed Books Ltd, 2006).

Ho, Kathleen, 'Structural Violence as a Human Rights Violation' (2007) 4 *Essex Human Rights Review* 2.

Hong Hai, Nguyen, 'Human Rights—Human Security—Human Development. Assessing the Inter-Relationships of Human Development, Human Security and Human Rights in Poverty Reduction in Vietnam', Document presented at the *Human Security Conference*, University of Thailand, Thailand, 2007.

Hoogensen, Gunhild and Kirsti Stuvoy, 'Gender, Resistance and Human Security' (2006) 37 *Security Dialogue* 2.

Howse, Robert and Ruti G Teitel, *Beyond the Divide: The Covenant on Economic, Social and Cultural Rights and the World Trade Organization* Dialogue on Globalization, Occasional Paper No 30 (Geneva Office, Friedrich-Ebert-Stiftung, 2007).

Hudson, Heidi, '"Doing" Security As Though Humans Matter: A Feminist Perspective on Gender and the Politics of Human Security' (2005) 36 *Security Dialogue* 2.

Humes-Schulz, Stacy, 'Limiting Sovereign Immunity in the Age of Human Rights' (2008) *Harvard Human Rights Journal* 21.

Huneeus, Alexandra, 'Courts Resisting Courts: Lessons from the Inter-American Court's Struggle to Enforce Human Rights' (2011) 44 *Cornell International Law Journal*.

Inglehart, Ronald F and Pippa Norris, 'The Four Horsemen of the Apocalypse: Understanding Human Security', The 2011 Johan Skytte Prize Lecture (2012) 35 *Scandinavian Political Studies* 1.

Instituto Tecnológico Autónomo de México (ITAM), *Migración centroamericana en tránsito por México hacia Estados Unidos: Diagnóstico y recomendaciones-Hacia una visión integral, regional y de responsabilidad compartida*, ITAM, Mexico City, 2014.

Jesse, Moritz, 'Missing in Action: Effective Protection for Third-Country Nationals from Discrimination under Community Law' in Guild, Elspeth, Kees Groenendijk and Sergio Carrera (eds), *Illiberal Liberal States. Immigration, Citizenship and Integration in the EU* (England/USA, Ashgate, 2009).

Jones, John F, 'Human Security and Social Development' (2004) *Denver Journal of International Law and Policy*.

Kaczorowska, Alina, *Public International Law*, 5th edn (Oxon and New York, Routledge, 2015)

Kaldor, Mary, *Human Security* (Cambridge, Polity Press, 2007).

——, Mary Martin and Sabine Selchow, 'Human Security: A European Strategic Narrative' (2008) *International Policy Analysis*.

Kapuy, Klaus, 'European and International Law in Relation to the Social Security of Irregular Migrant Workers' in Pieters, Danny and Paul Schoukens (eds), *The Social Security Co-Ordination between the EU and Non-EU Countries* (Antwerp, Intersentia, 2009).

Kardos, Gábor, 'Right to Peace, Right to Development, Right to a Healthy Environment: Part of the Solution or Part of the Problem?' in Rosas, Allan and Jan Hegelsen (eds, with the collaboration of Donna Gomien), *Human Rights in a Changing East-West Perspective* (London and New York, Pinter Publishers, 1990).

Kempen, Piet Hein van, 'Four Concepts of Security—A Human Rights Perspective' (2013) 13 *Human Rights Law Review* 1.

Kennedy, David W, 'The International Human Rights Movement: Part of the Problem?'(2005) 15 *Harvard Human Rights Journal*.

——, 'Law and the Political Economy of the World' (2013) *Leiden Journal of International Law* 26.

——, 'The International Human Rights Regime: Still Part of the Problem?' in Dickinson, Rob, Elena Katselli, Colin Murray and Ole W Pedersen (eds), *Examining Critical Perspectives on Human Rights* (Cambridge, Cambridge University Press, 2013).

Khaliq Urfan, 'Freedom of Religion and Belief in International Law: A Comparative Analysis' in Emon, Anver M, Mark S Ellis and Benjamin Glahn (eds), *Islamic*

Law and International Human Rights Law. Searching for Common Ground? (Oxford, Oxford University Press, 2012) 183–225.

King, Gary and Christopher JL Murray, 'Rethinking Human Security' (2004) *Political Science Quarterly*.

Klein Goldewijk, Berma, 'Why Human? The Interlinkages between Security, Rights and Development' (2008) 19 *Security and Human Rights* 1.

Koch, Ida Elisabeth, 'Dichotomies, Trichotomies, or Waves of Duties?' (2005) *Human Rights Law Review* 5/1.

Köpcke, Ma Isabel, '"La nueva Tierra Prometida": Derechos morales del inmigrante frente a la sociedad de acogida' in Bosch, JM (ed), *Migraciones económicas masivas y derechos del hombre* (Barcelona, ESADE, Facultad de Derecho, 2002).

Krause, Catarina and Martin Scheinin, 'The Right Not to be Discriminated Against: The Case of Social Security' in Orlin, Theodore, S, Allan Rosas and Martin Scheinin (eds), *The Jurisprudence of Human Rights Law: A Comparative and Interpretive Approach* (Turku/Åbo, Finland, Institute for Human Rights, Åbo Akademi University, 2000).

Langford, Malcolm and Jeff A King, 'Committee on Economic, Social and Cultural Rights: Past, Present and Future' in Langford, Malcolm (ed), *Social Rights Jurisprudence. Emerging Trends in International and Comparative Law* (Cambridge, Cambridge University Press, 2008).

——, Wouter Vandenhole, Martin Scheinin and Willem van Genugten (eds), *Global Justice, State Duties. The Extraterritorial Scope of Economic, Social and Cultural Rights in International Law* (Cambridge, Cambridge University Press, 2013).

Leach, Fiona and Sara Humphreys, 'Gender Violence in Schools: Taking the "girls as victims" discourse forward' in Terry, Geraldine and Joanna Hoare (eds), *Gender-Based Violence* (Oxfam GB, London , 2007).

Lemanski, Charlotte, 'Everyday Human (In)Security: Rescaling for the Southern City' (2012) 43 *Security Dialogue* 1.

Lerner, Natan, *Group Rights and Discrimination in International Law*, 2nd edn (The Hague, Brill-Martinus Nijhoff Publishers, 2005).

Lester, Eve, 'Socio-Economic Rights, Human Security and Survival Migrants: Whose Rights? Whose Security?' in Edwards, Alice and Carla Ferstman (eds), *Human Security and Non-Citizens: Law, Policy and International Affairs* (Cambridge, Cambridge University Press, 2010).

Lewis, Hope, 'Between Irua and "Female Genital Mutilation": Feminist Human Rights Discourse and the Cultural Divide' (1995) 8 *Harvard Human Rights Journal* 1.

—— and Rachel E Rosenbloom, 'The Boston Principles: An Introduction' (2011) *Notre Dame Journal of International, Comparative and Human Rights Law* 1.

Liebenberg, Sandra, 'South Africa: Adjudicating Social Rights under a Transformative Constitution' in Langford, Malcolm (eds), *Social Rights Jurisprudence. Emerging Trends in International and Comparative Law* (Cambridge, Cambridge University Press, 2008).

Liotta, PH Lanham, The Uncertain Certainty: Human Security, Environmental Change, and the Future Euro-Mediterranean (Oxford, Lexington, 2003).

Maas Weigert Kathleen, 'Structural Violence against Women' in Kurtz, Mariam M and Lester R Kurtz (eds), *Women, War, and Violence: Topography, Resistance, and Hope* (USA, Praeger Security International, 2015).

MacFarlane, Neil S and Yuen Foong Khong, *Human Security and the UN. A Critical History* (Bloomington, Indiana University Press, United Nations Intellectual History Project, 2006).
MacNaughton, Gillian, 'Untangling Equality and Non-Discrimination to Promote the Right to Health Care for All' (2009) 11 *Health and Human Rights: An International Journal* 2.
Mandela, Nelson, *Long Walk to Freedom* (Boston, Little, Brown & Co, 1994).
Martin, Mary and Taylor Owen, 'The Second Generation of Human Security: Lessons from the UN and EU Experience' (2010) *International Affairs* 86: 1.
——, Mary Kaldor and Narcís Serra (eds), *National, European and Human Security: From Co-Existence to Convergence* (New York, Routledge, 2012).
McAdam, Jane, *Complementary Protection in International Refugee Law*, Oxford Monographs in International Law(Oxford, Oxford University Press, 2007)
——, and Ben Saul, 'An Insecure Climate for Human Security? Climate-Induced Displacement and International Law' in Edwards, Alice and Carla Ferstman (eds), *Human Security and Non-Citizens: Law, Policy and International Affairs* (Cambridge, Cambridge University Press, 2010).
McClean, Emma, 'Human Security and International Law: Much Ado About Nothing?' in Banakar, Reza (ed), *Rights in Context: Law and Justice Late Modern Society* (UK, Ashgate, 2010).
McKay, Susan, 'Women, Human Security, and Peace-Building: A Feminist Analysis' in Shinoda, Hideaki and Ho-Won Jeong (eds), *Conflict and Human Security: A Search for New Approaches of Peace-building*, IPSHU English Research Report Series No.19, (Hiroshima, Institute for Peace Science-Hiroshima University, 2004) Chapter 7.
McNevin, Anne, 'Undocumented Citizens? Shifting Grounds of Citizenship in Los Angeles' in Nyers, Peter and Kim Rygiel (eds), *Citizenship, Migrant Activism and the Politics of Movement* (London, Routledge, 2012).
Merry, Sally Engle, *Human Rights and Gender Violence: Translating International Law into Local Justice* (Chicago, University of Chicago Press, 2010).
Miakhel, Shahmahmood, 'Human Security and the Rule of Law: Afghanistan's Experience' in Mason, Whit (ed), *The Rule of Law in Afghanistan: Missing in Inaction* (Cambridge, New York, Cambridge University Press, 2011).
Michael, Sarah, 'The Role of NGOs in Human Security', Working Paper No 12 (The Hauser Center for Nonprofit Organizations and the Kennedy School of Government, Harvard University, 2002).
Mitsilegas, Valsamis, *The Criminalisation of Migration in Europe: Challenges for Human Rights and the Rule of Law*, (Cham, Heidelberg, Springer, 2015).
Möschel, Mathias, 'Is the European Court of Human Rights' Case Law on Anti-Roma Violence "Beyond Reasonable Doubt"?' (2012) 12 *Human Rights Law Review* 3.
Mullally, Siobhán, 'Domestic Violence Asylum Claims and Recent Developments in International Human Rights Law: A Progress Narrative?' (2011) *International and Comparative Law Quarterly* 60.
——, 'Attending to Method in *Feminist Approaches*' in *IntLawGrrls. Voices on International Law, Policy, Practice*, Friday 19 October 2012, available at www.intlawgrrls.com/2012/10/attending-to-method-in-feminist.html.

Nasu, Hitoshi, 'Operationalizing the "Responsibility to Protect" and Conflict Prevention: Dilemmas of Civilian Protection in Armed Conflict' (2009) *Journal of Conflict and* 14 (2).

——, 'The Place of Human Security in Collective Security' (2012) *Journal of Conflict and Security Law*.

Navi Pillay, UN High Commissioner for Human Rights, 'The ICC in the International System', Remarks delivered during the event 'Retreat on the Future of the International Criminal Court', Liechtenstein, 17–18 October 2011, available at www.ohchr.org/en/NewsEvents/Pages/DisplayNews.aspx?NewsID=11562&LangID=E.

Nedelsky, Jennifer, *Law's Relations: A Relational Theory of Self, Autonomy, and Law* (New York, Oxford University Press, 2011).

Neuman, Gerald L, *Strangers to the Constitution: Immigrants, Borders, and Fundamental Law* (Princeton, New Jersey, Princeton University Press, 1996).

Ní Aoláin, Fionnuala, 'Some Caution in Reading Human Security Report', Monday 15 October 2012, Blog posted in *IntLaw Grrls. Voices on International Law, Policy and Practice*, available at www.intlawgrrls.com/2012/10/some-caution-in-reading-new-human.html#more.

O'Manique, Colleen, 'The "Securitization" of HIV/AIDS in Sub-Saharan Africa: A Critical Feminist Lens' in MacLean, Sandra J, David R Black and Timothy M Shaw (eds), *A Decade of Human Security. Global Governance and New Multilateralisms* (England/USA, Ashgate, 2006).

O'Sullivan, Maria, 'Human Security and the Protection of Refugees in Africa' in Abass, Ademola (ed), *Protecting Human Security in Africa* (Oxford, Oxford University Press, 2010).

Oberleitner, Gerd, 'Human Security: A Challenge to International Law?' (2005) 11 *Global Governance*.

——, 'Human Security: Idea, Policy, and Law' in Martin, Mary and Taylor Owen (eds), *Routledge Handbook of Human Security* (New York, Routledge, 2014).

Oberoi, Pia, 'Empowering Migrants: Human Security, Human Rights and Policy' in Edwards, Alice and Carla Ferstman (eds), *Human Security and Non-Citizens: Law, Policy and International Affairs* (Cambridge, Cambridge University Press, 2010).

Ogata, Sadako, Interview to former UN High Commissioner for Refugees (1991–2000) and President of the Japan International Cooperation Agency (2003–2012), in *Council of Foreign Relations*, 18 March 2008.

——, 'Empowering People for Human Security', Presentation at the 56th Annual DPI/NGO Conference (no date).

Okubo, Shiro, 'Globalization, Human Security and the Right to Live in Peace' in Okubo, Shiro and Louise Shelley (eds), *Human Security, Transnational Crime and Human Trafficking. Asian and Western Perspectives* (New York, Routledge, 2011).

Omorogbe, Eki Y, 'The Impact of the AU on Women in Armed Conflict in Africa', Conference delivered at the 5th Annual Conference of the European Society of International Law, in Valencia, Spain, 13 September 2012, personal notes taken.

Owada, Hishasi, 'Human Security and International Law' in Fastenrath, Ulrich, Rudolf Geiger, Daniel-Erasmus Khan, Andreas Paulus, Sabine von Schorlemer and Christoph Vedder (eds), *From Bilateralism to Community Interest, Essays in Honour of Judge Bruno Simma* (New York, Oxford University Press, 2011).

Owen, Taylor, 'Challenges and Opportunities for Defining and Measuring Human Security' in *Disarmament Forum*, three 2004—Human Rights, Human Security and Disarmament, 2004.

——, 'Human Security—Conflict, Critique and Consensus: Colloquium Remarks and a Proposal for a Threshold-Based Definition' (2004) 35 *Security Dialogue* 3.

Paris, Roland, 'Human Security: Paradigm Shift or Hot Air?' (2001) *International Security* 26(2).

Paupp, Terrence E, *Redefining Human Rights in the Struggle for Peace and Development* (Cambridge, Cambridge University Press, 2014).

Peers, Steve, 'Revising the "Dublin" Rules on Responsibility for Asylum Seekers: Further Developments', Professor of Law, Law School, University of Essex, in *Statewatch Analysis*, July 2012, available at www.statewatch.org/analyses/no-186-dublin.pdf.

Pelletier Quiñones, Paola, 'Análisis Sentencia Nadege Dorzema y Otros v República Dominicana, Corte Interamericana De Derechos Humanos' (2013) *Revue québécoise de droit international*, Hors-série.

Peroni, Lourdes and Alexandra Timmer, 'Vulnerable Groups: The Promise of an Emergent Concept in European Human Rights Convention Law' (2013) 11 *International Journal of Constitutional Law*.

Persaud, Christine and Hye Jin Zumkehr (eds), *Gender and Security: Guidelines for Mainstreaming Gender in Security Risk Management*, Briefing Paper, European Interagency Security Forum, 2012.

Pevnick, Ryan, *Immigration and the Constraints of Justice: Between Open Borders and Absolute Sovereignty* (Cambridge, New York, Cambridge University Press, 2011).

Pirjatanniemi, Elina, 'Missing Promises—No War Against Intimate Terror' in Scheinin, Martin, et al (eds), *Law and Security—Facing the Dilemmas*, EUI Working Paper Law 2009/11 (EU, European University Institute, 2009).

Pisarello, Gerardo, 'Los derechos humanos de los migrantes' in Añón, María José (ed), *La universalidad de los derechos sociales: el reto de la inmigración* (Valencia, Spain, Tirant lo Blanch, 2004).

Pitch, Tamar, *Pervasive Prevention. A Feminist Reading of the Rise of the Security Society* (UK, Ashgate, 2010).

Pogge, Thomas, 'Severe Poverty as a Human Rights Violation' in Pogge, Thomas (ed), *Freedom from Poverty as a Human Right: Who Owes What to the Very Poor* (Oxford, Oxford University Press-United Nations Educational, Scientific and Cultural Organisation, 2007).

Quilligan, James Bernard, *The Brandt Equation: 21st Century Blueprint for the New Global Economy* (USA, Brandt 21 Forum, 2002).

Ramcharan, Bertrand G, *Human Rights and Human Security* (The Hague, Martinus Nijhoff, 2002).

——, 'Human Rights and Human Security' (2004) *Disarmament Forum: Strengthening Disarmament and Security* 1.

Ranzi, Costanzo, 'Social Vulnerability in Europe' in Ranzi, Costanzo (ed), *Social Vulnerability in Europe. The New Configuration of Social Risks* (London, Palgrave Macmillan, 2010).

Reardon, Betty A, 'Women or Weapons: The Militarist Sexist Symbiosis' in Kurtz, Mariam M and Lester R Kurtz (eds), *Women, War, and Violence: Topography, Resistance, and Hope* (USA, Praeger Security International, 2015).

—— and Asha Hans (eds), *The Gender Imperative. Human Security vs State Security* (New Delhi, UK, 2010).

Reimners, David M, *Unwelcome Strangers. American Identity and the Turn against Immigration* (New York, Columbia University Press, 1998).

Remiro Brotóns, Antonio, *Derecho Internacional* (Valencia, Spain, Tirant lo Blanch, 2007).

Resnik, Judith, *Migrations and Mobilities: Citizenship, Borders, and Gender* (co-edited with Seyla Benhabib) (New York, New York University Press, 2009).

Reveron, Derek S and Kathleen A Mahoney-Norris, *Human Security in a Borderless World* (USA, Westeview Press, 2011).

Roberts, David, *Global Governance and Biopolitics: Regulating Human Security* (London, Zed Books, 2010).

Robinson, Fiona, 'The Importance of Care in the Theory and Practice of Human Security' (2008) 4 *Journal of International Political Theory* 2.

Robinson, Mary, 'What Rights Can Add to Good Development Practice' in Alston, Philip and Mary Robinson (eds), *Human Rights and Development: Towards Mutual Reinforcement* (New York, Oxford University Press, 2005).

Rodríguez, Cristina María and Ruth Rubio-Marín, 'The Constitutional Status of Irregular Migrants: Testing the Boundaries of Human Rights Protection in Spain and the United States' in Dembour, Marie-Bénédicte and Tobias Kelly (eds), *Are Human Rights for Migrants? Critical Reflections on the Status of Irregular Migrants in Europe and the United States* (New York, Routledge, 2011).

Rojas Aravena, Francisco and Moufida Goucha (eds), FLACSO-Chile/UNESCO, *Seguridad Humana, Prevención de Conflictos y Paz en América Latina y el Caribe*, FLACSO-Chile, Santiago, Chile, 2002.

Rosas, Allan, Review of the book, *Exploring Social Rights: Between Theory and Practice*, by Daphne Barak-Erez and Aeyal M Gross (eds) (Oxford, Hart Publishing, 2007), (2009) 42 *Israel Law Review* 1.

Rossi, Julieta and Víctor Abramovich, 'La tutela de los derechos económicos, sociales y culturales en el artículo 26 de la Convención Americana sobre Derechos Humanos' in Martin, Claudia, Diego Rodríguez-Pinzón and José A Guevara B (eds), *Derecho Internacional de los Derechos Humanos* (Ciudad de México, Universidad Iberoamericana Mexico City, American University Washington College of Law and Distribuciones Fontamara, 2004).

Rubio Marín, Ruth and Clara Sandoval, 'Engendering the Reparations Jurisprudence of the Inter-American Court of Human Rights: The Promise of the *Cotton Field* Judgment' (2011) 33 *Human Rights Quarterly* .

—— and Estrada-Tanck, Dorothy, 'Violence against Women, Human Security and Human Rights of Women and Girls: Reinforced Obligations in the Context of Structural Vulnerability' in Tripp, Aili, Myra Marx Ferree and Christina Ewig (eds), *Gender, Violence and Human Security: Critical Feminist Perspectives* (New York, New York University Press, 2013).

Ryngaert, Cedric and Math Noortmann (eds), *Human Security and International Law: The Challenge of Non-State Actors* (Cambridge, Intersentia, 2014).

Salomon, Margot E, *Global Responsibility for Human Rights: World Poverty and the Development of International Law* (Oxford, Oxford University Press, 2007).
——, 'International Human Rights Obligations in Context: Structural Obstacles and the Demands of Global Justice' in Andreassen, Bard A and Stephen P Marks (eds), *Development as a Human Right: Legal, Political and Economic Dimensions*, 2nd edn (Antwerp, Intersentia, 2010).
——, 'The Future of Human Rights' (2012) 3 *Global Policy* 4.
—— and Ian Seiderman, 'Human Rights Norms for a Globalized World: The Maastricht Principles on Extraterritorial Obligations of States in the Area of Economic, Social and Cultural Rights' in *ibid*.
Sassen, Saskia, *Losing Control? Sovereignty in an Age of Globalisation* (New York, Columbia University Press, 1996).
Schabas, William A, 'Freedom from Fear and the Human Right to Peace' in Keane, David and Yvonne McDermott (eds), *The Challenge of Human Rights. Past, Present and Future* (USA/UK, Edward Elgar, 2012).
Schachter, Oscar, *International Law in Theory and Practice* (The Netherlands, Martinus Nijhoff Publishers, 1991).
Scheinin, Martin, 'The Right to Enjoy a Distinct Culture: Indigenous and Competing Uses of Land' in Orlin, Theodore, S, Allan Rosas and Martin Scheinin (eds), *The Jurisprudence of Human Rights Law: A Comparative and Interpretive Approach*, (Turku/Åbo, Finland, Institute for Human Rights, Åbo Akademi University, 2000) Chapter 6.
——, 'The Right to Social Security", in Eide, Asbjorn, Catarina Krause and Allan Rosas (eds), *Economic, Social and Cultural Rights. A Textbook*, 2nd revised edn (The Netherlands, Martinus Nijhoff Publishers, 2001).
——, 'Human Rights Committee. Not Only a Committee of Civil and Political Rights' in Langford, Malcolm (ed), *Social Rights Jurisprudence. Emerging Trends in International and Comparative Law* (Cambridge, Cambridge University Press, 2008).
——, 'Terrorism and the Pull of "Balancing" in the Name of Security' in Scheinin, Martin, et al (eds), *Law and Security—Facing the Dilemmas*, EUI Working Paper Law 2009/11 (EU, European University Institute, 2009).
——, in collaboration with Ciarán Burke and Alexandre Skander Galand, *Rescue at Sea: Human Rights Obligations of States and Private Actors, with a Focus on the EU's External Borders*, RSCAS Policy Paper 2012/05 (Florence, Robert Schuman Centre for Advanced Studies, Global Governance Program, European University Institute, 2012).
Schopel, Bas, *On the Right of Exclusion: Law, Ethics and Immigration Policy* (New York, Routledge, 2011).
Scrinzi, Francesca, 'The Globalisation of Domestic Work: Women Migrants and Neodomesticity' in Freedman, Jane (ed), *Gender and Insecurity: Migrant Women in Europe* (Aldershot, Ashgate, 2003).
Sepúlveda, Magdalena, *The Nature of the Obligations under the International Covenant on Economic, Social and Cultural Rights* (Oxford, New York, Anvers, 2003).
Solanes Corella, Ángeles (ed), *Derechos humanos, migraciones y diversidad* (Valencia, Spain, Tirant lo Blanch, 2010).
Sorj, Bernardo, 'Security, Human Security and Latin America' (2005) *Sur. International Journal on Human Rights* 3, Year 2.

Ssenyonjo, Manisuli, 'Human Rights of Women in Africa: A Prerequisite for Human Security' in Abass, Ademola (ed), *Protecting Human Security in Africa* (Oxford, Oxford University Press, 2010).

St Marie, Joseph J, Samuel S Stanton, Jr and Shahdad Naghshpour, 'The Colonial Origins of Human Security: Economic, Geographic, and Institutional Determinants' (2008) 36 *Politics & Policy* 1.

Suhrke, Astri, 'Human Security and the Protection of Refugees' in Newman, Edward and Joanne van Selm (eds), *Refugees and Forced Displacement: International Security, Human Vulnerability, and the State* (New York, United Nations University Press, 2003).

Sunga, Lyal S, 'The Concept of Human Security: Does it Add Anything of Value to International Legal Theory or Practice?' in Frick, Marie-Luisa and Andreas Oberprantacher (eds), *Power and Justice in International Relations. Interdisciplinary Approaches to Global Challenges* (England/USA, Ashgate, 2009).

Tadjbakhsh, Shahrbanou, 'Human Security: 60 minutes to Convince', UNESCO, 13 September 2005.

——, 'Human Security: Concepts and Implications with an Application to Post-Intervention Challenges in Afghanistan' in (2005) *Les Études du CERI*, 117–18.

——, 'In Defense of the Broad View of Human Security' in Martin, Mary and Taylor Owen (eds), *Routledge Handbook of Human Security* (New York, Routledge, 2014).

—— and Anuradha M Chenoy, *Human Security: Concepts and Implications* (London and New York, Routledge, 2007).

Takahashi, Saul (ed), *Human Rights, Human Security, and State Security: The Intersection*, (USA, Praeger Security International, 2014) Vol 1.

Taran, Patrick A, 'Clashing Worlds: Imperative for a Rights-Based Approach to Labour Migration in the Age of Globalization' in *Mondialisation, migration et droits de l'homme: le droit international en question/Globalization, migration and human rights: international law under review*, under the supervision of Vincent Chetail (Bruylant, Collection of the Geneva Academy of International Humanitarian Law and Human Rights, 2007) Vol 2.

Tehindrazanarivelo, Djaboca L, 'The African Union's Relationship with the United Nations in the Maintenance of Peace and Security' in Yusuf, Abdulqawi A and Fatsah Ouguergouz (eds), *The African Union Legal and Institutional Framework: A Manual on the Pan-African Organization* (Leiden, Boston, Martinus Nijhoff Publishers, 2012).

Teitel, Ruti G, *Humanity's Law* (New York, Oxford University Press, 2011).

Terwase Sampson, Isaac, 'The Responsibility to Protect and ECOWAS Mechanisms on Peace and Security: Assessing their Convergence and Divergence on Intervention' (2011) *Journal of Conflict and Security Law* 16(3).

Thielbörger, Pierre, 'The Human Right to Water Versus Investor Rights: Double-Dilemma or Pseudo-Conflict?' in Dupuy, Pierre-Marie, Francesco Francioni and Ernst-Ulrich Petersmann (eds), *Human Rights in International Investment Law and Arbitration*, (Oxford, Oxford University Press, 2009).

Tomuschat, Christian, *Human Rights. Between Idealism and Realism*, 3rd edn (Oxford, Oxford University Press, 2014).

Tramontano, Mario Umberto, 'Is the Bossi-Fini Law (L.189/2002) in Compliance with Arts. 2 and 26 of the International Covenant on Civil and Political Rights?', available at http://es.scribd.com/doc/63794132/Is-the-Bossi-Fini-Law-in-Compliance-With-Arts-2-and-26-of-the-International-Covenant-on-Civil-and-Political-Rights.

Traschler, Daniel, 'Human Security: Genesis, Debates, Trends' (2011) *CSS Analysis in Security Studies* 90.

Triandafyllidou, Anna, 'Irregular Migration and Domestic Work in Europe: Who Cares?' in Triandafyllidou, Anna (ed), *Irregular Migrant Domestic Workers in Europe: Who Cares?* (Burlington, Farnham, Research in Migration and Ethnic Relations Series, Ashgate, 2013).

Truong, Thanh-Dam and Des Gasper (eds), *Transnational Migration and Human Security: The Migration-Development-Security Nexus* (Berlin, New York, Springer, Hexagon Series on Human and Environmental Security and Peace, 2011) Vol 6.

——, ——, Jeff Handmaker, and Sylvia I Bergh (eds), *Migration, Gender and Social Justice: Perspectives on Human Security* (Berlin, New York, Springer, Hexagon Series on Human and Environmental Security and Peace, 2014) Vol 9.

Turner, Bryan S, *Vulnerability and Human Rights* (Pennsylvania, Pennsylvania State University Press, University Park, 2006).

Vavoula, Niovi, 'Detention of Irregular Migrants—The Returns Directive Shows its True Colours In Mahdi (C-146/14 PPU)', in European Law Blog, 15 September 2014, available at http://europeanlawblog.eu/?p=2501

Vázquez, Daniel and Domitille Delaplace, 'Public Policies from a Human Rights Perspective: A Developing Field' (2011) 8 *Sur—International Journal on Human Rights* 14 (Biannual, English Edition) available at www.surjournal.org/eng/conteudos/pdf/14/02.pdf.

Veelke Derckx, 'Expulsion of Illegal Residents (Aliens) with Medical Problems and Article 3 of the European Convention of Human Rights' (2006) 13 *European Journal of Health Law* (electronic access through Ingenta Connect).

Verdross, Alfred, 'Jus Dispositivum and Jus Cogens in International Law' (1996) 60 *American Journal of International Law*.

Von Tigerstrom, Barbara, *Human Security and International Law: Prospects and Problems*, (Studies in International Law) (Oxford and Portland, Oregon, Hart Publishing, 2007).

Vonk, Gijsbert (ed), *Cross-Border Welfare State. Immigration, Social Security and Integration*, Social Europe Series (Antwerp, Intersentia, 2012) Vol 29.

Weissbrodt, David, *The Human Rights of Non-Citizens* (Oxford, Oxford University Press, 2008).

Wellman, James K and Clark Lombardi, *Religion and Human Security: A Global Perspective* (New York, Oxford, Oxford University Press, 2012).

Williams, Fiona, 'Towards a Transnational Analysis of the Political Economy of Care', SULCIS Working Papers, Stockholm University Linnaeus Center for Integration Studies—SULCIS / Scandinavian Working Papers on Economics, WP No 2011:6, 9 August 2011.

Xu, Qingwen, 'Migrant Workers in China: Rights and Security' (2010) 31 *RDD. Regional Development Dialogue: Assessing Human Security* 1.

Zwitter, Andrej, *Human Security, Law, and the Prevention of Terrorism* (London, New York, Routledge, 2011).

INTERNATIONAL AND REGIONAL LEGAL INSTRUMENTS AND PRACTICE

ACLU/National Human Rights Commission of Mexico, Humanitarian Crisis: Migrant Deaths at the US–Mexico Border, 2009.

Additional Protocol in the Area of Economic, Social and Cultural Rights to the ACHR (Protocol of San Salvador), signed 17 November 1988 and entered into force 16 November 1999.

African Charter on Human and People's Rights (ACHPR), adopted on 27 June 1981, Organization of African Unity Doc CAB/LEG/67/3 rev 5, 21 I.L.M. 58 (1982), and entered into force 21 October 1986.

African Commission on Human and Peoples' Rights, Resolution on the Right to a Remedy and Reparation for Women and Girls Victims of Sexual Violence, ACHOR/Res 111 (XXXXII) 07.

African Union, *Draft Strategic Framework for a Policy on Migration in Africa*, and *Migration Policy Framework for Africa*, EX.CL/276 (IX), adopted in the Ninth Ordinary Session of the Executive Council of the AU, Banjul, The Gambia, 25–29 June 2006.

Albrecht, Ulrich and Christine Chinkin, et al, 'A Human Security Doctrine for Europe: The Barcelona Report of the Study Group on Europe's Security Capabilities'. Study Group on Europe's Security Capabilities, Barcelona, Spain, 15 September 2004, presented to EU High Representative for Common Foreign and Security Policy Javier Solana, available at www.lse.ac.uk/Depts/global/Publications/HumanSecurityDoctrine.pdf.

—— and ——, et al, *A European Way of Security: The Madrid Report of the Human Security Study Group*, Human Security Study Group, Madrid, Spain, 2007, presented to EU High Representative for Common Foreign and Security Policy Javier Solana, available at www.lse.ac.uk/depts/global/studygroup/studygroup.htm.

American Civil Liberties Union (ACLU), 'ACLU's Immigrants' Rights Project', available at www.aclu.org/issues/immigrants-rights

American Convention on Human Rights, OAS Treaty Series No 36, adopted on 22 November 1969 and entered into force on 18 July 1978.

American Declaration on the Rights and Duties of Man (ADRDM), Organization of American States (OAS) Res XXX 1948.

Amnesty International, *Víctimas invisibles. Migrantes en movimiento en México*, 28 April 2010.

——, *'We Are Foreigners, We Have No Rights': The Plight of Refugees, Asylum-Seekers and Migrants in Libya*, November 2012, based on fact-finding visits to Libya between May and September 2012, at www.amnesty.org/en/news/libya-foreign-nationals-face-abuse-and-exploitation-2012-11-13.

——, *Culpables conocidos, víctimas ignoradas. Tortura y maltrato en México* (Índice: AMR 41/063/2012) 2012, 'Abusos Contra Migrantes'.

Basic Principles and Guidelines on the Right to a Remedy and Reparation for Victims of Gross Violations of International Human Rights Law and Serious Violations of International Humanitarian Law, adopted and proclaimed by UN General Assembly Resolution 60/147, 16 December 2005.

Beijing Declaration and Platform for Action adopted by the Fourth World Conference on Women: Action for Equality, Development and Peace, 15 September 1995.

Boston Principles on the Economic, Social and Cultural Rights of Noncitizens, 1 May 2011, Annotated Version, available at www.northeastern.edu/law/pdfs/academics/phrge-principles-long.pdf

Cartagena Declaration on Refugees, Colloquium on the International Protection of Refugees in Central America, Mexico and Panama, adopted by the Colloquium on the International Protection of Refugees in Central America, Mexico and Panama, held at Cartagena, Colombia from 19–22 November 1984.

Center for Human Rights and Global Justice, *A Decade Lost: Locating Gender in U.S. Counter-Terrorism* (New York, New York University School of Law, 2011).

Center for Justice and International Law (CEJIL), 'República Dominicana debe cumplir obligaciones en materia de nacionalidad y migración', 29 July 2015, available at http://cejil.org/en/node/7426.

Charter of the United Nations, signed on 26 June 1945 in San Francisco.

Civil Society Network for Human Security, initiative set up by the Dutch development organisation Cordaid and the Global Partnership for the Prevention of Armed Conflict (GPPAC), at www.humansecuritynetwork.net/organisations.

Court of Justice of the European Union (CJEU), *NS and Others v SSHD*, Judgment of the Court (Grand Chamber), 21 December 2011 in Joined Cases C-411/10 and C-493/10.

Commission on Human Security, *Human Security Now* (New York, Commission on Human Security, 2003).

Conference on Security and Co-Operation in Europe, *Final Act* (Helsinki, 1975).

Constitutive Act of the African Union, done at Lomé, Togo, 11 July 2000, available at www.au2002.gov.za/docs/key_oau/au_act.htm.

Convention (I) for the Amelioration of the Condition of the Wounded and Sick, Geneva on 12 August 1949, and entered into force on 21 October 1950.

Convention (II) for the Amelioration of the Condition of Wounded, Sick and Shipwrecked Members of Armed Forces at Sea, Geneva on 12 August 1949, and entered into force on 21 October 1950.

Convention (III) relative to the Treatment of Prisoners of War, Geneva on 12 August 1949, and entered into force on 21 October 1950.

Convention (IV) relative to the Protection of Civilian Persons in Time of War, Geneva on 12 August 1949, and entered into force on 21 October 1950.

Convention Determining the State Responsible for Examining Applications for Asylum Lodged in One of the Member States of the European Communities (Dublin Convention) 15 June 1990 [1997] OJ C254/1.

Convention on the Elimination of All Forms of Discrimination against Women (CEDAW), adopted 18 December 1979 by the UN General Assembly Resolution 34/180 and entered into force on 3 September 1981.

Convention on the Prohibition of the Use, Stockpiling, Production and Transfer of Anti-Personnel Mines and on their Destruction, adopted on 18 September 1997, 2056 UNTS 241.

Convention on the Rights of Persons with Disabilities, adopted by UN General Assembly resolution 61/106 of 13 December 2006 and entered into force on 3 May 2008.

Convention on the Rights of the Child, adopted and opened for signature, ratification and accession by UN General Assembly Resolution 44/25 of 20 November 1989 and entered into force 2 September 1990.

Convention relating to the Status of Refugees, adopted on 28 July 1951 by the UN Conference of Plenipotentiaries on the Status of Refugees and Stateless Persons convened under General Assembly Resolution 429 (V), and entered into force on 22 April 1954.

Convention relating to the Status of Stateless Persons, adopted on 28 September 1954 by the Conference of Plenipotentiaries convened by the Economic and Social Council Resolution 526 A (XVII), and entered into force 6 June 1960.

Council of Europe Convention on Preventing and Combating Violence against Women and Domestic Violence, adopted by the Committee of Ministers of the Council of Europe on 7 April 2011 and opened for signature in Istanbul, Turkey, on 11 May 2011, entered into force 1 August 2014.

Council Regulation (EC) 343/2003 of 18 February 2003 [2003] OJ L50/1 (Dublin Regulation).

Danish Refugee Council (Regional Office for the Horn of Africa &Yemen)/Regional Mixed Migration Secretariat (RMMS), *Desperate Choices: Conditions, Risks & Protection Failures Affecting Ethiopian Migrants in Yemen*, European Commission/ Swiss Agency for Development and Cooperation (SDC), October 2012.

Directive 2008/115/EC of the European Parliament and of the Council of 16 December 2008 on common standards and procedures in Member States for returning illegally staying third-country nationals [2008] OJ L348/98–107.

ECHR Blog, Grand Chamber Judgment in *N v UK*, Wednesday 28 May 2008, available at http://echrblog.blogspot.com.es/2008/05/grand-chamber-judgment-in-n-v-uk_28.html

ECHR, *A v Croatia*, Appl No 55164/08, 14 October 2010.

——, *AA and Others v Sweden*, Appl No 14499/09, 28 June 2012 (Final 28 September 2012).

——, *AA and Others v Sweden*, Appl No 14499/09, 28 June 2012 (Final 28 September 2012), Dissenting Opinion of Judge Ann Power-Forde.

——, *Aksu v Turkey* (GC), Appl Nos 4149/04 and 41029/04, 15 March 2012.

——, *Alajos Kiss v Hungary*, Appl No 38832/06, 20 May 2010.

——, *BS v Spain*, Appl No 47159/08, 24 July 2012.

——, *Bevacqua and S v Bulgaria*, Appl No 71127/01, 12 June 2008.

——, *Branko Tomašić and Others v Croatia*, Appl No 46598/06, 15 January 2009.

——, *Bygylashvili v Greece*, Appl No 58164/10, 25 September 2012.

——, *Chahal v the United Kingdom*, Appl No 22414/93, 15 November 1996.

——, *Chapman v the United Kingdom* (GC), Appl No 27138/95, 18 January 2001.

——, *Connors v the United Kingdom*, Appl No 66746/01, 27 May 2004.

——, *D v the United Kingdom*, Appl No 30240/96, 2 May 1997.

——, *Dahlab v Switzerland*, Appl No 42393/98, Decision of inadmissibility, 15 February 2001.

——, *DH and Others v the Czech Republic* (GC), Appl No 57325/00, 13 November 2007.

——, *ES and Others v Slovakia*, Appl No 8227/04, 15 September 2009.

——, *Gaygusuz v Austria*, Appl No 173/71/90, 19 September 1996.

——, *HLR v France* (GC), Appl No 24573/94, 29 April 1997.

——, *Hajudova v Slovakia* 2010, Appl No 2660/03, 13 November 2010.

——, *Hirsi Jamaa and Others v Italy*, Appl No 27765/09, 23 February 2012.
——, *Hoogendijk v the Netherlands*, Appl No 58461/00, Decision of inadmissibility, 6 January 2005.
——, *Horváth and Kiss v Hungary*, Appl No 11146/11, 29 January 2013.
——, *IM v France*, Appl No 9152/09, 2 February 2012.
——, *KAB v Spain*, Appl No 59819/08, 10 April 2012 (Final 10 July 2012).
——, *Kiyutin v Russia*, Appl No 2700/10, 10 March 2011.
——, *Kontrovà v Slovakia*, Appl No 7510/4, 31 May 2007.
——, *Kuric and Others v Slovenia* (GC), Appl No 26828/06, 26 June 2012.
——, *Leyla Sahin v Turkey* (GC), Appl No 44774/98, 10 November 2005.
——, *Maslov v Austria* (GC), Appl. No. 1638/03, 28 May 2008.
——, *MC v Bulgaria*, Appl No 39272/98, 4 December 2003 (Final 4 March 2004).
——, *MSS v Belgium and Greece* (GC), Appl No 30696/09, 21 January 2011.
——, *Muñoz Díaz v Spain*, Appl No 49151/07, 8 December 2009 (Final 8 March 2010).
——, *N v Finland*, 38885/02, Appl No 38885/02, 26 July 2005.
——, *N v United Kingdom* (GC), Appl No 26565/05, 27 May 2008.
——, *N v United Kingdom* (GC), Appl No. 26565/05, 27 May 2008, Joint Dissenting Opinion of Judges Tulkens, Bonello and Spielmann.
——, *Nacic and Others v Sweden*, Appl No 16567/10, 15 May 2012 (Final 24 September 2012), Partially Dissenting Opinion of Judges Spielmann and Power-Forde.
——, *Nada v Switzerland* (GC), Appl No 10593/08, 12 September 2012.
——, *Oneryldiz v Turkey* (GC), Appl No 48939/99, Judgment of 30 November 2004.
——, *Opuz v Turkey*, Appl No. 33401/02, June 9, 2009.
——, *Sufi and Elmi v United Kingdom*, Appl Nos 8319/07 & 11449/07, 28 June 2011.
——, *SJ v Belgium*, Appl 70055/10. Friendly settlement: 26 August 2014. ECOWAS Convention on Small Arms and Light Weapons, their Ammunition and Other Related Materials, adopted in Abuja, Nigeria on 14 June 2006, and entered into force on 29 September 2009.
Eide, Asbjorn, UN Special Rapporteur on the Right to Food, *The Right to Food (Final Report)*, E/CN.4/Sub.2/1987/23, 1987.
Equal Power–Lasting Peace. Obstacles for Women's Participation in Peace Processes, The Kvinna till Kvinna Foundation, Sweden, 2012.
EU, Council Directive 2004/83/EC of 29 April 2004 on minimum standards for the qualification and status of third country nationals or stateless persons as refugees or as persons who otherwise need international protection and the content of the protection granted [2004] OJ L304/12 ('Qualification Directive').
——, Directive 2008/115/EC of the European Parliament and of the Council of 16 December 2008 on common standards and procedures in Member States for returning illegally staying third-country nationals, *OJ* L 348/98-107.
EU Fundamental Rights Agency, *Fundamental Rights of Migrants in an Irregular Situation in the European Union*, 2011, available at http://fra.europa.eu/fraWebsite/research/publications/publications_per_year/pub-migrants-in-an-irregular-situation_en.htm.
——, /UNDP/European Commission, *The Situation of Roma People in 11 EU Member States: Survey Results at a Glance*, EU FRA/UNDP/EC, Luxembourg, 2012.
European Committee on Social Rights, Conclusions XIX-2 (2009), Luxembourg, 22 December 2009.

European Convention for the Protection of Human Rights and Fundamental Freedoms (ECoHR), CETS No 005, opened for signature by the Member States of the Council of Europe on 4 November 1950 and entered into force on 3 September 1953.

European Council, 'A Secure Europe in a Better World: European Security Strategy', 12 December 2003, available at www.consilium.europa.eu/uedocs/cmsUpload/78367.pdf

——, *Report on the Implementation of the European Security Strategy*, S407/08, 11 December 2008, available at www.consilium.europa.eu/ueDocs/cms

European Parliament. 2006. *Resolution on Development and Migration*, Doc. P6_TA (2006) 0319, 6 July 2006.

European Social Charter, CETS No 035, opened for signature by the member states of the Council of Europe in Turin on 18 October 1961 and entered into force on 26 February 1965.

Food and Agriculture Organization, Directrices voluntarias de la Organización de las Naciones Unidas para la Alimentación y la Agricultura (FAO) sobre la gobernanza responsable de la tenencia de la tierra, la pesca y los bosques en el contexto de la seguridad alimentaria nacional, 2009.

Framework Treaty on Democratic Security in Central America, adopted on 15 December 1995 by the States of Central America: Costa Rica, El Salvador, Guatemala, Honduras, Nicaragua and Panama, and entered into force 26 December 1997.

Friends of Human Security, at www.mofa.go.jp/policy/human_secu/assistance.html.

G8, 'Toyako Framework for Action on Global Health: Report of the G8 Health Experts', Group G8 Summit, Hokkaido Toyako Summit, Toyako, Japan, 8 July 2008.

Gallup's Potential Net Migration Index, available at www.gallup.com/poll/142364/migration-triple-populations-wealthy-nations.aspx.

Geneva Declaration, 'Tackling Violence against Women: From Knowledge to Practical Initiatives', Working Paper by Milliken, Jennifer with Elisabeth Gilgen and Jasna Lazarevic, Geneva Declaration Secretariat, Geneva, 2011.

GISTI, Groupe d' Information et de Soutien des Immigrés, 'Les notes pratiques. Sans-papiers mais pas sans droits', 5e édition, juin 2009, available at www.gisti.org/publication_pres.php?id_article=1615

Global Burden of Armed Violence 2011, Geneva Declaration Secretariat, Geneva, 2012.

Gobernanza y Seguridad Urbana y Humana en América Latina, ONU-Habitat, at www.onuhabitat.org/index.php?option=com_docman&task=doc_view&gid=37&tmpl=component&format=raw&Itemid=235.

Guidelines for the Policy of External Common Andean Security, Decision 587, adopted at the 13th Ordinary Meeting of the Andean Council of Ministers of Foreign Affairs (integrated by Bolivia, Colombia, Ecuador and Peru) on 10 July 2004.

Human Rights Ahead, 'What Next for Human Rights?' Working Paper. A Reflection on the 60th Anniversary of the Universal Declaration of Human Rights, Human Rights Ahead, Spain, December 2008, available at www.hrahead.org/our-agenda/promoting-human-security.

Human Rights Watch, *A Costly Move: Far and Frequent Transfers Impede Hearings for Immigrant Detainees in the United States*, 2011.

——, *Belgium: Abused Migrant Women Fear Deportation. Legal Loopholes, Inadequate Shelter Access Send Women Back to Abusers*, 8 November 2012.

——, *Costly and Unfair: Flaws in US Immigration Detention Policy*, 6 May 2010.

——, *Deportation by Default: Mental Disability, Unfair Hearings, and Indefinite Detention in the US Immigration System*, 25 July 2010.

——, *Detained and at Risk: Sexual Abuse and Harassment in United States Immigration Detention*, 25 August 2010.

——, *Detained and Dismissed: Women's Struggles to Obtain Health Care in United States Immigration Detention*, 17 March 2009.

——, *Hidden Emergency: Migrant Deaths in the Mediterranean*, by Judith Sunderland, Human Rights in Europe, August 2012.

——, *'If You Come Back We Will Kill You': Sexual Violence and Other Abuses Against Congolese Migrants During Expulsions from Angola*, 2012.

——, *Jailing Refugees: Arbitrary Detention of Refugees in the US Who Fail to Adjust to Permanent Resident Status*, 29 December 2009.

——, *Locked Up Far Away: The Transfer of Immigrants to Remote Detention Centers in the United States*, 2 December 2009.

——, *No Way to Live. Alabama's Immigrant Law*, United States, Human Rights Watch, 2011.

——, *Returned to Risk: Deportation of HIV Positive Migrants*, 29 September 2009.

——, *'The Law was Against Me: Migrant Women's Access to Protection for Family Violence in Belgium*, 2012.

——, *'Tough, Fair, and Practical': A Human Rights Framework for Immigration Reform in the United States*, 8 July 2010.

——, *United States—Forced Apart (By the Numbers): Non-Citizens Deported Mostly for Nonviolent Offenses*, 15 April 2009.

——, *World Report 2012. Events of 2011*, 2012.

Human Security at the United Nations, United Nations Trust Fund for Human Security, Human Security Unit, OCHA, New York, 2012.

Human Security Brief 2006, Human Security Centre, University of British Columbia, Canada.

Human Security Handbook, UNTFHS, OCHA, 2009.

Human Security Report Project, *Human Security Report 2005. War and Peace in the 21st Century* (Canada, Human Security Centre, University of British Columbia, Oxford University Press, 2005).

——, *Human Security Report 2012: Sexual Violence, Education, and War: Beyond the Mainstream Narrative* (Vancouver, Human Security Press, 2012).

IFRC, World Disasters Report 2012. Focus on Forced Migration and Displacement, Geneva, 2012.

Inter-American Commission on Human Rights (IACoHR), Access to Justice as a Guarantee of Economic, Social, and Cultural Rights: A Review of the Standards Adopted by the Inter-American System of Human Rights, Organization of American States, OEA/Ser.L/V/II.129, Doc 4, 7 September 2007.

——, Annex to Press Release 82/11, 'Preliminary Observations of the IACHR's Rapporteurship on the Rights of Migrant Workers on its Visit to Mexico', 2 August 2011, available at www.cidh.oas.org/pdf%20files/IACHRPreliminaryObservations%20Mexico2011.pdf.

——, *Human Rights of Migrants and Other Persons in the Context of Human Mobility in Mexico*, OEA/Ser.L/V/II. Doc. 48/13, Organization of American States, 30 December 2013.

——, *Jessica Lenahan (Gonzales) et al v United States*, Case 12.626, Report No 80/11, OEA/Ser.L/V/II.142, 2011.

——, *Maria da Penha Maia Fernandes v Brazil*, Case 12,051, Report No 54/01, Annual Report, OEA/Ser.L/V.II.111 Doc.20 rev, 2000.

——, Organization of American States, *Report on Citizen Security and Human Rights*, OEA/Ser.L/V/II, Doc 57, 31 December 2009.

——, *Pacheco Tineo Family v Bolivia*, Case No 12.474, referred to the Court on 21 February 2012.

——, 'Report on the Situation of Human Rights of Asylum Seekers within the Canadian Refugee Determination System', OEA/Ser.L/V/II.106, Doc 40 rev, 28 Feb 2000.

——, 144 period of sessions of the IACHR on 30 March 2012, at www.cidh.org/Migrantes/migrants.background.htm.

Inter-American Convention Against the Illicit Manufacturing of and Trafficking in Firearms, Ammunition, Explosives, and Other Related Materials, adopted 14 November 1997, entered into force 1 July 1998, OAS 24th Special Session.

Inter-American Convention on the Prevention, Punishment and Eradication of Violence against Women (Convention of Belém do Pará), adopted on 9 June 1994 at the twenty fourth regular session of the General Assembly of the OAS and entered into force on 5 March 1995.

Inter-American Court of Human Rights (IACHR), Advisory Opinion 18/03, *Juridical Condition and Rights of Undocumented Migrants*, Advisory Opinion OC-18/03 (AO 18/03) requested by the United Mexican States, 17 September 2003.

——, *ibid*, *Amicus curiae* presented by Jorge Bustamante from *Universidad Nacional Autónoma de México*.

——, *ibid*, Reasoned Concurring Opinion of Judge Sergio García Ramírez.

——, *Barrios Altos v Peru*, Merits, Judgment of March 14, 2001.

——, *Expelled Dominican and Haitian Persons v Dominican Republic*, Preliminary Objections, Merits, Reparations and Costs, Judgment of 28 August 2014 (formerly named *Case of Benito Tide Méndez and Others*).

——, *González et al ('Cotton Field') v Mexico*, Preliminary Objection, Merits, Reparations, and Costs, Judgment of 16 November 2009.

——, *Inés Fernández Ortega and Others v Mexico*, Judgment of 30 August 2010.

——, *La Cantuta v Peru*, Merits, Reparations and Costs, Judgment of 29 November 2006.

——, *Massacre of Mapiripán v Colombia*, Judgment of 15 September 2005.

——, *Massacre of Ituango v Colombia*, Judgment of 1 July 2006.

——, *Mayagna (Sumo) Awas Tingni Community v Nicaragua*, Merits, Reparations and Costs, Judgment of 31 August 2001.

——, *Miguel Castro Castro Prison v Peru*, Merits, Reparations and Costs, Judgment of 25 November 2006.

——, *Moiwana Community v Suriname*, Preliminary Objections, Merits, Reparations, and Costs, Judgment of 15 June 2005.
——, *Nadege Dorzema et al v Dominican Republic*, Merits, Reparations and Costs. Judgment of 24 October 2012.
——, *Plan de Sánchez Massacre v. Guatemala*, Merits, Judgment of April 29, 2004.
——, Provisional Measures, Haitians and Haitian Origin Dominicans in the Dominican Republic, Orders of 14 September 2000; 12 November 2000; and 26 May 2001.
——, *Saramaka People v Suriname*, Preliminary Objections, Merits, Reparations, and Costs, Judgment of 28 November 2007.
——, *Sawhoyamaxa Indigenous Community v Paraguay*, Merits, Reparations and Costs. Judgment of 29 March 2006.
——, *ibid*, Separate Opinion of Judge AA Cançado Trindade.
——, *'Street Children' (Villagrán-Morales et al) v Guatemala*, Merits. Judgment of 19 November 1999.
——, *ibid*, Joint Concurring Opinions of Judges AA Cançado Trindade and A Abreu-Burelli.
——, *Valentina Rosendo Cantú and other v Mexico* (Ser C) No 216, 31 August 2010.
——, *Velásquez Rodríguez v Honduras*, Judgment of 29 July 1988.
——, *Xákmok Kásek Indigenous Community v Paraguay*, Merits, Reparations and Costs, Judgment of 24 August 2010.
——, *Yakye Axa Indigenous Community v Paraguay*, Merits, Reparations, and Costs, Judgment of 17 June 2005.
——, *Yean and Bosico Children v Dominican Republic*, Judgment of 8 September 2005.
Inter-American Treaty on Reciprocal Assistance, adopted at the Conference for the Maintenance of Continental Peace and Security of the OAS, in Rio de Janeiro, Brazil, on 2 September 1947.
International Convention on the Protection of the Rights of All Migrant Workers and Members of their Families, adopted by UN General Assembly Resolution 45/158 of 18 December 1990, entered into force on 1 July 2003.
International Labour Organization (ILO), *International Labour Migration: A Rights-Based Approach*, 2010.
ILO Convention 189, Convention Concerning Decent Work For Domestic Workers, adopted by the General Conference of the International Labour Organization at its 100th session, 16 June 2011.
International Commission of Jurists, *Migration and International Human Rights Law*, Practitioners Guide No 6, ICJ, Geneva, 2011.
International Council on Human Rights Policy, *Irregular Migration, Migrant Smuggling and Human Rights: Towards Coherence*, Geneva, 2010.
International Court of Justice, *Case Concerning The Barcelona Traction, Light and Power Company, Limited, Belgium v Spain*, Judgment 5 February 1970.
——, *Case of Avena, Mexico v United States*, Judgment of 31 March 2004.
——, *Case of LaGrand, Germany v United States*, Judgment of 27 June 2001.
——, *Legal Consequences of the Construction of a Wall in the Occupied Palestinian Territory*, Advisory Opinion, 9 July 2004, International Court of Justice, Reports 2004.

International Covenant on Civil and Political Rights, adopted by UN General Assembly Resolution 2200A (XXI) of 16 December 1966, entered into force on 23 March 1976.

International Covenant on Economic, Social and Cultural Rights (ICESCR), adopted and opened for signature, ratification and accession by UN General Assembly Resolution 2200A (XXI) of 16 December 1966 and entered into force on 23 March 1976.

International Convention on the Elimination of All Forms of Racial Discrimination (ICERD), adopted by UN General Assembly Resolution 2106 (XX) of 21 December 1965 and entered into force 4 January 1969.

International Crisis Group, 'Working Paper on Preventing and Responding to Sexual Violence against Women Displaced by Conflict', by Donald Steinberg, 12 July 2010, available at www.crisisgroup.org/en/regions/op-eds/working-paper-on-preventing-and-responding-to-sexual-violence-against-women-displaced-by-conflict.aspx.

International Federation of Red Cross and Red Crescent Societies (IFRC), *World Disasters Report 2012: Focus on Forced Migration and Displacement* (Lyon, France/Geneva, Imprimerie Chirat, 2012).

International Law Commission, *Draft Articles on Responsibility of States for Internationally Wrongful Acts*, Supplement No. 10, UN General Assembly A/56/10, November 2001.

International Meeting on Women's and Girls' Right to a Remedy and Reparation, held in Nairobi from 19 to 21 March 2007, at www.womensrightscoalition.org/site/reparation/signature_en.php.

International Organization for Migration, World Migration Report 2011: 'Communicating Effectively About Migration', 2011.

——, 'Global Migration Trends 2015 Factsheet', IOM-Global Migration Analysis Centre, released 19 April 2016, available at www.iom.int/news/iom-releases-global-migration-trends-2015-factsheet.

——, World Migration Report 2015: 'Migrants and Cities: New Partnerships to Manage Mobility', 2015.

Kampala Convention for the Protection and Assistance of Internally Displaced Persons (IDPs) in Africa, entered into force on 6 December 2012.

Kjaerum, Morten, Director, European Union Agency for Fundamental Rights (FRA), 'Dignity and Rights of Irregular Migrants', *4th Fundamental Rights Conference*, Warsaw, Poland, 21–22 November 2011.

Maastricht Principles on Extraterritorial Obligations of States in the area of Economic, Social and Cultural Rights, adopted on 28 September 2011.

Medecins Sans Frontieres, *Urgent Delivery—Maternal Deaths: The Avoidable Crisis*, Special Report, 7 March 2012.

Mexican Ley General de Acceso de las Mujeres a una Vida Libre de Violencia, published in Diario Oficial de la Federación, Mexico, 1 February 2007, last reform published 20 January 2009.

Mexico City Commission of Human Rights (Comisión de Derechos Humanos del Distrito Federal), *Informe sobre Seguridad Humana en la Ciudad de México 2006–2008*, CDHDF, Mexico, 2009.

Meyer, Maureen, with contributions from Stephanie Brewer, *A Dangerous Journey through Mexico: Human Rights Violations against Migrants in Transit*, WOLA and Centro Prodh, December 2010, available at www.wola.org/publications/

a_dangerous_journey_through_mexico_human_rights_violations_against_migrants_in_transit.

Millennium Development Goals and Economic, Social and Cultural Rights; a Joint Statement by the UN Committee on Economic, Social and Cultural Rights and the UN Commission on Human Rights' Special Rapporteurs for Economic, Social and Cultural Rights, November 2002, at www2.ohchr.org/english/bodies/cescr/docs/statements/MDGandESCRs-2002.doc.

National Human Rights Commission of Mexico (CNDH), *Informe Especial sobre los Casos de Secuestro en Contra de Migrantes*, 2009.

——, *Informe Especial sobre Secuestro de Migrantes en México*, February 2011.

Office of the United Nations High Commissioner for Human Rights (OHCHR), 'Acting High Commissioner for Human Rights, in Address to Security Council, Calls for Action Against Impunity in Congo-Kinshasa', 7 July 2003.

——, 'Hear Our Voices—Children in Immigration Detention', 13 November 2012, available at www.ohchr.org/EN/NewsEvents/Pages/MigrantChildren Detention.aspx.

——, 'Of all places … a toilet', Monday 19 November 2012 World Toilet Day, available at http://www.unric.org/en/latest-un-buzz/28033-of-all-places-a-toilet-world-toilet-day-19-nov.

——, 'The International Convention on Migrant Workers and its Committee', Fact Sheet No 24 (Rev 1), United Nations, New York and Geneva, 2005.

Open Society Justice Initiative/CEJIL, Summary of the Initial Petition in the case of *Emildo Bueno Oguis v Dominican Republic*, presented to the Inter-American Commission on Human Rights, 1 June 2010.

Opening Statement of Magdalena Sepúlveda Carmona, Special Rapporteur on Extreme Poverty and Human Rights, Human Rights Council 20th session, Geneva, 21 June 2012.

Optional Protocol to the Convention On The Rights Of The Child On The Sale Of Children, Child Prostitution and Child Pornography, adopted and opened for signature, ratification and accession by General Assembly Resolution A/RES/54/263 of 25 May 2000, entered into force on 18 January 2002.

Optional Protocol to the ICESCR, adopted by the UN General Assembly, A/RES/63/117, December 10 2008, not yet entered into force at the time of writing.

Optional Protocol to the UN Convention on the Rights of the Child on the Involvement of Children in Armed Conflict, adopted by UN General Assembly Resolution A/RES/54/263 of 25 May 2000 and entered into force 12 February 2002.

Organización de Estados Americanos, Consejo Permanente, OEA/Ser.GCP/ACTA 1293/01, 19 Septiembre 2001 (available only in Spanish).

Organization of American States (OAS), 42nd regular session of the General Assembly, held in Cochabamba, Bolivia, 3–5 June 2012, resulting documents available at /www.oas.org/en/42ga/.

——, Declaration of Cochabamba on 'Food Security with Sovereignty in the Americas', AG/DEC. 69 (XLII-O/12), adopted at the fourth plenary session, held on 5 June 2012.

——, Declaration on Security in the Americas, OEA/Ser.K/XXXVIII, 28 October 2003.

——, General Assembly, 'Inter-American Convention Against the Illicit Manufacturing of and Trafficking in Firearms, Ammunition, Explosives, and

Other Related Materials', AG/RES 2094 (XXXV-O/05), resolution adopted at the fourth plenary session, held on 7 June 2005.
——, General Assembly, 'Excessive Commodity Price Volatility and its Consequences for Food Security and Sustainable Development in the Americas', AG/RES. 2757 (XLII-O/12), agreed at the fourth plenary session, held on 5 June 2012.
——, Non-Aggression and Common Defence Pact, adopted on 31 January 2005.
Organization for Economic Cooperation and Development (OECD), Armed Violence Reduction: Enabling Development, OECD, Paris, 2009.
Organization for Security and Cooperation in Europe (OSCE), Ministerial Council Decision No 15/05 Preventing and Combating Violence Against Women, MC.DEC/15/05, 6 December 2005.
——, 'Helsinki Final Act signed by 35 participating States', OSCE, 1975.
——, Office for Democratic Institutions and Human Rights (ODIHR), *Gender and Early Warning Systems: An Introduction*, OSCE/ODIHR, 2009.
Platform for International Cooperation on Undocumented Migrants (PICUM) Bulletin 11 July 2012, available at http://picum.org/en/news/bulletins/35405/.
Procuraduría General de Justicia del Distrito Federal, 'Acuerdo A/015/2012 del C. Procurador General De Justicia Del Distrito Federal, por el que se emite el Protocolo Para La Búsqueda Inmediata de Personas en Situación de Extravío o Ausencia, en Especial de Mujeres, Niñas, Niños y Adolescentes', *Gaceta Oficial del Distrito Federal*, 4 October 2012.
Protocol Additional to the Geneva Conventions of 12 August 1949, and relating to the Protection of Victims of International Armed Conflicts (Protocol I), adopted on 8 June 1977 and entered into force on 7 December 1978.
Protocol Additional to the Geneva Conventions of 12 August 1949, and relating to the Protection of Victims of Non-International Armed Conflicts (Protocol II), adopted on 8 June 1977 and entered into force on 7 December 1978.
Protocol Additional to the Geneva Conventions of 12 August 1949 relating to the Adoption of an Additional Distinctive Emblem (Protocol III), adopted on 8 December 2005 and entered into force on 14 January 2007.
Protocol on the Status of Refugees, approved in New York on 31 January 1967 and entered into force on 4 October 1967.
Protocol to Prevent, Suppress and Punish Trafficking in Persons Especially Women and Children; and Protocol Against Smuggling by Land, Sea and Air, both supplementing the United Nations Convention against Transnational Organized Crime, 'Palermo Convention', all three instruments adopted and opened for signature, ratification and accession by UN General Assembly Resolution 55/25 of 15 November 2000. The Protocol Against Trafficking entered into force on 25 December 2003 and the Protocol Against Smuggling on 28 January 2004.
Protocol to the African Charter on Human and Peoples' Rights on the Rights of Women in Africa, the Maputo Protocol, adopted by the 2nd Ordinary Session of the Assembly of the Organization of the African Union in Maputo, 11 July 2003, entered into force on 25 November 2005.
Regional Program in Latin America of UNIFEM (today incorporated into UN Women), 'Ciudades Seguras: Violencia hacia las Mujeres y Políticas Públicas' ('Safe Cities: Violence Against Women and Public Policies'), available at www.americalatinagenera.org/es/index.php?option=com_content&view=article&id=295&Itemid=170.

Report of the UN High Commissioner for Human Rights to the Economic and Social Council, E/2010/89, 1 June 2010.
Report of the UN Independent Expert on the question of human rights and extreme poverty, Magdalena Sepúlveda, UN General Assembly, A/64/279, 11 August 2009.
Report of the UN Special Rapporteur on Extreme Poverty and Human Rights on the Obstacles to Access to Justice for Persons Living in Poverty, UN General Assembly Resolution A/67/278, 9 August 2012.
Report of the UN Special Rapporteur on the Human Rights of Migrants, Jorge Bustamante, to the UN Human Rights Council, A/HRC/7/12, 25 February 2008.
Revised European Social Charter (RESC), CETS No 163, opened for signature by the member states of the Council of Europe on 3 May 1996 and entered into force on 1 July 1999.
Rome Declaration on World Food Security, 1996, available at www.fao.org/wfs.
Rome Statute of the International Criminal Court, adopted on 17 July 1998, 2187 UNTS 90, and entered into force on 1 July 2002.
Ruggie, John, *Guiding Principles on Business and Human Rights: Implementing the United Nations 'Protect, Respect and Remedy' Framework*, presented in the Report of the Special Representative of the Secretary-General on the issue of human rights and transnational corporations and other business enterprises, UN Human Rights Council Resolution A/HRC/17/31, 21 March 2011, and endorsed by the UN Human Rights Council in June of 2011 and in UN General Assembly Resolution 17/4 'Human Rights and Transnational Corporations and other Business Enterprises', 6 July 2011.
Save the Children/World Vision, *Ending the Everyday Emergency: Resilience and Children in the Sahel*, July 2012.
Speech by Morten Kjaerum, Director, European Union Agency for Fundamental Rights (FRA), 'Dignity and Rights of Irregular migrants', 4th Fundamental Rights Conference, Warsaw, Poland, 21–22 November 2011. Available at http://fra.europa.eu/fraWebsite/attachments/MK-Speech-FRC-NOV2011.pdf.
Statements by F Crépeau at the debate The Management of the External Borders of the EU and its Impact on the Human Rights of Migrants: The Italian Experience'. A Consultation between the UN Special Rapporteur on the Human Rights of Migrants, Mr François Crépeau, Civil Society, and Academia, organised by the Migration Policy Centre, Robert Schuman Centre for Advanced Studies of the European University Institute (EUI), with the support of the Open Society Foundations, and held at the EUI in Florence, Italy on 3 October 2012.
Statement by Gulnara Shahinian, UN Special Rapporteur on Contemporary Forms of Slavery, its causes and consequences, to the UN Human Rights Council at its 12th session, 15 September 2009.Statute of the International Court of Justice (ICJ), annexed to the Charter of the United Nations, 1945.
Study Group on Europe's Security Capabilities, *A Human Security Doctrine for Europe: The Barcelona Report of the Study Group on Europe's Security Capabilities*, presented to EU High Representative for Common Foreign and Security Policy Javier Solana, Barcelona, 15 September 2004, available at www.lse.ac.uk/Depts/global/Publications/HumanSecurityDoctrine.pdf.

The Platform for International Cooperation on Undocumented Migrants (PICUM), data on rights of undocumented migrants, available at http://picum.org/en/our-work/undocumented-migrants/.

The Responsibility to Protect, Report of the International Commission on Intervention and State Sovereignty (ICISS) (New York, December 2001).

The Stanley Foundation, *R2P: The Next Decade* (The Stanley Foundation, New York, 2012).

Universal Declaration of Human Rights (UDHR), adopted by the UN General Assembly on 10 December 1948, Resolution 217 A (III).

UN, 'The Second Interagency Workshop on Implementing a Human Rights-based Approach in the Context of UN Reform', Workshop Report, Stamford, 5–7 May, 2003.

UN Center for Regional Development, *RDD. Regional Development Dialogue: Assessing Human Security* (United Nations Center for Regional Development, Nagoya, Japan, Spring 2010) Vol 31, No 1.

UN Commission on Human Rights, 'Report on the Human Rights of Migrants Submitted by the Special Rapporteur of the Commission on Human Rights', A/59/377, 22 September 2004.

——, Sixty-second session, E/CN.4/2005/WG.15/CRP.2, 24 November 2005, Working group established in accordance with Commission on Human Rights Resolution 1995/32, Eleventh session, Geneva, 5–16 December 2005, 'General Provisions' of the Draft UN Declaration on the Rights of Indigenous Peoples.

UN Committee Against Torture, Concluding Observations on Philippines, CAT/C/SR.887 and 888, 12 May 2009.

——, General Comment No 3, *Implementation of Article 14 by States Parties in its address of Non-Discrimination and the Right to Redress*, CAT/C/GC/3, 19 November 2012.

——, *Sonko v Spain*, CAT/C/47/D/368/2008, 27 January 2012.

UN Committee on Economic, Social and Cultural Rights, *Concluding Observations of the Report Submitted by the Dominican Republic*, E/C.12/DOM/CO/3, 19 November 2010.

——, General Comment No 3, *The Nature of States Parties Obligations, (Art 2, para 1)*, 14 December 1990.

——, General Comment No 4, *The Right to Adequate Housing (Art 11 (1) of the Covenant)*, 13 December 1991 (Contained in document E/1992/23).

——, General Comment No 7, *The Right to Adequate Housing (Art 11 (1) of the Covenant): forced evictions*, sixteenth session 1997, Contained in document E/1998/22, annex IV, 20 May 1997.

——, General Comment No 9, *The Domestic Application of the Covenant*, E/C.12/1998/24, (General Comments), 3 December 1998.

——, General Comment No 12, *Right to Adequate Food*, E/C.12/1999/5, 1999.

——, General Comment No 14, *The Right to the Highest Attainable Standard of Health (Article 12 of the International Covenant on Economic, Social and Cultural Rights)*, E/C.12/2000/4, 11 August 2000.

——, General Comment No 19, *The Right to Social Security (Article 9)*, E/C.12/GC/19, 4 February 2008.

——, General Comment No 20, *Non-Discrimination in Economic, Social and Cultural Rights (Art 2, para 2)*, E/C.12/GC/20, 10 June 2009.

UN Committee on the Elimination of Discrimination Against Women, General Recommendation No 19, *Violence against women*, Contained in document A/47/38, 29 January1992.
——, General Recommendation No 26, *Women Migrant Workers*, CEDAW/C/2009/WP.1/R, 5 December 2008.
——, General Recommendation No 28, *The Core Obligations of States Parties under Article 2 of the Convention on the Elimination of All Forms of Discrimination against Women*, CEDAW/C/GC/28, 16 December 2010.
——, General Recommendation No 32, *General recommendation on the gender-related dimensions of refugee status, asylum, nationality and statelessness of women*, CEDAW/C/GC/32, 14 November 2014.
——, General Recommendation No 33, *General recommendation on women's access to justice*, CEDAW/C/GC/33, 3 August 2015.
——, *AT v Hungary*, Communication no: 2/2003, 26 January 2005.
UN Committee on the Elimination of Racial Discrimination, Concluding Observations of the Committee on the Elimination of Racial Discrimination: Dominican Republic, UN Doc CERD/C/DOM/CO/12, 16 May 2008.
——, General Recommendation No 11, *Non-citizens (Art 1), Gen Rec No 11 (General Comments)*, Contained in document A/46/18, 19 March 1993.
——, General Recommendation No 30, *Discrimination Against Non-Citizens*, 1 October 2004 (General Comments), available at Compilation of General Comments and General Recommendations adopted by Human Rights Treaty Bodies. Addendum, HRI/GEN/1/Rev.7/Add.1, 4 May 2005.
UN Committee on the Protection of the Rights of all Migrant Workers and Members of their Families, Concluding Observations on Argentina, (CMW/C/ARG/CO/1), 2011.
——, General Comment No 1, *Migrant Domestic Workers*, CMW/C/GC/1, 23 February 2011.
——, General Comment No 2, *The Rights of Migrant Workers in an Irregular Situation and Members of their Families*, December 2012.
UN Committee on the Rights of the Child, Concluding Observations on Thailand, CRC/C/SR.1698, 3 February 2012.
——, Concluding Observations on Togo, CRC/C/OPSC/TGO/CO/1, 8 March, 2012, Fifty-ninth session, held on 16 January–3 February 2012.
——, General Comment No 6, *Treatment of Unaccompanied and Separated Children Outside their Country of Origin*, CRC/GC/2005/6, 1 September 2005.
——, General Comment No 13, *The Right of the Child to Freedom from all Forms of Violence*, 2011.
UN Department of Economic and Social Affairs (DESA), 'Data on global migration', available at http://esa.un.org/migration.
—— and OECD, *World Migration in Figures*, October 2013.
UN Development Fund for Women (UNIFEM), The Regional Program in Latin America of UNIFEM (today incorporated into UN Women), 'Ciudades Seguras: Violencia hacia las Mujeres y Políticas Públicas' ('Safe Cities: Violence Against Women and Public Policies').
UN Development Program (UNDP), 1993 Human Development Report, *People's Participation*, New York, 1993.

——, 1994 Human Development Report, *New Dimensions of Human Security*, New York, 1994.
——, 2004 National Human Development Report on Afghanistan, *Security with a Human Face: Challenges and Responsibilities*, UNDP, 2004.
——, Arab Human Development Report 2009, *Challenges to Human Security in Arab Countries*, UNDP, Regional Bureau for Arab States, New York, 2009.
——, *At Risk: Roma and the Displaced in Southeast Europe*, UNDP Regional Bureau for Europe and the Commonwealth of Independent States, Bratislava, 2006.
——, Human Development Report 2009/10, Occupied Palestinian Territory: Investing in Human Security for a Future State, 2010.
——, *The Human Security Framework and National Human Development Reports*, National Human Development Report Series, NHDR Occasional Paper 5, by Richard Jolly and Deepayan Basu Ray (Institute of Development Studies, Sussex), UNDP, Human Development Report Office, National Human Development Report Unit, May 2006.
UN Economic and Social Council (ECOSOC), Resolution 1985/17 of 28 May 1985.
UN General Assembly (UNGA), A/64/291, 16 July 2010.
——, AG/RES. 2757 (XLII-O/12), agreed at the fourth plenary session, held on 5 June 2012.
——, A/RES/66/290 'Follow-up to paragraph 143 on Human Security of the 2005 World Summit Outcome', 25 October 2012.
——, A/RES/70/1, Resolution adopted by the General Assembly on 25 September 2015, *70/1. Transforming our World: The 2030 Agenda for Sustainable Development*.
——, Declaration on the Human Rights of Individuals who are not Nationals of the Country in which they Live, adopted by Resolution 40/144 of 13 December 1985.
——, Declaration on the Right to Development, General Assembly Resolution A/RES/41/128, 97th plenary meeting, 4 December 1986.
——, Declaration on the Right of Peoples to Peace, General Assembly Resolution 39/11, 12 November 1984.
——, *Implementing the Responsibility to Protect*. Report of the Secretary-General, A/63/677, 12 January 2009.
——, Informal thematic debate held on 14 April 2011, in implementing GA Resolution A/64/291 of July 2010. Personal account taken.
——, Millennium Development Goals, adopted by the UNGA in 2000, available at www.un.org/millenniumgoals/gender.shtml.
——, *Special Session of the General Assembly on HIV/AIDS:* Report of the Secretary-General, UN GAOR, 55th Sess, Agenda Item 179, A/55/779, 2001.
——, *World Summit Outcome*, Resolution A/RES/60/1, 24 October 2005.
UN High Commissioner for Refugees, Statement on the Right to an Effective Remedy in Relation to Accelerated Asylum Procedures, 2010.
——, 'Submission by the Office of the United Nations High Commissioner for Refugees in the case of *MSS v Belgium and Greece*', June 2010, available at www.unhcr.org/4d4bfebe9.pdf.
——, 'Thriving after a Crisis: Security and Empowerment in Dadaab', 2012, retrieved from www.unhcr.org/4f9947df6.html, UNHCR, Protection: A Safety Net.

—— and UN Office for the Coordination of Humanitarian Affairs (OCHA), *Guidelines for Gender-based Violence Interventions in Humanitarian Settings: Focusing on Prevention of and Response to Sexual Violence in Emergencies*, 2009.

UN Human Rights Committee (UN HRC), *A v Australia*, Communication No 560/1993, CCPR/C/59/D/560/1993, 30 April 1997.

——, *Delgado Páez v Colombia*, Communication No 195/1985, 12 July 1990.

——, *Dias v Angola*, Communication No 711/1996, UN Doc CCPR/68/D/711/1996, 2000.

——, General Comment No 15, *The Position of Aliens under the Covenant*, CCPR General Comment No 15 (General Comments), 11 April 1986.

——, General Comment No 22, Article 18, *The Right to Freedom of Thought, Conscience and Religion*, CCPR/C/21/Rev.1/Add.4, 30 July 1993.

——, General Comment No 23, *The Rights of Minorities (Article 27)*, CCPR/C/21/Rev.1/Add.5, 8 April 1994.

——, General Comment No 29, *States of Emergency (Article 4)*, CCPR/C/21/Rev.1/Add.11, 2001.

——, *Karakurt v Austria*, Communication No 965/2000, UN Doc CCPR/C/74/D/965/2000, 4 April 2002.

——, *ibid*, Individual Opinion by Committee Members Sir Nigel Rodley and Mr Martin Scheinin (partly dissenting).

——, *Sayadi and Vinck v Belgium*, Communication No 1472/2006, 22 October 2008.

UN Human Rights Council, 'Accelerating efforts to eliminate all forms of violence against women: ensuring due diligence in prevention', A/HRC/RES/14/12, 30 June 2010.

——, Draft Declaration on the Right to Peace, contained in Human Rights Council, Report of the Human Rights Council Advisory Committee on the right of peoples to peace, A/HRC/20/31, 16 April 2012.

——, *Guiding Principles on Extreme Poverty and Human Rights*, (contained in the Final Draft submitted by the Special Rapporteur on extreme poverty and human rights, Magdalena Sepúlveda Carmona, UN General Assembly Resolution A/HC/21/39, 18 July 2012), endorsed by UN Human Rights Council in Resolution 21/11 of 27 September 2012.

——, 'Promotion of the Right to Peace', A/HRC/20/L.16, 29 June 2012, and adopted on 5 July 2012.

——, Resolution A/HRC/RES/14/12, 30 June 2012.

UNICEF, Strategic Priority Action Plan 2010–2012, available at www.unicef.org/gender/files/Strategic_Priority_Action_Plan_2010_to_2012.pdf.

UN International Human Rights Instruments, HRI/MC/2008/3, 6 June 2008, available at http://uhri.ohchr.org/about.

UN Office of Drugs and Crime, *Drug and Crime Report*, United Nations, Austria, 2010, available at www.unodc.org/documents/data-and-analysis/tocta/TOCTA_Report_2010_low_res.pdf.

UN Office of the High Commissioner for Human Rights / Europe Regional Office, *Rights of Migrant Domestic Workers in Europe*, 2011.

——, *Human Rights for Everyone Everywhere*, at www.ohchr.org/Documents/AboutUs/Leaflet_OHCHR_EN_print.pdf.

——, Human Rights Indicators: *A Guide to Measurement and Implementation*, HR/PUB/12/5, UN, New York and Geneva, 2012.

——, 'Towards the Establishment of an ASEAN Human Rights System', available at http://bangkok.ohchr.org/programme/asean/Default.aspx.

——, *UN OHCHR Report 2011*, Geneva, 2012.

UN Security Council (UNSC), Note by the President of the Security Council, UN Doc S/23500, 31 January 1992.

——, Resolution 1325, S/Res/1325, 31 October 2000.

——, Resolution 1820, S/Res/1820, 19 June 2008.

——, Resolution 1888, S/RES/1888, 30 September 2009.

——, Resolution 1889, S/RES/1889, 5 October 2009.

——, Resolution 1960, S/RES/1960, 16 December 2010.

——, Resolution 2106, S/RES/2106, 24 June 2013.

UN Secretary General (UNSG), *An Agenda for Peace. Preventive Diplomacy, Peacemaking and Peace-Keeping*, Report of the Secretary-General pursuant to the statement adopted by the Summit Meeting of the Security Council on 31 January 1992, A/47/277—S/24111, 17 June 1992.

——, Kofi Annan's Address to the European Parliament upon receipt of the Andrei Sakharov Prize for Freedom of Thought (Brussels), 29 January 2004, at www.europa-eu-un.org/articles/en/article_3178_en.htm.

——, Report of the Secretary-General on the work of the organization, supplement to an agenda for peace: Position Paper of the Secretary-General on the occasion of the fiftieth anniversary of the United Nations, A/50/60—S/1995/1, 3 January 1995.

——, Report of the Secretary-General presented to the Human Rights Council, UNGA Doc A/HRC/21/36, 21 September 2012.

——, Report of the UNSG, In Larger Freedom: Towards Development, Security and Human Rights for all, A/59/2005, 21 March 2005.

——, Report of the UNSG on Human Security, A/Res/64/701, 8 March 2010.

——, Second Report of the UNSG on Human Security, 'Follow-up to General Assembly Resolution 64/291 on human security. Report of the Secretary General', UNGA Resolution A/66/763, 5 April 2012.

——, Third Report of the UNSG on Human Security, 'Follow-up to General Assembly Resolution 66/290 on Human Security', A/68/685, 23 December 2013.

UN Special Rapporteur on Violence Against Women, its Causes and Consequences, report of 2006, Integration of the Human Rights of Women and the Gender Perspective: Violence Against Women. The Due Diligence Standard as a Tool for the Elimination of Violence Against Women, report prepared by Yakin Ertürk in accordance with Commission on Human Rights Resolution 2005/41, 20 January 2006.

——, Report of the UN Special Rapporteur on Violence Against Women, UNGA A/66/215, 2011.

UN Special Session of the General Assembly on HIV/AIDS: Report of the Secretary-General, UN GAOR, 55th Sess, Agenda Item 179, A/55/779, 2001.

UN Trust Fund for Human Security, human security global data, at http://ochaonline.un.org/Home/tabid/2097/Default.aspx.

——, *Human Security in Theory and Practice. Application of the Human Security Concept and the United Nations Trust Fund for Human Security*, Human Security Unit, Office for the Coordination of Humanitarian Affairs, United Nations, 2009.

——, Human Security Unit, *Human Security at the United Nations*, OCHA, New York, 2012.

——, Human Security Unit, *Strategic Plan 2014–2017* (United Nations, 2014).

Vienna Convention on the Law of Treaties, adopted in Vienna on 23 May 1969, entered into force on 27 January 1980, in United Nations, Treaty Series, Vol 1155, 2005.

Vienna Declaration and Program of Action, UNGA, World Conference on Human Rights, A/CONF.157/23, 12 July 1993.

World Bank, *Guidelines for Assessing the Impacts and Costs of Forced Displacement*, World Bank, Washington DC, 2012.

——, *Migration and Remittances Factbook 2011*, 2011.

——, *Migration and Remittances: Recent Developments and Outlook*, Migration and Development Brief 26, 2016.

——, *World Development Report 2011: Conflict, Security and Development*, 2001.

——, *World Development Report 2012: Gender Equality and Development*, 2012, available at http://econ.worldbank.org.

World Commission on Environment and Development, *Report of the World Commission on Environment and Development: Our Common Future* (Brundtland Report), UN Doc A/RES/42/187/Annex, 2 August 1987.

World Health Organization, 'Maternal Mortality', Fact sheet N°348, May 2012, available at www.who.int/mediacentre/factsheets/fs348/en/index.html.

MEDIA AND COMMUNICATION SOURCES

CNN, 'Obama Administration to Stop Deporting Some Young Illegal Immigrants', 16 June 16, 2012, available at http://edition.cnn.com/2012/06/15/politics/immigration/index.html?hpt=hp_t1.

Digital Granma Internacional, 'Cuba advierte en ONU sobre amenazas a la Seguridad Humana', in *Digital Granma Internacional*, La Habana, 5 June 2012.

Dudley, Stephen, 'Parte III: La Ruta del Peligro', in *Insight Crime. Crimen Organizado en las Américas*, 28 November 2012, available at http://es.insightcrime.org/investigaciones/migrantes-centroamerica-mexico.

Eilperin, Juliet, 'Interior Dept. official at MMS resigns' and 'Independent Probe of BP Oil Spill in Works', *The Washington Post*, 17 and 18 May 2010, respectively, available at www.washingtonpost.com/wp-dyn/content/article/2010/05/17/AR2010051702123.html.

——, 'US Exempted BP's Gulf of Mexico Drilling from Environmental Impact Study', *The Washington Post*, 5 May 2010, available at www.washingtonpost.com/wp-dyn/content/article/2010/05/04/AR2010050404118.html.

García, Judith, 'Cada 24 horas muere un mexicano al querer pasar a EU ilegalmente: SRE' in *El Sol de México*, 5 August 2012, available at www.oem.com.mx/elsoldemexico/notas/n2645139.htm.

Godoy, Emilio, 'México, escala de terror para inmigrantes centroamericanos', *Ipsonoticias*, 28 abril 2012, available at http://ipsnoticias.net/nota.asp?idnews=95272.

Gómora, Doris, 'Cae presunto autor de muerte de 72 migrantes en Tamaulipas', *El Universal*, 8 October 2012.

IASW, 'ALBA Attacks Justice, Human Rights', *IASW*, Tuesday, 12 June 2012, available at http://interamericansecuritywatch.com/category/nicaragua/.

——, 'OAS Rights Body Facing Criticisms, Dissolution", Friday, 8 June 2012, available at http://interamericansecuritywatch.com/category/nicaragua/.

Interview with Mehrnaz Mostafavi, Officer in Charge of the United Nations Human Security Unit, New York, 8 April 2011 (personal interview).

Interview with Sadako Ogata, former UN High Commissioner for Refugees (1991–2000), co-chair of the Commission for Human Security (2001–03) and President of the Japan International Cooperation Agency (2003–12), in *Council of Foreign Relations*, 18 March 2008, available at www.cfr.org/search/?Ntt=human+security&submit.x=0&submit.y=0.

Lara, Ivonne, 'México tiene su propia (gran) crisis migratoria', *Hipertextual*, 11 September 2015, available at http://hipertextual.com/2015/09/crisis-migratoria-mexico.

La Bestia, documentary by Pedro Ultreras, on Central American migrants trying to enter Mexico by train through the southern border, available at www.youtube.com/watch?v=YgHR1-5HptA

Los Angeles Times, 'In Arizona, Cheers and Disillusionment Follow Immigration Ruling', *Los Angeles Times*, 25 June 2012, available at www.latimes.com/news/nation/nationnow/la-na-nn-supreme-court-immigration-arizona-20120625,0,1865769.story

Nelson Mandela Centre of Memory, 'Transcript of Mary Robinson's Nelson Mandela Annual Lecture. Freedom, Truth, Democracy: Citizenship and Common Purpose, 5 August 2012, available at www.nelsonmandela.org/news/entry/transcript-of-mary-robinsons-nelson-mandela-annual-lecture.

Peña, Alex, 'Migrants Face Higher Risks Illegally Crossing the Border', *NBC Latino*, 20 September 2012, available at http://nbclatino.com/2012/09/20/migrants-face-higher-risks-illegally-crossing-the-border/.

PICUM, Bulletin of 9 May 2012, reports on Arizona Law SB 1070 from *The Guardian*, 24 April 2012.

——, *Undocumentary*, web-documentary on irregular migrants, October 2012, available at www.undocumentary.org.

Terraferma, movie by Emanuele Crialese on North African migrants attempting to reach Italy by sea (not available through internet).

The Global Herald, 'Leaders Celebrate Anniversaries of Conventions on Refugees and Statelessness', *The Global Herald*, By News Desk; published on Wed, 7 Dec 2011, available at http://theglobalherald.com/leaders-celebrate-anniversaries-of-conventions-on-refugees-and-statelessness/26122/.

The New York Times, 'Death Toll of Migrants 2012', at www.nytimes.com/2010/01/21/world/americas/21deathtoll.html.

The Times, London, 'Criminal Court', 6 March 1862.

——, 'Daylight Air Raid. 76 Killed and 154 Injured', Monday, 28 May 1917.

——, Monday, 20 June 1842 (title not visible);

——, Saturday, 20 January 1858 (title not visible).

——, Wednesday, 18 October 1848 (title not visible).

——, 'Widow-Burning in India. Letter to the Editor from and East India Proprietor', *The Times*, 1831 (exact date and page not visible).

Vega, Arturo, 'El infierno de los inmigrantes centroamericanos' (2011) *Periódico El Universal*, available at www.eluniversal.com.mx/notas/736080.html.

Index

Please note that references to Footnotes are indicated by the letter 'n' following the page number. References to Tables are in *italics*

www.ingramcontent.com/pod-product-compliance
Ingram Content Group UK Ltd.
Pitfield, Milton Keynes, MK11 3LW, UK
UKHW020133290926
15471UKWH00003B/458

9 781509 928804